THE STRANGER WHO WAS MYSELF

THANKS

I started writing when I was almost seventy. I am now eighty years old. *The Stranger who was Myself* is my third book.

I am grateful to all the people and places, the accidents of fate, the lucky gifts and chance encounters that have brought me to this place.

I give thanks to:

Yvonne Lafond, for the gift of life and for your fierce, protecting love.

Paul for your everlasting love. You bring boundless happiness. Every day.

Rhiannon, Gareth, Carys. You are my manna, my heart, my treasure.

Gordon, Matthew, Harriet, Angelique for saying yes.

Siân, Paul, Jack, Skye, Hugo, Elle, John, Beatrix, Solomon. Miracles of hope, joy, promise.

Annette, Carol, Anthony for cherished childhood.

David, Thora, Philip, Vivian, Dinah for immediate and continuing embrace.

Pappy for never letting on.

Jeffrey for us growing up together.

My biological father for half my DNA.

Trinidad and Tobago. This brilliant, bravez-danger, outrageous, unbelievable, generous, gifted place where I was lucky to be born and am privileged to call home.

Cymru / Wales for a home from home.

The Bocas Lit Fest, The Cropper Foundation and The UWI St Augustine for unimagined openings.

The Bookclub for a sustaining sisterhood.

Jeremy and Hannah at Peepal Tree Press. For your friendship and unwavering support, thank you. Again.

THE STRANGER WHO WAS MYSELF

BARBARA JENKINS

PEEPAL TREE

First published in Great Britain in 2022
by Peepal Tree Press Ltd
17 King's Avenue
Leeds LS6 1QS
England

ISBN13: 97818452325345

Printed in the United Kingdom by
Severn, Gloucester,
on responsibly sourced paper

Love after love

The time will come
when, with elation,
you will greet yourself arriving
at your own door, in your own mirror,
and each will smile at the other's welcome,

and say, sit here. Eat.
You will love again the stranger who was your self.
Give wine. Give bread. Give back your heart
to itself, to the stranger who has loved you

all your life, whom you ignored
for another, who knows you by heart.
Take down the love letters from the bookshelf,

the photographs, the desperate notes,
peel your own image from the mirror.
Sit. Feast on your life.

— Derek Walcott

We walk through ourselves, meeting robbers, ghosts, giants, old men,
young men, wives, widows, brothers-in-love. But always meeting
ourselves.

— James Joyce, *Ulysses*

If you know whence you came, there are absolutely no limitations
to where you can go.

— James Baldwin

We all have to make our own arrangements with the past

— Ian McEwan

For Sian, Paul, Jack, Skye, Hugo, Elle, John, Beatrix, Solomon
and those yet unborn with so much love and gratitude for
the gift of you

CONTENTS

This is my arrangement with much of my past. With few exceptions, all the people mentioned here are real people I know as well as anyone can know anyone else. I'm not sure how much of myself I know after this exploration into the past.

GREET

Is there a way in which all of us are fictional characters, parented by life

and written by ourselves?

James Wood

THE TIME WILL COME

I understand now what you saw when you looked at it. I followed your gaze as your eyes took in the white lettering on the two blue enamelled street signs set at right-angles to each other on a concrete post, the low wall curving round the two streets, the green twisted-wire fence that topped it, the gallery that mirrored that curve and the jutting bay room that anchored it on the right, the fretwork-fringed *porte cochère*, the little oval blue enamelled street number plate fastened to its front, the steeply sloping corrugated galvanize roof streaked red-brown by time, the finials at the ridge-ends pointing fingers to the sky: at each feature your eyes widening, your smile broadening. It is… it is… exquisite, you said. Exquisite.

I didn't see exquisite. I saw an old-fashioned house built of the wattle and daub we here call nuggin, and wood too – wood floors, wood windows, wood partitions, everywhere wood, ordinary wood, a wood that looked solid until you touched it and your fingers felt no resistance, felt something thin like paper that you could punch through to reveal secret tunnels, branching and interlocking; a separate nuggin and wood kitchen shed outside; a separate wood latrine out in the back. Everything about it shaming and shameful. It did not have the tiles, the solid concrete blocks, the glass, the everything-anyone-needed kitchen, proper facilities like a bathroom with a shower and flush toilet. It wasn't the modern everything I'd aspired to when I lived there.

Many years into the future when we had not just the one – she straddling your hip that morning as we stood on the pavement at the corner of Reid Lane and Pelham Street, Belmont – but three little ones, Sundays would find you donning your wide-brimmed burgundy West Indies cricket hat, piling a chair, a tripod and a camera bag into the car trunk. You'd be leaving home to trawl through the streets and lanes of Belmont, Woodbrook, Gonzales, Laventille, Piccadilly, Corbeau Town and beyond in search of suitable subjects. On finding one you would park, stand on the chair on the pavement and in the street, adding to your six-foot height for a better view, and methodically document on film – and written notes – whatever you could of it, so that over time you had a record of perhaps a couple of hundred or more of those fast-disappearing, exquisite houses. I would, on those Sundays, recall that love-at-first-sight moment when that future must have reached back in time to tap you on the shoulder, that day when you pronounced my childhood home exquisite.

In the years before that day, those early years of our life together far away from here, I hadn't told you anything about the house where I grew up. I don't know why, but somehow it had never come up in conversation. Did it seem as odd to you then as it now does to me? After all, I knew your family home and there must have been lots of opportunities for me to make comparisons or reflect aloud about my old home. But then again there was so much about me, about my past, that I didn't talk about, that you didn't know about even after the almost nine years we'd been together. But that day we were there and I was glad you could find out for yourself all you had perhaps silently wondered about my old home and, perhaps, about me.

The red concrete steps leading to the gallery, the green sweet-oil tins lining the steps, were as bright as if Marmie had painted them the day before, but the palms standing in the tins, their branches withered brown and brittle, told a different story, a story of Marmie's absence – as if the deep grey dust that registered the soles of our shoes in the gallery, like a burglar's shoe-print in wet soil outside an open window in an old-fashioned whodunit, wasn't clue enough. I marvelled at how excited you were to be there, how much you wanted to explore, to see everything, anxious to ask me questions and get answers about the life of the house, my life in the house. But oh, how I now regret I didn't try to match your enthusiasm. I felt heavy, as if the weight of the empty present and the too-full past had seeped from the very pores of the house to fall on my shoulders, squeezing all vitality out of me, rendering me silent, dull.

Shall we go round the back? you asked. We went down the steps and there, walking past Marmie's front garden, a sharp burst of minty fragrance distilled from her chrysanthemums dispelled my churlishness. I smiled up at you, you squeezed my hand, and it was with a lighter heart I continued along the side of the house, stepping on moss cushions, deep and springy from the lack of human tread, rounded the corner, and there we were, in the backyard.

The back doors of the main house were bolted shut, but, across the yard, the kitchen, lacking doors, was wide open and out of that doorway there hurtled a screeching something. The apparition landed on the top step of the house, its plumage so black, so glossy, it gleamed purple. It shook a cape of gold from its crown, extended its wings like one of those birds of prey on a coat of arms, stretched its neck to the sky, lifted its head and trumpeted a burst of territorial crowing. At that summons, a fussy, compact little brown hen emerged from the doorway and around her peep-peep-peeped three or four yellow chicks. Remember how our little one wanted to get closer, to pick up one of the chicks, but I was too afraid to let her? That cock's crowing was not a warm welcome, not with those powerful wings that would allow him to fly at us like a real bird, not with those calculating yellow-ringed eyes beneath that scarlet comb carried like a triumphant warrior's crown, blood-red wattles swaying under his chin, not with that dagger of a beak and heel-spurs like drawn knives.

Marmie had always had a few fowls scrabbling about in the yard, but she'd been gone such a long time that these could not be ones she'd left; these must have been several generations down the line, and without Marmie there to scatter corn on mornings, I guessed that each new generation must have got fewer and fewer in number, reverting more and more to their original wild state. They'd survived through that ceaseless peck-peck-pecking in the ground that comes instinctively, feasting on their natural fare of insects, lizards, frogs, congarees and worms. I've seen chickens catch butterflies and cockroaches in flight – the meal in flight, I mean, not the diners. I remember Marmie opening a drawer and finding that a mouse had nested there, taking the drawer out into the yard and tipping it over. The chickens, with a mad fluttering, had scrambled towards the shredded paper, old Christmas cards, rubber bands and bits of geometry tin contents and, scratching through these, revealed a half-dozen or so squirming pink blobs, like animated cartoon marshmallows. They skewered them with their beaks, lifting their heads, and swallowing them whole. These now in the yard hadn't starved, they weren't homeless, they'd adapted to change. I thought about that for a while and it seemed to me that whatever resilience and acumen it requires to take an evolutionary backward step in one's habits, and learn to look after oneself in changed circumstances, these chickens certainly showed they had it.

I'd left a home far away where I was happy and comfortable and returned to this home of my pushed-aside past in this strange yet familiar country. I hadn't come back alone. I brought you and her, my family – my precious other selves. To you and her everything about this place, this country, was new. I looked at the fowls, who by now had gone about their own business as if we weren't there, and I wondered whether I, too, had hidden in some primeval part of my being the endurance, the ability to become as adjusted as they to this place where we found ourselves. I wondered even more how you, how she, how we, would adjust.

Back on the pavement, I took a last look at the house. It was locked but it wasn't abandoned. In it lived my life from girl to woman. In it, too, were Marmie, Annette, Carol and Tony. There was my grandmother, my aunts and uncles, friends and family, neighbours. There was Pappy too. This is the house that grew me, and it is to all that happened while I lived there, and all that I learned when I lived there, that I must return if I am to make sense of who I was then, who I am now, and how I have become myself.

DOOR

Pappy asked my aunt's husband to tell me that he was going to sell the house. So what about Marmie? I asked. He replied that Pappy said that since it didn't look like she was coming back, he had to make a decision. What if she does come back? Where would she live? She could decide for herself, he said. Pappy would give her half of what he got for the house to do with whatever she wanted.

It was the second week of my return home, July 1971. My husband's work permit hadn't yet come through and he was under threat of deportation, even though he had a government job on a three-year contract. I was due to take up teaching in a matter of weeks, a requirement of my scholarship contract. We were staying with my aunt, my mother's sister, at her home, with six of her seven children and her husband, Pappy's go-between. We were looking for a place of our own to rent while still searching for suitable day-care for our two-year old. We had no car since the Hillman Hunter we'd bought new with our slender UK savings and a local loan was stolen a couple of days after we'd visited the house in that first week of our arrival. That's how things were with us, with me, when Pappy dropped on me, not in person, but through an intermediary, the news of his intention.

I hadn't seen my old home for the decade of my life away. It held the memories of my growing years, and now, before I could even properly reconnect with it, Pappy was going to sell it. At the time I didn't question why he'd waited for my return to do this. I had been away for so long that I was out of touch with family and with people's ways of thinking and doing things, so much so that I was effectively a stranger. I suppose I may have taken it for granted that Pappy wanted us all, all four of our mother's children, to be present and in agreement with his plan before he acted. It was a quick and naïve assumption, and it was only later that I saw how much I had erred.

I mean how present were we as a collective called Marmie's children, as collaboratively concerned with seeking our mother's interest, anyway? I asked them, my siblings, how they felt about Pappy wanting to sell the house? Well, it's his. He can do what he wants. That seemed to be their position and how could it be anything else? I'd left Marmie with her children as a unit, but I had come back to find her gone and her children scattered. Annette and Carol were married with husbands and children of their own, both living in Diego Martin, some distance from Belmont, and Tony, now twenty-one, lived nearby in Belmont with family friends, and there was I, newly arrived and not alone, staying with family until we found a place of our own. I didn't rally them, my two sisters and brother, to look more closely at the implications of our easy dismissal of interest in Pappy's intention. They had their own lives to get on with and it could be that they felt some relief in imagining that this house sale would sever their last link to him. After the house was sold, it became clear to me that I had walked into a trap, a set-up, contrived and carefully laid by Pappy himself, very likely with my uncle-in-law's connivance, and that I had, by my quick and easy agreement to the sale of the house, allowed myself and my siblings to be accomplices in defrauding our mother of what was her due by virtue of her many, many years of investment in her home.

I was eleven when we moved into 74 Pelham Street. From the road, where the open-tray Ford truck pulled up with us and our belongings, my mother and we children saw a cream, single-storey house with a long narrow-roofed extension over the front path, steps leading up from the path to a wide gallery backed by three sets of double doors, with big clear knobbly-patterned glass panel inserts. 74 Pelham Street also had another address, 10 Reid Lane, for it was a corner house, and the gallery wrapped round to give views over both streets. I wanted to believe, to hope that all of it was ours as we walked through the gate, but Marmie didn't go up the steps to the gallery to enter the house by either of the double glass doors, or by the solid wooden door to the bay room. We children followed her round a path between the side of the house and a tall galvanize fence that separated the house spot from the next-door house, past the bay room to the backyard. Marmie handed baby Tony to me, and we children stood in the yard while she climbed four plain concrete steps to a closed door. At the top step she unbolted the door, which turned out to be only the top half of the door. She swung it open and latched it against the outside wall. She then reached in to unbolt the lower half. She swung it back and walked in.

This was our future home. Two rooms at the back, behind the bay room. Those two rooms were to be our everywhere space, for sleeping, sitting, eating. Everything else we needed was shared with the other occupants of the house. How it was worked out that ours was the right-hand part of the kitchen shed behind and separate from the house, and the right-hand stall of a two-compartment, single-pit latrine outhouse further behind, I don't know; perhaps we simply inherited those arrangements from the former occupants of our part of the house.

There was just one kitchen sink, shared by all the tenants. This was a deep concrete structure built on the outside wall of the left side of the kitchen shed and reached from the inside through an opening in that wall.

There was one brass tap, and a hole at the base of the sink for the wastewater to fall directly into the concrete drain that ran out into the street gutter. Vivid green algae flourished in that drain. I would watch its long lush strands like mermaids' hair waving in an underwater world as water from the sink rippled through.

The open-to-the-sky shower, which was everybody's, was a simple affair of three walls of galvanised sheeting leaning against the wall of our side of the kitchen shed. One sheet, fastened to the others by hinges, swung as a door. A galvanised pipe, bent overhead, was intended as the water supply, but as water was always scarce, bathing was often simply dipping from a metal bucket the water fetched from the standpipe on Reid Lane. There, against the law, grown men, barely recognisable through the thick white suds covering them from head to toe, naked but for drawers, stood on mornings rubbing extravagant handfuls of foaminess under arms, over bodies and reaching down their hands massaging clean the unseeable bits, and, sloshing whole bucketsful over themselves, emerged clean and gleaming. As years went by, a carelessly dropped zaboca seed germinated, grew and flourished just outside the shower, giving it a shape-shifting, living roof of branches, leaves and fruit.

Our half of the kitchen and our compartment of the latrine was also used by Miss Cobus, the occupant of the bay bedroom at the front of our two rooms. That first day, she told my mother she had one child, a son, living in America. She showed us his picture – a sepia print of a young man in a military uniform. In the other half of the house, in the original living and dining rooms and the gallery, lived a family of mother, father, and three children. We didn't see them on the first day. They had the left latrine compartment and the left side of the kitchen shed, the side with the shared sink. Also in the back, next to the latrine shed, was a guava tree that seemed to produce year round such an abundance of fruit that I could never understand why the phrase 'guava season' means hard times, because, daily, passers-by would call out, Neighbour, I just picking up some guava here, and a woman would come in with a basin to collect fallen fruit to be made into jam or guava cheese for home use or sale. Marmie, too, would collect fruit and make guava jelly, gifts for family and friends, rows of jars of clear red jelly, as pretty as jewels. When sunlight shone through Marmie's guava jelly, I thought it more beautiful than a stained-glass window in church.

Our proudest furniture was Marmie's parting gift from her disappointed mother – a handsome three-piece mahogany bedroom set. These were set up in the innermost of our two rooms, the room that had a common wall with Miss Cobus's bay room. Taking up the most space was a massive bed where Marmie and the younger three children slept. Under the bed was storage – numerous cardboard boxes of clothes that one or other of us had outgrown and were awaiting a younger one to grow into, boxes of rags, a couple of cardboard grips, boxes of old newspapers to wrap things in – and also to be torn to size for the latrine. Also under the bed resided an enamel posie for night-time use, as we children were not allowed to venture out to the latrine in the dark.

The second furniture item was a dressing table with three deep drawers on either side where our folding clothes went, and one, longer, shallow one in the middle for our mother's jewellery. In the space under that middle drawer there was a matching stool. A big round mirror was attached at the back, and over the drawers was a wide surface where our mother placed three embroidered, lace-edged, delicate, fine linen doilies – an oval one in the middle and a smaller round one on each side. These she alternated with ecru crocheted ones as the seasons changed from festive to ordinary. On the doilies she set a tortoiseshell backed hairbrush, a matching hand mirror and comb set, which were never used, her talcum power, her face powder and a hairbrush and comb for regular daily use.

The big matching mahogany wardrobe, the third piece, had two doors, each with brass handles and a tiny brass keyhole into which a pretty little key fitted. Inside ran a long brass rail for hanging clothes. We never had enough hangers. Hangers were of wood with a wire hook and, on these, three, sometimes four garments were hung, one over the other, so that to find a particular dress, you peeped under the skirts, peeling them apart to find the one you wanted, hoping it wasn't too far under, because you'd have the task of lifting the others off, taking the one you wanted and putting the others back, one at a time, steupsing all the while, knowing you had to leave things just as you found them. Above the rail was a shelf, half the depth of the wardrobe, where Marmie put her hats, our church hats, her handbags, including those whose clasps were broken or straps were beyond repair, for in these she stored important documents such as birth certificates, ours and hers, rent receipts, receipts for purchases, receipts for pawned jewellery, letters, ration cards and the like. A lower shelf was for shoes. The wardrobe and dressing table drawers were lined with cedar whose fragrance hit you so powerfully right in the centre of your forehead when you opened the doors, that you only had to close your eyes to feel yourself not there at all, but somehow magicked off to an unknown, faraway, mysterious place.

There was a pair of jalousie doors between our two rooms, but these were never closed. In the second room, the one nearest the backyard, there was a wire-mesh-sided food safe, a canvas folding cot where we sat, if we ever needed to sit indoors during the day, and where I, as the privileged eldest child, slept at night. In this back room, too, stood Marmie's precious foot-pedal Singer sewing machine, an oilcloth-covered wooden table and two wooden chairs. The partition walls between the rooms, our two and those of the neighbours in the adjoining rooms, were made of upright wood planks. These walls didn't quite reach the ceiling. Slender, regularly spaced square-section wooden rods bridged the wide gap. Lower down, halfway along the walls ran a narrow ledge, very useful as a shelf for small objects, a bar of Palmolive soap for bathing, a bar of yellow Sunlight soap for washing clothes, a tin opener, a small flat round tin of Vicks vapour rub, a small tub of Vaseline, boxes of matches, safety pins and hair pins.

In each room there was a pair of jalousie windows that could be flung open and these were flanked by jalousies that could be pushed to close and held in place by a long pin that fitted into a hole in the frame. I spent many a happy childhood hour opening and closing jalousies, seeing how they all moved together, working out the way the parts fitted together, astonished at the clever, simple closing mechanism. The houses on Pelham Street were so close together that whenever I was idly singing, Mr Bones, the father of the Portuguese family in the next-door house, would call out and ask me to sing the *Ave Maria* for him, and after I'd sung it he'd want to hear it again. Our one door, the one that opened to the back yard, was split in two across the middle, a stable door I learned later. It was kept fully open when any of us was at home. At night, we slid a bolt into place on the inside of each half and when we went out, we slid shut the one bolt on the outside. Why only one bolt, I wondered. I examined the door, opening and closing it, marvelling at the ingenuity of the simple and effective design that made this possible.

Marmie cooked our meals in the kitchen shed on a two-burner pitch-oil stove placed at one end of a long narrow table. On the rest of space, she stacked an iron stewing pot, one big metal boiling pot with a lid, two big bowls, one metal pot spoon, a sharp knife, and our plates, cups, deep soup plates with rims and an odd assortment of spoons, knives and forks.

After a few years, when Miss Cobus moved out to join her son in America, we got her room, and when the other people moved out sometime after, we were able to occupy the whole house. Perhaps that's when Pappy bought the house from Mr Sarvary. I must have been in my mid-teens at the time. I don't think any of us children had any sense of either being tenants or becoming a family of homeowners when the change happened. Pappy didn't live with us but he was the person in charge and as he was always secretive about his real life and his dealings, I never knew whether he'd bought it outright with cash or had taken out a loan, whether he bought it when the other tenants left or whether his buying it occasioned their leaving. I wonder now whether Marmie knew any more than I. Whatever had been the cause, we simply spread as new space was opened up to us. Miss Cobus's bay room became Marmie's bedroom and her bed moved in there. Another bed was purchased or made for the room she'd vacated, and when we got the other half of the house, it slowly reverted to its original functional design as living room, dining room and gallery for cooling off, looking at the street and chatting with passers-by, with a bannister for Marmie's little clay pots of African violets and ivy. Along each side of the red steps leading to the front door, she put large sweet-oil tins, painted green, and grew tall, yellow-stem palms.

Marmie sent a message to Sidney a cabinetmaker from up the Valley Road. They talked a bit and he went away. At the time she was working six days a week as a cashier in a Chinese grocery in Charlotte Street, for nine dollars a week; from this she put one dollar a week in a sou-sou. She took the first hand so that Sidney could buy the wood and start to build the furniture – a mahogany, curved-arms morris chair set, an oval dining table and harp-back chairs. These would bring the drawing room and dining room to life. After that sou-sou cycle had finished and a new one started, she once again took a first hand to pay Sidney for his workmanship. Sacks of ticking stuffed with coconut fibre and beaten into shape with a long hooked *bois* became seat cushions. These and stylish floral cretonne cushion covers and lace curtains for the long French doors came with the rhythm of the sou-sou cycle.

We children took it all in our stride, this flowing into new space and having new things. But while I hadn't felt particularly deprived before, I did feel a lift in moving up in the world, but there was no way I could match Marmie's joy and satisfaction in her huge accomplishment. For Marmie, who had fallen further and further from grace with her family with the arrival of each of the four of us, and the increasing diminishment of her circumstances as her burdens grew, this was a big step. Marmie, at last, had a home she could be proud of. She worked hard over the years to keep up to this standard; she made improvements to the kitchen, maintained the yard and created a pretty garden at the front.

And to think that Pappy had decided to sell her home while she was away, working as a domestic and nanny in Brooklyn, an illegal alien there, unable to come home and fend for herself. How could she come back? She would be denied re-entry to the land of opportunity if she left. And to think that Pappy had waited for me to come back home to break this news to me, not in person, but manipulatively through Marmie's sister's husband. And to think he was expecting me to give him my blessing – which I did – with the promise, relayed through the intermediary uncle-in-law, that he would give her half of the twenty-eight thousand Trinidad and Tobago dollars that he got for it – a promise he didn't keep, because he said he'd used it up by the time she was able to return home to fix up her papers to go back up north, no longer an illegal alien but a green card holder.

About a dozen or so years ago, I started going back to Belmont. I would always take the same route. Turn left off the Savannah after the Queen's Hall roundabout on to Belmont Circular Road, passing the new police station on the rising slope to the left, the Belmont Secondary School, on the spot where the Catholic Youth Organisation once stood, past the grand old family homes, now subdivided into boutique studios and offices, and Providence Girls' School, once just a single grand and charming traditional gingerbread building, scrupulously maintained, now with the addition up the slope of a cluster of new charmless sprawling concrete buildings. Then I'd take the next right down into Pelham Street, turning second right onto Clifford Street, to my destination, the home of a childhood friend, with whom I'd recently reconnected.

But before I got there, driving along Pelham Street, I'd slow down a short way before the junction with Reid Lane so as to be at a steady crawl when passing number 74. From the street side I could see that the house had undergone some changes, had been modernised. The gallery was now enclosed, with burglar proofing wherever there was an opening to the outside. But the shape of the house, the steep pitched roof, with its white finial topping the crest at the front and back – like the twin exclamation marks that bracket statements of surprise and outbursts in Spanish – the fretwork fringed *porte cochère*, the bay bedroom, the twisted-wire fence above a low solid wall, the way the house sat and presented itself to the world, was instantly, heart-clutchingly, indisputably, *home*.

There was never anyone about and the windows and doors seemed to be always closed, so I wondered whether anyone lived there, though I could see it wasn't abandoned; everything looked too tidy, too well kept for that. Perhaps, I thought, they were there, indoors, sealed off in the comfort of air-conditioning – for who is out and about on the road on a weekday in the middle of the hot morning?

But one day there was someone. A man. His back towards the road, he was concentrating on sweeping the drain outside the house. I braked and wound down the passenger-side window. Morning. Excuse me, I said. Is this your house? He paused in his sweeping, stooped to brush whatever he'd gathered into a scoop, pulled himself up along the broom handle, leaned against the broom steadying himself, before he turned to face the car. I felt I could read him sizing me up. Old white car, clearly a roll-on-roll-off, grey-haired woman maybe ten years older than himself, brown like himself, she wearing a tatty T-shirt and unfashionably un-ripped jeans, so perhaps not an estate agent, or insurance salesperson, or developer, or lawyer or anyone of that predatory ilk who, trolling through such neighbourhoods, buy up old property from the vulnerable elderly, to tear down and put up blocks of apartments.

So, not suspicious but puzzled, he took his time to gather his thoughts, the Corolla engine purring softly along with him, before he answered. It belongs to my brother. He's away. I'm staying here. I could sense an unasked question, Why do you want to know? And I offered, I used to live here once, dramatizing, by borrowing a Jean Rhys' story title, to cover my suddenly felt embarrassment at intruding on an old man on a Saturday morning and making him reveal to a total stranger his relationship with a house and his status as someone dependant on a foreign-based sibling for somewhere to live and his exposing his gratitude for this privilege by keeping the place and its surroundings nice. I felt the need to say more, to make up for my flippant explanation of my curiosity. I grew up here, I said. I see your brother made some changes. It's different. But it's still nice. He nodded as if he understood what the house would mean to me even after all this time. I wanted him to say, Would you like to come in? Would you like to see inside? To see what is different? But he didn't and I understood that the conversation had nowhere else to go. I said, Thank you. Have a good day. As if he was a customer and I a Hi Lo cashier.

I think often about that encounter and how I could have made it go differently. Should I have asked to be shown around? How would he have received such a request? Supposing he had a wife or significant other there who would have wondered at his bringing a woman, a stranger, into their home? And what sort of woman would ask a strange man to take her into his home? What would his neighbours think of him? What if he'd refused!

I don't go to Belmont much anymore. Not since my childhood friend died. The picture of 74 Pelham Street in my head shape-shifts between my seared knowledge of it from my childhood and my more recent brushing acquaintance with it, depending on whether my thoughts are in the then or in the now. As is the case with my thoughts on anything and everything, I guess.

Except that, more recently, long years after I had last gone past the house, John Robert Lee, a St Lucian writer whom I knew only by reputation and through his literary email newsletter, but had finally met in person at Carifesta in Port of Spain a couple months earlier, sent me an email.

> Am sending you, on impulse, some recent poems coming out of my recent stay in Belmont. All inspired by my own photos taken as I walked to and from the savannah.

I didn't know he'd stayed in Belmont and I don't think that he knew that I was from there, so I was curious to see what of my old stomping ground had caught his attention and inspired poems. Before reading the poems, I flipped through the attached photos and when I got to a particular one, my breath caught in my throat. There among them was 74 Pelham Street. The poet had been staying at a newish guesthouse built on the site of the Chinese grocery of my childhood. The photo, taken from his second floor bedroom window opposite my old home, showed the house almost exactly as I'd last seen it, except that the *porte cochère* had vanished and the perimeter wall had been raised, swallowing the space where the green twisted-wire fence once allowed passers-by views into the front garden and the golden startle of Marmie's chrysanthemums.

PHOTOGRAPHS

Chuichi Nagumo, born 25 March 1887, Vice Admiral of the Imperial Japanese Navy, lifts binoculars to his eyes. A wintry sun rising over the Pacific horizon casts a feeble shaft of light on to the rail of the aircraft carrier. Six aircraft carriers, forty torpedo planes, forty-three fighters, forty-nine high-level bombers and fifty-one dive-bombers are assembled, primed and poised, awaiting his signal.

Seven thousand miles away in Upper Belmont Valley Road, Yvonne Lafond, born 25 March 1917, is sitting on a low bench by the water cistern. She places a basin under the tap and lifts the lever to let the water flow on to the last batch of new muslin diapers, flannel belly bands and tiny pastel cotton chemises she's sewn and embroidered herself. The noonday sun spins out a blinding dazzle from the twisting stream of water and, as she looks down into the basin at the rising water level, bright pinpoints of swirling constellations pull her into their spinning. She grips the edge of the basin. Steadying herself, she leans over, tips the water away, gathers the little clothes in both hands and squeezes them into a ball. She must hang the little things on the clothesline. She makes to get up, but can't. Every muscle in her body is tensed against the pain that holds her belly in its iron grip.

In the early afternoon of Thursday 4th December 1941, on her mother's bed in her grandmother's house in Upper Belmont Valley Road, Belmont, Trinidad, a baby girl is born.

Her first cry startles two mockingbirds feasting on clusters of fragrant fruit hanging from the tree outside the bedroom window. As they lift off, the rebounding branch disrupts the air, deflects a morpho's smooth glide into a frenzied flutter of iridescent blue, sends a curl of aromatic air through the canopy of leaves to be caught in a rising thermal and transported in the trades across the Gulf of Paria into the Caribbean sea, through the Panama canal and onward to the Pacific, where three days into its journey the tang of chenettes tickles the nostrils of the Vice-Admiral of the Imperial Japanese Navy. At that moment he orders three-hundred and fifty-three Imperial Japanese aircraft to a surprise rendezvous with the American naval base at Pearl Harbour. On Monday 8 December 1941, Trinidad declares war on Japan. Britain and the United States of America do too. With Europe already consuming itself with rage, North America and Asia are drawn into further embroilment.

The mother and the baby girl drift in and out of sleep on their first day as two, wrapped together as if still one, snatches of radio broadcasting from London in another room flowing through the ear of one and reverberating in the head of the other. *A village in wartime… is innocence enough… parents' messages to evacuee children in Canada… Calling the West Indies… Christmas greetings from London from two young Trinidadian airmen, Mr Mervyn Cipriani and Mr Ulric Cross, invited by Miss Una Marson.* Hardly in the world, yet the world is already pressing the newborn with the urgency of its preoccupations. The whole world is at war. And so are the baby girl's mother and her mother. The new mother is twenty-four when the girl is born. Not young, at least not too young to be a mother. Already her twin sister is the mother of four, another sister of two; a third is expecting her first. All younger, all married.

Did she feel left behind, left on the shelf, I wonder. Was that why she, unmarried, had me for a man whose name I did not know until I was fifty, when she, on her deathbed, unable to speak – her larynx and much else surgically gone – at my asking at this last minute, wrote the name of the man who had planted his seed in her, rousing her waiting egg to acceptance, to become me. On that day, almost the last day of her almost seventy-five years, she wrote his name with care on a child's magic erasing slate and, on my reading it, she lifted the clear plastic sheet so she could write more, and that brisk parting of the sheets took his name away, and he was once again gone, swiftly erased. Overlying him was an explanation, an elaboration: that they were in love, they were to be married, that his parents had whisked him off abroad to study, to prevent him being tied down with wife and family. All this she wrote, her scribble wilder and wilder, lines sloping off the plastic page that she lifted and lifted again. And I, there, was looking under each page, trying to get back to where he was, where he'd gone, buried under newer words, overlain by newer stories. I often wonder whether the implantation of half of me was as swift, as casual, as my fleeting sight of the reality of him, a name on that magic slate.

My mother was born in the same house where I was born. I like to imagine it was the same bed, so that I can claim the full weight of the biblical issue of blood connection with my grandmother. She, though disappointed about the shame the news and views of the impending arrival brought upon the family, once I was no longer the visible bulging evidence of her daughter's downfall, but a separate, guiltless person, my grandmother loved me.

Growing up in my grandmother's house I saw my grandmother as an old woman – but how could that be? She couldn't have been more than fifty, and now I'd give my eyeteeth to be back there, back at fifty, fifty years young – but what the child me saw as old were threads of steel-grey woven through that single thick dark plait hanging down the exact middle of her straight back, her daily siestas in the darkened bedroom with only the shrill scraping of cicadas for company, a stifling torpor seeping from under the closed door, invading the whole house where we all fight against yet must succumb to sleep, too, as if in a fairytale castle. Above all, in my eyes, my grandmother's advanced age lay in her unquestioned authority over everyone – her still-at-home sons, the visiting grandchildren, the household workers and the tenants on the land. Even her adult daughters living elsewhere, with husbands at home to answer to, children of their own to answer to them, reverted to a childlike helpless state in her presence. But she must have been young once, and there is a story of her early life.

From what my mother told my youngest daughter, her mother was born in Venezuela to parents who were on the wrong side of one of the many civil upheavals in that land during the eighteen hundreds. As descendants of the original people of the land fighting for what was then called native rights – the word indigenous, with the authority of being as much an inalienable part of the landscape as the trees and rivers and soil, was not yet a label of indisputable rights – my grandmother's parents were both killed. My orphaned grandmother, their daughter, and I do not know if only child, was smuggled out of the country and secreted away to be adopted and raised in another family.

When she was about twelve, my daughter, while interviewing my mother, taped that story. In the process of some minor personal upheaval many years after, I, *mea culpa*, must have thrown away that cassette tape, which I had never heard, and was the only record of my mother's voice speaking about a critical part of her immediate ancestors' life. The tape lay jumbled among unidentifiable and indistinguishable tapes of calypso, parang, the Supremes and Grease, and when I committed that unpardonable error, cassettes were obsolete, and I was fighting a lost battle with a plague of termites that had tunnelled and granulated whole wardrobes and chests of drawers. So, at that time, my watchwords were to throw out, discard, minimize; now I know examine, select, preserve would have been a more judicious motto. Here I am with enough time on my hands and the interest to be able to take an unlimited numbers of cassette tapes to a specialist and have them put on CDs, or a memory stick, or whatever is the latest thing, and listen to the recordings at leisure. But no. Dear Carys, I am truly sorry that I did not treat your initiative with the respect it deserved. I have deprived us all of a proper ancestral story.

What else does my daughter recall of that interview? That her great grandmother had grown up in one of the islands to the north, St Kitts, maybe, and was adopted by an English family involved in colonial administration, and that it was at an event after their new posting to Port of Spain that a young Frenchman, a court interpreter, her future husband, was presented to her, my young grandmother-to-be. Given the privileged circumstances of her upbringing, somewhere there must be old family albums, and among yellowing black and white and faded sepia photos, a darker skinned presence, a Dido Belle among the pale Anglo-Saxons whose descendants now perhaps gaze in puzzlement at her image. The only picture I have of her is a copy of a much later photo in an aunt's family album.

It is a formal family photo taken outdoors, perhaps in the front yard of their Belmont home. My grandmother dominates the photo. She is sitting upright, hands folded in her lap; her hair, cut to just below her earlobes, frames a strong, determined face. It is the face I see on every portrait of a warrior Taino, Aruac, Warrao, Kalinago, who inhabited these islands in the millennia before the cataclysm of 1492. It is a deal with me if you dare kind of face. Both her feet are firmly planted on the ground, as if she'd stamped them there to assert her right to that space. Even seated, she is a head above the man in the chair next to hers. He is slouched in that careless louche way of those white men of that time who were not descendants of land-granted cedulites, not of that proud entitled aristocracy, not formerly owners of chattled human beings. He is sitting with the kind of pulling in, the trying to minimise themselves, that men like him seemed to adopt when photographed with their family. That slightly-built, pale Frenchman, my grandmother's husband, the grandfather whom I never knew, had disembarked in the Port of Spain harbour when a ship from Marseille had anchored offshore, awaiting bunkering on its way to Brazil. Then he – ship's boy or runaway, independent child immigrant or transported, indentured minor, aged thirteen or fourteen or fifteen – was taken or captured or adopted at the docks by a securely settled Portuguese merchant whose family name, Pestana, and confident profile are memorialised on an oval bas-relief complete with laurel wreath on the back wall of the family plot in Lapeyrouse Cemetery Port of Spain, where he, my grandfather, was to be buried some forty something years later. Also seated in the photo is another man who is discernably half Chinese, round-faced, mixed with African and something else. He is Moon, my mother's twin sister's husband.

Standing behind and flanking this front row are the Lafond children, very pale and at first glance seeming somewhat uncertain. My Uncle Carmie, the eldest, the only boy in long trousers, stands slightly aside, observing the others, as if already aware that responsibility for their wellbeing would fall on his shoulders, and he's trying to discern which of them he'll have to take care of. The other boys, Tebeau and Véné are in formal knee-length trousers. Véné, hands in pockets, the artist-to-be, carries off an air of insouciance. Tebeau is a boy. That's all. A boy-boy. Maybe thinking of the game of marbles he's been called from to get bathed and dressed for this formal family photograph. There are four girls. The twins, my mother Yvonne and her sister Yvette, can be distinguished apart only because Yvette is holding a baby, my eldest cousin, Lenfar. Yvonne and Yvette, probably just eighteen, sport flapper hairstyles, shoes and dresses, as if ready to go to a dance and are looking forward to doing the Charleston. Nissa is there, in plaits and big floppy hair-ribbon bows, looking down and away, not looking at the camera. And there's Fiette, the baby of the family, holding a doll and standing in that belly-thrusting-forward way of little children. These are the names I know them by, and not a one is the name on their birth certificates.

When I was ten, my mother handed me an envelope to take to school to present for registration for the College Exhibition Examination. I opened the envelope before handing it to my teacher and that's how I saw my birth certificate for the first time. I read the first column. Child's Name: Barbara Magdalen. Next column, Mother's Name: Thalitha. I stop reading. My mother is Yvonne. Who is this Thalitha? I am the eldest child of Yvonne Lafond. Am I who I think I am? Does Thalitha know that someone called Yvonne has me and says she is my mother? Maybe this Thalitha person was a friend of my moth… a friend of Yvonne's and Thalitha got sick, very sick, and she left me with Yvonne before she died. That's to prevent me being sent to the orphan home. When I peep through the gap where the galvanised fence around the orphanage has pulled away, I see the orphans running around the yard. They wear a uniform even if it isn't school time. Rita, who lives on Belle Eau Road near the orphanage, says that's so people can recognise them if they try to run away. Rita says that sometimes ladies get very sick when they are having a baby and if they die the baby is put into the orphanage. I wonder whether Thalitha died while she was having me.

I slipped the paper back in the envelope so no one else could see it. When Mrs Thornhill called for the birth certificates I handed mine in like everyone else. I sat there in class all morning, but it was as if I wasn't there, yet at the same time not aware of being anywhere else, as if I was asleep not dreaming, with eyes wide open. And then, as I began to notice where I was and what was going on, I started to try to work out the puzzle of the names and eventually I decided that maybe Thalitha was another of my mother's names, just as I had two, a first name and a middle name, and that for some reason she chose not to put Yvonne on my birth certificate. I had never heard anyone call her Thalitha. She was always Yvonne. What strikes me now as particularly sad about how I felt at that time, what I went through that long confused morning, is that when I got home, still thinking, still trying to agree in my head with what I had worked out was the reason for my mother's different name, I put away the envelope with my birth certificate in the old grey handbag in the wardrobe where Marmie kept precious papers, and when Marmie got home from work that night I did not ask her about it.

One by one as they died, my mother's siblings' true names were revealed on their funeral programmes. It was as if at death they were born again to their intended identity, that their life here with those other names was just a temporary sojourn. I tried to imagine what different life reclusive sibilant Nissa might have lived if she had been called instead by her definitive, explosive Merle. Or Tebeau – 'Ti Beau, handsome little one' – if he'd worn his more macho Leon name, would he have been bolder, more self-assured? And Fiette – Fillette, little girl, indulged to the last – who would she have been as Nyce? Or maybe that's not so different. I certainly believe that had my mother been called Thalitha – all three syllables of it with that repeated *th* sound which demands care and attention in its articulation, tongue between the front teeth twice in one eight-letter word, the open-mouth for the *ah* sound also twice, the stretched lips for *lee* – she would have been treated with more respect and my birth certificate would not have read Father's Name: Illegitimate.

Auntie Nissa named me Barbara because she was a fan of the movie star, Barbara Stanwyck, and considering the shameful circumstances of my conception, perhaps nobody else cared enough to bother to suggest an alternative. Marmie and all the family always called me Babs; my children, Babsies. I get Barb, Barbie, from friends, but mostly it's Barbara. But Auntie Nissa must have been doubly inspired. When I was fourteen or so I visited a friend who had the Catholic calendar, a big paper poster, pinned up just inside her front door and, as the dates of many feasts depend on the moon, they change every year (Easter, Good Friday, Corpus Christi, Pentecost and so on), so you need to buy a new calendar every year to know when those important feast days fall. Such a calendar was not an item in which Marmie could invest a whole shilling. So while waiting for my friend, I idly glanced down the list of three hundred and sixty-five feast days and saints' days. When my eyes landed on my birthday, they couldn't believe what they were reading. It turns out that my birthday is the feast of St Barbara, virgin, martyr. It is a fixed feast day, every year, same date. I felt marked, singled out in some way and not in an altogether nice way either. More like an invisible mark on my forehead. I don't know whether she's still venerated, St Barbara, that is. The Catholic church purged dozens of dubious characters from its list of saints after I left it, and I haven't checked on her fate since. I wouldn't be surprised to discover that there was a double purge – of both my eponymous saint and me. I've never told anybody that coincidence of my name, for who would find it as full of foreboding as I did? I don't know what criteria my Lafond grandparents used to name their large family; I don't think any of their names are of those of saints.

Papa and Maman – Puppah and Mummah to their children – my grandmother was Frances, my grandfather, Eugene. He was a linguist, speaking and interpreting French, Spanish, Portuguese, Italian and English. Could he have been a ship's boy for many years and picked up in the quick easy way that children do the many languages of crew and passengers before that final fateful disembarking. With this facility he worked in the Trinidad courts interpreting back and forth for the polyglot inhabitants and transients of this Babel of a British colony who brought their matters, or had their matters brought, to His Majesty's Courthouse at the end of the 1890s and the early 1900s. This is in the known record of my grandfather's life. It is said he later added a smattering of Hindi and Bhojpuri, but not for use in an official capacity. His other vocation was the garden. He was an ardent horticulturist.

On land in Upper Belmont Valley Road, he set out to create a new Eden, carving out a space on the riverbank and on the forested slopes of that cool tightly bound valley to cultivate, not food for his growing family, but prize hybrid roses, gladioli, dahlias and carnations from cuttings, slips, bulbs, corms and tubers imported from Holland, as it was then called, ordered by handwritten letter in English with a postal order in pounds sterling, and brought in the holds of ships tenderly packaged in paper and corrugated cardboard. This last I learned from my Uncle Carmie, who along with my mother inherited the gardening gene. Uncle Carmie himself continued to grow temperate flowers in a tropical land to the day he died.

I like to imagine my grandfather in the soft afternoon sunshine in that quiet garden. He is wearing a straw hat and walking among the flowerbeds, removing excess side shoots from roses to encourage air circulation and sturdy upward growth; banking up at its base a top-heavy gladioli, its spike a row of fat buds about to burst open; dead-heading dahlias past their best to encourage the new buds to open. Or at night, in the flickering flame of a pitch-oil lamp, head bent over the latest illustrated catalogues that had been left at the post office in town for his collection, poring over the pictures, descriptions and prices of the newest species and hybrids to choose for his expanding garden. It is only there and in the courthouse that I can see him as autonomous, in charge, and fully himself. Not the awkward displaced person I see in that single snapshot story, slumped in his chair, his native-blood wife towering over him.

Widowed young, with a large brood of barely educated dependants, children and household help alike, and no visible means of support, what could Frances Lafond, my grandmother, do? This much I know from my own childhood. The boys continued the garden, but whereas their Puppah grew flowers for the joy of it, for the showing and sharing of them, they tried to turn the garden into a commercial venture, cycling into town early every morning with handle-baskets full of freshly cut flowers in bud to deliver to the two flower shops there, but the few cents for a perfect bloom didn't multiply up to enough to keep everyone afloat, and I suspect that as young boys with other interests they didn't have the passion for flowers that their Puppah had. My grandmother was therefore forced to make hard decisions.

She had three unmarried sons and three spinster daughters at home when her husband died and his monthly salary came to an end. She had the house they lived in, a grand red concrete structure up on the hill and reached on foot by a narrow dirt track. There was electricity supplied by a kerosene-fired Delco generator and spring-fed, year-round running water stored in a large concrete cistern. She had support staff to feed, house and pay – a cook, a washerwoman, a yardman and a general maid – for who else was there to clean the cistern, remake the path in the dry season, clear the aggressive bush around the house, peel and cook and pound ground provision for food, scale the fish, kill the hog and salt it in wooden barrels, feed, fatten, kill, pluck, season and cook the chickens, mend the broken plumbing, clean the gutters, clear away the fallen fruit that littered the yard, wash, starch and iron the clothes, polish the furniture and floors, and sweep mop and cobweb the house?

She had a smaller house further down the hill, nearer the dirt road, where the family moved to in the torrential wet season when the footpath to the big house flowed swift, sloughing off its packed earth skin, gouging it clean of loose soil, leaving sharp stones and bare, entangling tree roots to trip up and shatter the bones of the unwary. And she also had the land. Acres and acres of land curving around the head of this fertile cul-de-sac valley and reaching to the crest of the enclosing ridge, mainly virgin forest with some secondary growth on the lower slopes where, under the giant immortelles blazing orange at Christmas, there were well ordered cocoa trees, their pendulous pods a reminder of when, not too long before, cocoa was king and fortunes were made in trading beans worth their weight in gold. Yes. She had the land.

I imagine she was encouraged by her sons who, after a couple of years perhaps, saw little future in flowers and in any case may have seen themselves about to leave home and start families of their own, and what could their mummah do left by then with one spinster daughter and all those servants to look after if she didn't have a dependable monthly income? They saw an opportunity in what was going on further down the valley, in the village once called Freetown which was growing and densifying apace, with its runaway snaking paths and its new, pretty little gingerbread style houses. There was a real and increasing demand for a piece of land to put down a board house, raise a family, and go to work as carpenters, joiners, masons, stoneworkers, metalworkers, electricians and plumbers, clerks and messengers, hewers of wood and drawers of water. This demand came from the land-denied descendants of the enslaved who were swarming into the city, people who had been shut out of possible agricultural employment by the recruitment from British India of indentured workers, shut out from the very lands where generations of their enslaved ancestors had worked for centuries as the property of their masters, without reward or reparation, while the slaveowners were compensated for the loss of their human property when enslavement ended. The ex-enslaved people were joined by new arrivals, Africans fresh from the homeland, who'd been on intercepted ships bound for the Caribbean after the slave trade had been officially abolished, but an illegal trade still flourished. These newcomers brought with them their languages, their gods and their rituals, rekindling the sparks of ancient memory in those who'd long been here, resurrecting meaning in their own diluted and syncretised practices. Those already here grounded the newcomers by welcoming them to a blurred but familiar space. News of this busy world was brought to their mother by her sons; they moved freely between the big red house hidden in the hillside and the bigger world outside. They brought tales of the liveliness, the hustle and bustle of the expanding village down below, so that my grandmother either decided or agreed to let small parcels of the land to tenants.

Access to the family land, even when I was quite grown up, was by a dirt road since the paved road ended some half a mile away from the house, but in the absence of cars that wasn't a problem, because the rare mule cart with its huge iron-shod wheels, as well as horses, donkeys and bicycles could negotiate the ruts and humps and, of course, everyone with the benefit of functioning legs walked. This dirt road ended at my grandmother's house. Soon, however, it sprouted branches of dirt tracks up the slopes to the small houses of raw wood and corrugated galvanize newly dotting the hillside. I remember the land rent for each tenant as being sixpence a month and this was paid by the tenant in exchange for a receipt torn out of a book where a carbon copy resided as the only means of record keeping. Over time, these houses were made wider and higher as clay blocks and concrete blocks replaced wood, but even though the tenants' fortunes increased, the land rent stayed the same – small enough before, it had become a mere nuisance, a peppercorn.

When I think about my early childhood, the years that I remember most fondly are those spent up the Valley Road with my grandmother, my uncles and my cousins during the long school holidays. The taxi our mother hired for the journey would deposit us with our bags and baggage where the pitch road ends and the dirt road begins. We stand in the black puddles of our noonday shadows and watch the taxi reverse, whining back down the road until it finds a place to turn and its sound fades until we can no longer hear it, and the silence of where we are seeps into the space that's left, a soundless presence. Only then do we turn away and set our sights ahead. The sun is bright, but I can barely make out the dirt road ahead as it bends away from us into deep shade. There is something mysterious about the darkness and the tightly packed trees with dense intertwining crowns. I am a-tingle with the fear and excitement you feel in the cinema, watching that part of a film when explorers on an expedition in the jungle are about to enter a world they know nothing about – an older, different world.

On the visit I'm now thinking about, my mother is carrying baby Tony in her arms, a bag hooked over that crooked arm and the other hand holding the hand of the second to last child, Carol, then three or four. But even so, burdened as she is, Marmie seems lighter, younger. She is excited, pointing out familiar sights, anxious for us to remember this place, to be one with her in her joy at coming home. Davis' house, she says; remember? She points with her chin upwards to a house perched on a steep slope above us. I say nothing, I don't know why it matters, but I nod in agreement and look away to peer down at a level piece of land at the side of the stream that borders the road along which we came. Down there sits a squat pink concrete structure. In faded blue over the door I can make out these letters: *ose ow*. I say, ose ow? I say h-ose ow-l. I look again and say, nose own. And lose how. Marmie gives me one of her trying-hard-not-to-laugh looks. Rose Bowl, she says. That's the name. I am looking for roses and bowls. I see a misguided bois canot that has taken root in a crack in the front wall near the roof. The surroundings are overgrown. There are no roses. And no bowls either. I wonder about names. If you name something Rose Bowl, there ought to be at least one rose and one bowl. It's confusing. Bois Canot. Razor grass. Those are more truthful names. Marmie waits while I puzzle over the Rose Bowl; only when I lose interest and turn away do we carry on walking. On the right, down in a hollow, there's a compact little wooden house like a storybook elf's cottage. Marmie calls out, Dédette, oohhoo, Dédette! At the window a round, creased face, looking every inch the expected elf, appears. A mouth opens and a high fine voice says, Yvonne, is you? Marmie says, Yes, is me. The elfin person says, but look how big the children getting. Marmie stops to name us for Dédette and we children stand silently and look at the ground through this ritual which I, the eldest at ten or so years old, and therefore the one with the longest memory, know will be gone through over and over again in the weeks ahead.

I am carrying two bags, Annette, aged seven, one. We walk at Carol's pace as she alternates between stopping to look at every patch of moss, every puddle, every shiny mica stone and dragging at our mother's dress, tired, begging to be picked up. I'm too irritated at her whining, and too tired from the bags getting heavier and heavier, to pay attention to the moment when we enter my favourite part of the journey, where the road suddenly turns again and, as if a stage curtain has been pulled back, Ta-Da!, we are in a pool of light where a gap in the dense cover of nameless trees allows the overhead sun to enter at this time of day. The little stream alongside is glittering as it slides by. I stoop close to catch sight of a cluster of tadpoles doing headbumps in a circle, tails waving behind. This is the point on the road where my mother stops, too, and lets out a loud shrill sustained whistle – *Ah quooooookie a quooo coo.* Everything around us is still, holding its breath like me, as we wait. She whistles again *Ah quooooookie a quooo coo*. Trees shake, leaves tremble, parrots screech, butterflies flit upwards, as out bound our two uncles, Véné and Tebeau. They swoop down, sweep a child under an arm, take our bags and run away, lost to our sight. By the time they get back for Tony and me, we're almost there, standing near the foot of the grand steps, looking up at the family home, waving to our grandmother who has come out onto the encircling verandah to see us arrive.

I find it hard to pinpoint what we did in that long, unstructured six-week spell of the rainy season school holidays at the house in Upper Belmont Valley Road, yet it is stored in the deepest parts of my memory as an idyllic time. There was bathing in the river and bathing in the rain, there was acting out dolly house with cousin Marilyn's dolls, combing out Granny's hair during her siesta and trying to plait it back, watching the man clean the cistern of moss and debris, learning how to pound plantain in the wooden mortar and pestle, and eating buckets and buckets of ripe mangoes and chenettes picked in the forest by Gabriel who, on one otherwise indistin- guishable day, fell out a tree and was raced by jogging uncles on a makeshift hammock stretcher to the pitch road where a car took him to the Colonial Hospital to fix what turned out to be only a broken arm.

The adults in the house went about their business, looking after us in that casual way one looks after pets that live outdoors and have lives independent of their owners, with little or no noticeable supervision or interference. Somebody must have cooked our meals, washed our clothes and made sure we were all in by dark, but I don't remember any instructions or prohibitions, so we were free to roam and do as we liked. At night, we fell asleep anywhere and everywhere and would wake up in places we didn't remember being in before falling asleep. Some nights I would hear, through my sleep, sound coming from far away, drumming, patterns of tap, tap, tapping of palms and fingers on drums, skin on skin, drums sounding like different voices talking to one another, a conversation weaving through my dreams. I would wake next morning and the sound would be gone and I'd convince myself it was only dreaming.

There was nothing to make anyone suspect that the smooth operation of that household rested on a very precarious foundation – land rent from the tenants. It wasn't long before that income proved to be inadequate. I don't know what was the big expense that my grandmother faced – it could have been as simple as a final demand for back taxes on the land, but something sudden forced her with no alternative but to go to The Building and Loan Society to mortgage the land. By then just two of them were left in the big house up the hill; the smaller house down the hill had been for many years occupied by one of her daughters, estranged from her husband. Véné and Tebeau had left, got married and had families of their own, so she was there with one son, Carmie the eldest. He had been injured or infected, bitten or stung, attacked or invaded, by something unknown, some thing with a paralysing venom, some thing with a fever that flamed his joints, some thing with a chill that froze his bones. He'd been lost for a fortnight in the forest and left a cripple. The fingers of his left hand were bent immovably into his palm, the fingers of his right hand not quite so tight, the index only bent, not immobile, the other fingers bent quite far in but with some mobility and the chance of a gap, so that forever after he had to use his knuckles and free thumbs, index finger and the space in his right hand to hold things. His right foot had been left so twisted back at the instep, like a foot-bound Chinese girl, that he had to wear a roomy shoe with a wide tongue that laced from deep in the toe box, so that the shoe on that foot had its front half tilted up, empty, and the tread of that part of the sole, never trodden, would remain deeply grooved and clean.

I think of my grandmother marooned up there in later years when I, old enough to be left at home in the holidays to take care of the others, no longer went for extended periods. The red of the house had faded to patchy pink, the white balusters on the grand steps leading up to the top floor had grown dingy with red dust, windblown from the dry season baked laterite. There were strategically placed rainy season buckets and basins on the floors to catch the rivulets and cascades where the galvanise-sheeted roof, reduced to red rust, leaked. There was just one helper, an old retainer who stumbled uselessly about, so that the bush overtook the yard, the chickens refused their coop under the house, roosting instead in the encroaching trees from which their eggs dropped like alien fruit, smashing below, slimy and golden, useless as food for people, but slurped up by the waiting Cinderella, Uncle Carmie's pet dog. He said hunting had made he and Cinderella swap life chances; she was a rags-to-riches stray hound who'd wandered, emaciated and depressed, forgotten or lost by one of the hunters who roamed the hills following the spoor of deer, manicou, lappe, agouti and quenk, but now she was at the big house, not required to work for her living, leading a charmed life, while he? Well, what more was there to say about his very different post-hunt metamorphosis?

And my grandmother, dishevelled, neglected, her now pewter hair escaping from its restraining plait, refused to leave the house of her marriage to go to live with one of her married daughters, until a bout of fever rendered her incapable of resistance and she was moved out of her Upper Belmont Valley Road home to a smaller rented house in Champs Fleurs, with running water and electricity that required no management on anyone's part, a paved road in front and a shop nearby, and cars running as pirate taxis all day and night, right in front of her gate. With the weight of day-to-day property responsibility off her shoulders, my grandmother became a new person. She started to visit her children and grandchildren, all too busy and grownup themselves to make the trek to see her, spending two days by one, a week by another and returning, refreshed by what she saw and did in new city locations – St James, Mucurapo, Boissiere, St Francois Valley Road, Maraval and Woodbrook – full of astonishment at the success at school and other achievements of her couple dozen grand-children. The introduction to new places ignited in her an urge to move home often. It seemed that every few years she lived in a different place. Champs Fleurs was followed by La Pastora and then La Seiva. She never went back to her Upper Belmont Valley Road home. Ownership of the land slipped away into other hands, to one daughter's husband, to another daughter, to the tenants and to the mortgagors.

I was twelve and had just started school at the convent, when my mother, silent and serious, took me, me and her alone, by hired car to a place on Long Circular Road. It was a series of low wooden buildings surrounded by a wire fence. Someone was waiting for us on the other side of the fence. Her flapping cotton nightdress reached to halfway down her calves, bony and shrunken. Stick-thin arms hung from too-large sleeves, her hair sparse, totally grey, limp. On seeing us she smiled, and only by the smile that sparked bright her face did I know the apparition to be Granny. She didn't put up her hand to touch mine when I pressed it against the wire mesh and my mother quickly pulled my hand away, placing my arm firmly at my side. I was forbidden to tell anyone, least of all Pappy, that we had gone there, that we had been to see my grandmother.

Not long after, the head nun at the convent came to my classroom and beckoned the teacher. They spoke quickly, glancing towards where I was sitting. The teacher called me to the door. The nun told me to pack up and go home. I was wanted there. When I got home I saw my mother slumped on the edge of my cot, the little ones huddled around her. Everyone was quiet as if there was nothing they wanted to say, so I didn't ask Marmie what had happened. I just knew it was something terrible that I didn't want to hear. She said, Babs, Granny died.

News of the death of 'ole lady Lafond' travelled through Belmont with such speed that hardly had Marmie come back from making arrangements at the funeral home than neighbours and passers-by began to call out from the back gate to offer their sympathy. Where was the Dead House, they wanted to know. It wasn't here, in our home and I don't remember whether Granny spent the night in the home of another of her six children until her funeral the next day. It probably wasn't in her own home up the Valley Road where one son lived alone, crippled and unable to make necessary provi-sion; nor at any of her other daughters – their husbands or circumstances wouldn't allow; and of her two remaining sons, I can't imagine either of their wives permitting the level of disruption such an accommodation would cause. Marmie had the responsibility for everything as the eldest daughter, even though she was oldest only by the few minutes that separated her from her twin sister. She was the one who went to the funeral home, but even so, she didn't arrange to have Granny brought to our two rooms. How could she? She had no jurisdiction there, she wasn't the one paying the rent, so I'm guessing that Granny stayed at the funeral home until she was brought to the church for her funeral service.

I think, now, that at the time Marmie must have been overcome with remorse that she couldn't do more for her mother in death, that she couldn't bring her home. But I think she comforted herself that it was only her mother's body in the funeral home and her spirit was anywhere it was welcome, and that her mother would understand she was doing her best. My mother acted as if her mother was indeed laid out in her coffin right there in our home. We children watched, not understanding, as Marmie dragged out a cardboard box from under her bed and pulled out old dresses, old school uniforms, old curtains and the worn-through bed sheets that were stored there. She shook each piece free of folds, held it at arms' length, looking at it briskly up and down, separating the pieces into two piles. The bigger pile she folded and replaced in the box, then pushed the box away back under her bed. She covered the big round mirror on her dressing table with an old dress of hers, so that it looked as if the mirror was wearing the dress. The two smaller wing mirrors were dressed in my old Tranquillity school overalls. It took two curtains draped over the mirror on the inside of her wardrobe door to shut out its reflection completely when the wardrobe was opened. We had no pictures of people hanging on our walls or else they would have been turned to face the wall. Our one picture, a grocery calendar for that year, 1954, was a scene of a mountain peak with snow on top and black and white cows standing in very green grass sprinkled with little white flowers. Cows didn't count as people, so the calendar remained facing outward.

That evening people came by to pay their respects. How many of the couple dozen folks who gathered in our yard knew Granny personally? I would guess just one or two. It wasn't even as if Granny's body was lying in state in our home as an excuse for people to gather, saying they wanted to see her for the last and how they'd heard their cousin, uncle, nenen, tantie say what a nice lady she was and how life strange, and you never know when it's your turn, and the Lord knows best, He giveth and taketh away, and at least she didn't suffer long, she lived a good life and now she has earned her reward. Few had known her, yet our yard was full of people and poor Marmie in her confusion of grief was fighting up to host a wake. We brought out all our chairs, neighbours came with their own, our little table was brought out and another sent for. Someone brought out a pack of cards, a game of All Fours started. Marmie brought out the remaining half bottle of Vat 19 and glasses, and sent one or other of us to beg a neighbour with a fridge for a tray of ice. Another little table appeared, another pack of cards was cut and a rival All Fours game began, cigarettes were passed around and there were calls for more liquor.

It was after seven, the Chinese shop across the road was shut as required by law, but Uncle, the proprietor, was not averse to facilitating favoured customers. So you called out and listened for the clap-clap-clap of the wooden soles of Uncle's sapats on the concrete path as he approached the gate. After a whispered exchange, a big brown paper bag containing a bottle of Vat 19, a bag of ground coffee, two tins of condensed milk, a five-pound paper bag of three-for-cent Crix, a pound of cheese and seven candles was handed over the gate, and the total added to our curling trust paper on Uncle's wire hook. Now our Marmie could hold her head high that she'd not neglected her duty, except that after everyone had finally gone home and she and I were replacing the furniture, clearing away the glasses and scraping up the candle drips, she said, I would have like some prayers, but nobody wanted to say even one decade of the rosary.

At the time it did not cross my mind that one day in the future my own mother would die and that I, the eldest, would have the responsibility that I saw shouldered so naturally that night. And I reflect that when it did come to pass, some almost three decades ago, how different it all went down with Marmie and me, and I wonder, when my turn comes to go, how will my three deal with it from afar, and where will I be and where will I be put? It's not with worry that these questions come to me, only with a mild curiosity, especially now that the family plot has been legally transferred to only one branch of my grandparents' children's families, to the family of Fiette, their last child to die. It's something about the deceased others being tenants in common, so that the families of their other six children, my mother's and mine as well, are alienated from the right to occupy that plot in death. But in my grandmother's case she is there by right of ownership, and it is at her funeral that I first become aware of the Lafond plot at Lapeyrouse Cemetery.

At four o'clock on the afternoon of the next day, the hearse with my grandmother inside arrived at St Francis Church, Belmont. We children were encouraged to go to the open casket to see her for the last time. I looked in the white, satin-lined box to say goodbye. But Granny wasn't there. Someone had made a statue, a statue like the ones in the church, but not out of marble, out of wood. What was in that box was fixed and solid. Whoever had made that model – looking a little like my Granny – had made it hard and shrunken; the face was pulled in tight and I could tell it was an imitation Granny lying in that box. I turned away without saying goodbye and followed my mother and the others into the church. When I knelt at the pew I couldn't stop thinking about it, all through the service with the priest chanting in Latin and the waving of the smoking incense censer over the closed casket, and the thou art dust and unto dust thou shall return in Latin, the sprinkling of dust in the shape of a cross on the casket, and my mother beside me, her shoulders shaking with the strength of the crying that had been fighting to get out, and she'd been holding back, but couldn't, so the little ones were streaming tears because Marmie was crying. When I thought about it, what came to me was the idea that what makes a person a person is a special force inside, like a light burning in a lamp, something different from a soul because a soul is like a slate on which sins are written – some big, some small, and rubbed off or not, depending on whether you go to confession or not and get absolution and do penance or not – but what makes a person a person is different from that. It is the thing that makes the body move and do things and think things and shine to be who the person is, and the light of every person is different from the light of any other person and when that light inside goes out the person is gone and what's left is like a lamp without a light; it is an ornament but of no use, and when the light goes from a person what is left is a shape like the person, but not the person. I was crying because seeing my Granny like that, like a useless wooden statue, made me realise that her light was truly gone out and would never shine again and that was something to really, really to cry hard about, because that light had been mine for twelve years, the only grandparent light I ever had, and now, now it had been put out.

At the front of the cortege was the Haynes and Clark hearse, its roof straining under the dozens of wreaths; it was followed by a couple of cars ferrying some who couldn't or wouldn't do the procession. Behind the hearse were Granny's children, their spouses, their children, the tenants on the land, friends of the family, all of us, everyone dressed in black, or white, or mauve. We walked two or three abreast from St Francis Church Belmont, down Belmont Circular Road, along Jerningham Avenue, around the Savannah and down Victoria Avenue to Tragarete Road and to Seventh Street, Lapeyrouse Cemetery, to plot 916-919, its two-foot high grey walls topped by cast-iron railings, through a heavy cast-iron gate, to where a nine-foot deep trench had been dug. People anxious for another last glimpse filed past the coffin to gaze through its oval glass pane before that window was closed, screwed shut, and the coffin, minus its silver cross – prised off as a sacred memento – was lowered into the pit by four gravediggers with ropes passed under the coffin and through the handles.

I looked to see whether her soul – that part of her with its sins erased by the sacrament of Extreme Unction – would rise then, before the coffin was covered with dirt, but even as I concentrated hard to conjure it up – something flimsy, insubstantial, smoke, mist, a shimmer of heat warping the air – I could see nothing. Each member of the family took a handful of the dirt piled around the hole and threw it on the coffin and when that was done, the gravediggers did the job more quickly with their shovels till the hole was filled, then they heaped the remaining dirt into a mound over the grave, patting it smooth with the back of the shovels until it resembled a loaf of newly risen bread dough. And with that thought I felt comforted by the idea of something risen, as her soul must surely be, risen straight to heaven. The other thought that came was of the bread that is turned into the body and blood of Christ at consecration during Holy Mass, and I felt then that Granny had put those thoughts into my head and it was going to be all right for us because she was looking after us from heaven. Everyone took the wreaths and laid them over the grave, over and around until the whole plot was a blanket of tightly packed flowers, mauve and white, pink and yellow and I was sure that Granny, looking down from heaven, was happy to see it and to remember the days when her husband wandered among his roses, dahlias, carnations and gladioli while she looked down from the verandah of the grand old house.

I knew and loved all my mother's siblings, but my absolute favourite was Uncle Carmie and I would like to believe that I was his favourite among his many nieces and nephews. As I've mentioned, he'd become crippled in the forest while hunting and although he'd adapted to his new state and could do everything for himself – cooking, washing, looking after his flowers, getting around on his bicycle – he felt it would not be fair to his fiancée if he married her. He thought she could do better. Angela Del Piño was a close family friend – it was she who was chosen to be my godmother and, as the story goes, she was heartbroken by Carmie's refusal to marry her. Try as she might, she couldn't persuade him that they could build a happy life together in spite of his crippled state. I remember her as a sweet, kind, if distant godmother who gave me my middle name, and then she disappeared out of our lives, back to the Main where she'd come from. Uncle Carmie never married, was never a father and I think this is why he took a special interest in me, whom he perhaps saw as in some respects fatherless. I think, too, that in spite of his perceived physical limitations, Uncle Carmie, as the eldest, also saw himself as the protector of the family.

Some of his siblings didn't need his support. I think his brothers, Véné and Tebeau, with competent wives, managed without him. Two of his sisters married men who were steady and could provide; another, in constant danger of falling apart, was often too proud to accept help; and then there was Yvonne, my mother, for whom the one constant in life was uncertainty. Uncle Carmie didn't have a job, but he never stopped working. He kept a flower garden all his life. This meant continuing to do, as his Puppah did, ordering stock from catalogues, clearing them from the docks, putting them in the ground, tending them with weeding, pruning, harvesting, transporting them by bicycle, and delivering cut blooms to the same flower shops as he'd always done. He'd be paid the following day for the flowers he'd delivered the day before, in cash – dollar bills and coins stuffed into his trouser pocket by the flowershop girls.

On his way to the family home in Upper Belmont Valley Road from which he'd never moved, he would stop by our home on Pelham Street. I'm thinking about the time in my mid-teens when we'd spread into the whole house. I can see him now, turning into Reid Lane to bring his bike to a halt just in from the junction. He'd perch his foot, the bad foot, on the low wall, balance himself on the saddle, hold with his right hand onto the green twisted-wire fence that topped the wall, and whistle – *Ah quoooooookie a quooo coo* – then he'd call out, very loudly, Anybody home? It would be obvious that somebody must be in, with the breeze billowing the long lace curtains out of the wide-open French doors of the drawing room into the gallery, but confirming presence wasn't the real intention of the call. It was the protocol in those days that you never called a person's name out loud in the street. One of us would come out and Uncle Carmie would ask, *Your Marmie there?* And if Marmie was at home, Uncle Carmie would dismount, wheel his bike along the lane, push it through the back gate, lean it up against the wall, and go into the kitchen.

My mother would be in there, perhaps clearing up after breakfast or preparing lunch. You want something to eat? she asks. Whatever you have, he says. Sometimes there'd be nothing left of breakfast, nothing ready for lunch yet. But often enough she could say, It have a little buljol from this morning. You want that? Whatever it is, he'll have it. He then calls one of us and tugs at the side of his pants pocket. Put your hand in and take some money and go to the shop. Yvonne, what you want? She says she's got what she needs for today. He says to which ever of us is there, Go and get two hops bread, one ounce of butter, and four slices of salami. These my mother makes into two sandwiches that he eats, clutching the bread in his more open hand and balancing it with the other tight one. My mother pours boiling water over a big teaspoon of cocoa powder in a large enamel cup. She puts the cup, a spoon and a punched tin of condensed milk on the table next to his sandwich plate. Uncle Carmie puts down the sandwich, takes the milk tin between his hands and tips it over the steaming mug. The thick milk flows like white lava into the cup. He gives it a twist and the flow is cut off. He places the tin on the table, reaches for a spoon with his hand, grasping the handle between thumb and palm. He stirs the cocoa until its dark brown gets lighter and lighter. He sets the spoon down on the table. He leans over and takes a slurp from the cup, smacks his lips and continues with the sandwich. When the cup is cool enough to hold, he takes it in both hands and finishes the cocoa to the last drop. All the while he's eating and Marmie is doing something in the kitchen, they are talking, talking, talking, talking, sharing what's new, bringing up what's old.

When my own youngest was about five and very chatterbox, Auntie Jeanette, the woman who cared for us when our children were young, said to her, Child, you is a real Lafond, to which my daughter, the talkative child, looked puzzled, not knowing that Lafond is my maiden name, and asked, What is a Lafond? Is it a kind of parrot? This has passed into family legend and I see and read the smirks that my now adult children exchange when I start talking, talking, talking. Now don't you start, dear reader, OK? This is my life and I'll tell it with as many diversions as I wish.

So when Uncle Carmie starts with, I hear…, you're pretending to do whatever you were doing before, but it's to him you're paying secret attention. I hear they talking of cutting a road through the swamp by Laventille. Marmie nodding, thinking, taking her time to ask, to go where? Well, says Uncle Carmie, I suppose from Wrightson Road to connect with the Churchill-Roosevelt. And Marmie chews on this a little before, but that is right through Shanty Town, right by the dump. Yes, says Uncle Carmie, they will mash down the shacks where the squatters and them living, but is what they will do with the people? I, too, chew and swallow what I hear, but can't digest the idea of a new road building in a place where people living. Will the people be moved to somewhere else? Will they just be warned to get out of the way? Will they be told that a road is coming to cut through where they live? While I'm figuring out what could happen, the conversation has moved on. Uncle Carmie is already updating Marmie on current political affairs. He would start with something like, Gomes get vex in the Legco and throw himself on the ground, and Marmie would laugh and say, So what they do? And Uncle Carmie would say, Is not what they do, is what they couldn't do. Since that man weighing a good three hundred pound, you know nobody woulda try and move him. And Marmie, still amused, would say, I woulda leave him right there too. Big people behaving like lill chirren.

But while they would be entertained at the daytime antics at the Legislative Council, matters happening at night downtown were taken very seriously. The Doc was in the square last night – Uncle Carmie pauses to make sure Marmie is listening and when she looks up he carries on. Like that man doh get tired at all. He talk for at least two hours straight. It had plenty people? Marmie asking. Plenty? Man, the place was jam-pack. The square full up, people on the pavement outside and not a man making a move when the doc talking. So what he say? Is history lesson down the line. He name the square The University of Woodford Square and he say he there to teach people their own history that they ignorant about. The priest say Doctor Williams is a communist, Marmie says in her worried voice. Uncle Carmie says, Chuts! Priest? Is not only the priest. You eh see what the papers say? Babs, go and get the papers from mih bike. I'm so excited to be included that I'm there and back in seconds. He can't easily turn the big floppy pages of *The Trinidad Guardian* and he asks me to open at the editorial. He peers at it and raps his knuckle against a paragraph. Read that bit. I read aloud:

The jungle of Woodford Square has been used before for sniping at lions and tigers, though it is an open question whether any bags have actually been made. Now it is being employed as the stalking ground of an aspirant for political honours, who, if not the lineal descendant of a certain bearded demagogue, nevertheless follows him in trouncing and denouncing those he deems to be his enemies, and using the occasion to win political kudos for himself.

I understood practically nothing of what I read. I don't remember hearing about any jungle or zoo with lions and tigers in Woodford Square, nor anyone making bags there either. The aspirant for political honours is Dr Williams, I'm guessing, because what I read is about Woodford Square and that is what Marmie and Uncle Carmie were talking about, about the Doc being there and that's why Uncle Carmie sent me for the papers. What is a certain bearded demagogue? I want to know, but I don't ask. Uncle Carmie says to Marmie, *The Guardian* sayin right here that The Doc followin Communism. I am suddenly very frightened. Just that morning I had read on a piece of paper in the latrine that in California in America twelve, or maybe it was fourteen people were found guilty of being Communist spies and were sentenced, but while I don't remember for sure whether it was execution they were sentenced to, my mind is telling me it is. Americans kill people on electric chairs, which is the modern way, not like here where people are hanged. I wish I'd paid more attention to the story when I was reading it, since our papers are saying that Communism is happening here, but I can't now go and find the piece of newspaper because I had used it and dropped it down the hole, among the creatures whose names I do not know that I can see squirming just below the latrine's oily surface. I don't want the Doc to be found guilty of Communism and be executed, because Marmie and Uncle Carmie like him. So I am frightened for the Doc and for Uncle Carmie and Marmie and even for me, who may be guilty of following a Communist.

I know that to follow Communism is bad. Father Graham said so. He said that the Virgin Mary came to the three shepherd children in Fatima and told them that they must tell the world how bad Communism is because Communists are atheists. Atheists are people who don't believe in God and God doesn't like that. He smiteth the godless. I am afraid that he might smite Dr Williams. If he does, will he also smite Uncle Carmie and Marmie who like Dr Williams, even though Marmie isn't godless. She goes to church every Sunday though she isn't allowed to go to communion because she is excommunicated for having children out of wedlock, but that doesn't make her a Communist to be smitten. I don't think Uncle Carmie is an atheist. He doesn't go to church but I think he believes in God as much as he believes in Dr Williams, but not in the same way, because I think that believing in God is Faith because you can't see Him, but believing in Dr Williams is more like Trust, because you can see him and you're trusting

that he is who you think he is. At least that's what I think. A word doesn't
have to mean the same thing every time you use it. For example take *love*.
You can say, I love God and mean one thing and say, I love ice cream and
mean something different. The Sunday school teacher said if you love God
you should be prepared to die for him, like our new saint, Saint Maria
Goretti, who was killed because she didn't want to commit a sin of the flesh
against God's commandment: thou shalt not commit adultery. I asked the
teacher whether Saint Maria Goretti was married and she said of course not,
she was twelve years old, and that there are different kinds of adultery, the
married kind and the not married kind. I don't think anyone could love ice
cream enough to die for it. I wouldn't. Not even for barbadine ice cream.

Uncle Carmie might have trouble opening a newspaper and turning to
the right page in a hurry, but it is obvious that otherwise he can manage on
his own; he's had years and years of daily practice. I never heard him once
refer to his condition, nor indicate he couldn't do something because of it.
At the end of the meal he motions to his trouser pocket and says to Marmie,
Take something. Buy something for the children. What he means is, I want
to make sure you have enough money. This is not said, but it is understood.
It allows both Uncle Carmie and Marmie to come out of the transaction
with their dignity intact.

Uncle Carmie lived simply. A couple pairs of long khaki trousers, a few
short-sleeved merinos, a khaki cap like the Yanks wear, one pair of tall top
gym-boot style watchekongs. Some pairs of underpants. His domestic setup
was simple. He lived in one room of the big house. The other rooms he
rented out to a variety of floating ne'er-do-wells who were perpetually
unemployed. He looking for work, he'd say when a visiting sibling, out of
concern, asked whether so-and-so ever paid rent. Things hard for everybody
now. And the visiting sibling would see the so-called jobseeker sitting on the
front step, nicely showered, clean merino and khaki shorts, absently picking
his teeth with a bit of hibiscus twig and gazing meditatively into the distance
across the valley, and they'd follow his line of sight to check what work he
could possibly be looking for across there. But no one could hassle Uncle
Carmie too much about it. His generosity extended to everyone and it made
no sense to make him feel bad about it, to indicate that they felt he was being
taken advantage of, for what good would that do? The most the solicitous
visitor could manage is, Huh! he too wutless, in reference to the alleged
jobseeker. Uncle Carmie wouldn't agree or disagree. The visitor was a here-
now-soon-gone passer through. The residents were there all the time.

The set up in his room was a single metal-frame bed with a layer of metal
springs hooked into the frame, a coconut fibre mattress and sheets made
from white flour bags printed in sun bleached red and blue MAPLE LEAF
FLOUR MILLS, one sheet to lie on and another as cover if the night was cold,
a small table with a pitch-oil lamp, a box of matches and a radio.

His wardrobe was a clothesline strung across the room, on which his clean dry clothes were draped. There was no electricity because no one contributed to paying the bill and it had been disconnected. But he paid the water bill himself, a flat rate, saying that it would be the same if it was just him or twenty people and you can't begrudge a person a glass of water. The caring sibling might point out it wasn't a glass of water they were using. The one flush toilet was shared by all occupants, as was the one outdoor shower, a lean-to against the back of the house, two sheets of corrugated galvanise, one open side as doorway, the open sky above; a galvanised pipe bent overhead let down a single stream of water when the valve was opened. The runoff simply ran off alongside the dirt track leading down from the house.

The house was built on a slope so that while the back rested on low concrete pillars, the front pillars were at least some fifteen feet high, creating a big under-house space, like a cave. There the stray fowls, black, white, black and white, red-brown, brown and white, the thin, strutting roosters with magnificent glossy plumage and the plump nervous hens, belonging to no one in particular, after pecking about the yard and foraging in the bush around the house all day, came in for the night, scratched hollows in the packed red earth, laid eggs, hatched chicks of mixed and varied parentage and led their own parallel casual existence. Uncle Carmie shared this under-house space with them.

Outside, at one corner of the front of the house, he had set up on a base of concrete blocks a small water barrel with a tap. Just under the house, in shelter, was his kitchen – a low wooden bench, and another taller bench on which a one-burner pitch-oil stove sat. Under this bench he stored a bucket and a basin. Hanging on nails driven into a strip of wood between two pillars were his kitchen utensils and tools – a two-handled iron pot, a frying pan, a big pot spoon. An old sideboard with a missing leg, propped up by a flat river stone of suitable size and balance, had found its way there and in the drawer was where he kept knives, spoons, a can opener and matches. On top rested a bottle of cooking oil, salt, black pepper, a tin of condensed milk resting in a saucer of water and a tin of cocoa powder. In the lower part, where there used to be hinged doors, lived his plate, cup, a bowl and any dry foodstuffs like garlic, rice, flour and ground provisions, though he never had much of these, preferring to buy small amounts for each day as needed. The other feature of this space was a hammock, a stitched together affair of woven jute sugar bags, suspended by ropes tied round two pillars.

Uncle Carmie washed his clothes himself in a basin under the water barrel. With blue soap he scrubbed out the day's sweat and draped the washing over a clothesline he'd strung under the house, sheltered from the rain. There they'd drip overnight – he couldn't wring out the excess water – and next morning they'd still be damp, but he had another set of clean, dry clothes and that freshly washed set would be ready in his room for the day after.

He cooked his own meals on the pitch-oil stove. Everything he cooked was a one-pot dish. He'd set the pot a third full of water on the stove and light the burner. While it was heating, he'd settle on the low bench to prepare the ingredients for his soup. Let's say he's making a thick split-peas and vegetable soup, a favourite of his. He's assembled what he'll need, small paper bag with dry yellow split peas, bowl, pot spoon, small knife, cup, three eddoes, two green bananas, small bag of flour, three cloves of garlic, four fat leaves of Spanish thyme plucked from a bush on the side of the path, two bird peppers, ditto. He pulls the basin from under the bench and positions it on the ground between his feet.

He grasps the bowl and secures it between his knees, picks up the bag of split peas in both hands and pours about a handful into the bowl. Puts the bag back on the bench. Takes the bowl and rests it on the ground under the tap, and runs water to cover the peas. Picks up an eddoe and traps it between thumb and closed fingers of left hand, reaches over and slips the knife handle into the gap between palm and fingers of right hand and peels the eddoe. The peel falls into the basin at his feet, the slippery eddoe slides down. He peels the second, the third. He peels the green bananas. He reaches down and tips the bowl by pressing gently on the rim until the water runs off. It is cloudy with the floury dust from the dry peas. More water, a further rinsing until the water runs clear. He picks up the bowl and tips it into the now seething water in the pot. A few peas are stuck to the inside of the bowl. He adds water from the tap, swirls it around, they loosen and fall into the pot. He shoves the basin under the tap with his bad foot, turns on the tap, the skins and peeled vegetables separate. He reaches down and transfers the vegetables to the bowl and into the pot, tips the basin over and the water and peelings flow away to the open drain. The chickens, standing around, now squawk excitedly, flapping over to the drain to fight over the peelings and the few escaped peas.

He stirs the pot, puts on the lid and turns down the flame. The flour is at hand and he tips some into the bowl wedged between his knees, places his cup under the tap to catch a half cupful of water. He adds this to the flour, reaches over and picks up the saltshaker in both hands and adds a little salt. He puts his whole fist into the bowl and pummels at the water-flour-salt mixture until it becomes a dough. He hammers the garlic cloves with his fist and the skins split. He teases out the pulp with a crooked finger and brushes it with one hand into the palm of the other. He opens the pot, drops in the garlic, the thyme and bird peppers, sticks the knife into whichever bit of provision is visible to check its progress and, if satisfied, picks up the spoon and uses it to cut scoops of soft dough, dropping them into the soup to make dumplings. Ten minutes later, he turns off the stove. The soup is ready.

Uncle Carmie must wait for it to cool a little before he can handle the pot to serve himself. From his vantage he can look down the valley. The sun is low. Its slanting rays gild the edges of banked violet clouds. He watches its swift glide downwards until falls behind the ridge. Evening has come. Cool air slips down the hillside, a light chill begins to settle in the valley.

One of the residents walks up the path. Like yuh makin soup, neighbour? he says. Yuh feelin for some? Carmie asks. Well, I eh eat nutten since morning, comes the answer. Take the bowl, Carmie offers. The guest serves himself. The host reaches up and, with an old merino serving as gloves, grabs the pot by both handles and lifts it off the stove. The pot will serve as his bowl tonight. The guest tells of his day. Carmie listens. They talk sport and politics. The hens come in and fussily settle to sleep. The guest leaves. Uncle Carmie piles the dishes into the basin, runs the tap, rubs a cloth over the bar of blue soap and washes up his wares. The young new moon has risen and set. It's too dark to do any more. With his bad foot he pushes the basin of clean wet dishes under the tall bench. He'll put away things tomorrow. One more thing, though.

He fishes out from his pocket a couple dollar bills and places them on the sideboard, securing them from blowing away by lifting the milk tin saucer and pushing the corners of the bills under it. The bills will be gone by next evening, but the pitch-oil bottle that feeds his little stove will be full and so will his water barrel, with its lid tightly secured to keep out dust and breeding mosquitoes.

He can find his way to his room in the dark, but tonight there is the pure light of a billion bright stars in a crisp, clear untroubled black sky. He takes off his clothes and gets into bed, reaches over and, pressing down on the top of the radio to steady it, he fumbles with the bent right index finger to click the switch to catch the news. Several minutes of roaring and shouting from what he can see in his mind's eye is a packed crowd in Woodford Square, The *University* of Woodford Square, he corrects himself. When that subsides, the voice comes on again, This is The Peoples National Movement. Uncle Carmie looks up at the ceiling. History happening.

There were four girls in the Lafond family. I say girls because all except my mother were wives at fifteen, sixteen or seventeen and moved out of the family home into their husbands' family homes. I think of these young, soft, malleable, gentle Lafond sisters from the quiet, relaxed, fairly privileged country life of Upper Belmont Valley Road thrown into three very different sets of circumstances with men whom they hardly knew and a family of in-laws – a new mother and father, new brothers and sisters – some of whom were welcoming, some hostile – into an unscripted history of quarrels, friendships, backstories and ongoing feuds they would know nothing of, and be expected to fit into. It's a risky business trying now to assess how these girls coped. They didn't talk about their lives. All are dead now so I can't make up for my earlier oversight in failing to extract from them their stories, in their own words. But I knew all of them in my growing-up years and after, as an adult myself, and I can try to say how they seemed to me.

The youngest of the sisters, Auntie Fiette, was the last Lafond of that generation to be born and the last to die. In her latter years I saw quite a bit of her, and one day she told me a story that, from the first quarter of the twenty-first century, seems like something out of medieval times.

Mummah and Puppah, the Lafond parents, used to order their groceries from United Grocers in town and get some other supplies, perhaps wine, from a wholesale and retail alcohol outlet at the corner of Prince and George Streets, owned by an Indian man and run by him and his son. Was it by going, perhaps with a brother, into that latter establishment that Fiette first saw her future husband, one of the sons of the proprietor? How did they court? How did they agree to marry? She didn't say, but this story is of the day they were going to be married as she told it to me.

I came down early that morning and sat on a bench on the customer side of the shop, waiting for Pa to let Shaffick finish work so he could go with me to the Red House. But it was a busy day and when he told him he could leave and we got to the Red House to get married the clerk at the registry told us it was too late. They had finished registering marriages for the day. He pointed to the big clock on the wall. It was ten past twelve. Shaffick returned to the shop and I went back home. I came down the next day and waited. When things were a little quieter, Pa told Shaffick he could go. We went back to the Red House and got married. My sister Yvonne, your mother, was a witness and one the clerks was the other witness. Shaffick and I then walked back to the shop. Shaffick went behind the counter and continued to work and I sat on the bench. When the shop was closed for the day we all went to his home together. It was the first time I saw where he was living and where I was going to be living too.

As a child I often went to spend the day at the house that became home to Auntie Fiette. One of a pair of identical cream two-storey concrete houses, with an upstairs balcony overlooking the road, my aunt's home seemed grand and imposing, not so different from the house she grew up in. It was certainly the grandest among the mostly single-storey houses nearby. 15 and 15A Mucurapo Road, St James backed onto the sea. When you opened the back gate, blue crabs, with massive upraised gundies and startled eyes swivelling on stalks, scrambled down holes that pocked the black mud extending as far as you could see to meet the white edge of lapping wavelets. In the distance, along the coastline, thick mangrove and coconut trees stretched a long, long way, and just visible on the hazy horizon were the five islands and the white sails of fishermen's pirogues. If there were other buildings, you couldn't see them; they would've been hidden by trees.

My aunt and uncle Shaffick and their children lived with Pa, a widower, one unmarried son who was a lawyer, and an unmarried daughter who sewed garments for a select clientele. Another daughter was married and lived nearby; another son, also married, lived not too far away. It was a very close, hierarchical Muslim family with Pa at its pinnacle. My aunt had been brought up Catholic and while her children were baptized Catholic, the ethos of the household was Muslim. There were rules about no shoes in the house, no bare feet outside, no playing of cards, and set names by which you addressed older people, and who was allowed to eat at table and who was served first. There was haram and halal which I didn't really understand, where your feet could touch and could not touch, and which hand was used for what and other things that everyone seemed to know without being told – as natural as who peed standing up and who sat down to pee – things about what boys were allowed to do and what girls were not, and where they could go and with whom and when. But I didn't see that as a marker of religious difference, but more as the habits of a particular family, and so they were not difficult to adjust to. In those days I don't recall that there was what we would now label an essentialist ethnic identity. At least, not among urban dwellers like my aunt's family by marriage. The women dressed like ordinary women everywhere in the colony with aspirations of becoming more and more western in dress and manners.

When I suggested that the cousins and I go out the back to catch crabs as we did on holiday in Toco, it was met with silence and covert glances until my uncle explained that Muslims don't eat food with shells. No shrimps? No crabs? And no pork, ham, sausage, salami, bacon either, he said, but that didn't disturb me as much as the shrimps and crabs, both of which I loved. They had food taboos, but they were modern in their eating habits; they had plates and spoons and knives and forks when many people still ate with their hands off sohari leaves, something then considered very low-class but has since become fashionable among the wealthy because it affords a rare opportunity to combine identity-origin-affirmation with a conspicuous virtue-signalling display of environmental awareness. My cousins went to whatever school of whatever religious denomination was available and, as far as I remember, they didn't go to mosque. The neighbours in the other big house were more observant of their faith; the women, though wearing ordinary dresses, pulled a light veil over their heads when they left the house. At the time, this seemed to me no more than fashion, like my mother's dress-up hats, and definitely not as serious as the compulsory head covering for us girls and women before we were allowed to cross the threshold of the Catholic church.

This aunt, my Auntie Fiette, became the most prosperous of all the Lafond siblings, and she was generous and shared her good fortune with those of us who were less well-off. I don't think she had money in her hand, but she always had a well-stocked larder. There were many times when Uncle Carmie would come by with two tins of condensed milk or a can of corned beef and say to Marmie, I pass by Fiette today to see how she is and she send this for you. At Christmas, every one of her more than a dozen nieces and nephews got a present, a personal individual gift wrapped in pretty Christmas paper, with a personalized card. From: Auntie Fiette and Uncle Shaffick. To: the child's name. The two of them would drive around from family to family distributing gifts a few days before Christmas. She must have spent a long time choosing each gift, matching gift to child and then wrapping and labelling them, but that didn't cross my mind at the time as I eagerly but carefully unwrapped mine on Christmas morning. Their presents were always toys, not anything we needed like new socks or school books. It was always something nice, something to make us feel special. A doll, a doll's tea set, a book of lavishly illustrated fairy tales or *Gulliver's Travels*, a pull-along train, a kaleidoscope or a Viewmaster with its set of circular cards of transparent photos of scenes of exciting places, like Mt St Helen's or the Statue of Liberty or New England in the Fall. Nice things to treasure. She also brought a family gift – a big tin of Huntley and Palmers biscuits, which we eked out through the season.

Her children got no gifts from any of us, nor do I imagine from any of their other cousins on their mother's side of the family. None of us could afford gifts like those Fiette gave us, not even for one another. Our mother couldn't. What we got from her at Christmas was a new outfit. When I got a scholarship for a free high school place, Auntie Fiette gave me a pair of gold cameo earrings. I still wear them, almost seventy years later, one of the few things I have from my childhood. I know that at the time they cost around nine dollars because a similar pair caught my eye when I was window-shopping on Frederick Street later that year. In those days my mother's weekly pay, as a grocery cashier, was exactly that – nine dollars.

I'm guessing that as a daughter-in-law my aunt Fiette was subject to the dictates of her in-laws, particularly since she lived in their house and her husband worked in his father's shop under the direction of Pa, from the time his mother died when he was twelve, until the old man himself died, but I don't suppose that, while it may have been restricting, it was unkind. I think her new family helped to raise her, to shape her into someone who knew how the world worked and how to make it work for you. They gave her ideas about commerce, about the business world and she learned well. She had seven children, all but the last born when they were still living with her in-laws. She was so absorbed into her new family that, to me, she even started to look like them. Her children looked like their father's family, with not a trace of their mother as she was, the little girl in the old family picture, not a semblance visible in any of them.

There was a close bond and intimacy within Auntie Fiette's family among the children and their parents and an understanding of the boundaries of acceptable behaviour that I haven't seen in many other families. Uncle Shaffick once related to me an incident involving himself and the aspiring suitor of one of his daughters. The young man had approached him in the shop and said he had seen that particular daughter, that he liked her and wanted to marry her. After he'd checked the suitability of the young man's parents and satisfied himself about his other credentials, Uncle Shaffick thought about how he would introduce the young man to his daughter.

I decide, he said to me, that it would be a good idea for them to get to know one another before they get married. I tell the boy he could come home and have dinner with the family. That way we could hear how he speak and see how he behave. Afterwards, I let him come some evenings and sit in the porch with my daughter. But I make sure one or two of her sisters there too. I even let him take her and her sisters to the cinema. The matinee show on weekend, you understand. Going there all together in his car and coming back together right after the show. I tell you something, he continued, Pa didn't like that at all. You allowing too much liberties, he tell me. Anyway I didn't see anything wrong with that, so I let them go. Then the week before the wedding the young man ask me if he could take my daughter to the cinema alone. I look at him good. I wonder what kind of fool he take me for. I tell him, have patience. When the two of you married, you could take her cinema every night if you want, but until then, no. In the end, he wait and they get married. At this point in the story Uncle Shaffick looked at me and smiled a knowing kind of smile. I don't know how much cinema they go to after that.

Auntie Fiette and Uncle Shaffick were inseparable. They went everywhere together. He admired and respected her and she flourished. Somehow they got into racchorse ownership. As part of a syndicate at first, I heard, then outright. They would go to England to the big racecourses and the big races. They went to America. Everywhere they would meet breeders and examine bloodstock. They imported horses with distinguished pedigrees. There are photos of Auntie Fiette smiling, as elegantly dressed as if at Ascot, leading a winner back to the paddock at the Queens Park Savannah, the horse with a garland around his neck. I was away in those years and so missed out on the class elevation this bestowed on the family, but there are albums of photos that my cousins pored over with me so that I could share in reminiscences of vanished glory.

When, finally, they could move out of the family home and build a house of their own, my aunt took an interest in house design. This she honed into a fine skill and soon they were into land development and house construction. She was exacting with her builder, making sure that every house she built was one in which she would be happy to live herself, which she often did, to iron out the kinks that appear only after occupation. She limited the sale of her houses to friends or highly recommended friends of friends, because she saw the transaction as much a gift of her time and interest as a business.

It is only in recent years that it struck me that while my aunt's husband's family did not consume alcohol and none was allowed in their home, nor was served at their four daughters' weddings, no matter how posh the hotel venue, or the social class or religion of the couple hundred or so guests, the family fortune, as it grew from humble beginnings over the years, was founded on a shop in the unfashionable east end of the city whose sole business activity was the selling of alcohol.

In my view, the other two sisters did not fare quite as well. My mother's twin sister, the first of the Lafond girls to leave home, married a prison officer, a man of half Chinese descent. They lived in St Francois Valley Road, the neighbouring valley to Belmont. I remember Auntie Yvette as relentlessly hardworking. With a husband and seven children, all but two boys, how could she not be? I picture her day like this: the daily scrubbing of her husband's two-piece khaki uniform – heavy, bulky clothes – by hand, the boys' long khaki school pants, the shirts, the vests, the merinos, the drawers, the socks, the bleaching out of stains on the patch of round stones out in the yard in the open sun, the rinsing, the wringing, the hanging to dry, the bringing in when rain falling, the taking back out when rain stop, the sprinkling of clothes, the ironing, wrinkles to disappear, seams to create right down the exact middle of each trouser leg, collars to smooth, sleeves to open, epaulettes to flatten, inside pockets to flatten, turn-ups to flatten, self to flatten; the choosing of a chicken, the chasing of the chicken, the catching of chicken, the wetting of the stone, the sharpening of the blade on the whetstone, the running for the basin, the baring of the neck, the putting of the basin under, the cutting of the neck, the squawking, the little prayer for forgiveness, the checking the blood draining into the basin, the boiling of water, the dipping of the chicken into the water, the hurried plucking of feathers, quick-quick, fingers burning, the slicing down the front, pulling out guts, liver, gizzard, the minding not to burst the gall bladder, the heart, oh the heart with valves stronger than hers, the digging into the pelvic girdle to extract kidneys, the freeing of soft spongy pink lungs, the separation of thigh from body, leg from thigh, foot from leg, toenails from toes, upper wing from chest, lower wing from upper wing, neck from chest, breast divided above the breast bone in two, wishbone intact, lower breastbone in two, the back in four – how many pieces?

Enough for everybody. Singe the feet, peel the skin off the feet, cut open the gizzard, remove the little stones, and the lining skin; wash in lime juice, season with salt, pepper, thyme, oregano, rosemary, chopped onion, crushed garlic, lime juice; brown the sugar in oil, drop in the pieces – quick stir, mustn't let it burn and get bitter – lower the flame, put on lid, put on pot of water – rice or provision today? – rice: check pot with chicken, stir, add water, put on lid, raise flame, wash rice, lower flame – that's rain, run outside, pick up clothes, run back in – pot sticking, lift lid, add water, lower flame, put rice in pot with water – rain stop, hang back up clothes, run inside – stir rice, put on lid, lower flame. What else, Auntie Yvette, what else, look round the kitchen good. Oh yes, stew the blackeye peas you put to soak since last night. They come home. They sit to eat. You serve them. You serve yourself the neck and lots of gravy and liver, heart and gizzard, feet and toes. It's my favourite parts, you say. Yvette, don't tell me you forget to season the blood to make pudding?

My other aunt, Auntie Nissa, has always been something of a mystery to me. Separated young from her pharmacist husband, she came back home to live in the lower house with two of her four children; the other two lived in their father's family home with their father, grandparents, an aunt and her children, their cousins. The arrangement seemed to be fluid as the children moved from one parent to the other with whim and circumstance. I see this aunt as being somewhat dreamy, impractical, emotional, loving too much, with ideas about horoscopes, and the stars and the moon and coincidence and fate, and foretelling and foretold – and green. Green was bad luck. Nothing green was allowed. No green in curtains, cushion covers, dresses, shirts, hats, handbags, shoes, not even a button. No green in wall paint, railings, roof. No green jewellery. But oh, my dear Auntie Nissa, in your stubborn pride, you steeped the young green leaves of the soursop tree in boiling water and added sugar to give to your children to quell their hunger and bring sweet dreams; you hid yourself in the dark rooms of the house set among the dense green of Upper Belmont Valley Road, and then, when the children grown up and all but the last gone, you took off and went to work in America, for greenbacks. Nissa wasn't more than forty-something when she took on caring for other people's children in New York, and she was there long enough to imagine some of the boys she'd looked after being among those stiff shrouded mummies she witnessed on TV news being offloaded from cargo planes flying in from Vietnam every night. Indeed, her spirit broke with the futility of her investment of time and love and care and life and my mother was sent for to look after her sister while she recuperated. This took my mother, at just fifty, away from her own dead-end futility to adventure and a new life in New York. All this was while I was away, hands and heart tied elsewhere, with news, as distilled as I've written it, getting to me.

The uncles got married and went away. I saw little of them, so little in fact that one day, when I was ten or so, while walking along the pavement with a friend, the friend said, You see that girl, the one on the left, that one is your cousin. I looked at the two girls coming towards us. The one on the left looked half Chinese, half white. My cousin? Yes. Your uncle daughter. By then they'd caught up. My uncle's daughter looked at me. I looked at her. We passed each other and continued on our way.

My Uncle Véné had married a Chinese woman. She worked in a bank. Her mother didn't approve of Uncle Véné, an artist. He didn't have a proper career like her daughter. Erratic income. Feast and famine. Odd jobbing at a nascent ad agency. Selling his paintings. Decorating ladies' dresses. Designing and making evening gowns for Carnival Queen contestants. They had children, that girl and two boys. One boy died young. They divorced. He remarried, went to live south. I met the new wife when I was already an adult. More children. I remember little boys, all with cherubic faces. Later on, much, much later on, I became friends with that girl. The one whom I'd walked by on the pavement decades before. Her own life echoed that of her parents. Fragile and fraught.

What of Uncle Véné is left? The last name, Lafond, crops up on Facebook, attached to female and male first names. These Lafonds are friends of a Facebook friend so I was emboldened to contact one such friend of a friend, a female I gathered from the name on the thread, and seemingly based in south Trinidad. I sent her an inbox message. *Sorry to intrude*, I wrote, *but your last name is the same as my maiden name. Are you by any chance related to Véné Lafond? I ask because he was my mother's brother.* A week later, a cool brief response. *I asked my grandfather*, it says. *He says that was his father.* End of conversation. So, it turns out she is Véné's great-granddaughter. I wonder why she is so distant. Did she maybe think I had an ulterior motive for contacting her? I suppose I can't really blame her for dismissing my little overture. Can't trust anyone these days. All those scams and identity thefts. Or maybe it was just millennial or gen x or gen z indifference to familial ties? I promise her that one day she will rue this lost opportunity to follow the bright red thread of blood that connects us, just as I am now kicking myself for neglecting to ask people stuff they probably had answers to while they were still around.

But I haven't completely lost my Uncle Véné. I have two of his paintings. One of Auntie Yvette's daughters, Lenfar, the baby in the family photo, seems to have collected a lot of art. From her I got a painting of an orchid by him. The other painting, of hunting dogs at rest, was given me by a friend whose husband, a hunting pal of Uncle Véné's, was gifted it by the artist himself. When my friend sold her country house, the painting didn't suit the décor of her city home. Uncle Véné's two hunting dogs now guard the entrance to my home.

Uncle Tebeau I knew better. He lived in Belmont until he and his wife and their children emigrated to Florida. He'd built a house not far from the family home in Upper Belmont Valley Road. By then the paved road had extended way past the old house, right up the head of the valley to meet with the Lady Young Road that runs along the ridge from the Savannah to Morvant. It bypassed the centre of Port of Spain, at which the city took umbrage and scrambled in unseemly haste to infill and spread and envelop, so the once-imagined bypass is now a main road looping, swooping and climbing along a ledge carved out the side of a sierra, from which rockfalls and landslips and mudslides add to the sudden surprises of snapshot-worthy scenic views as your car inches in traffic. Where the Belmont Valley Road meets the Lady Young Road, there's a dirt track leading to the house in Cascade, the neighbouring valley, where I lived for many years with my husband and family and where my mother stayed when she came from New York to visit us. When my mother was in Cascade, Uncle Tebeau, with a daughter or two would walk from Belmont to visit us. Then I lost sight of them, hearing later that Florida had claimed them all.

I moved from Cascade to Diego Martin almost thirty years ago, but a curious thing happened a couple of months ago. One Saturday, when I was at a workshop in St Ann's, a district adjacent to Cascade, I walked a short distance to a vegetable shop to get some bananas for emergency lunch. While I was paying at the counter, a woman came into the shop and walked up to me and said, You're Barbara. I looked at her closely. Never saw her before. Yes. I said. Sorry but I don't think we've met. She said, I'm your cousin. Portia. Oh my god! Portia! Uncle Tebeau's daughter! What are you doing here? Don't you live in Florida? Yes. I do. I'm visiting. Staying with a friend. And would you believe, I had just said to her – she's driving, she's in the car waiting outside – I'd just said to her I wonder whether I could find Barbara's house while we're in the area. Find my house? I haven't lived in Cascade for a long time. But Portia, how did you know me? Portia laughed. I was in the car just looking out and I saw you walking. Recognised you from the back. Asked my friend to stop. Jesus, Portia, how long you here for? Just a few more days. I'm here with Sandra. Here's my number, I said. Put it in your phone now. Let's talk. I'll come and pick you both up. Have lunch with me before you go back. It worked out. It was just magical. Cousins Portia and Sandra – lost and found.

None of Auntie Fiette's children emigrated. All continued to live in Trinidad and raise their children here. Of Auntie Nissa's four, two stayed, two went; of Yvette's seven, three stayed; all of Uncle Tebeau's four went, then he himself; not sure about Véné's tally, though I know the daughter lives away; and of my mother's four, all four of us away at one time, she herself too, and now only I, myself alone, living in the country where we were all born and grew up.

I've been trying to figure out why some families scatter and some stay, and while I'm sure that big studies have been done and many learned papers in sociology and economics have been written about the phenomenon of diaspora, I have only to do an empirical study of the families I know to conclude that family wealth, especially business wealth, is a major influence in decision-making about emigration. If a family has a business to pass on, complete with a network of business connections and a banking history, it doesn't matter what level of education the children receive, they move seamlessly into either running the family business or starting up something else upstream, downstream or tangential with increased opportunities as times and tastes change. So, the father is into selling haberdashery and what does son and or daughter do? Neither is going to stand behind a counter measuring fabric or helping a customer choose buttons. No. Buy some sewing machines and hire a few girls to make ladies' garments for the new dress shop your sister has opened. And if dad is into wholesale and retail alcohol, son and or daughter open a chain of cocktail bars. Grocery families morph into restaurant tycoons, vegetable stall owners become catering barons, or get a foreign fast food franchise. Those with free primary, secondary and almost free tertiary education, can become doctors, lawyers, engineers. The rest of us, lacking social and financial capital, go away to seek our fortune in places where the sacrosanct myth is that everyone can pull themselves up by their own bootstraps.

BREAD

My mother had four children. I, the eldest, was fathered by somebody other than the father of the younger three, Pappy, who yet was father to the four of us. I didn't really know Pappy wasn't my real father until long after he died, but I now think that everybody else knew. My aunts and uncles knew, of course; maybe my cousins knew but never said; strangers knew or guessed correctly, but only I and, I believe, my siblings didn't. So complete and effective was the *Omerta* on the subject of my paternity that, at twenty-three, I put Pappy's name on my marriage certificate in the column *Father's Name*.

I think it is important to stress that my ignorance of my true paternity, of my true situation in respect to everyone around me, allowed me to go through the early, most vulnerable part of my life without feeling any different or disadvantaged with respect to my family. It allowed me to accept Pappy, my siblings and Marmie without questioning or measuring how we treated one another. Punishments and rewards were accepted as they related to the deeds that prompted them and were not coloured by analysis of family relationships. For that I am very grateful as an adult who now knows. No one lied to me, no one needed to, because I didn't ask the question until my mother was dying.

My gratitude to Pappy for treating me as if I was his child – as if I was just like Annette, Carol and Anthony – cannot, must not, extend to forgiveness for the way he treated our mother. What about her, I wonder, made her the target of his pervasive, relentless, raging cruelty? Hey! Stop right there. What about *her* you ask? How about if you put *Pappy* in the witness box, in the spotlight, under the microscope. What if you ask instead: why did Pappy, my father, torment Marmie, my mother?

When my mother died, four years younger than I am now, her shaking had got less, very much less. There were even times when it wasn't there, when you had to look for long minutes to see if it would manifest. She'd had twenty-four years, almost all of them in America, as a free woman, earning her own living, depending on no one and having no dependants, with financial resources to distribute as she pleased, with a network of mainly diasporic friends to count on and to count on her. Twenty-four years to shake off the shaking and it still hadn't completely gone.

Parkinson's was the quick brown fox jumps over the lazy dog diagnosis, but it wasn't that. It wasn't Parkinson's. Only her head shook. From side to side. As if always saying, no, no, no, no. In denial. Disapproving. Fast-fast-fast, a constant glancing left, glancing right, left-right-left-right, looking at what, looking for what, looking for whom? I first noticed it when I was about nine and over the years it became more rapid, more frequent. I wanted to hold her head. Hold it steady. To force it to stop. But I couldn't because even then I knew it was best to pretend you didn't see it. Isn't that what you do when someone has a different physical characteristic or whatever it's safe to call it now. They know they have whatever they have, it's you to whom it's new, so don't draw attention. It's unkind. So I looked away from the shaking, hoping others would too. It got worse over time; all her energy seemed to go into the constant metronome of her head, keeping time, marking time. Biding time.

His absence was more powerful than his presence. He kept us all under surveillance, even though hardly ever there. But he could arrive, he would arrive, he did arrive, at any moment. Like god. Any day and every day could be Judgment Day. And so everything you did, everything you thought of doing, was weighed against his possible displeasure. The possible transgressions were many. It could be anything – friends, neighbours, activities, clothes, food, drink, time, place. He had a fundamentalist, a zealot's idea of what his woman should be like, what his children should be like, but he never showed us the template. It was like walking through a minefield. There were no signposts. You would only know you'd stepped on a mine when your leg was blown off, or you lost your life.

Pappy was East Indian, like Uncle Shaffick, my Auntie Fiette's husband, and they knew one another quite well. Maybe they were acquaintances, but not friendly, because I now think that Uncle Shaffick may have considered Pappy somewhat low class because of his way of life, but I do know that they shared similar expectations of their women and children. I wonder whether Pappy looked at how Shaffick's household was run – that happy, harmonious household's acquiescence in the expectations of the patriarch Pa, the uncles, the aunts, the deeply felt religious tradition – and wanted us to be like them. Maybe he did. But that would have been merely fanciful on his part, for, whereas their household was built on solid rock, ours was on quicksand.

Pappy had a married wife, with whom he lived as his official address. He had another woman whom he visited regularly, his outside woman. And there was my mother, neither inside nor outside, more like on the side, but also belonging to him. My mother had the recognition, responsibility and risk of being the mother of the only children he fathered. Pappy worked on the docks as a tally clerk for a big merchant company. He drove a car, a big American left-hand drive, registered as a taxi, which he sometimes plied when visitors arrived at the docks and wanted to be taken for a scenic drive or to a beach. He had another car, a taxi too, that someone else, a man called

Satnarine, drove for him. I've listed his possessions, us among them. We children knew about the cars and the job, but we only belatedly got to know about the wife or the outside woman. For a long time we only knew that he lived somewhere else, not with us – that was until Pappy decided that we children should be presented to his wife

Was this some kind of deliberate thought-through decision or a mere vaps? I don't imagine it was discussed with Marmie, but she must have known where he was taking us. Of course, we weren't told what was the plan. Only that Pappy was taking us for a drive. This was so rare that we were too excited to be puzzled. Our Marmie dressed us carefully. Church clothes, clean shoes and socks, tidy hair with ribbons. We sensed that it must be somewhere special. Could it be for a treat like milkshakes at The Dairies? We'd only heard about milkshakes, never been inside The Dairies. With the four of us seated in the back, he drove into the heart of town, down Charlotte Street, along Piccadilly Street, which winds alongside the Dry River. We were now in the area of The Plannings, a public housing development of several streets of walk-up, three-storey apartment blocks. Pappy turned into Queen Street and down Duncan Street and stopped. This wasn't The Dairies. He opened the backdoor and signalled with a jerk of his head that were to get out. We slid out, one by one, dragging our bottoms along the seat, no one urging the others to hurry up. When we were all assembled on the pavement, Pappy locked the car, jiggled his keys, looked at them, put them in his pocket and walked away. We followed him to a door on the ground floor of a tall building, where he stopped. He took out his keys, chose one, put it in the lock, turned it, opened the door and gestured to us to go in.

I went in first. Inside was dark. There were heavy curtains over the windows – I suppose so passers-by couldn't see in. There was a woman seated on a rocking chair at the far end of the room. Pappy guided me by my shoulder towards her. She was dressed up, as if about to go to church, in a pinkish, peachy, silky, long-sleeved blouse with a ruffle down the front and a plaid pleated skirt and, even though at home, she was wearing stockings and black polished shoes with a little heel. Her hair wasn't pressed straight, it had its natural curly texture. It was parted in the middle, pulled back behind her ears and secured at the back of her neck. Her hands were folded in her lap. She looked as if she herself had been carefully dressed, like us, and placed on the rocking chair ready for inspection. Pappy said, This is the biggest. Barbara. Then he introduced Annette and Carol. Then Tony. The last one, he said, and the only boy. She smiled at each of us in turn. She had a nice round, calm smooth face, with powder of a shade that was too light. She didn't have on lipstick. He told her who we were, but he didn't tell us who she was. Didn't say her name. Didn't say why he'd brought us there.

We sat down. She said to Pappy, Give them something to drink. He went out of sight and came back with a tray with six glasses of red soft drink. My glass had a line-drawing of flowers in red. You could feel the outline of the flowers when you held the glass. The lines felt like they were painted on. On the other glasses the flowers were drawn in different colours. Six glasses all the same pattern. A matching set. And ice in cubes from a fridge, not chipped from a piece you got from the shop when you had guests. I was impressed. We sat in silence, sipping the cool drink. Carol started to swing her legs back and forth while drinking. I gave her a hard stare. I was afraid she would spill her drink or drop the glass and break it and that would spoil the set. When we had finished drinking, Pappy collected the glasses and disappeared again. He came back and said to the woman, We going now. She nodded. She hadn't moved in all the time we were there. He signalled us to get up. We did. He opened the door and we filed out, onto the pavement. He locked the door. We went to the car, got in and he drove us home. He stopped the car with the engine still running, reached over the back of his seat and opened the door nearer the pavement from the inside. We got out and went into our yard, round the back to our two rooms. He didn't turn off the engine. He didn't get out. He didn't follow us home. He drove off.

We never saw her again. We never spoke about the visit. Not among ourselves. Not to our mother. Not to him. But I was left with a diffuse feeling of sadness and I wasn't able to locate it anywhere, not on any one person or any one thing. I still can't figure out why he took us to see her. Was it to show her that he could father children even though she didn't have any of her own? I somehow don't think so, for she didn't seem to be hurt by our presence in her home. She was clearly dressed to receive us and she wanted to show us welcome and hospitality. I wonder whether it was she who instigated the visit, wanted to share in some way in his other life, the one with growing children, a life she didn't herself experience. And had my mother agreed to this because she felt she owed this sharing of her children with the wife of the man who had fathered them? I don't think that Marmie was unwilling to let us go to visit Pappy's wife. I think she may have thought of it as some sort of atonement for whatever wrong she thought she might have done to her. Maybe it was Marmie's way of saying, look, something good has come of this, see how nice these children are? This is what I would like to believe.

Our meeting with the outside woman was different. It was Carnival Tuesday and Pappy said he was taking us to see mas'. I think our mother suspected where he was taking us; she knew the outside woman lived somewhere downtown, and she was not happy with us being taken there or anywhere without her on a Carnival day. But she got us ready. Other girls and women wore pants and shorts at Carnival, but not us. It was an article of creed among some Indian men at that time that women and girls were forbidden to wear those garments. I used to think that such men thought that if women wore pants they might get bossy and feel they were as good as men. Wearing pants signalled authority. So who wearing the pants in this house? was a common assertion by men of that time. But now I'm of a different view. It's about women's role in leading men astray. A pair of shorts or long pants shows where the inflammatory crotch is. That sight could inflame passion. A man could not be held responsible for what he would be incited to think or do, and therefore we girls were not to lead any innocent unsuspecting man into temptation by wearing pants. So we were got ready, not quite Sunday best, but in good clothes for Pappy to take us to see mas'. Our mother added one festive touch. She got out her lipstick and painted us girls' lips red and painted a big red disc on each cheek. Not smudged to blend like rouge, but distinct circles like a clown. Even Tony got the clown discs, though not the lips.

Pappy took us to Marine Square, a place I knew from my Saturday morning trips to the Wm. H Kennedy & Co warehouse where he worked and where I was sent to collect the weekly allowance he sent Marmie to mind us. But we didn't go there. We stopped at another building along Marine Square. There were many people there already. It was noisy. People were talking loudly to one another over the sound of the Wurlitzer in the corner playing something I couldn't make out, and I could hear the radio on the wall playing, I going to bite them young ladies, pardner, like a hot dog or a hamburger, a calypso the priest said we were not allowed to sing, because the calypsonian was singing about wanting to come back as a bedbug when he died, and Catholics did not believe in Reincarnation and it was a sin to sing about things to do with other religions. It was only hymns we should be listening to, like the one that Marmie and I liked from the radio, 'Rock of Ages, Cleft for Me, Let Me Hide Myself in Thee'. That sounded like poetry and the Thee part made it sound holy, and furthermore bedbugs were bad things worse than cockroaches, even though many people got them in their beds and even soaking the coconut fibre mattress with a Flit spray gun didn't kill all – even though you could smell the DDT weeks after the soaking – because you knew they were back when you woke up with tiny red bites like a rash wherever your body touched the mattress when you were sleeping. All the while I was thinking those things, we were following Pappy among tables where mostly men were sitting around drinking. They looked as if they were having a nice time. Some were playing cards. One man, leaning against a counter and talking to a lady pouring rum into little glasses, called out to Pappy. Jimmy, come and fire one with we. Pappy answered, Later, and jerked his chin towards us, trailing behind him. The man smiled a kind of man smile and said, Allrrriiiiiight, in a slow, drawn-out way.

I could see the dark-wood bannister of a staircase way at the back of the room. I wondered whether that's where Pappy was headed and why he didn't stop to fire one. Upstairs was where we were heading and it had a lot of people too. There were lots of ladies, like ladies I'd never seen before in real life. These ladies looked glamorous like movie stars. Some had their hair piled up in upsweep styles like Hedy Lamarr, who was in *Samson and Delilah*, a picture I went to see twice just to see the ending again, when Sampson, his eyes blinded with a red hot bar of iron, got back his strength, which Delilah had destroyed by cutting his hair, and Samson, broke the chains that bound him, got up and pushed apart the tall pillars that held up the massive stone building, which fell down, killing everybody, mostly evil people, which was good, and even Samson, himself, who wasn't evil, except he had allowed himself to be led astray by a wanton woman. The ladies wore lipstick and rouge and eyebrow pencil, and one had her eyes outlined in black with a little tail on the outside corners, like Cleopatra. I don't think anyone had ever told *them* they couldn't wear pants or tight dresses that showed their knees or allowed you to see up the inside of their legs when they sat down. One of them, who had very black hair done like Jane Russell, sort of short and bouncy at the front and sides but longer at the back, came up to us as we walked in. So, Jimmy, these are the kids, she said. No one had ever called us kids before; we were always children. But it was a modern word from the Yanks at the base who said kid and kids, and I felt we were somehow elevated by the new label. She then said, which of these pretty little kiddies is which. Tell me your names. Pretty. That was new too. People didn't talk about whether someone real was pretty or not. You could say that, let's say, Ava Gardner was beautiful, or the latest Carnival Queen was beautiful, but we were not like them. They were white people. So the word pretty made us bashful and we didn't answer. Pappy got angry. He had a way of getting a sharp look on his face and his body going hard as if he'd turned into a cutlass blade. He didn't shout, but his low voice made us more frightened than shouting. So what happen? Is a set a dummies I bring here? I saw Tony's lips begin to tremble and I was afraid he would cry and make Pappy even more angry. So I named all of us for the lady. She didn't say our names back at us like some people do to make sure they heard it right, but she smiled, and Pappy nodded without smiling. I felt they were both satisfied.

The lady then reached into Pappy's shirt pocket and took out his packet of Anchor Special. Her nails were long with shiny red Cutex on them. Cutex was another thing no one at home was allowed. She tapped the pack against her hand and three cigarettes came out a short distance. She pulled out the one that was longest, placed it between the fingers of her left hand and put the pack back into Pappy's pocket. I could not believe what I was seeing. Someone had dared to touch one of Pappy's things, taken something of his. I looked at Pappy, expecting him to be angry. Maybe even slap her. But he seemed quite unconcerned. Still holding the cigarette, she placed it between her lips and nodded at Pappy. He reached into his pants pocket and took out his silver lighter. He flicked it, she bent to the flame, the end of the cigarette caught fire, she lifted her head, sucked in and blew out a cloud of smoke. A man lighting a lady's cigarette with a lighter was like something in a movie. Black and white. Just the heads and shoulders. Humphrey Bogart wearing a hat and Lauren Bacall looking up at him after she'd blown out the first puff of smoke. I never saw real people do that before. Everything was unreal. The place, the people, Pappy, nothing, nobody seemed real. I felt as if I was Alice in Wonderland, as if I'd fallen into a strange new place, or a different country where the rules and manners were different. Maybe I was in a dream, or sitting in the Olympic Cinema. Nothing, nothing, here was real.

Pappy took us to the other side of the room where one wall was made up entirely of open glass-paned windows. Some people, mainly children, kids, were sitting on chairs looking out. He showed us where we should sit and he went back to the other side of the room. I followed with my eyes where he was going and what he was doing. He picked up a bottle of rum that was on a table, opened it and poured some into two glasses. He gave one to the lady with the cigarette and took one himself. I saw them do cheers and they sat together at the back, looking towards where we were seated. She was talking and laughing and he nodded at what she was saying and put his arm around her waist. I didn't want him to think I was minding their business and get him angry, so I turned around to look at what was going on below on Marine Square.

There was one time when Marmie was also part of Pappy's display. A ship's captain on one of the small steamers that ferried cargo between our islands and the islands up the chain was a friend of Pappy's – in the way that everyone on the docks was friendly with one another. This ship's captain was a foreigner, as all captains were, maybe he was English. This man took a liking to Pappy, and I wouldn't be surprised if he saw Pappy as a person who was reliable and solid. I think he saw how efficiently Pappy worked for his employer, since his meticulousness and strictness extended to all the areas of his life where he was in control. I'm thinking, now, that maybe the captain, from his observation of Pappy at work, surmised that Pappy's family life somehow corresponded to his, the captain's, and he invited Pappy to bring his family to lunch at his home one Sunday.

We – Marmie and the four of us – were taken to a nice house in Barataria where the captain lived with his lady and their daughter. This was the first of quite a few Sundays there, where we were presented as a nice normal family without skeletons in closets. The lady, whom I only ever knew as Miss T – oh my goodness, now I'm thinking, could that have been Misty? Unlikely, as we children would have had to call her Miss Misty and we didn't. Miss T was a brown-skin woman, the child, an only child, a girl, was very light-skinned, red we called it, with coppery hair that fell in neat tight springs, each coil spun with the end of comb from neatly parted, equal sized squares of hair. She was like a life-sized doll in a frilly pink organdie dress, with a wide skirt, white sash and white shoes with socks that were turned over to show a little pink and white frill at the edge.

This child had many books. Huge illustrated books. Like comics, but not floppy. They had hard covers and the pages were not stapled like comics, nor were they glued; when you opened the book and peeped down the little gap between the cover and the back of the pages you could see that the pages were sewn with thread into the back of the book behind the spine. This little child was much younger than me, but clearly my superior in every other way. That first visit, she let me read one of her books, with the warning that I was not to dirty the pages, or tear them, or crease them, or put them down spread open to damage the spine, or pull out another by the top of the spine. I swear to god that this bossy child is the reason why all, every single one of the hundreds, nay, thousands of books I now own is as fresh as the day they were bought, except for things outside my control, like the brown stains of time, the dust of ages and the tunnels of silverfish. Dear biographer, I leave for you no marginalia, no downturned ears marking a significant page, no highlights, no underlinings; my books are sterile territory. There are no nuggets of insight into my mind to unearth from any of their pages. But oh the rewards at that time: Billy Bunter. Greyfriars School. Harry Wharton. The Owl of the Remove. The Headmaster, whatshisname, Jesus wept, I can't remember.

I couldn't wait for the next visit to Barataria to sit in a corner and read. Even though it was that little girl's image that rose to supply a mental picture of Violet Elizabeth Bott – an equally spoilt and bossy brat, whom I met later when I became immersed in the Just William series in our public library, I am forever grateful to that child for letting me open her treasured books and enter a very, very, different and alien world, an introduction that led seamlessly to P.G. Wodehouse, Bertie Wooster and Jeeves, and gave me an early, solid idea of the England where I wanted more than anything to go to study to be a doctor and live in when I was grown up.

At some point in his friendship with Pappy, this ship's captain had the idea of expanding his business from merely transporting other people's cargo to setting up a wholesale and retail business of his own with St Vincent as the headquarters, and that Pappy was the right person to handle that side of the business at HQ while the captain was at sea. I think St Vincent because Miss T was from there and maybe she wanted to go back home. To continue the fantasy of respectability that Pappy had created with these Sunday visits, Pappy would have to take Marmie and us four and set up a family home in St Vincent. This he agreed to do. I guess the prospect of being a boss instead of a lackey, combined with the freedom to travel back to Trinidad on the said steamer and secure his other interests here, without the bother of Marmie being around, must have had a strong appeal. And Marmie, she went along with the idea. If she felt she had any say in the matter, I'm guessing she must have weighed up the advantages of a safe stable life, guaranteed by proximity to the ship's captain's family, against the security of her own family, friends and her familiarity with place that a move to another island would force her to surrender.

We children told everyone we were going to live in St Vincent. Our aunts and uncles first of all; then our neighbours, the Boneses, the Josephs, the Marks, Alonzos, Fordes and the Clarkes, the Pantins down the road next to the church – who were cousins of cousins; the Adamses who were the cousins of those cousin-cousins; then Uncle and Tantie, the Chinese shopkeeper and his wife opposite, then Marmie's boss at the Chinese grocery on Charlotte Street (this when I passed there on the way to Marine Square one Saturday and made Marmie disappointed in my big mouth that has no cover on it); then Miss Gibbings, the lady round the corner who was the sou-sou banker, and who sewed carnival costumes for Saldenah; then Zanda, the shoemaker across the road (who let me watch how he sewed the leather sole of a man's shoe to the leather upper through little holes he pierced with something like an ice pick, making nice even stitches of white thread that he first ran through beeswax); Nurse Rivers the midwife; Sam the man who made Christmas trees out of twisted wire and unravelled rope dyed green and a red blob at the end of each branch (who let me watch him do that, twisting the wire so the flat rope swirled out like a bottle brush); Miss Clara who sold black pudding and souse from a tray outside Zanda's shop on Saturday nights; Miss Maud who washed and ironed men's long-sleeved shirts for six cents each and long pants for the same six, even though they were bigger than shirts, but shirts had so much more work in them to get clean and get smooth, especially the collars; and Miss Ivy, the Warner's servant and her son, Dennis, who was sixteen and a half pounds at birth (so Nurse Rivers the midwife said, and his mother was so damaged she never had another child), who grew and grew and grew to a giant of a young man who came to push the heavy metal floor polisher across our drawing room floor on Saturday mornings while we were too small to do it ourselves.

Of course, we had to tell our seamstress too. Marmie bought yards and yards of material for her to make new clothes for all of us, for you know what you leaving, but you don't know what you going to find when you get there, and we knew how good Miss Francis does sew and who knows whether there are sewing machines in those small islands, let alone seamstresses who could run a tape measure over you, look at a picture of a dress and make something that looking good and fitting big enough to grow into. It was a big investment this moving away, and Uncle Carmie, overjoyed at the favourable turn in his favourite sister's fortunes, stumped up the cash to pay for it all. I suspect he must have hastily joined a sou-sou and drawn out an early hand because the amount it would have cost, Peace and Queen Elizabeth roses couldn't have paid for in one go. We were leaving behind all that we knew but, truth be told, a lot of it wasn't good. Wasn't hopeful. We were going away to a new island, a new life, a new future for us all.

I am now going to make a confession. Uncle Carmie, wherever you are, please forgive me. I don't know why I did it and I am now, as an old woman, not foolish enough to try to find excuses and explanations for what I, as a fourteen year old, did to you, the person who at that time loved me more than anyone else in the world except Marmie. The day you propped your bad foot on the wall, balanced on your bike and leaned into the twisted wire and called me over and asked – Babs, you remember the time your Pappy was going to take you all to live in St Vincent? I looked down at the ground and I answered, no. He said, you don't remember? I didn't look up. I said again, no. He said, you really don't remember and you have such a good memory. I said, I don't remember. He pushed off the wall with his bad foot and cycled up the lane out of sight. I should have listened for a cock crowing thrice. I'm certain, one must have done. This was hardly two years after the plans to move had collapsed.

Of course I remembered. I remembered the shame we all felt. The disappointment. The quiet grief. The deep sense of loss for a brightly imagined, more hopeful future that we weren't, after all, going to have. None of us knew why it didn't happen. I don't suppose Pappy told Marmie any more than, We not going again. I don't really have any desire to speculate, although it's tempting to lay blame on any and all of the actors in this humiliating scenario. But just as I said to my beloved Uncle Carmie sixty something plus years ago, I don't remember. Plenty, plenty important people who oversee, nay, are the instruments of the debacle of huge business empires and the loss of fortunes and life to many large and small, sit in commissions of enquiry and say with straight faces, I don't remember, and, I don't recall, both here and in places bigger and ostensibly better than ours. So who is me?

Apart from that farce with the sea captain's family, we never went anywhere as a family. That is we never went out in public to an event together, Pappy, Marmie and the four of us children. Marmie and we children went out sometimes. She took us to the bandstand in the Botanic Gardens on Sunday afternoons to hear the Police Band play. But she went to five o'clock mass and we children to seven o'clock on Sundays. We went to school and she went to work. But we did see neighbouring families going out together, to family get-togethers with their cousins, to the sea, to children's birthday parties. Pappy had two cars, but they weren't for us to use. So when he said he was taking us all, Marmie and all four children, to

the Sunday matinee to see *White Christmas* we felt that at last we were going
to be like everybody else. We bigger girls were joining Bing Crosby in
singing *I'm dreaming of a white Christmas* every time it came on the radio. We
didn't get new clothes but Marmie prepared our best clothes as if we were
going to the governor's Christmas garden party.

The Sunday came and we ate lunch early. Marmie said we should
because she didn't want anyone getting a tummy-ache from excitement.
She made us have a little lie down and then got us up to dress us. We three
girls had white dresses with little sprigs of blue flowers, all of the same
fabric, but made into different styles. Tony had a white, long-sleeved shirt
and brown short pants. Marmie had a dusky-pink silky dress with a wrap
front top and flared skirt. It had a belt of the same material. She wore sheer
stockings and white peep-toe shoes with wedge heels. The show was to
start at half past four and Pappy said he would come at quarter to four. At
half past three we were absolutely ready, checked over by Marmie once
twice three times. Every hair ribbon in place, every sock turned over just so.
We were warned not to run about and get untidy, not that we wanted to
anyway. We girls lifted our dresses at the back before we sat down so they
wouldn't get creased. Even little Tony sat still. We didn't have a clock and
the only way to tell the time was by Marmie's watch. It was a delicate little
gold wristwatch with an oblong face and an interesting way of fastening at
the back. I used to play with that clasp for hours when she wasn't wearing
it. I saw her looking at her watch, putting it to her ear to hear its ticking,
winding the little screw at the side, looking at its face, putting it to her ear,
over and over. I wondered why the time was going so slow. We seemed to
be waiting forever. Eventually Annette asked, Is it quarter to four yet?
Marmie looked at her watch again and said, It's half past four. Nobody
asked the time again and Marmie never looked at her watch again. We sat
there in silence. It got dark outside. Nobody got up to turn on a light. It got
darker and darker with only the candleflies switching themselves on and
off. Tony rested his head on the arm of the chair. Marmie got up and turned
on a light. She didn't have to tell us it was time for bed.

In that one picture I have of Marmie as a young woman, the family
picture with her parents and siblings, she is dressed fashionably for the
time. Short hair with a curl on the forehead and what we called kiss curls
at the temples, flapper style, like Isadora Duncan. But that was long before
I was born. My earliest memory of her is of her having long hair with a side
parting and clips above her ears holding the hanging sides off her face.
Pappy had a thing about hair. At least about our female hair. It must not be
cut. Mine, curly and springy, never grew beyond my shoulder blades. But
Marmie, Annette and Carol had hair that grew right down to their hips.
Actually, having hair of different texture from my siblings was something
that I remember a man, a complete stranger, once remarking on when we

were all four together. We were waiting outside a store downtown and this man stopped, looked at us and said, Allyuh is brother and sister? I said yes. He said, Same mother, same father? I said yes. He said, Then how come them, his pointing index moving from one sibling to the other, his face triumphant as if he'd somehow caught me out, how come them hair soft and your hair so hard?

He was right, of course. They had soft hair, my hair was hard. But even while that was many, many years before I would come across Gregor Mendel and his experiments with smooth and wrinkled peas, tall and short stalks, purple and white flowers and I did not have at my fingertips any solid support in genetics to account for hair texture difference in mixed-race children of the same parentage, the questioning of strangers never led me to doubt the certainty with which I agreed to – same mother, same father. To me we were but peas in a mixed pod.

Anyway back to hair at home. Of course, hair was never worn loose. Why yuh looking like a Warahoon, Marmie would declare if we had our hair flying untidily all about. We girls wore ours in plaits or a ponytail. Marmie, whose hair was thin and fine, had different ways of making plaits and coiling them round her head like a crown, or winding it round and round to make a bun at the nape of her neck.

I do not know how or why or who, but one day Marmie had her hair cut to shoulder length. It was a very nice style. It made her hair look fuller, less old-fashioned, and it made her face look younger, less tired. She was happy about it and everyone complimented her about how much it suited her. She didn't ask Pappy and she didn't tell him, so when he arrived some days later and saw it he let her know that he disapproved. We got home from school that afternoon to find our Marmie's face swollen and bruised, one eye purple and could hardly open, her cheeks blue-black and puffy, her arms and legs livid with raised red wheals. There were bleeding cuts where his belt buckle had struck. He had also taken scissors and chopped off chunks of her hair right down to its roots so that there were big gaps where her scalp showed. Marmie would not have screamed. She would not have shouted. It would have been shameful to expose herself in that way to all who could hear. Did the neighbours know? They would have heard the slap of leather on flesh. They would have heard the scrape of chairs as she ran between them to duck from the rain of blows. They would have heard his grunts of satisfaction as he grabbed her by the hair and dragged her, trapping her between his knees to show her what he could do with hair. Marmie never wore her hair long again. She had it cut short.

When she was about twelve, my sister Annette, always the bravest of us all, started, bit by bit, to cut inches off the end of her hair, so that instead of it looking as if it was growing, it looked to us at home as if it was shrinking. She was clever, though, because she changed from plaits to wearing it in a high ponytail, which makes hair look shorter anyway. She shortened her hair so gradually you didn't notice the ponytail getting shorter and shorter. At least I don't think Pappy did. I think if he had he would have let Marmie know in his usual demonstrative way.

Sometimes Pappy slept where we lived. He slept in Marmie's bed that her mother had given her when she left home after I was born, but before Annette was. It was a big bed and when Pappy was there, Tony was lifted up fast asleep from where he slept and placed with the two younger girls in their bed. I remember Tony waking up one morning in what was for him the wrong bed. I had already got up, folded away my canvas cot and come to wake the others. Tony was sitting up between the two still sleeping girls, rubbing his eyes and looking puzzled. I decided to tease him, even though I knew why he was there. I hadn't seen him being brought there, but I woke up in the night when Marmie passed through our bedroom with that white enamel thing like a vase with a red rubber hose that smelled of vinegar that she got out when Pappy was there and which was always otherwise put away out of sight. I said to Tony, what you doing there? He hung his head and shrugged his little shoulders. I said, You don't know? Maybe you walked in your sleep? He looked up surprised and pleased that he could do such an amazing thing. For weeks afterwards, in broad daylight, he would walk around the house, his eyes closed and his arms outstretched, mumbling, even though I'd said nothing about him talking in his sleep, which, it is said, only I did, often. What did I say, what did I say, I would ask, but no one would tell me.

When Pappy slept in our home we walked around on tiptoes, our nerves on edge. His presence, unexpected, unannounced, uncomfortable, so disturbed our regular life that we didn't know how to proceed. If it was a school day, we stumbled through getting ready, forgetting to brush our teeth, drink our cocoa, comb our hair. We put left feet into right shoes, didn't pack our books and got to school late, dishevelled, hungry and out of sorts. I would walk back home slowly after school on such days, praying that he would have gone by the time I got there. He always was, he had his own life to get on with, but with him, you never really could be sure. If it was on the weekend, let's say a Saturday night, he would have arrived in the very early hours of Sunday morning. Those nights I would hear him retching and Marmie would be hurrying through our bedroom with a frothy basin that reeked of acid and rum, return with it emptied and rinsed and back again, and again. Then the enamel vase thing. I wouldn't sleep much on a night like that. I hated him most of all on those nights when I got older and knew what it was all about. I hated her too then. Why didn't she leave him. Take us and go where he couldn't find us. Why didn't she take the big kitchen knife and push it under his ribs, hard, at an angle, up under the left side, Marmie, thrust it deep as he slept. As I wanted to.

On the mornings after the nights he spent where we lived, I would wake up to see on the table everything he had emptied from his pockets. A white handkerchief, a black pocket comb, a Parker 51 pen, a big ring of keys, a brown leather wallet and loose change. Money. Visible money in plain sight of those who had none. But we knew, somehow we knew. That we had to contend with not only Almighty God with the long white beard looking down out the clouds, or Father Christmas who knows when you are sleeping, knows when you've been bad or good, but a too real Pappy, and we knew why he had put everything there. It was bait. To catch Marmie with the wallet contents, to catch us children with the loose change. I had seen him pick up his things when he was dressed and ready to leave. He would pick up each item and examine it. The pen. Ink level same in the bladder. The handkerchief, any alien snot? The comb, any long hairs? The wallet. All bills there. Keys, ditto. The loose change, not just counted correct, but actual coins of unchanged denomination. At least that's how I, in judgement of him, read his careful reclaiming of his possessions.

On such mornings, Marmie would send one of us across to the shop for a sachet of Nestle's instant coffee, on trust, make a cup for him, adding precise milk and sugar, put it on the table along with the ashtray, a white one he had brought home that said in white letters on a blue oblong band CINZANO. I had no idea what that meant. I thought it was a foreign word like Spanish because it ended in an o. I thought it meant 'Cheers' – though why an ashtray should say Cheers was a mystery. Our mother would be busying herself doing things nearby while Pappy sat and smoked and drank his coffee. She wouldn't be too close in case he felt she was crowding him, but not so far away that she would not hear if she was needed. Then he would get up and go, without a goodbye. Just walk out and drive off. If it was a Saturday morning I might not have seen him leave because I would be washing myself in the shower, to get dressed and ready, to catch a bus to go down to Pappy's place of work to receive from him the sometimes twelve, the sometimes fifteen dollars he sent Marmie to mind us for the week.

If for some reason – my tardiness, his having gone elsewhere early before I got there – and I got back home with no money, Marmie would have a quick conversation with Uncle, the Chinese grocery proprietor, and trust would be extended for another week. It was really trust he placed in his debtors, because Pappy wouldn't make up for the missed week when the next weekend came. It was like that saying about the things that don't come back – the word spoken, the sped arrow. Marmie's nine-dollar pay for a week's work at the Charlotte Street Chinese grocery would have to stretch somehow to keep us going, to bridge the gap over the two-week period. But there was always Uncle Carmie, arriving on his black Humber bicycle with a tin of something from Auntie Fiette, or some cash from his pants pocket to get something for the children, or Marmie would have a sou-sou hand to cash in, or her gold bracelets to pawn – although those last two options were for Marmie like savings in the bank, for specific big purchases, for an event like Christmas or please god no, for very dire straits. Marmie would always manage to straddle the gap between have and have not and bring us all safely over to the other side.

Hey you, Mr or Miss or Mrs or Ms Politician, sitting there on your well-cushioned backside, tapping your well-manicured fingers on your well-polished desk. Want to know how to manage a country? Go to the poorest part of your realm. You don't know where that is? Tut-tut – and you so smart you win election? So, if you don't know, well do like we tell little children: Don't know comes before find out; so raise your fat ass off that Charles Eames chair, put your coiffed head out the door and ask – minions know these things, somebody will be able to tell you where that place is, because you certainly wouldn't have spotted it while passing through the edge of town, with your head bent over your cellphone while you swish through, police escort sirens and outriders clearing peasants out of the way for your swift passage. Then, once the secret of the location of poorest slum in your jurisdiction has been revealed to you, go there (hold your nose against the stench), find a family where a woman is raising children, feeding them, keeping them clean, and sort of safe, sending them to school, and study – is study I saying not watch – study that woman for a year and you will learn something, apart from the onliest thing it looking like yuh know, which is how to win election.

Look, I've been around a long time, and if is one thing I learn is that not everybody have the same advantage in life. Maybe I was just lucky to be born hand-to-mouth, even though we weren't the really very poor (there were plenty plenty people poorer than us who were exposed to ways of living off breeze and sneeze and a lil something else), our Marmie catching where catch can, and maybe is not your fault your life experience so limited, so I going to be kind. I going to ease you into the task I set you, prime you up for the shock by letting you in on how Marmie managed to feed us.

When I was twelve, I witnessed a boy of my age with a tin of Vienna sausages. I hope I don't have to explain what those are to anyone; just to say it has no connection in social class with either waltzes or psychiatry. This boy looked into the opened tin, poked his fingers in, extricated one of the plump pink wobbly contents, held it up, tilted his face and popped the whole entire thing in his mouth. Chew, swallow. Looked in the tin, plucked out another. I turned away after the third. I could tell where this was going and I felt sick. Not because I didn't like Vienna sausages. I loved them. I'd watch salivating as Marmie ran the tin opener up and down the rim of the tin, leaving a small piece of the lid attached to hold the lid in place, tilt the tin over the sink and drain away the liquid, prise back the lid, drop the five sausages onto a plate and slice each one across until there'd be about thirty sausage discs. In the iron pot she'd pour a little coconut oil, add a chopped onion, two clove of garlic crushed with the grinding stone, a diced tomato and a couple finely chopped Spanish thyme leaves; stir the lot till the onions are clear, add a little water and drop the sausage slices in. Put a cover on the pot and let it simmer a bit. Serve on to five plates each with a hops bread cut across and buttered. A cup of sweet cocoa tea. Special breakfast. And Marmie always had a lil bit lef back in the pot. In case. In case what? In case somebody pass by while we eating. Dat is why. And if we finished eating and no one had come, the few remaining bits of sausage would be divided equally to the last quarter inch among us four children. So I want you to tell me how come a lil boy could open a tin a Vienna sausage and eat the whole ting, the whole entire blessed ting by he one and only self, jusso jusso?

So if a tin of Vienna sausages could stretch to breakfast for a family of four children, their mother and maybe a casual passer-by, what could a pound of beef liver or beef kidney or tripe do? I loved the way liver gravy had a kinda graininess to it. I used to think of it as bits of the organ surrendering separate cells, but later I worked out it was simply blood coagulating, which is why in the UK they dip slices of liver in flour and fry it, not make a gritty stew like we did at home. Kidney is made up of smooth round balls joined together by white stringy tissue which you had to cut away otherwise the stew would have a faint whiff of pee. And as for tripe. So much variety of texture in those slabs of pale white, rubbery, bloodless meat. I loved to examine the pieces of tripe, layers of fibres running at right angles to the layers above and below it, like plywood. I loved how it looks like coral, some parts like brain coral, some like pineapple coral, and the surfaces, oh my, such a range of textures. When there's tripe in a sancoche you'd eat all the provision first, then the liquid soup and leave the best for last, the tripe. You would hold a piece of tripe in your mouth without chewing, just so your tongue could run over the surface and relish a sensual pleasure that is usually enjoyed only by your fingers, your tongue exploring textures like velvet, corduroy, going into craters and along ridges that put you in mind of soft honeycomb. Liver, kidneys, tripe, heart – the stuff that's called offal – how and why did it go out of fashion? Don't cattle have those body parts any more? Maybe they don't. You never know with factory farming. Birds that can't fly, too breast-heavy to stand up on weak legs, fruit programmed to produce sterile seeds, so why not offal-less cattle?

Our special feasting day was Sunday. Since she worked all day Saturday on the grocery's busiest day, Marmie would make market early-early Sunday morning and get back in time to go to five o'clock mass. She would come home from the market with one pound of beef or pork, or sometimes half and half. That would be for lunch. She would rest it in a bowl, wash it along with a length of lime peel, cut it up into dice, add salt, black pepper, chives, onion, garlic, French thyme and a squeeze of lime and cover the bowl with a plate and set it aside. She'd go to the shower, lift the stone off the piece of tin that covered the bucket, slide off the tin, and attend to the blue crab that had been living there for the past week, feeding on vegetable peelings to purge out whatever swampy nastiness he'd been foraging on in his freedom before. She'd distract him with a stick aimed at its front, which he'd grab hold of, she'd snatch its back quickly with her other hand – the crab's antenna eyes swivelling around too late – take it with its legs and two treacherous gundies flailing to the concrete sink, hold a plate with her other hand to make a shield between her hand and the gundies, and twist off its back. When the crab stopped moving, she'd scrape off the stiff hairs on its legs, chop off the needle tips of the gundies and legs, wash the dozen or so pieces with lime and leave them to sit in a bowl.

She'd then measure out two cups of rice, pour it in a heap on the table and set one of us to pick the rice – that is to drag from the heap a few dozen grains of rice, spread it over the table, and look through it for the broken black grains. These you'd deftly pull aside to the right with a dragging right index finger while sweeping the whole clean white grains to the left with the left hand until the pile has been picked through and there's a heap of unblemished rice on one side and a small heap of discards on the other.

Marmie, across the table from you peeling the stalks and ribs of dasheen bush leaves, would then nod and you'd get up, brush the discards into your hand, go into the yard, click your tongue against your palate until the yard fowls came fluttering and you'd throw the grains for them. They'd hang around expectantly because they knew you well enough to know that when you set the bowl under the edge of the table and swept the clean rice into it, some grains would escape onto the floor and they'd flap over the drain into the kitchen for a lagniappe.

A pound of meat and chunks of potato stewed brown and tender in rich caramelised-sugar gravy, grainy boiled rice, boiled plantain pounded to a dense paste by one of the little ones who fought for the honour, pounded with a long heavy wooden pestle in a huge mortar carved out of a tree trunk, the mortar the height of a two-year-old child and the weight of a teen, and callalloo flavoured with crab and a piece of salt kine or brined pigtail. That was Sunday lunch.

And even though it was special, a meal into which much love and care and thought and time and resources had been poured, we seldom would sit at the kitchen table or at any table to eat. Marmie would call, Food ready, and we would come to the kitchen and she would serve us and we would take our plates and sit anywhere we felt like, most often on the back step, or a bench in the kitchen, and we would eat there, talking and laughing and moving around to get more, or to pass bits from one plate to another, throw something in the yard for the chickens or the dog – an unwelcome blade of chive or a woody thyme stalk, long bitter stems of cressles, a piece of pork skin, a chunk of fat, a beef bone sucked clean of slick, tender marrow. There'd be one of us, all of us saying, That smelling nice fuh so or That looking nice, but there'd be no requirement for table manners or grace, no polite conversation or seating plan. We didn't know about such, no please, thank you, if you don't mind or excuse me. But I think we were, in our own unconscious, untutored and rubbing-full-belly-that-nice-too-bad way, grateful to Marmie, to one another, to those who provided the ingredients and to whoever was in charge of keeping the world spinning to make it all come together, for that day's special Sunday lunch.

Mr/Miss/Mrs/Ms Bigshot Politician, I still talking to you. You ever cook a Sunday lunch like that? Oh ho, the cook does? You order in? You eat out? Well try it, nah? Get the children involved; it's a fun family thing, like going to Disneyworld without the long lines, the high cost, the tawdriness, the ephemeralness, the excess. Think of the skills, the sharing, the knowledge, the togetherness, the sheer blissful freedom you're missing out on. But here does not end the sermon, because while I'm in the mood to berate the higher-ups, to speak truth to power, I want to say something to god.

Dear god, and I mean dear god in the kindest most respectful way, not like I'm uttering a mildly irritated blasphemy, OK? Dear god, why did you do this to Marmie? Who controlled Marmie's fate? Who ordained that good people like my mother see hell on earth while the wicked around her enjoyed the fruits of creation?

Is anyone listening? I'm not getting an answer. We follow horoscopes, read tea leaves, read cards, read palms; we wear crystals, chant for things, breathe deeply and exhale while sitting cross-legged; we follow gurus, charlatans, cult leaders. And we do things we wouldn't like done to us. We slaughter one another for land, metal, oil, for a cellphone, a car, a perceived insult, a skin colour, the sound of an unfamiliar language. We walk into a church with an assault rifle, chat with the pastor, then mow him down along with the congregation and walk away unscathed; we drive our car to climb a pavement at speed into whole families wearing a different garb from ours. We do these things because we look at what befalls good people like Marmie and know there's really no justice, no fairness, no comeuppance for wrongdoing in the world.

But my Marmie, though neglected by fate, still believed in fairness and justice. She was sure that one day things would work out for her and above all for us her four children if she just kept faith. Marmie placed her faith in a god whom she couldn't see, though he was said to be everywhere. She believed he had an earthly agent, the Holy Roman Catholic Church, and its visible, ordained representatives, the archbishop and the priests. That institution and its creeds shaped Marmie's view of the world and decreed her place in it.

In his account of this incident in Cuba, the Catholic priest, Bartolomé de las Casas, Protector of the Indians, reported that Hatuey, the Taíno Cacique, at the point when he was about to be burned alive for inciting insurrection against the Spanish enslavers, when reminded that if, at his final moment, if he were to agree to being baptised Catholic, he would go to heaven after death, Hatuey, tied to the stake, dry timbers piled at his feet, a flaming torch held at the ready, asked whether there would be Spaniards there, and on being told that, of course, heaven was full of Spaniards, he Hatuey emphatically declared he'd rather be in hell.

Centuries later, god's agent told my Marmie that because she had bastards she couldn't go to communion; her mortal sin was so heinous it was forever etched on her soul. Her bastards had to be baptized on Thursday, not Sunday, so everyone would know the child was stained forever. She still loved god and trusted him and went to church. She sent us, each clutching one copper penny (the sacrificed purchasing power of two hops bread or five salt prunes or two guava syrup shave-ice presses) to be surrendered from our reluctant sweating palms to the purple velvet bags whose greedy poles reached right to the furthest kneeling parishioner at Mass. She sent us to sit still and listen to that priest, that reputed interferer of his acolytes, reminding us, not that god loves us and will save us his children from eternal damnation, but that next Sunday was the silver collection, an announcement to make us shrink with shameful knowledge that there wasn't a hope lasting longer than spit on a pitch road at midday in July that silver would cross our palms next Sunday. My Marmie went to five o'clock mass in the dark so that she, the sinner, wouldn't offend the eyes of the pious, for whom the gala mass was reserved at eight. She wouldn't send us to the six or eight mass because to do so would run the risk of being told to remove ourselves from a seat we'd unwittingly occupied when the owner, whose family name was inscribed on a brass plate fixed to the pew, turned up and turfed us out, head bent to hide tear-brimming shame, to stand at the back with those who didn't have a seat at the lord's table. And even if mass had started and the owner hadn't come, you'd better not relax and feel safe, because the pew owner could come in at any time, even after the Gospel, when officially you're too late to claim you've fulfilled your obligations – or does that rule not apply to people who own pews?

Marmie has long gone from here and I like to imagine her arrival at the pearly gates. St Peter opens his big book. It is ruled in two columns. Thumbs up and thumbs down, like Nero at the coliseum in olden days or voters on You Tube performances nowadays. Her thumbs-up list runs for page after page after page. Thumbs down has one entry: repeated fornication leading to four bastards. St Peter summons Bartolomé de las Casas, Head of Border Control for Arrivals from the New World. B de las C asks, Did you repent? Marmie says, The fornication and production of my bastard children happened in Trinidad, a country ruled by a ruthless zealot, but I have lived for the past two decades in Florida, a jurisdiction of more ambiguous, more ambivalent morality. There I confessed my sin, received absolution and was welcomed as a faithful communicant. B de las C smiles as he escorts Marmie to the heavenly throne. I, too, managed a similar squeeze through, he confides. In my latter years I renounced all kinds of enslavement, indigenous as well as African and now I am revered back there as an early human rights advocate.

Yesterday, my Facebook page was flooded with reports that Pope Francis is in favour of same sex civil unions. All I could say is, well, look at dat!, and wonder whether all those souls in the fires of hell, where they were consigned as abominations, would now have their eternal sentences changed to what? Maybe purgatory, then heaven if they get judged on other aspects of life not to do with sex. But who knows?

I don't want you to go away with the impression that Marmie was unhappy. She wasn't. Not in the way that people are unhappy and brood and are depressed and uncommunicative. Marmie, I think, lived by an understanding that she had made her bed and must lie on it. She had become pregnant with me for a man who escaped responsibility and that changed the course of her entire life. All that befell her afterwards, her having three more children for a man who abused her, her precariousness and her dependency, all these were the natural consequence of that fall from grace, and she accepted her lot with fortitude and stoicism. She had friends, neighbours, family and got from them a certain enjoyment in life and quiet support. And when we were grown up and getting on with our own lives, she escaped, had some years of unexpected freedom, money, and a sufficiently open heart to embrace her change in circumstance without spoiling it with regret that it hadn't come sooner. She took it all in her stride, every setback, every tiny gain.

Her own growing-up years were easy, I think. She spoke of holidays by the seaside with brothers and sisters and friends and their brothers and sisters. It must have been a carefree time, her teens, the years between the two big wars. She spoke about long holidays at Los Iros on the south coast, she and friends meeting up in a big guest house, girls with names like Cooksie and Bunty, Cora and Grace, girls I never met, because Marmie spoke of them as going to the Main or marrying a man from the oilfield or a Yank and disappearing for good. Cousins have pictures of the Lafond girls at the seaside long ago. I see them in swimsuits, trousers, shorts, carefree, happy, young, unencumbered. I heard Marmie being teased from time to time when she and her sisters got together and were in conversation about friends from the past. One sister would say, Yvonne, you remember so-and-so? Yes, him, he wanted to marry you, remember, and you didn't want him? Well, he… And another would say, You pick and pick and choose and choose and… Those years of time spent by the seaside were precious to her and she tried to give us something like that too.

There must have been a time when she felt secure enough to pawn her precious gold bracelets, a gift from her father; sure that she would be able to redeem them after her splash of what could be seen as spendthrift behaviour. This was when Marmie rented a small house on the hill at Trois Roches on the Toco coastline every year in my latter years at school, when Tony was old enough to be reasonably independent and we'd go there for the full month in August. She gave us those days of learning to swim by battling waves surging between the many more than three rocks, catching crabs at full moon with boys also on holiday nearby, walking on the hot black pitch road in the late afternoon to the fish depot when the sails of returning pirogues signalled that a catch would soon be laid out on the long plank for inspection. She gave us that, I think, because she had her treasured memories of Los Iros and wanted us to lack for nothing of joyous childhood memories of our own. And just as she tried to give us holidays to cherish, Marmie celebrated every festival so that they meant something big and important to us. Thanks to Marmie, we as adults feel the significance of celebrating festivals so strongly that we in turn transmitted the importance of particular festivals to another generation, to our children. Christmas was especially important to Marmie. No. Christmas was everything to Marmie. And so, to us.

Many families own houses; some also own land. This they use as collateral to secure loans from banks or other financial institutions. Till the day she died, Marmie had neither house nor land. But that didn't mean Marmie had no collateral. Not-at-all-at-all; Marmie had her bracelets. Her heavy pair of twenty-four carat gold bracelets; her financial institution was the pawnshop at Y De Lima jewellers. She also had a savings facility, the neighbourhood sou-sou. Between the pawnshop and the sou-sou hand our Christmas was as splendid as anyone's who had house and land and bank.

Marmie liked to start Christmas preparations early, from the end of October. Little by little she'd be putting aside the ingredients for the black cake – one pound of currants one week, one pound raisins the next, later one pound of prunes. I'd be the one to spread the raisins and currants on a tray and pick out the hard little stalks that were either attached to the fruit or loose among them. Then I'd take a small knife and cut up the prunes to remove the stones. Marmie would then check my work, nod her satisfaction and rinse the dried fruit. The big stoneware jar with a tightly fitting lid, a relic from the old house up the valley road, would then be taken from the top of the wardrobe where it had rested since the December before, and be thoroughly washed and dried. She'd then put the clean dried fruit into the jar, pour in most of each of a bottle of cherry brandy and one of rum, give the jar contents a good stir and put the lid securely on the jar. The jar would sit on the top of the china cabinet and be taken down once a week until the eve of Christmas Eve to have an alcohol top up as the dried fruit swelled with absorbed liquid.

With the cake in train, Marmie would turn her attention to the house. The requirement for new cushion covers for the morris set and new curtains for the doors and windows took her to Frederick Street for patterned cretonne and white or ecru lace, yardage cut in the shop and put aside, a deposit paid, and small amounts paid off every week until, debt liquidated, the fabric was collected and dropped off for the seamstress to begin sewing. These, the fruit soaking for the cake and the investment in soft furnishings, as I now know they're called, constituted the advance foray of Marmie's Christmas preparations. The main onslaught started in late November. First up was to be measured for new clothes, all four of us children. Timing was a fine balance; leave it too late and the new clothes wouldn't be ready in time, too early and our growing bodies would have inched into the measurements so that garments that we would be expected to gradually grow into and continue to fit as our special clothes until the following Christmas, would begin to strain at the seams before the end of the August holidays, rendering them unfit for purpose.

The final items – the oilcloth for the kitchen table, the other cake ingredients, the pastelle ingredients, the fresh pigeon peas, the ginger, the sorrel – were purchased in the week leading to Christmas Day and finally, on the eve of Christmas Eve, there was the purchase of the real five-foot at a-dollar-a-foot-imported-from-distant-Canada Douglas fir. This was deco-rated by us children with very fragile, very breakable – careful, careful – ornaments of thinnest coloured and decorated glass, in shapes of minarets, domes, churches, stars, angels, icicles, globes and crescent moons. Then the strings of fairy lights that blinked and bubbled coloured liquid up candle-shaped tubes, and the big star at the top and angel hair spread like a wispy veil over all, making everything seem dreamlike, with the lights shining through, as if through mist, their overlapping haloes blending into rainbows.

The week before Christmas saw us in a frenzy of preparation. Ginger to be scraped free of skin, grated, placed in a glass jar with boiling water, a stick of cinnamon, a sprinkle of cloves and a curl of lime peel and set in the sunshine to intensify the flavour for ginger beer. Finger-staining bright crimson sorrel sepals had to be separated from prickly seedpods, washed and dropped into a pot of boiling water and left to draw with cinnamon and cloves. There was the whole business of cake-making, the beating of a dozen eggs, the sifting of flour with baking powder, the washing of the salt butter followed by the creaming of butter and sugar, the putting together of everything along with the alcohol-soaked fruit and citron and spices. There is no fragrance, no taste, no sight, no feeling to match that of Christmas. Nothing comes close to the blended aromas of new curtains, new cushion covers, French-polished morris furniture, Mansion-polished floors, needles and resin of the tree.

I locate my own ghost of Christmas past in the time when I was more grown up and working, and Marmie finally had a fridge and a stove with an oven. There I am transported into the richest most evocative of realms. When it was my turn to create Christmas, I did it all with my children and with Paul, my Welsh husband, who embraced it with the zeal of the convert. But now alone, I don't do any of it any more. I don't need to. The fragrance of ginger, of cloves, of cinnamon, of rum vaporising from an oven where a black cake is slowly baking, the sight of red sorrel in heaps, green banana leaves waiting to be wilted over an open flame and turn into wrappers for pastelles and I am back there, young, happy, carefree.

I don't know where she got the courage from, her trust that everything would work out if only she could hold on and persevere with us and with her circumstance. Maybe it came from her belief in a god of love, a god of redemption, but since that was not the god we got in church, that confidence must have come from somewhere within herself. We didn't do family prayers, nor did we go to the same Sunday mass, so I never saw Marmie at prayer, or at least in a pose of communion with her god except on Old Year's Nights when the neighbours gathered at the crossroads to see in the New Year. Only the adults took part; it was they whose precarious lives were being offered up to god or fate, in the hope of a change in fortune in the coming new year. I always wanted to join the adults in this Old Year's Night ritual, but maybe Marmie wanted that time to be hers alone, a private time for her own thoughts without the impediment of a child who might be sleepy or cranky and spoiling it for her. But one year I did join her at the crossroads.

It is the December I've just turned twelve, and nothing will stop me from being with the big people when the New Year starts. All through that Old Year's Day I can't eat, I can't play, I can't do a thing. The whole day I'm waiting for the sun to go down so I could focus on my plan, which is to stay awake all night. What if I lose concentration and fall asleep at ten or eleven and no one wakes me? I can just picture Marmie seeing me lying there on the couch, fast asleep in my waiting-for-the-new-year dress, and I can almost hear her saying, Let the poor child sleep. She must be tired. I can't bear to imagine this New Year coming in and me not being there for it and having to wait three-hundred-and-sixty-five nights for another chance.

I keep asking Marmie, What's the time, what's the time? She says, Why don't you listen to the radio. But she's telling me anyway, it's ten, and later when I ask again, quarter past ten. Only? That can't be right. An eternity has passed in that quarter hour. I continue to pester her, until, at eleven o'clock, she tells me to get dressed. I choose my new dress, the green organdie one with the puffed sleeves, as if I'm going to Holy Innocents Mass again. Marmie is looking nice too, in her new church dress. She puts on her lace mantilla and drapes another over my head. As we're walking out, I flip my two plaits forward to lie on my chest. I don't want their crisp, new taffeta ribbons hidden by my veil.

At the crossroads, Mr Joseph is checking his wristwatch. Twenty-seven minutes to go, he says. The moon is full that night, big and gold. I search for the man in the moon. I don't see him. Star light, star bright, first star I see tonight, I whisper, but I don't know which is the first star I see; there are millions and millions of them. I have never been outside this late before. The quiet, the calm, the wispy veil of moisture in the air that is settling on my skin, making it chilly and bumpy, all that makes me feel that everything, even time, has stopped and everything is waiting, expecting something big, like an apparition, to happen, so that I won't be at all surprised if St. Peter or a lagahoo or some spirit of the crossroads appears before us.

The grownups don't talk. Everybody seems to be lost in their own thoughts. They are so serious that I'm guessing they are thinking about the year that's about to end, going over in their minds what good things had happened, what bad had befallen them, where they went wrong, and where they'd been wronged. And they are trying out thoughts for the year to come, wondering whether they dare to shape in their heads all their hopes, their wishes for the coming year, because you can blight yourself, put goat mout on yuhself, bring all manner of bad luck upon yourself, by imagining good things for the future. As the song says, the future's not ours to see, *que sera, sera*, although the Sunday school teacher says that's a bad song because God has a plan for everyone and nothing that happens to you is *vye-qui-vye*. No. Nothing happens by chance, she says. My own head has none of these past or future thoughts. I'm simply waiting for one year to go and a new one to come and to be here, awake for it, to feel for myself the old going and the new one coming. The silence feels like a weight. Marmie must have sensed my anxiety for she holds out her chaplet for us to share. Rolling the beads through my fingers, the silver cross dangling between Marmie and me, makes me calmer. I think about what Marmie is probably praying for. She's saying in her heart, Lord give me strength, for whatever trials are to come. She'd be saying, Lord, let this be a year when we are safe. She'd be saying, grant us the comfort of Thy mercy, Lord. And at the end of every wish she'd add, if God spare life, for she wouldn't want God to think that she was so presumptuous that she was taking even a moment of life in the future for granted or that she was confident He'd grant her hopes and wishes for the year ahead.

A ripple passes through our little group, a little shuffling of feet, a little adjustment of bodies and I look around for its source. It's Ma Darceuil making her entrance. You couldn't miss her among the other women. They are wearing hats and mantillas; she is in the big white head-tie done up like an Arabian Nights turban, just as if this night was one of those Saturday nights when she would spread a white tablecloth on the ground under the wide eaves of Uncle's grocery away from the settling dew, place a vase of red ixoras and a lighted candle on the tablecloth, ring her big brass bell and preach out loud for all to hear. Father Graham says that it is a sin to listen to her. She was sent by the devil to turn us away from the true faith.

Mr Joseph is calling, Six minutes to go. Hurry up if you want to hear the countdown. I am not sure if I can count sixty seconds times six to get the exact time, at the exact moment. I must-must-must know it. I must know what it feels like to be there when a year dies and a new one is born, I want to know if I will see the skeleton in a hooded robe like a monk carrying a scythe and walking away, and a stork flying in, carrying in its beak a shawl hanging like a hammock in which a smiling baby is lying, just like the cartoon drawings. Mr Joseph says, Four minutes to go. Mrs Wallace waddles off to her house to turn up the volume on her Rediffusion, and suddenly, our quiet hush is hammered by the hearty voice of Sam Ghany booming out live from the Old Year's Night party at the Country Club.

... and on the ballroom floor, who do I spy? It's our lovely Carnival Queen, tripping the light fantastic with her charming escort ... and what an elegant couple they make... the band has stopped playing... the dancers... to their tables... waiters... buckets of champagne... paper hats... whistles poised... toasts at the ready...

At the ready, at the corner of Reid Lane and Pelham Street Belmont, we stand, holding out, not toasts, but our tentative dreams for change in our lives in the New Year. We pay no attention to Sam Ghany's jolly commentary from the Country Club. We are listening intently only for the countdown. A chorus of excited voices crackle over the airwaves, *Ten... nine... eight...* At our crossroads, we do not count. We are silent. I grip Marmie's hand, squeezing it hard. *Seven...* The chaplet beads imprint stigmata on my palm. *Six... five... four...* Marmie closes her eyes. I do too. I stop breathing. *Three... two... one... HAPPY NEW YEAR!* There are screams and shouts coming over the radio, shrill whistling, popping corks, merry laughter. Loud, slurred, competing voices rising in *Should auld acquaintance be forgot...* We do not know that song and we do not join in. We hear the bells of Queen's Royal College on the other side of The Queen's Park Savannah ring out its Big Ben midnight chimes; anchored ships hoot forlornly in the harbour.

It's happened. Really and truly happened. 1953 is gone and now it's 1954. And I am here at the very beginning, at the first second of it. I feel light and excited as if I've been given the present of this brand new year all for myself. We are hugging our neighbours and wishing, Happy New Year, and May God bless you. Ma Darceuil places her hand on the crown of my head. She closes her eyes and I close mine. Eshu Legba Elegbara, she says. When she lifts her hand I look around for The One With the Pointed Horns and the Cloven Hooves to appear, but he does not, and I feel relieved about that because it means that it wasn't a bad thing I let happen to me and I am suddenly aware that I am somehow specially chosen to have an unusual blessing bestowed on me for the year ahead. And I am hoping that Marmie, too, will get a blessing through her own prayers.

I think Marmie used to pray a lot, silently to herself all day long. She would send up her prayers to God, Jesus, Mary, St Ann, St Anthony, St Jude depending on what she was praying for. She would persevere while not knowing whether they'd be answered or even received, and from the way life went, it was hard to tell. She would smile when people said humorously, Lord, put a hand, put a foot, send a man, come yourself, but I'm guessing that there were days of quiet desperation when that would've been her most fervent prayer. But it wasn't only prayers she relied on to give her grounding in her daily life; Marmie had other means of glimpsing into her future.

Marmie used to want to know in advance what was going to happen in her life, whether it was going to be good or bad. She couldn't do anything about it, because what is going to happen is going to happen and even if you try to change it, what eventually happens is what was going to happen anyway. Even your trying to interfere was in the plan. Marmie didn't have powers of divination. She didn't need it. She had Nora. And what Nora had was her ability to cut cards with deadly accuracy. Nora wasn't one of the Lafond siblings; I think she may have been related to that Pestana person on the cemetery wall. Auntie Nissa said she was a cousin, but I never heard Marmie say so. After all, if both your parents claim to be only children, there couldn't be any cousins, could there? But anyway, if anyone was one of Marmie's kith and kin it was Nora.

It is a Thursday morning during the school holidays. Marmie hands me a folded piece of paper and points with her chin towards the shop across the road. I run across and hand the paper to Uncle. Uncle unfolds the paper, squints at it, hands it back. What Marmie want? Marmie knows that Uncle cannot read English. Marmie knows that I can shop for many more than four items without a written list. But Marmie can't talk. Or won't talk. She has gone into a sort of trance. I read aloud Marmie's shopping list for Uncle: a bottle Vat 19, 10 Anchor Special, a pack cards, 1 coffee. Now I know. It's like a detective story where a specific set of numbers is the code for a combination lock and when the bank robber turns the dial click, click, click, the safe door swings open. Nora is coming.

Uncle goes from one part of the shop to the other, assembles the items, puts them in a brown paper bag, unhooks the wire from the nail driven into the door frame, looks through the curling squares of brown paper threaded through it, finds one, adds a sprinkling of Chinese symbols to those already crowding the paper and passes the bag to me.

Without a word Marmie takes one end of the morris couch, I the other, and we move it out of the way, across to the dining room. I lift the vase of flowers and the crocheted doily off the little centre table and rest them on the dining table. Marmie and I move the two morris chairs closer to the little table. I know the routine. I fill a glass jug with water and place it on a tray with two glasses. That I rest on the dining table. By now Marmie is dripping wet, her thin hair clinging to her scalp and neck in black tendrils, showing pale rivulets between. Half moons darken her dress underarms. She looks at me and nods. Drips of sweat fall on the front of her dress. She looks at her dress, turns and goes out. I hear the splash of water against the galvanise walls of our open-air shower. Marmie comes out, pulling a fresh dress over her damp head. She's still tugging hard at it where it's sticking to the bits of her that she hasn't taken time to dry properly, when the back gate pushes open and Nora steps in the yard.

I like Nora. I like the way that when she comes to see Marmie everything else stops. I like the feeling that something big is going to happen and you must sit still and wait for it. It's like sitting in a dark cinema and you're there to see a film, but before it starts, right at the beginning, the first thing that comes on the screen, even before the title of the film, is the lady wrapped in a sheet, her arm stretched up, holding a bright light with long rays coming out of it and the music comes on and it makes you feel excited and nervous at the same time.

Nora is the thinnest person I know and I know plenty thin people. People say to my mother when she and I are together, But how she so magga? Meaning me. Nora's clothes are all the same style. Just different colours. Today her skirt is black. On her it looks like black paint on a stick. Her blouse is like a shirt with a collar and buttons, but without sleeves and it is tucked into the skirt waistband, but not tight; it spills over in a pink puff all the way round. She is wearing black flat sandals with criss-crossing straps that come to halfway up her calves, like someone in a bible-story film with Roman soldiers. I think she's very brave to wear something like that. But Nora lived in New York and that means she does many things that are normal and ordinary there but not so here. And I don't think Nora notices that those things are not ordinary here. I also don't think that if anyone told her that it's different here she would change. She isn't the sort of person who bothers about stuff like that.

Nora is white. Not pale like Marmie, who is not white but sort of beige. Nora is so white her skin is transparent. I think that comes from living a long time in the cold and not seeing sun. When I am studying to be a doctor, which is what I'm going to be when I grow up, I'm going to ask Nora to let me study her body for live anatomy lessons. You could trace every blood vessel under the skin. You could follow the blue lines in their many branchings and joinings; even on her face you can see little ones feathering out from her jaw up along her cheeks. Where her lower leg meets her ankle you see long tight fibres straining. These are either tendons or ligaments, I'm not sure. But it's her hands that are most interesting. The bones stand out like the ribs of a breadfruit leaf. Her fingers are long and thin. At every joint you can see where the end of one little bone swells for the next little bone to slot in. But best of all are her fingernails, long and shiny red with Cutex. She cut the tips to make a point like an arrow. I think Nora wants to look like Marlene Dietrich because her eyebrows are very thin and are shaped like two rainbows way above the edge of her eye sockets. I don't think that shape can be natural. I think she plucks them but I can't get close enough to her face to look for the little bumps that show when you pull out eyebrow hair by the roots with tweezers. And her lips are shiny and red like Marlene's in the film posters. Even her hair is done like hers. But her hair is not the same colour. I think Nora dyes her hair. Red is not a real colour for hair, except for Rita Hayworth. I look at Nora's hair roots where they show but there is no difference, so I can't tell for sure. Marlene's hair is blonde in the posters. I don't think she dyes hers. She is German. You pronounce her name Mar-lay-nay, not Mar-leen, to rhyme with Kath-leen, like Kathleen Poon in my class at Tranquillity. Nora may be very thin but that doesn't stop her from being a very striking person. I can imagine her walking along the street and people turning to stare at her but I cannot imagine anyone laughing at her, only admiring her.

When Nora comes in she doesn't talk. She just nods and walks towards the chairs and little table. She always sits on the same chair. The one with her back to the gallery. If it was me, I would choose the one facing the gallery so that I could look through the wide open doors at everything passing by on the lane outside. Before Marmie sits, she brings a glass, the new bottle of rum, the pack of cigarettes, a box of matches, the new pack of cards and the Cinzano ashtray and puts them on the table. Marmie picks up the bottle and twists the cap to break the seal. She tilts the bottle and a splash of rum falls on the floor. I can smell the vapour rising up from the puddle. It goes up my nose and my eyes water a little. Marmie then screws back on the cap and puts the bottle on the table before she sits. While she was doing this, Nora has pulled the little cellophane string around the cigarette pack and the two perfectly packet-shaped pieces of cellophane fall off. She opens the pack, takes out a cigarette, puts it to her lips, strikes a match and lights it. She shakes the match like a wand and it goes out, but I know the tip will still be hot enough to give a little round burn that blisters; I once touched one to check whether, since it was black, it wasn't hot and I now know for sure that isn't so. For a moment a thin veil of grey sulphury smoke hangs around Nora. She places her cigarette in the little groove in the ashtray where it balances. She picks up the bottle and pours some rum into the glass. I'm looking at the cigarette. There is red lipstick printed on the end where her lips were and also red at the other end, but a sparkling red with pretty blue smoke curling up, making letters and patterns that move and change before I can read the letters or make out the patterns. I sneeze and they both look up from whatever they were thinking and Marmie lifts her chin towards the door. I know that means I must go and find something to do. I am not allowed to mind big people business.

When I think about those episodes, Nora's visits, the careful preparation, the seriousness of the encounter, the long thoughtful silences Nora left in her wake, the way Marmie moved in a more cautious way for weeks after, her listening for something, her watching for something, her gathering of us, her searching of our faces, touching our foreheads, I return to a puzzle, an unease about it. What drove my Marmie to bypass that self and church-imposed mandate to put everything in god's hands? What drove her away from that blind trust to seek through a medium a glimpse of what was to come? There must have been a more than usual worrying uncertainty, a shifting of her tenuous hold on her ground, an inkling of the coming of things that she feared would push her over, things she needed to know about and steel herself against, something that no priest no saint no god would give her insight of, she not being Bernadette nor Lucia, Jacinta nor Francisco.

I'm guessing that Nora, who knows and sees all things, must have warned Marmie in advance about many things. Some good. Some not. She may have warned Marmie in advance about an upcoming bout of Pappy's violence, but knowing something and acting on it is not the same thing. In any case, what could Marmie do? I'm asking this as an old woman at the start of the third decade of the twenty-first century when women still don't act on domestic abuse. It doesn't help to say to them, leave him. He's no good for you and the children. You'd be better off without him. You feel they don't know that? Jesus wept! That is the one and only thing they *do* know. But the gap, the gap, the gap they are constantly minding is a Grand Canyon that separates knowing from doing. They do not need knowledge. They have knowledge in spades, in high-low-jack-game. They could write Volumes 1-10 of the Encyclopaedia Violencia Domestica if they had the time. So knowledge is there, they don't need that from you with the Power Point bulleted five by seven list. Want to do something? Something real? Something hard? Something bigger and better than pontificating? Build a bridge, throw a rope, hold out a helping hand across the canyon. They need a home, a safe place for themselves and their children, money of their own – no strings attached, protection, new confidence, skills. Help. Not advice. So Marmie had warnings, she had experience, but she didn't have help. No bridge over troubled water. So while she lived on this island, while she lived under the menace of his shadow, she was stretched taut, her head shaking from left to right, left to right, left-right, left-right. No fight left, right. No-no-no.

WELCOME

Many of the best lessons that have lasted me through my long life are those I learned at Tranquillity Girls' Intermediate School in the late forties and early fifties. I still marvel at the twist of fate that, to my eternal gratitude, gave me the gift of Tranquil. I was maybe eight or so when we moved from Bournes Road, St James, where my sister Carol was born, to Saddle Road, Bossiere Village Number Two, Maraval, to three rooms on one side of a house rented from the Cupens, owners of a nearby hardware store. While we lived in St James I went to Miss Vanderpool's kindergarten on Western Main Road, but by the time we got to Boissiere I was already able to read and write and was therefore too old to be sent to sit in someone's gallery and chant the abc and times tables and to write my letters and do addition and subtraction sums on my slate. I had to go to a real school with books to read from, and double-line copybooks to write in.

I may have had a stint at nearby Mucurapo Girls' RC School after Miss Vanderpool, but that is hazy, though I do remember a music festival there and grownup sisters named something and something Carimbocas singing a duet about a bambino, and someone singing, 'Where the Bee Sucks, There Suck I', but I don't put much trust in that memory, though why is it so clear that I remember the words and where I was standing in an open hall full of children, and a stage where the singing was happening? But I don't remember anything else, not the uniform, not the teachers, nothing but a music festival. However, once we were settled in Boissiere Village, in the unstated but tacitly understood care of an older child of the neighbours in the other half of the house – was his name Errol? – I was despatched to the Boissiere Village RC Primary School. How long my stay there lasted I have no idea. It could've been weeks, months, or even terms. I remember nothing of it except one incident.

The route the neighbour's son took me along from home to school and back again was away from the paved road. I'm guessing now that it wasn't because the road was particularly hazardous – there were few cars in those days, people used bicycles to get around and people walked, even though there weren't pavements outside the city, but that off-road route to school was a shortcut, one side of a triangle with the bent road on the other two sides. In those days the Maraval River wasn't in a paved channel, and that stretch of the Saddle Road, built on slightly higher ground, hugged the steep valley sides, first on one side, then on the other, crossing the river at two points in doing so. Between those two bridging points the Maraval River wended its careless, meandering way through a low lying basin that I can now identify as a little flood plain. Our route through the flood plain was along a narrow dirt path leading from just before the first bridge on the Saddle Road and emerging just beyond the second.

I can't say I was a dreamy child but, looking back, I can see that I was somewhat detached from reality. I saw things and heard things around me, and I paid close attention to them, but I didn't attach meaning to them. No more meaning than I could make of the news about the sitting of the Legislative Council or 'Chattanooga Choo-Choo' coming from the neighbour's Rediffusion. I think, though, that the stories and nursery rhymes that were read to me at Miss Vanderpool's had more reality because the words that were there had pictures next to them. *Mary had a little lamb; its fleece was white as snow.* And there was a picture of Mary and her lamb. I could see them and name them. And if I was ever to see a Mary or a lamb I would be able to name them. And when I saw snow on Christmas cards I could recognise it and name it. White I knew already. I knew all the colours, even purple and orange, though I puzzled why the colour orange was so named because oranges are green whether green or ripe.

My own world did not have pictures or stories or rhymes about it and so I did not have many names for the things around me. I cannot say what were the names of the flowers, the bushes, the grasses, the trees that we passed on our way to school, just to say that it was overgrown, and we called all that collectively bush, that there were cows and donkeys tied to bushes and trees among long grass, and lots of birds, some big, some small, but nameless. But ignorance didn't stifle my curiosity. I would often pause to grasp the long stalk of a grass just below its seed head, wide and fluffy like a bunch of feathers, and pull it gently upwards out of its enclosing sheath so that the tender pale lower part of the stalk slid out of the main plant without breaking. I would chew on one of these brackish-sweet stalk-ends and then another. From time to time Errol, who was way ahead, would stop and look back at me, urging me with hand signals to hurry up and I would become aware that I was dawdling and run to catch up.

One morning he went off leaving me behind in the shortcut wilderness. I'd spotted a procession of ants carrying pieces of leaves over their heads like flags and I was following them through the tall grass. They were going along a trail, their own little path, no wider than the part in my hair. I watched for a while. I picked a thick grass stalk and laid it across their path, blocking their way. The first ant crashed into it and stopped. It walked alongside the grass stalk for a little distance, back and forth a couple times. Then it came back to where it had first stopped and simply climbed over back on to the path. The others behind, who were waiting for the first ant, then crossed over without stopping to investigate, as if the obstacle wasn't there. I then pushed aside an ant, pushed it away from the procession and the others behind followed it, going in the new direction for a while before the line gradually eased back to the old route. Some ants without flags were coming in the other direction, and when they bumped into the ones I was looking at they stopped and rubbed heads with each ant in turn, before hurrying along. I was bent down to find out whether they were kissing or whispering when a loud snort and *Ha-haw, Ha-haw* made me jump. Right behind me was a huge head, long ears and big yellow teeth. I ran until I found the shortcut path and continued running all the way to school.

The schoolyard was strange that morning. It was not as I was accustomed to seeing it. Nobody was skipping rope. No one was hopping through the chalked hopscotch squares. No *lavay* hand-clapping. The only children I saw were standing in a line, quiet, quiet. I stood behind the last one not knowing why or what it was about.

Whap! Whap! Whap! Pause. *Whap! Whap! Whap!* And a mewling sound like a cat when you accidentally stand on its tail. The line moves forward. *Whap! Whap! Whap!* Pause. *Whap! Whap! Whap!* The mewling gets louder and I'm not sure if it's a cat or a person. The line moves forward again. With each set of whaps, I get closer and closer to the schoolroom door. I could now see the headmaster, standing just inside the schoolroom. A boy, the one now first in the line, is standing facing him. The boy's head is level with the middle of the headmaster's chest. The headmaster gives a brisk nod of his head. The boy holds out his right palm. The headmaster lifts his right arm as if he is about to bowl at a cricket game but he isn't holding a ball. He slams a brown strap down on to the boy's hand. *Whap! Whap! Whap!* The boy curls his palm and tucks the fist into his underarm. *Mew mew mew* comes from his mouth. There is dribble running down the side of his chin and dripping onto his blue shirt. And tears down his cheeks. The headmaster nods and the boy holds out his left hand. At the end, the boy's chest is heaving as if there is something trapped inside fighting to escape, but his lips are caught between his teeth and nothing comes out. He tucks the second hand under his armpit and stumbles into the schoolroom making room for the next pupil in the line.

Like a lamb to slaughter I stayed in the line and my turn too came. Shame made me, like the others, not cry out, but I didn't go into the schoolroom afterwards. I ran out the school gate and ran back home, through the shortcut, not stopping for donkey, ants, birds, sweet grass, nothing. My mother looked at my red puffy hands in disbelief. Who did this? How many lashes? With what? But she was as powerless as I. Knowing her own rickety status with respect to the religious institution that governed the school, and perhaps not wishing to subject herself to possible abuse and reference to her harlot state and my own bastard one, for which she could have no rebuttal, visibly pregnant as she then was with her fourth illegitimate child, my mother weighed her options and decided she would not fly down to the school with her raging self to confront the Headmaster and maybe rain some buss head on him, but she would simply not send me back there. I would be sent somewhere else. And as neither money nor school places for an eight-year-old grew on trees, she was faced with a problem.

Not averse to pulling strings at the best and worst of times, she may have searched long and hard for some connection with someone who could help to find a school place me, but she must have come up empty-handed, because she decided to aim for the best and to throw herself at the mercy of the headmistress of Tranquillity Girls Intermediate School. Miss Umilta Mc Shine, daughter of a judge, maiden sister of the eminent physicians, the two Drs Mc Shine, the legal luminary Mc Shine, and assorted well-established top-drawer folk, the educated coloured aristocracy of the colony, Miss Umilta Mc Shine was the indomitable headmistress of Tranquillity Girls' Intermediate School all through my time there and long after. Yes, Miss Mc Shine took me in, a nobody girl from nowhere, and I was placed in Standard Two in the care of Mrs Granderson.

On mornings, summoned from whichever part of the yard we were playing by the ringing of a big brass handbell, we girls lined up in the courtyard class by class, our soft, pale, wide-brimmed Panama hats with their dark blue grosgrain ribbon bands shielding our upturned faces from the hot sun. Mrs Olga Maynard, sitting at the piano in the school building, would be ready, waiting for the signal to start playing. We would march in, class by class, passing through a passage where we would hang our hats by their chin elastic on hooks along a wooden louvred partition, then continue into the wide open building. Along the far wall was a series of raked benches, the transepts, as they were called. There, the whole assembled school stood and sang loud and lustily, *So, here hath been dawning another blue day,/ Think! wilt thou let it slip useless away,/ Out of eternity this new day is born,/ Into eternity at night will return*. There's no mention of birds in the song or of flying, but now as I sing it in my head, I am transported back there, standing on those steps feeling in my chest the same rise of birds and flying, soaring up as I felt then. I think it is the music that gives that feeling, not the words. At the time I didn't think about the words; the singing was just a way of creating and releasing an uplifting feeling. Later, long after, I reflected on the sentiments expressed in the words and wondered why I had let them pass me by unnoticed. The words may have slipped me, but not uselessly, for the whole ethos of Tranquil was shaped around the song that started our day.

The big open space was subdivided into classrooms by double-sided blackboards and jalousie-style screen partitions, high enough so a girl couldn't look over, but low enough so that the head of the teacher in the neighbouring classroom could appear and with a glance quell any disturbance that might arise in a roomful of unsupervised girls.

There were a few private primary schools and these were patronised almost solely by the families of the French Creole class; the offspring of the English administrative class were sent to boarding schools in England, so schools like Tranquillity Girls catered for the whole spectrum of society minus those others. There, the daughters of respectable, stable, home-owning middle-class salaried workers and professionals sat in benches alongside girls like me. I suppose that girls like those others brought with them standards of speech and modes of behaviour that we others unconsciously modelled ourselves on, but I would claim that it was the teachers and Miss Mc Shine who set the tone, standards and expectations and showed us ordinary girls that there were other ways of being. This was not consciously taught; it was simply absorbed, a kind of cultural osmosis by association, but it served as the foundation on which the school built its excellence in both the proper raising of girls and in academic achievement.

By the time I left Mrs Granderson, I could recite the times tables to twelve times twelve, and I could do subtraction, addition, multiplication and division of numbers, in plain numbers and in money – pounds (£), shillings (s) and pence (d); weight – ounces (ozs) pounds (lbs) hundredweight (cwt) and tons (t); in volume – pints, quarts and gallons (pts, qts, g); and in linear measurement – inches, feet, yards, furlongs and miles (ins, ft, yds, f, mls). In Standard Two we learnt the names of the continents and could point to them on the world map, a large varnish-coated canvas map on a wooden rail hanging by a string from a nail driven into the wall. On that map, which stretched a globe world into a big rectangle, we would be called up one by one to locate the oceans and seas, identify the major countries coloured pink that splashed across every continent, and find the dot that was Trinidad. We learned to read, to write legibly in capital and common letters in our double-line exercise books. We could spell and read aloud, enunciating clearly. We learned the names of the parts of a plant and the names of the visible parts of our body. Tranquil girls did not leave that institution saying *foot* to mean the entire limb from hip to toe, as was common then. We knew leg and foot and its subparts: thigh, knee, shin, calf, ankle, instep, toe, and similarly there was no ambiguity with respect to hand and arm either. We did quizzes, mental arithmetic and spelling. We said please, thank you, good morning, good afternoon, yes miss, no miss.

I was skipped a class and was sent to Standard Four with Miss Ward. Long division and long multiplication and comprehension entered my life, as did *The Students Companion* by Wilfred D. Best. This must have been an all-time bestseller among schoolbooks in Trinidad and Tobago. It was a compendium of useful information, a mini encyclopaedia of proverbs, seasons of the year, comparatives and superlatives of common adjectives, abbreviations, masculine and feminine of nouns, names for the adult and young of animals, occupations, single words for phrases, prefixes and suffixes, quotations, highest mountains, deepest ocean, historical facts and so much more. It became the handbook from which we learned a whole rash of stuff. We would be given ten personal nouns, let's say, and made to learn their masculine and feminine forms overnight for a test the next day. Thereafter, no one would look at a large bird with a big flat beak and webbed feet and say, that's a duck, without adding, or it could be a drake. I'm sure any Tranquil scholar who went into poultry farming would have named a favourite male duck Sir Francis. We revelled in show-offy puns too.

There was another book I remember from that time. It was a big book of history, big in that the dimensions, length and width of the book, was large, not that it was thick. I can't recall the name, but I do remember the pages being smooth and shiny and that each chapter was illustrated by a colour plate with intriguing titles like *When Last Did You See Your Father*, which was the title of the picture of a small boy in a white long shirt standing with his hands clasped behind his back, in a room with lots of books and lots of serious men dressed in black and wearing tall hats and tall boots. A man seated behind the desk seemed to be the one asking the question. Another picture was called *Ophelia*, and it was of a young woman, fully dressed, her dress reaching to her ankles, lying in water, her eyes closed, flowers strewn around her floating in the water with her. That's how I floated in the sea, no flowers of course, but with my face sticking above the surface of the water. Hers wasn't. There was one of the men in white robes cutting mistletoe from a tree with a silver knife. Was there a silver platter for it to rest on? But that one was called, I think, *The Druids*. Do I also remember a *Boadicea*? A woman in white robes on a small open chariot? The one called *The Empress of India*, an oval black and white, was of a rather stout old woman who was sitting with a tiny crown perched on her head, like a topknot. Another showed a procession of blond children dressed all in white, the lead child carrying a large cross and that picture was about angels or was it angles, going against the infidel, something about Saracens and The Crusades – but the title has slipped from me. I didn't make much sense of the history but I spent hours looking at the pictures.

Mrs Thornhill came next, Standard Five, the exhibition class. Her task was to prepare us to sit the very important annual College Exhibition Exam, from the results of which a successful student would gain one of the few government-funded free places to one of the, at that time, just four secondary schools on the island, two schools for boys, two for girls.

Dear Mrs Thornhill, how did you do it? How did you, year after year, face up to thirty-five ten and eleven-year-old little girls of diverse abilities and situations and teach relentlessly from morning to afternoon, setting tests and marking books, and rewarding and punishing and nurturing, keeping calm and involved and caring? You checked our nails, straightened our blouses that crept up after vigorous play, tidied the pleats in our overalls, smoothed back messy hair, retied ribbons and made us stand on the bench for bad behaviour or badly done work; you made us clean up our blue-black ink spills when we accidentally tipped over our little white ceramic inkwells set in holes in the tops of our desks. If you saw we didn't have anything to eat, you shared yours from your wide-mouth thermos flask. You knew our mothers and our siblings by name. Mrs Thornhill's two daughters, Myrna and Maureen, were also at Tranquil; I was in class with both. Her son, Terrance, was at Tranquillity Boys on the next-door compound. While I was in her class, Mrs Thornhill was expecting her fourth child. I think it turned out to be a boy, but as I'd already left I'm not sure. Mrs Thornhill must have been among that first wave of female teachers who were allowed to continue in their profession as married women and, as a pregnant married woman.

Set in an upper-class residential neighbourhood and occupying a massive piece of land, maybe an acre, between two wide avenues, Victoria and Stanmore, with spacious grounds dotted with shady trees and flowering shrubs, Tranquillity Girls offered unlimited opportunities for free play and exploration. A favourite place was at the back of the grounds where there were enormous tamarind trees. The ripe pods fell on the ground and if you picked them up not long after they'd fallen, they'd be free of burrowing insects, especially a kind of weevil whose presence in a pod you could detect by careful search of the brittle brown shell for the tiny holes they made to gain entry or maybe exit. One tamarind tree in particular seemed to be always in season. Groups of us girls scrambled around collecting pods, our skirts lifted at the front to act as sacks. We spent much of the lunch break sitting on the network of hard knobbly exposed roots shelling the pods, teasing with tongue and teeth each seed from the long fibres that hold them together, sucking off the brown sticky acid sweet pulp and collecting the brown seeds, hard and shiny like polished wood, perfect squares with rounded corners, patterned with radiating lines of a lighter shade of brown, beautiful to look at, as smooth and satisfying to the touch as a rosary bead. I think we really ate tamarind for the seeds, because these we packed into small cloth sacks that we hand-stitched ourselves from the rags of old clothes so we could play the then very popular game called bean bag. In this, two girls standing about twelve feet apart throw the bean bag to each other but aiming to hit any and eventually all of a dozen or so girls running from one end of the field of play to the other, they running between the girls throwing the beanbag, their numbers diminishing as a girl struck by the bean bag must leave the field of play, until only one target is left and she too is hit and given out. The sacks were never too tightly packed with seeds because this would have made them a weapon. It is with amusement that

I note that a beanbag is now a huge sack filled with styrofoam beads on which one slouches in front of a TV screen.

Tranquil was the place to which trainee teachers from the nearby Government Teachers Training College came to do their practical training. Home Economics and Art must have figured highly on their curriculum because I remember one visiting teacher teaching us to peel – I had that skill already – and grate – a new skill – raw cassava, squeeze the grated root to extract the juice, and put the juice in a basin out in the sun for the liquid to evaporate, leaving a residue of white powder. This is starch, she said. You can starch your clothes with it. We each got a piece of brown paper to make a twist of a small amount of cassava powder to take home. Marmie put it in a saucepan, added a little water and brought it to the boil and yes, as she stirred, it turned from opaque to clear and became gluey. It was really starch, enough to make a school blouse stiff and smooth to iron. Another teacher showed us how to fold paper to make things other than the boats and dunce caps we usually made; with her we made pretty things like aeroplanes and birds. She also gave us each a piece of a raw potato and showed us how to carve a shape in it and how to dip it in a shallow saucer of ink and stamp it on paper to make printed patterns. It did really trouble me at the time that something to eat, potato, was used in this way; that a food item could be so casually used for a purpose that had nothing to do with nutrition. And I must confess that even now I'm not sure that I am untroubled by it. Oddly though, the idea of cassava, also a food, being used for making starch didn't unsettle me then, and doesn't now either.

There must have been an outbreak of tuberculosis in the island while I was at Tranquil, and that some sort of BCG campaign had been launched, because one day a team of nurses from the hospital came to school. We girls were lined up and were shown how to turn up the left sleeve of our blouses until our upper arms were exposed to the shoulder. As we filed past the little table set up in the schoolyard, one nurse dipped a small piece of cotton wool into a little white enamel bowl and rubbed it across the top part of your arm. It smelled very strong like rum but was it was clear like water. The next nurse scratched the rubbed spot with something like a pin and that was it. You moved along and rolled down your sleeve. The following week the nurses came back to check our arms. On some of us you couldn't tell there had been a scratch. On others there was a large red swollen boil. The nurses wrote down in a book what they saw on each of us. I think the girls with swollen arms got an injection, but I'm not sure, as I wasn't among them; my scratch had disappeared.

Tuberculosis was the cause of death of a friend, a neighbour from down the Saddle Road, not far from my home. I don't remember her name – was it Lucille? – but I do remember the occasion. We children went to see her at her home where she was waiting for us. I remember her coffin, the outside covered with white velvety material with an embossed pattern of roses. She was due to make her first communion, as was I, a couple of weeks later at Easter, but she died before she could. Lying deep into the pleated white satin of her coffin, opened so people could see her for the last time and say goodbye, she was dressed in her white first communion dress, a white veil and a coronet of white artificial roses, her white prayer book clasped in her folded hands. She was the first dead person I saw – this was before my grandma's death – and I remember that I was more curious than upset by it. I thought it was lucky that her mother had got her all dressed up and lying so perfectly with prayer book and all before she died, so that she was ready and waiting for the coffin to be brought home and just be lifted into it. She looked peaceful, as if she was already in heaven, where we all prayed to go, and her dying only meant that she had got there before us.

All three of us Lafond girls went to Tranquil. When it was just Annette and me there, we boarded out for lunch at Mrs Blanche's on Tragarete Road. There we met up with other children under a shed in her backyard, where we sat on long benches at a table. Mrs Blanche gave each of us a spoon and a plate of rice, beans and chopped stewed meat, either as separated items or as a cookup, or we got a bowl of sancoche, the thick yellow split peas soup with floating islands of dumplings and ground provision. An older man, respectably dressed in a long-sleeved shirt and tie, an office worker from the nearby Government Printery, ate by himself just inside the house proper, sitting at Mrs Blanche's closed sewing machine on which she'd spread a small broderie anglaise tablecloth. He ate his lunch with knife and fork, tools none of us rough children knew how to use. These superior dining implements scraped against the plate as he cut his food. We children would start up chanting, *ka-chow, ka-chow, ka-chow*, imitating the sound of cutlery against the plate as he chopped up his meat and the cucumber, lettuce and tomato salad. When we saw him pause to turn his head and glare at us, we stopped our chanting and all he could see was half a dozen or so schoolchildren paying close and silent attention to their food, but the minute he turned his back and continued eating, the chant would start up again. This must have upset him and he may have threatened Mrs Blanche that he would leave, because she warned us that she would tell our mothers about our behaviour. I don't think she did. How could she? Neither she nor we had a phone and she would have had to send a message to Marmie through one of us miscreants. Marmie never mentioned it and Mrs Blanche continued to accept the dollar a week per child that Marmie sent. But her threat was enough. We stopped our nonsense.

There's a lot I learned from that experience about gang behaviour and bullying, not then, but long, long after, and even now I can't brush it off by thinking we were only children, we didn't know better. I'm wondering now whether it's because there weren't then specific labels like *gang* or *mob behaviour*, *bullying* and so on and whether the phrase *bad behaviour,* which was all that was ever used, was too vague and general and so just didn't have any impact. We never considered how our cruel childish behaviour could have hurt the grownup and perhaps important and certainly harmless man we were making fun of, or how the threat of his leaving because of us could have affected Mrs Blanche who was providing a service to our hardworking mothers. Are such considerations arrived at only as adults, and then only after reflection or personal experience? I think that consideration for others' feelings – empathy – can be, should be, taught at an early age. I never heard the word empathy used when I was growing up. I remember sympathy, but that was what you offered someone when a family member died. I think if someone had said to me, Put yourself in Mrs Blanche's shoes and think about it. Put yourself in that man's shoes. And if that person had taken me through the process, so much of what I did and so much of what I failed to do all through my life might have been different. But big people didn't talk to children back them. They corrected them when they stepped out of line and you'd be lucky to get away with a talking-to instead of licks. And I'm not sure how much or even whether that has changed. I guess that may come over as a self-serving excuse for my self-centredness and yes perhaps it is. Ah boy. Many of life's lessons are learned too late. What good does my shaking my head in regret do, eh? I ask you.

After lunch at Mrs Blanche's, I sent Annette back to school by herself – and here I see a lack of empathy for my little sister. Lord, I better stop this here and now or else I'll want to call her in Jacksonville Florida and ask her pardon, and have to go into long reams of explanation and clues to prod her memory – and risk having her nail me with other examples of slights, neglect and carelessness towards her that I have forgotten but am almost certainly guilty of. Let sleeping dogs lie. After lunch, with Annette dispatched back to school, I would stand on the pavement on Tragarete Road under someone's slatted jalousie window to listen to 'Second Spring', a radio serial. The introduction ran like this: *Can a woman who has once loved completely, ever find true love again? Can she find A Second Spring?* Then there was a short burst of anxious violin music followed by the voices of the actors in the drama. I stood glued to the spot until the fifteen-minute episode was over, then I went back to school.

When Carol was old enough to join us at Tranquil, Marmie bought an enamel three-container stacking food carrier in which she packed lunch that she'd woken at four in the morning to prepare for us to take to school. As the eldest I was in charge of taking the carrier, making sure the two little ones ate, and of bringing it, rinsed free of food particles, back home.

Because of this change in our lunch routine I never found out whether a woman who has once loved completely ever found her second spring.

When I moved on to the convent school, the food carrier was abandoned and forgotten. Long, long years after, while backpacking through India in my mid-fifties, I came across such food carriers, dozens of them at a roadside metal-goods shop. I bought one; nostalgia is a powerful goad. The vendor weighed the stainless steel one I chose; I fished out the requisite rupees from my waist wallet, squished the contents of the rucksack to accommodate the bulky uncrushable purchase, hoisted it on my back, lugged it for a month across the subcontinent and brought it home in triumph. One of these good days, eschewing current vegetarian lifestyle, I'll put rice in one, red beans in another and stew beef in the third, lay a table cloth, unstack the carrier, serve myself and relive a period of my life about which I thought nothing at the time, but which now is loaded with an accretion of heartaches and pains of regret that are in need of gentle soothing.

Except for the journey to and from school and for lunch, I hardly saw Annette. Carol, six years younger, was different. Some years ago, I was at a greengrocer's in Cascade and in came a woman whom I had been to primary school with. We hadn't seen each other for long decades. We had one of these long-time-no-see, so-what-you-getting-up-to type of exchanges and then she said, You know what I remember best about you? I said I'd no idea. She said, Your sister Carol. She used to come to find you every recess time. I didn't realise until then that a huge chunk of my childhood was defined by others through my relationship with my sister Carol. But it was true.

I was in the exhibition exam class when Carol entered kindergarten. The pupils of the exhibition class were often still in the classroom during recess, finishing off some serious work. And there would be my sister Carol, standing at the bottom of the steps, wailing in a most plaintive little voice, Barbara, I want my tea. I would pretend I hadn't heard, too engrossed in working out a square root or parsing a sentence. That served only to heighten her distress and cause her to call more loudly, Barbara, Barbara, give me my tea. Everyone in class was sniggering by then. Heads were buried in the copybooks to hide the laughter. I squirmed in shame, sliding down the bench until my head was below the level of the desk. Mrs Thornhill called out, Barbara, go and see about your sister. I got up from my desk and went to the bench where all the bookbags were kept, pulled out a thermos flask from my bag and walked down the classroom steps with it. I could hear Mrs Thornhill saying to the class, Hurry up and finish that exercise or you will get no recess at all, and the giggling behind me subsided.

Carol was such a skinny child that people would say a breeze could blow her away, but I, coming down the steps to her thin, forlorn little self, wanted only to strangle her, the cause of my humiliation. Our mother had combed her hair that morning in two long neat plaits that ended in two crisp white bows. The taffeta ribbons were braided into the hair so that they would not fall out and be lost. The crying and distress had somehow made one of the plaits come undone. The bow was intact, but the braiding had come loose and the bow was hanging on by a few long strands of hair. I sat on the bottom step and she sat beside me, her hands curled in her lap, waiting for me to do what I must. I unscrewed the outer cap of the thermos and the inner stopper and poured the milky cocoa into the outer cap, which served as a cup. While she held the cup in both her little hands and sipped the hot drink, I tugged out the dangling bow, harder than I needed to, undid the ribbon and smoothed it, replaited her hair, braiding in the ribbon.

By the time the bow was done, she had drunk the cocoa and was holding out the cup for more. Her face was streaked with tears, the corners of her mouth stained with cocoa. I should have felt some kindness, some fellow feeling towards this needy little sister, but all I could feel was rage for the shame she had brought me in front of others who had no little sisters calling for them. I told her she'd had enough, that she would get more at lunchtime and to go back to her classroom. I screwed back on both caps as she walked away, looking down at her feet and dragging her shoes in the playground dust. I walked back into the classroom, still angry with her and upset with myself for being angry with her. I didn't care who was casting sly glances at me or whether I had completed the schoolwork exercise. I sat at my desk, put my arms and my head on the desk and sobbed and sobbed.

My sister Carol died on Carnival Monday last year, in Orlando, Florida, where she'd lived for more than half her life. It grieves me that I didn't tell her how sorry I am that I wasn't kinder to her as a little child those long decades ago at recess time in Tranquil. I can only hope that she didn't remember, or if she did, she didn't dwell on it, for we were loving, mutually supportive friends as adults. Not that I think that has given me the absolution I still need. Maybe then, March fourth, the anniversary of her death, is the date for that food carrier christening? I could even make cocoa tea and fill a thermos. A small gesture of atonement?

For the exhibition exam, each candidate was allowed two tries. The first time I sat and the number of exhibitioners who got a free place to high school was one hundred and twenty-five. I was placed one hundred and sixtieth. The following year when I sat the exam again and the number was increased to one hundred and seventy-five, my name was there among the lucky ones. This made an unquantifiable change not only in my own schooling and in my life prospects, it also radically changed our family life.

I think Marmie must have been hanging on by the skin of her teeth up to the day I sat the exam, because soon after, as the long holiday intervened, she didn't take us to Upper Belmont Valley Road to spend time with our grandmother and cousins, but instead we were split up and parcelled out. At the time, Tony was a baby and Marmie took him with her. I think I heard afterwards that Annette was with people in San Fernando and now I can't ask Carol where she was sent. I was taken in by the Chong Tais, a Chinese family, a widow who owned the grocery next door. Of her six children, Monica, the second girl, was my friend.

I remember the feeling of powerlessness, the cold cramp clenching your belly tight when you find yourself abruptly on the edge of 'know' and look down into the dark pit of 'not-know'. My mother didn't tell us what it was about and at the time that didn't seem strange. Big people didn't explain things to children. They didn't have to. What prompted that dispersal I never knew, perhaps because I never asked. You took for granted that what happened, happened, and that was it. It is with some sadness that more and more I've come to realise that I journeyed through my childhood without a map or directions and that this suited our lives, all of our lives, because we had no real destination except staying alive while getting older.

It was not an unhappy time at the Chong Tais. Auntie Phyllis simply made space for me in the girls' bedroom and at the table and I was fed and looked after in the way she looked after her own children. I learned what went on behind the scenes in a grocery shop household and learned lots of new card games like Rummy and All Fours, which we children played with discarded burnt matchsticks as our stakes. I learned how to pour a tot of rum, measured out in a small glass and decanted into a larger one for the customers who sat on long benches at a long table and drank and played gambling card games. I learned about what I thought was Chinese cooking but was really Cantonese cooking – lots of tiny bits of meat and shredded vegetables barely wilted and served on boiled white rice or boiled noodles in a bowl to be eaten with chopsticks. It became passing a holiday with friends instead of family and after my initial discomfort and fear I was fine, though I heard nothing about the rest of the family, not Marmie and certainly not the younger ones. If Auntie Phyllis knew more than I, she didn't tell me. Maybe she told Upin, the eldest girl, or my friend Monica, or even the boys between Upin and Monica, Keong Fatt and Keong Hon, but if she did, no one shared the information with me.

My poor, poor Marmie. How she must have held her breath waiting for us to grow up, waiting for us to come out of childhood unscathed. She didn't do it alone. She knew she couldn't. I'm leaving it to God, I often heard her say. She'd recite her rosary, whisper prayers, It's in God's hands, through our measles, my mumps, Carol's pneumonia, appendicitis and broken arm, Tony's ear infections, Annette's teeth, and, after years of haemorrhaging, her own hysterectomy at the Seventh Day Adventist Hospital on Stanmore Avenue not far from Tranquil while I was still a pupil there. I'd pass in to see her on my way home with the little girls and she'd tell me what to do, what to give the others to eat when I got home, after passing along Belmont Circular Road to pick up Tony from Nennen who minded him in the day, God will provide, when there was no money and she had to face Uncle in the shop, to ask for trust. All of these things she weathered and I saw her go through worse, physical and mental assault from Pappy, yet nothing had led her before to scatter us as she did that time. So what was it, what was so insurmountable in 1953, that she did what she would have considered unthinkable in our normal unpredictableness, and put each of us little girls to live among practical strangers?

For many years I tried to find a reason, and all I can come up with is a feeble sort of explanation. Maybe Marmie wasn't working and perhaps Pappy had stopped paying the rent and we must have been evicted, though had bailiffs come to turf us out, I'm sure I would have remembered, or we must have gone quietly, as royalty and peasants alike are expected to, but sometimes refuse and kick up an unseemly fuss. Why didn't I ask her? If I had a dollar for every kick I've given myself for not asking questions of my mother in the many years I knew her after my childhood, I'd have enough to pay a privately practising doctor to treat my self-inflicted black and blue bruises. But it's too late now and all I can do is put two and two together and come up with all sorts of answers.

The exam results came out and I was placed first in the colony. My picture was on the front page of the newspaper. At the moment she was unfolding her morning paper, spotting the good news on the front page, Miss Umilta Mc Shine heard a bird singing in the garden of her St Ann's Fisher Avenue home. She sat at her piano and composed a piece of music, using as a recurring motif the birdsong she'd heard. She called the piece *Barbara Ann* and played it at assembly that very morning. It must have mattered a lot to her and to the school, though I was too young and too naïve to be aware of it. I do know that I was later called to read a poem for a live radio programme. The poem, *I hear America singing, the varied carols I hear,* I must have recited parrot fashion, the words meaning nothing to me and it's only recently, sifting through the memory of that time and disinterring this particular one that I looked it up, read it, and saw the significance of its provenance. Though I do know why I was chosen, I now wonder why that poem and why a radio recitation at all. It doesn't read like a poem that would interest a local listening audience. Could it be, I'm now wondering, that it was for WVDI, the American radio station beamed from the big American naval base at Chaguaramas? The time of year, which has to be between September and December, was too late for their July Fourth celebrations; maybe it was for Thanksgiving Day? Anyway, 1953, the year when our then new queen, Elizabeth II, was crowned, Mt Everest was conquered, the molecular structure of DNA was discovered, matchbox toys and James Bond made their appearance – all triumphs of England, the Mother

Country – was the year in which, with Americans still occupying bases throughout this colony, I, the minor-celebrity-of-the-moment, was called on to recite an uplifting patriotic poem on the radio for an American audience. Such are the ties that bind us and blind us.

In that term, relaxed because the results were out, trips out of school were arranged. We set out from Victoria Avenue and headed north, crossed the road to the Savannah (at the cannon ball tree where the Queen's Park Hotel taxi drivers in crisp white shirts and black, long trousers hung out playing cards and waiting for the bellhop across the road to summon one of them to take a hotel guest somewhere), walked along the pitch walk past the row of very grand houses where very grand people lived, and then to the very grandest of all, first past Queen's Royal College with its foreign masters and specially bright boys, past the homes of the Anglican bishop, the Catholic archbishop, the British Council, and finally Mr Stollmeyer's Castle, all the way past Nutmeg Ravine and The Hollows (not stopping at its ponds with lily pads, guabins and tadpoles), to the Botanical Gardens past the grand Governor's House with its long driveway of royal palms (straight trunks painted a stark white from ground to above my height, so they looked like important military figures with tall white socks and feathered helmets standing to attention as a one-legged guard of honour for the governor to pass through), and wandered among the trees that were brought in as tropical specimens from all over the empire (not that we knew that, as we didn't even know our own native species, or cared to know), before settling down to a picnic of sandwiches we'd brought from home instead of our usual regular lunchtime cooked food (you couldn't pull out a sandwich made from hops bread with saltfish buljol or black pudding inside, that would be very low class – it had to be soft white bread, butter bread, sliced, buttered and with cheese or ham or salami and lettuce and cut into triangles so that it looked like a proper sandwich, that is like a sandwich you had seen in a picture or a film). While I enjoyed the picnic in the gardens and continued with such visits many years afterwards, what I really, really loved, what was as new and exciting to me as going to a foreign country, was another school trip that involved my first train ride.

Early one morning, before the sun was really up, we girls, the whole of Mrs Thornhill's class, met at the big railway terminus downtown. We were taking the train all the way to the end of the line, to Rio Claro in the south of the island. The railway station is near the docks where big ships come in from faraway places. I am with Mrs Thornhill and a few girls waiting for the rest of the class to arrive. The railway station is a big khaki-coloured concrete building with so many people hurrying in and out of the high, wide-open archways that it makes me think of the Colonial Hospital where I was last year Carnival for a whole two weeks, because of mad blood. From where I am standing I can see the long sloping roof of the Wm. H. Kennedy & Sons warehouse on Marine Square where Pappy works as a tally clerk, there and at the docks when cargo ships come in. When I look to my right there is the Cathedral, and behind everything the Northern Range stretches all across the bottom of the sky. The Northern Range is light blue now. (I wonder why it wasn't called The Blue Mountains, like the mountains in Jamaica). But the Northern Range isn't always blue. In the daytime it looks green because of the trees, and at night it is so black you can't see it. I think that if you name a thing a colour and the colour changes you'd have to keep changing the name, and for the Northern Range that would be three times a day. Maybe the Blue Mountains are always blue. If someone asks you what colour is the sky, you would say blue. But that's not true. Sometimes it's white, sometimes, grey, sometimes it's black and at sunset it is every colour you can imagine. It's not like school shoes that are white and that's that. But even that's not really true, because I can only say my washekongs are white when I've just sponged on blanco, which I have to do in the afternoon when I get home from school. I wonder whether... There's a shout, Barbara! I turn. I see Mrs Thornhill signalling me to hurry up. I glance around. I am alone. I run towards her and we hurry to the platform and climb aboard.

The carriage jolts. I find a seat, rest down my paper bag and I join the others in sticking our arms out of the open windows to wave and shriek as the train pulls away from the station. We keep on looking out and pointing out what we see – buildings along the railway line and then small huts of galvanise and cardboard and piece-a-board walls, barefoot children, barebottom little boys in too-small open shirts, little girls in only panties who stare at us as we stare at them, mud, mud, mud. On the other side, there's coconut trees, the smell of smoke and an awful smell like rotting rubbish. We make a big fuss and cover our noses with our hands and make vomiting noises and Mrs Thornhill says, Behave yourselves, and we giggle, but as the smell goes on in the air for a long while, we don't find it interesting any more. There's more smoke and I can see people walking on the piles of rubbish, then a shimmer of water, mud, trees, trees, trees – and soon we have had enough of that. We withdraw from the windows to sit and chat, and gradually the carriage settles down to a low hum.

I do not lose interest in the world outside as the train chugs along at a speed no faster than a car, alongside trees with silvery leaves that look as if they just stepped off the land and decided to walk across the water, pale brown roots poking upwards from the water like comic-strip earthworms basking in the early morning light. We pass through a strange landscape of pale green cane shoots twice as tall as me, along a wide plain that stretches forever in all directions, completely covered in waving cane. Everywhere you look, the same tall, pale-green waving cane like grass. Over there in the distance, a tall chimney, then another rising straight up from the ground it seems, past clusters of carat-leaf thatched-roofed ajoupas, clay walls, some reddish earthen, a few daubed white. A woman in a long pink skirt is walking and, as we chug past, she draws an ohrini across her face with her free hand; the other balances a wide basket on her head, the light catching a thick silver bracelet around the ankle of her bare foot. Across a wide smooth brown river, a wide-eyed child no older than ourselves leads two big horned zebus up the bank. Suddenly, I remember Parbattie, the girl in the bed next to me in hospital. I don't know where she came from, but it wasn't as near as Belmont. Maybe it was somewhere like here? I don't remember why she was in hospital, but I do remember we took chairs out to the railings and sat there to watch the mas go by on Charlotte Street. Wilfred Strasser played 'One Penny'. His float was all copper-coloured just like the penny. He too. Completely one colour just like a real penny only very, very big. He sat perfectly still like Britannia on his seat, like the person on the coin. I wondered how he got himself and his robes and everything to be the exact colour of the penny. The words ONE PENNY was in the correct place on the side of the coin that was facing us as Strasser sailed past us that Carnival Tuesday afternoon. I wonder what became of Parbattie.

We are now at a place called Jerningham Junction. There's a Jerningham Avenue in Belmont. It joins Belmont Circular Road to the Savannah and it is an important street, which is why it is called an avenue not a street. There is the Jerningham Silver Medal and the Jerningham Gold Medal. I wonder who is Mr Jerningham and why are so many things named after him? Come to think of it, who is Reid? Who is Pelham? I know Victoria, a queen of the British Empire, where I belong.

Then we are passing through hills that are like big waves, up and down, all covered in cane too, but the train doesn't go up and down like a road would, it goes level, so sometimes you are down in a dip and can see some way towards another low rise but sometimes you can't see anything except the walls of rock. In an open area, a bull cart piled high with long sheaves of razor grass bumps away from us; a wiry man with a white beard, his head wrapped in a white turban, a curved grass knife in his hand, is sitting very calmly right at the top of the neatly laid green stalks, their feathered heads hanging over the back of the cart bouncing in rhythm with the jolt of big wheels. He sees us, we wave, he waves. The train goes dark all of a sudden; we are going through a tunnel and we scream, then laugh nervously, then we are onward, hemmed in by big trees you could lean out and touch, more small huddles of wooden houses and a little stream with big blue flowers on the bank and more close forest, more scatterings of houses, more dark forest, more tangled forest, more green forest, tall-tall trunks, some straight, some branching, and vines thick like the ropes that tie up ships, and small plants with big leaves on branches and dark damp places with low flashes of orange and red and white flowers and big blue butterflies. A sudden break in the trees and we are there. It's the terminus, the end of the line and we get out.

We take our bags and follow our teacher to a shed where we undo our packages and have our picnic lunch. Other passengers get off too. Two men lift jute bags onto a trolley on the platform and pull it along past us and then disappear through a passage. Two others offload a kerosene stove, a bolt of patterned cloth and a stack of enamel buckets onto another trolley. They too disappear. Trolleys come in the other direction laden with tightly packed jute bags. As they drag the bags onto the train wagon, the air smells different all at once. I can smell coffee beans, cocoa beans and tonka beans, smells I recognise from going to the warehouse on Saturday mornings to collect our allowance from Pappy. I always wondered where the trees were that grew the beans that sit in sacks in the warehouse waiting for a ship to come in and take them away to England. And now, at the end of the railway line, I know. We walk around for a bit, stretch our legs and make our way along the platform. In the meantime, the engine has made its way round the linking track to get to what was the back of the train on our way down, hook up what was the last carriage and now would be the first. We clamber on board once more and start our journey back home. Once again we pass the closed-in views of scattered villages, forest, more villages, more forest, and then more open, wider views through the cane fields. The lowering sun makes flashing swords of coconut-palm leaves; waves of red flow across the blue sky as flocks of scarlet ibis come in to roost in the tangled canopy of mangrove in the swamp islands; the neatly earth-bunded squares of watery rice paddies turn gold, then pink and purple, and our eyes, which have seen so much newness and strangeness in one day, are brimful, making a blur of everything, pulling down heavy eyelids as the train pulls into our station.

My exam success spurred surprising creativity in another direction. Even though on our birth certificates we were only our mother's children, and none of us shared his last name, Pappy must have been so overwhelmed by the massive outpouring of congratulations he would have received from his friends and co-workers (those who knew his life story) that, to take shame out he eye, he quickly found us somewhere to live and reunited the family, we three scattered girls, our Marmie and baby Tony, all now strangers to one another, in two rooms at the back of a house in Belmont, which he rented at nine dollars a month.

So, while my Tranquillity years were Boissiere Village, Maraval years (except that one last term after exam results came out in September, but before the new school year started the following January), 74 Pelham Street, Belmont was my home while I was at St Joseph's Convent Port of Spain.

Even though we were reduced from three rooms to two, the move to Belmont was good for Marmie. She could more easily see her siblings. Her twin sister, Yvette, lived in St Francois Valley Road, a half hour walk away, two brothers were still up Belmont Valley Road, Tebeau in his own home and Carmie in the upper family home, with sister Nissa in the lower family home. Now some of her many nieces and nephews, our cousins, visited, and so became our first friends in Belmont. Familiars passed by and called out and I think that Marmie felt she had in some way come back home to stay.

One frequent visitor was one of her many godchildren, Lawrence Cross. Marmie asked him to teach me to ride a bicycle in this interlude between schools. By that time, though, Marmie's bike, a lady's bike, had already been repossessed by the hire purchase company and Lawrence's bike was, of course, a gent's, and he, quite a bit older than me, was already a long lean six-footer to my under five feet, so the saddle and handlebars on his bike were way, way up there. Neither of those considerations seemed to bother Marmie or Lawrence, so I didn't query it.

Lawrence decided that Upper Clifford Street – that is the stretch between Belmont Circular Road and the Pelham Street junction – was to be the cycle training course. It is a wide street, and Clifford Street had pavements. That meant a passing car had room to manoeuvre around a novice cyclist and pedestrians were protected from my possible misadventures. Not least, Clifford Street had a good steady downward gradient from the top where it starts at the Circular Road, all the way down across the major road, Pelham Street, and on to Norfolk Street at its other end.

Lawrence swung one long leg over the cross bar, sat on the saddle, balanced himself, lifted me to sit sidesaddle on the cross bar and pedalled from my home down Pelham Street to Clifford Street He parked the bike with one pedal on the edge of the pavement and lifted me onto the saddle. I've never sat on a horse but if I ever do in my imminent dotage it won't be unfamiliar because that's how I felt up there on Lawrence's bike, gripping the handlebars to prevent myself from falling off, as if pulling on the reins of a big horse. With one hand holding the back of the saddle and the other on the handlebars, Lawrence guided the bike away from the pavement and on to the road. He then walked quickly down the road for a bit before letting go of the handlebars so that I alone was steering, occasionally pulling me back when I went off course, steadying me when I wobbled, and securing the bike when a car was also sharing the road with us. He pulled the bike to a stop at the major road, Pelham Street, and with me again sitting sidesaddle on the crossbar, he cycled back to the top. After a few goes like that, he stopped restraining the bike and allowed gravity to let it pick up speed down hill with him at a fast trot alongside, still holding on to the saddle. Up hill and down hill and suddenly I was flying. He had let go of the saddle and was racing alongside, only catching hold of the saddle to stop the bike just as I got the junction and was about to hurtle across Pelham Street into the right of way. He showed me how to slow down by using the brakes. He told me not to squeeze them too hard or the bike would stop suddenly and I would fall off. I looked down from where I was perched at the grey asphalt way below and decided that it was advice worth heeding. After about an hour, Lawrence had had enough of running downhill at speed and cycling with the weight of me up hill and he took me back home.

Over the course of a couple weeks, Lawrence must have become much fitter, built some muscle and improved his cardiovascular health. You see, I'm trying to think there was some benefit for this poor patient young man, apart from pleasing his godmother and imparting an essential skill to his little god sister. For my part, I learnt to balance, to steer and to slow a bicycle. I couldn't say I had learnt how to ride a bike, because getting on and off, moving from standstill, stopping safely and parking, Lawrence couldn't teach me with his method. These skills came later. Lawrence went abroad not long after to study agriculture and it was many years before I saw him again – by which time I was a reasonably accomplished cyclist. There was, though, the time when I was happily coasting down Upper Frederick Street alongside Memorial Park on my way to school when I tumbled *killkaytay* over the handlebars on to my head in the middle of the road outside the Royal Victoria Institute and was hospitalised with a concussion. The piece of metal that connects the back fender to the frame had somehow broken away and lodged itself between the spokes of the back wheel, causing the bike to come to a sudden stop. At least I had a bike story to tell Lawrence when he came back home from foreign.

During that spare term between the exhibition results and my starting at my new school, and well before the financial demands of Christmas took precedence, my mother got me ready for my next stage at school. My winning a place meant she didn't have to pay school fees for me. There was also a twenty-four dollar allowance for books. That money didn't come in hand; Muir Marshall & Sons, a downtown bookstore where the booklist was lodged, managed it, so that you could get items from the booklist up to the value of twenty-four dollars. Apart from textbooks and copy books there were other items – a padlock and two keys, separated, one labelled with pupil's name, a geometry set, a ruler, coloured pencils, a tin of Reeves water colour paints, three sable brushes of different sizes, a fountain pen and ink, pencils, eraser, sharpener.

The bookshop handed us a sheet of paper with labelled line drawings of the uniform – white blouse, blue overall, blue puffy knickers for everyday wear; grey overall, beige shirt, grey knickers and blue sash for PE; white long-sleeved dress uniform for special feast days, a white net veil for everyday along with instructions on what was the correct fabric for each garment and where to buy it. Waterman's was the store that stocked the bolts of blue, white, grey tobralco and the white linen, the blue woven sash and matching tie. The veil was to be bought at the convent. Buying fabric for the many different uniforms and paying someone to make them was a personal expense and could have deterred my mother from accepting the school place I had won, since there was no way our fragile family finances could have accommodated it. As an adult, I have heard stories of others who had to decline exhibitions because their families could not afford these extras. Marmie pawned her bracelets and the twenty dollars she got for them, along with a generous gift from Uncle Carmie, made sure I had everything I needed.

I'll say now for the record that I didn't want to go to the convent. I would have preferred Bishop Anstey High School. I liked their uniform, a dark blue skirt and white blouse and a red and black striped tie. They also had distinctive smart-looking dark-blue felt hats in a tricorne, like Napoleon's. The Bishops girls, too, seemed bolder than convent girls; my friend Monica was there already, and from her I learned things the girls talked about openly, like their bodies and its puzzling functions. I think, too, that I was a little afraid of the prospect of the convent. I think I might have felt intimidated by what it represented in my eleven-year old mind about privilege and one's place, an unformed awareness of hierarchy, about servants and madams, some sense of front doors and back doors that I picked up from what happens in church when you kneel at someone's pew where their name is on a brass plate and without words being exchanged you had to get up and leave, and maybe, too, from overhearing conversations among customers in Auntie Phyllis's grocery, customers who worked in a kitchen, or looked after children, or took care of a garden belonging to a madam. Of course, none of this was discussed or explained. It was the way the world worked and you just took it in with the air. I said nothing to anyone about this unease, and no-one asked me how I felt about things, beyond the simple question, So where you want to go?

But Father Graham, the Irish parish priest, arbiter of all matters concerning the ultimate fate of one's colonised Caribbean Catholic immortal soul, told my mother that if I went to that Protestant school, he wouldn't let me be confirmed. Poor woman, her eternal fate already sealed because of four bastards, she loved me and would do anything to save me from the everlasting torments of the unquenchable fires of Hell where she was already destined. I understand, eh Marmie. You and Toni Morrison's Sethe cannot be unique among mothers who would rather kill their child than have it go into eternal bondage. Except, dear Marmie, while you imagined I would escape the fires of hell by your surrendering to the priest's ultimatum, I must have done so anyway, because the blistering six-year sentence without parole I served at the convent was its own form of purgatory and has probably secured my place in heaven, regardless of what I've done since, in my many, many years of a long, happily unforgiven, trespassing life.

I turned twelve early December and just before Christmas there was another change. I showed Marmie my panties with the stain of blood at the crotch. She looked from the object in my hand to my face. She seemed worried and sad at the same time. She said, Oh. She went to her bedroom and came back with a piece of white cloth, which she folded into a rectangle. Put on a clean panty and put this in it. She left me sitting on the bed and went away. When she came back she sat next to me and pulled from her bag a length of wide elastic, two big safety pins and several pieces of white cloth, which she laid on her lap – smaller pieces of thin cotton, others larger, thicker material, also cotton cloth, like the diapers my little brother wore when he was a baby. I watched as she folded one of the smaller pieces into a small rectangle and wrapped it in the thicker fabric to make a long rectangle with the folded piece of smaller material in the middle. The elastic she knotted into a circle.

She bunched up my dress under my arms and held it there with one hand. She motioned me to step into the elastic circle, pulling it up until it was around my waist. Hold your dress, she said. She pulled down my panties and removed the square of white cloth, now with a red blot in the middle. She placed the newly folded cloth between my legs and pulled up the two ends – one at the front, the other at the back. She folded the front end over the elastic and pinned the loose end to the front. She turned me around and must have done the same at the back. She pulled up my panties and pulled down my dress. Then she turned her attention to folding three or four more cloth pads. You must change it when it gets dirty. You are a young lady now, she said. Don't let any boy put his thing down there. She pointed at where the cloth pad now lay within my panties. Or you will make a baby. You are too young for that. I was twenty-four years old when I had you. She picked up the soiled panties and the soiled cloth and went outside. I saw them soaking in a basin of soapy water on the bathroom floor when I was washing myself later that day. I dropped the dirty cloths there as I changed them. The stains went from browny-red to greeny-yellow in the soapy water. My mother spread the soapy cloths out on the bed of stones that was the bleach for our yard. There, on the hot stones, if you paid attention, you could see the stains shrinking and fading in the bright sun even while you were watching. My mother rinsed the cloths and draped them over the wire clothesline to dry.

BOOKSHELF

That first January school morning I got up, put on my new white blouse with the Peter Pan collar, my new blue overall, new white belt, new white washekongs and new white socks, put my books in the saddlebag of my new bike (a reward from Pappy), and rode down to St Joseph's Convent, Port of Spain. I knew where it was on Pembroke Street, but I had never been into the convent before. When I got to the high buff walls I slowed down, not knowing what to do next. There was a wide, open gateway with tall pillars on either side. I watched as girls got off their bikes and walked them through. So I did that too. There was a big shed to the right. They went there. I looked at how one girl pushed the front wheel of her bike through a slot in a long rack. I did the same. They then walked towards a gap between two very tall buildings. I followed them. I came to a big open paved space surrounded on three sides by connected tall buildings making a U shape. Across the open side, but not attached, there was a very long, high building with stained-glass windows like a church. I followed the girls along a wide corridor that edged the buildings. It was not bare concrete, but paved with cocoa-brown square tiles. One girl stopped at something like a small hand-wash basin, the kind you find in places that have flushing toilets. She pressed something and water squirted up. She lowered her head and drank. The water that passed her lips flowed into the little basin and went away. I didn't want to try that. I wondered whether the water that drained away would come up again like the water in the fountain in the middle of Woodford Square downtown, and I wouldn't want to drink that.

A nun stepped out of one of the buildings. She was completely covered in white from the veil over her head covering her forehead, and wrapped around her face, over her ears and neck, all the way down to her feet where only the tips of black shoes peeped as she walked. It was hard to make out her face and hands, the only bits of her not covered in white cloth. They were as pale and as white as her clothes. I knew about nuns. One came to my old school to teach catechism once a week. That one was brown and wore brown with a black veil. This nun, the one in white, looked at me with eyes like blue-glass marbles. You arrr a new gurrl? I said, Yes, sister. Some girls in a group chatting nearby looked at me, turned away and sniggered.

Mother, the nun said. Go upstairs to your classroom. She pointed to a corridor. Yes, Mother.

I saw a set of wide wooden stairs that reached up and branched into two. The steps were covered with a kind of green cloth in the middle showing only the dark wood on the sides of each step. Looking over the staircase where it branched was a statue of Mary, mother of God. She was dressed in white with a blue robe over that, the same blue and white as my new school uniform. The mother of God, Immaculate Mary, wore a gold crown on her head. My foot was on the soft material of the first step when I heard a shout. Not therrre, stupid child. It was the same Mother. The Mother pointed to the doorway behind the staircase. Therrrre! I felt myself go hot and then cold. I hung my head, afraid to look up or look around at whoever was there witnessing my stupidity. How was it that everyone else knew what to do, where to go? Why was I the only one to get it all wrong? I didn't expect to dislike anything or anyone on the first day, but that nun was my first lasting dislike in my new school.

I went *there*, to the corridor and came across another set of stairs, brown tiled stairs that matched the corridor and I took those. Upstairs, I saw big rooms, all looking the same. There were long doors with glass panes, not smooth but with a raised pattern of daises. The doors were open to the corridors on two sides. A third wall had a long row of open windows right along it. The fourth wall was unbroken. There was a blackboard fixed to it, and above that a big square-faced clock that showed the short hand just past VII and the long one resting right on IV. I liked how, to tell the time, you had to take time to work it out, like breaking a code, or solving a puzzle. Not just changing the roman letters into real numbers but also working out the value of the long hand numbers, and knowing before and after. Above the clock was a big black crucifix with a silver Jesus, perfectly shaped like a little doll, hanging on the cross from real nails through his open hands and his crossed feet. When I looked at the Jesus doll, at the drops of silver blood coming from where the thorns in his crown pierced his temple, I wondered, since his head was tilted down, lolling towards his chest, why were the drops of silver blood sloping to where they would flow if his head was upright? Was that a miracle to show the heathen Roman soldiers that he was the son of God, really God himself, the second person of the Trinity, and so his head would always be upright, even though to us mortals it would look fallen forward? That seemed a satisfactory explanation, so I turned my attention to the room layout. There were wooden double desks in four rows facing the wall with the blackboard, clock and crucifix, and under those was a platform supporting a big desk and chair. It all looked so clean and neat and tidy. So orderly.

I went into one room and looked through a window. Below was the big open space I'd seen downstairs. I could hear excited voices coming from another room and I looked in. Girls in little clusters were chattering and laughing, but there was nobody I could recognise so I walked on and went to the next room. Inside that room there were lots of girls like myself, standing silent, not looking at one another, also in crisp, new, too-big uniforms that we were expected to grow into during the course of the year. I looked around to see whether there was anybody from my old school. I saw Kathleen Poon. She was talking to Annette, her older sister who had been at this school for a year already. She did not look my way. A group of fair skin girls in what looked like older, tighter-fitting, washed-out uniforms, stood chatting among themselves, but not with anybody else. I went in and stood alone, like the others, not looking at anyone, just waiting for I didn't know what. I don't think that any of us girls in too-big, new uniforms did either, although at the time I was sure that only I knew nothing.

A nun came in the room and sent us to line up in the corridor. She opened a big book and called our names one by one, pronouncing our names in a strange way. This, in my old school, would have made me giggle and nudge my neighbour to join in with me, but somehow I was too frightened to find it funny. I even wondered whether we were saying our own names wrong all along and this was the right way. When we went in, she pointed where we were to sit. I was to share a double desk with a girl called Monica, just like my friend from Boissiere, who at that moment was in her own classroom in Bishops, where I wasn't. We were told to open our desks and put our things in them. I looked over to watch how Monica was arranging her things in the deep well of her desk, to see if there was a right way that was different from my way, so I wouldn't do something wrong again, but we both put the copybooks in a stack on the right side near the back and the text books stacked biggest at the bottom to smallest on top, on the left, with all the little things at the front – the tin of paints, the geometry set, the pencil case and the little bottle of Quink royal-blue ink.

When we were done, the nun called our names again, this time with the name of the house each of us was assigned to. It seemed there were four houses. My name was called when she reached the third house, a saint whose name I'd never heard before. We were told to line up in houses at the big desk. When I got to the head of the line, I didn't have money to pay for my badge, so I couldn't get the blue metal badge with the red strip for my house, St Xavier. Monica's badge had a brown strip overprinted with the words St Theresa, in silver. I was glad my house had a red strip and not brown, even though I knew more about a St Theresa than that other one. We were told to copy the timetable from the board. Then the nun rubbed it out and called one of the fair skin girls to write something on the board for us to copy. It was the Hail Mary. In French.

The group of fair skin girls were not new to the school like the rest of us. They had come up from the lower part of the convent school for which their parents paid fees. They did not have to win a place from a free government primary school like the rest of us. One of them, a girl called Ruth Ann, was our class prefect. She wore hanging gold earrings shaped like the fat bud of a little flower we children picked from roadside shrubs to pop like mini balloons on our foreheads. The real flowers are red; we called them forehead poppers. The rest of us who had pierced ears wore little gold, ball-shaped studs or small gold hoops, nothing as pretty as hers. This girl with the forehead-popper earrings was in charge of us; she knew what we were supposed to do and had the responsibility of making sure that we knew, too. An electric bell sounded and the nun got up from the chair. Ruth Ann came to the front of the class and signalled us to stand. We did. She then said, Thank you, Mère Rose. And we too said Thank you, Mère Rose, joining the other girls from the convent lower school in echoing Ruth Ann. Mère Rose left the classroom. I made to sit as did a few of us new girls. Then Ruth Ann said, In the name of the Father, and of the Son and of the Holy Ghost Amen, while crossing herself. So were we expected to stay standing? Then she started on Hail Mary in English and we all joined in. She signed herself again at the end and so we all did. She went to her own seat and we sat down. Another nun came in. Ruth Ann and the convent familiars stood, and so did we others. Good morning Mother Anna, the familiars chanted. We others joined in with Good morning Mother when the greeting started but couldn't finish. Then the nun called Mother Anna greeted us, sat at her desk and told us to take out our maths books. I did. She told us to work on the problems on the first page. We set to work and I realised I needed my geometry set too and I hadn't taken it out. I lifted the lid of my desk to get it out and was stopped by, You gurrl. Close that desk at once. I did. Stand up. I stood. What is your name? I told her. Your house? St Xavier's. You are getting a mark against conduct for not asking permission to open your desk. Yes, Mother Anna, wherever you are, you are the second person on whom I wished ill, on my very first day at the convent.

The first day ended at lunchtime for the whole school. It was a long-standing tradition that new pupils paid a visit to their old primary school in the spanking new uniform of the new school. I felt so distressed and ashamed at how my first day had gone, all the unpleasant surprises I met and my ignorance of everything around me that I didn't know how I could face Mrs Thornhill with my failures. I got on my bike and pedalled slowly towards my old school, wondering what I would say if my old teacher asked me how my first day went.

When I entered the old classroom, so welcoming, so familiar, and saw Mrs Thornhill, she said to her little seated ten- and eleven-year-olds who were regarding me with the wonderment reserved for some character out of a book or a film, if you study very hard and pass the exam, you could win a place at big school too and be just like her. The horrors of my first day at the convent suddenly no longer really mattered. My old school was proud of me. My old teacher wanted her new little girls to be like me. I felt very grown up and very accomplished. I told myself that I'd go back to that frightening place. I'd try to learn its ways. Maybe things would work out.

The girl I was put to sit next to was Monica Francis, daughter of Dr Francis and niece of Miss Francis. From the first day I could see that my desk mate was someone to learn from. Monica came prepared for the convent even though she hadn't come through the convent lower school. She had read *David Copperfield*, our literature set book, during the holidays and knew the meaning of the word posthumous, a word that appears in an early paragraph in Chapter One, and which had stumped me along with caul, mariner, presumptuous, all of which she understood. She was a bright girl, and I guessed that at home she had real books in a real family library, and of course *The Oxford English Dictionary*. Since I never saw inside her home on Phillips Street, a world apart from Belmont, I could only guess because she knew so many books, their names and the stories in them. She was not raised vye-qui-vye on a diet of borrowed comics, not the Just Williams and Nancy Drews and Hardy Boys, which was all that my local library afforded me. So in a short time, with Monica as my mentor, her extensive vocabulary was quickly absorbed into my own, which was as porous and as empty as a dry sponge.

There were lots of new things at school – like foreign languages. I loved French, Spanish and Latin, even though the first things we learnt in all of them was the 'Hail Mary' and the 'Our Father', which slowed us down a bit in getting to all those new words, all those masculine and feminine and neuter, different endings, genitive, dative and ablative, and verbs at the end and translations back and forth and prepositions that take one case or another. In English literature we underlined words we didn't know in *David Copperfield* and copied them in our exercise books along with their meanings which we looked up in the *Concise Oxford Dictionary*. In English language, we wrote essays. What we made in cookery bore no resemblance to actual real food. The teacher wrote a recipe on the board; we copied it in our exercise books. It was what we were going to cook in the next class. We were put into groups of three; each girl had to contribute an item or two from the list of ingredients in the recipe. I can remember us making short crust pastry and when it was done, we put jam in the middle; macaroni cheese, a pale dish in a white floury sauce with grated cheese on top; and a bread pudding using stale white bread, milk, eggs and raisins. These I couldn't replicate at home. They needed an oven. In any case, I couldn't see the point of learning how to make any of them. Let's say you feeling to eat some jam, some nice ruby guava jelly your mother just make, why not take a teaspoon and scoop out some from the jar and eat it just so, or if you want to do things proper, why not just take a piece of bread and put jam on it, why the fuss and bother to make and bake a special shape just to put the jam in? As for the other two dishes, I knew macaroni very well and I loved macaroni. Marmie used to cook macaroni all the time. When she was stewing beef or pork she would snap a few long brittle tubes of macaroni into shorter lengths and drop them in the gravy when the meat was almost done and the macaroni came out soft, brown and delicious, tasting of meat gravy. It helped stretch the meat to serve all of us, and she also dropped macaroni in soup so that it picked the flavour of the soup and you sucked scrumptious thick soup through the floppy tubes like they were straws.

The bread pudding puzzled me most. For that recipe I had to bring in the bread. Stale bread. You sure is stale bread they want, Marmie asking. I show her the recipe. Hmm. What kind of bread? Marmie, Is butter bread they want. Issues: 1. Bread never got stale in our house 2. We usually ate cheaper hops bread. 3. White bread, or butter bread as we called it, was more expensive and not as filling, so Marmie seldom bought it. But, Marmie not going to let down her exhibitioner and make her shame in front the whole class. Marmie gone over by Uncle and come back with a loaf two days before the class and rest it down in its brown paper bag to get stale for cookery day. I remember the little ones at home eyeing the bag and salivating at the thought of the unseen, untouchable loaf that I was taking – the whole loaf – to school to cook with and worse yet, it had to be stale first.

The wasted loaf bothered me, yes, but worse for me was the milk and eggs. Milk we rarely had, liquid milk that is; it was a rare luxury bought from a barefoot Indian woman who walked through the streets selling cows milk by the dipper from a galvanized bucket. Our cocoa tea was sweetened with a spoonful of Nestle's condensed milk, which also whitened the drink. And eggs! We rarely ate eggs as eggs, like you saw in pictures. Boiled, fried, scrambled, sunny side up were terms we knew, of course, but never a personal experience even live by sight. Two eggs stretched for an omelette for all five of us if the hens in the yard laid and we could find their eggs. Eggs were too precious to simply lose them in bread and milk and for what? To make more bread? It seemed a wasteful, time-consuming trick. Who does these things in real life? And why? There were some useful things, though, in cookery. We got to know about proteins, carbohydrates and fats.

For cookery and needlework the class was split in two so you did each in alternate weeks with only half the class. In needlework we sewed a pillowcase, and it wasn't like any pillowcase I'd ever met before. The setting up of the fabric was quite complicated because, before stitching up the sides, you had to fold over quite a large piece and then fold the raw edge of that twice to make a hem. The difficulty was you had to figure out not only wrong side and right side on unpatterned fabric that offered no clue, but you had to picture how it would end up when that extra bit was folded in to keep the pillow stuffed inside. I had to rip out my backstitched side seams because the flap bit was not folded correctly and I fell far behind in class because I never bothered to try to catch up at home. It just didn't seem important enough.

In class, you got a length of white cotton fabric on which a purple pattern had been stencilled. You could make out the outline of flowers, leaves and stalks that you were to fill in or stitch over with embroidery thread. Flowers you didn't know, but you knew they were the real genuine honest-to-goodness Garden of Eden flowers, not the irrelevant nonsense like the hibiscus and sweet lime, the bougainvillaea and gloriosa superba, the canna and ixora that jumbled up your front yard. As far as you knew, only the artist Glen Byam took any interest or pride in those everyday common flowers. It was not until I was twenty and the botany teacher in a far off cold land took our group on wildflower walks that I realised our tiny red, drooping, bell-shaped flowers on that long-ago pillowcase were meant to be blue, and the ones at the back were wallflowers that I shouldn't have done in purple. The daffodils I got right, quite by chance, even though I hadn't got to Wordsworth yet.

Monica was the only person in our class whose art was looked at and given a favourable written comment, Good, and a four or five out of five by our art teacher, Miss Atteck. I was an adult before I got to know that Miss Atteck was not just an art teacher; she was a renowned artist in her own right. She didn't bring her work to show us, she didn't teach us how to look at things, how to interpret them, how to present them. Actually, did she ever speak to us? I don't think I ever heard her voice. She would write on the board – I remember this exercise well – *A Market Scene*. That's it. Nothing else. Which market? Where? I'd never been to a market. I'd seen people selling on the road, yes, but surely that wasn't a real market? So I drew something from a book or a film, nothing like a market in Trinidad, nothing like the street vendors who were familiar to me. Most of us did. Our work was inhabited by well-dressed white people standing in orderly structures selling apples and grapes. Monica drew fat black women with head-ties and colourful print dresses, mangoes and melongene and bananas spilling out of huge woven baskets on to the ground. This was the kind of scene I knew well on my Saturday trips downtown. I don't think Monica had ever been to a market either, or even along Charlotte Street as I had, but she knew what Miss Atteck wanted.

Many years later I became acquainted with the work of Sybil Atteck, a pioneer of the postwar Trinidad art scene, and I saw how she and her contemporaries were revolutionaries in depicting the life and work, celebration and play of ordinary people in Trinidad. That was what she wanted from us – Shouter Baptist women in white carrying flambeaux; barefoot children playing hopscotch; African drummers, their faces pouring sweat;

Limbo dancers, bodies arched backward till their heads almost touched the ground, inching their feet sideways under a nine inch bar; heavily ornate tadjas, their carefully placed decorations glinting in the night, carried in procession to be surrendered to the sea; big hardback black men with huge steelpans slung around their necks playing infectious music, chipping along the road at Carnival. She didn't want foreign, sanitised work, but how were we to know? Nobody told us. Nobody showed us. She was the only person, the onliest person in that entire school, who in her own work validated us, us ordinary people, as real, visible and worthy people and she wanted us to do the same, to claim our place and make ourselves visible, but somehow either she was incapable of expressing that to us, or the institution we inhabited was incapable of allowing her to, or we ourselves were incapable of receiving it, so we didn't know. But Monica knew. Perhaps Miss Atteck's paintings or the work of other artists of the time had found a home in her home and Monica was exposed to a way of seeing our world and of honouring its validity that we weren't.

I'm thinking again about Miss Atteck. I've recently seen photos of her in her life outside the convent school. There are photos of her going up mountains and into caves, hanging out with cocoa-farming peasants in far rural districts and seated among bongo drummers in less salubrious urban spaces. In the photos, our silent, uncommunicative Miss Atteck seems happy, gregarious, adventurous. Was the convent a hateful assignment for her? Did she feel resentful and impotent when she entered the school gates? I wouldn't be surprised if somewhere in her diaries of that time there are entries expressing her antipathy to her job, for it must have stung her to the depths of her daring, imaginative soul the way her subject was treated at the convent. After our second year, girls who failed maths were not allowed to continue with it. They were assigned to domestic science aka cookery and entered in that subject for Senior Cambridge two years later. Girls who failed Latin were despatched to art. Monica, the most promising artist in our year group, passed Latin.

We had our own little art activity, though. We cut out paper dolls, Monica and I, long strings of girls holding hands and we dressed each one differently, different hairstyles, different shoes, different dresses, different features. My comic book education, especially the Archie comics, came in useful here, with Veronica and Betty as sources of inspiration, Daisy Mae of the Lil Abner comic didn't model the kind of wardrobe I wanted for my paper dolls. In an English Composition, title: *My Most Memorable Holiday*, Monica wrote – and I remember this as if it was yesterday – she wrote about going with her mother to Venice, the canals, gondolas, *O Sole Mio*, everything. This did not go down so well with the teacher. Did you go to Venice? No, Miss. Then this can't be your Most Memorable Holiday. The beautiful writing, even handwriting – for Monica had a fat, round lettering style – the evocative descriptions, the emotions expressed and aroused, all that counted for nothing. But had Monica prophesied her own future in that essay? After we left school, she went to Italy, married an Italian, had two Italian children, lived in Rome and ended her days there as a celebrated sculptor. Perhaps the Latin was useful after all.

Nuns dominated school life. In the years I spent at the convent, most of my teachers were Irish nuns, with a sprinkling of local nuns, a scant couple of European ones and a few local lay teachers. Of the local nuns, Mother Francis Xavier was the Principal in my first years there, and there was Mother Helen, of whom perhaps more later if I can summon up enough venom. Suffice it to say that I got dressed, got in my car and went to her funeral service at the Convent chapel a couple decades or so ago, just to make sure she was really, finally now and forever more, amen, dead. Mother Helen, was the choir mistress, and Mother Mary taught, lord knows what, maybe English. The nuns from Europe were Mère Rose, French teacher, Madre Marina, Spanish teacher and Mère Francois, French, who was in charge during needlework. Notice I didn't say taught, only in charge. Hardly any of that passel of white-robed chaste brides of Christ knew or wanted to know about us or about our real lives. Some were harmless or sweet like Mère Rose and Mother Angela; a few, and I single out here Madre Marina, made a huge effort and perhaps actually loved us as fellow sufferers, because she struck me as chafing at her lot herself, but most were downright arrogant, dismissive, even contemptuous. If I hadn't had the good fortune to meet real Irish people later, loveable charming people who sing, write lyrical poetry and startling, revealing prose, dance and make reckless love, drink, fight, cuss and blaspheme, people with hot red blood in their veins, I would have gone to my grave hating a whole nation based on that select sample of cold, judgmental men and women who entered holy office when I was growing up.

One or two of the lay teachers I quite liked. One of them was particularly kind to me when I needed help. And it was right at the beginning of term, in January, when I saw blood on my panties for the second time. What to do? Who to tell? Our Latin teacher was expecting a baby. I could see she was, because she was wearing a long, wide, pleated blouse over her skirt and the pleats opened up wide over her middle. I knew she must have let somebody put his thing down there. She would know about blood on panties. I went to the staffroom to look for her. I found her seated at her desk next to one of the many long glass-paned wide-open doors that surrounded every room in the school. I said to her, Excuse me, miss. She looked up. I didn't know what to say next. I hung down my head. She said, Is something wrong? I said, Blood. I got blood. She closed the book she was reading, got up and joined me in the corridor. Come with me, she said. I followed her to a door under the stairs. She opened the door and there was a toilet. She closed the door after us. She unrolled a wad of toilet paper and handed it to me. *Use this*, she said, and she left me in the toilet alone. I placed the toilet paper within my panties and for the remainder of the afternoon I walked with my thighs pressed together to prevent the bloodied toilet paper from falling out. When it happened again in February, I went to the same teacher. She said, This will come every month. You must mark the date and be ready for it. I didn't want to have to go to the teacher again, so I put on one of the cloths a few days before the twenty-fifth of March, just in case. I was glad I did because the bleeding came before the date. I was ready, too, in April. Thank you, Mrs Dolly Moore.

It was a long time afterwards, when I read in a *Seventeen* magazine about the twenty-eight day menstrual cycle, that I understood that the actual date wasn't as important as counting four weeks, like you do for working out when to expect a particular phase of the moon, like new moon for Eid or full moon for playing whoop in the yard. It was from what I read in magazines that I began to pay attention to my body, its rhythms and its warning signals. Words like the curse, cramps and periods came later. The magazines advertised Kotex sanitary pads and Midol for menstrual pain but none of that was relevant to me. For belly pain, as we called it, my mother gave me Veganin tablets from an orange and white tube and she let me stay home cradling a rubber hot water bottle when the pain was too much for me to even walk.

For the six years I was at school, every month I would take my folded cloths in a brown paper bag, leave the bag on the lid of the overhead toilet tank in a particular cubicle in the row of toilets, and fetch down the bag to change the cloths during the course of the day and take home a bag of soiled cloths in the afternoon – to be soaked, bleached, washed and dried, folded and used again. The bag was never discovered, or if it was, nobody interfered with it and that was lucky because if the bag had been found and a search had been conducted to locate the owner, I swear I would have disowned it and placed my poor Marmie in the position of having to conjure up a new set of cloths.

I note with wry interest that my then holy grail of disposable sanitary towels, the Moddess and Kotex of high grocery shelves and magazines, and I suppose in common use among all the other girls at school, are now deemed environmentally unfriendly, even hostile to the planet, and there is a small but impactful green movement towards sustainable feminine products including pieces of folded cloth, promoted as healthier than bleached natural and synthetic fibre disposable pads, with the added advantage of being reusable and financially sustainable. Between that and the shame-producing latrine, now lauded as a forward-looking, water-conserving, fertiliser-enhancing compostable toilet, I wonder now how much comfort I can squeeze out of switching the narrative from poverty-driven expediency to environmentally-friendly choice, especially now that those days of secrecy, hiding and shame are a lifetime in the past. Even though I did manage my periods at school without humiliation, that didn't spare me all the ways in which the convent conspired to pull me down. Me and my like.

One of the most humiliating experiences at SJC was to have your hair checked for lice. OK, so nowadays you can say hair checked for lice in a school in the UK and it's fine. I've heard Green-voting, progressive, Remain, nice middle-class Brighton mums say casually, while picking up their little kids from school, Oh she's got nits, as if nits is not louse eggs that hatch into blood-sucking lice, but something entirely different, as different as flu is from Covid 19. Anyway, in my day, having lice and their incubating offspring was a huge, huge social crime, akin to getting drunk and rolling in one's vomit in the gutter, no, worse, because the drunk can sober up, bathe, put on fresh clothes and join his circle again, no, it's more like leprosy. With lice, one was unclean, one was a pariah; why aren't you wearing your warning bell? Lice crawl from head to clothes, to other clothes, to other heads. They are catching. So they are not a good thing and must be eradicated and, trust me, no one is more fully in agreement with that than me. Lice? Ugh! Jesus wept, just typing this and I'm scratching my head. Here's how St Joseph's Convent dealt with the possibility of lice in their sanctum sanctorum.

Lice Day had its own vibe. Of course you weren't warned, no letter to parents. The first indication was a nun coming in and whispering something to your teacher in the middle of a class. The teacher would nod and the nun would leave. Then you'd see the girls from the classroom next to yours file out, looking uncomfortable. I once saw an animal rights video of cattle being taken to the slaughterhouse. You can see that the animals sense that romping in lush green pastures by still waters is not the plan. They pull back, they bellow, they plead with low moaning to be spared – as we girls sensed it wasn't for soursop ice cream we were being lined up. At this point, if like me you did sometimes have lice – and no amount of fine-tooth comb, no amount of grated mammie sepote seed treatment ever eradicated an infestation for long – believe me when I tell you that if you thought you might have lice you'd be losing bladder control.

So before your class was summoned, you'd put up your hand and ask to be allowed to go to the toilet. There you'd deal with the bladder and, most important of all, you'd fill your cupped palms with water and run your wet hands over your head. This had the effect of calming the feeding lice, causing them to lie low, to be camouflaged among dark follicles and dark scalp, not be roaming around hunting for new spots to dig their mandibles into and suck blood. By the time you got back upstairs, your class was already lining up. But here's the thing. Not everyone went into the

examination room. The insect vector control assistant nun would walk along the line and indicate to each girl whether she'd be examined or allowed back to the classroom.

Separating things and people wasn't new. In real life you had to pick out and throw away little stones and broken or mouldy dried beans before soaking the good ones to cook, and I'd also by then met lots of stories about separating groups into two or more, mainly in parables. There's the grain and the chaff that's winnowed out, the crop versus the weeds that get thrown into the fire, and the sheep and goats on Judgement Day. That last one was a puzzle then and still is. I like both sheep and goats, both their young have nice loveable names, both give milk to be made into cheese; both can be eaten, so why are sheep good and goats bad? Is it because sheep follow without question and goats are own-way, self-willed, bad mind? With yellow eyes and knowing looks that have a hint of malevolence and sly laughter? We say, *Doh put goat mout on me, doh put goat mout on my plan*, to mean don't spoil things? But back to that nun who decided at a glance which girls were to go back to the classroom and which to be sent for head lice inspection.

What were her criteria? Look at who were sent back and who were sent for scrutiny and formulate your own hypothesis. The few obviously African girls and the fair skin girls went back to the classroom. We mix-up girls, along with the Chinese and Indian girls, were sent along the corridor, past the set of stairs beyond which only nuns were allowed to go, and put into a kind of Checkpoint Charlie, maximum security no-mans-land limbo of a small room where a small, shrivelled old nun earned her keep by performing this task. Wearing fancy-sailor white cotton gloves, see her seated with a white cloth spread over her habit. In front of her is a low bench where you kneel with your head bent over Mother's lap – you will have taken out your hair elastic and undone your plaits or ponytail by now. This nun, who seems so frail, has remarkably strong hands – you could tell by the way she pulls at your hair and opens it in random batches and looks through it for the scurrying of disturbed incumbents. All this time you're telepathying to your resident colony, Keep Still, Don't Move. If she doesn't find any lice running for cover, you'll be tapped on the shoulder, a signal to stand. She then checks the cloth on her lap to see if any fleeing lice have abseiled down a hair shaft in the hope of escape. If none are found, she gives the all clear with a dismissive flick of her hand. In all my years at SJC, my native lice were never discovered. Oh that our First Peoples had had that skill!

Here's my hypothesis. Who was sent for scrutiny. Only girls with straight hair or hair in the waves light to moderate range. But why not the fair skin girls then? They have straight hair! Or at worst, slightly wavy. Ah! You see, the fair skin girls were clean, from good homes. They wouldn't, they couldn't have *lice*! And girls of African descent? Ah ha! Kinky hair was

not thought to be a hospitable environment for lice. There are other explanations for the latter exemption I'm sure, but I'm not going to explore them. There are too many other areas of nineteen-fifties SJC life where those other explanations are more pertinent, more valid.

But I am going to touch on privilege slightly here. Many years ago, one lovely relaxing Sunday on Maracas beach, blue skies and gentle breeze, my friend Maritza introduced me to a friend of hers, a slightly younger man who was a student at The College of The Immaculate Conception – CIC – aka St Mary's College, the brother school to SJC, just across Pembroke Street from us. We were chatting about school days and I had mounted my hobbyhorse about the nuns and racial and class discrimination. He said, You feel you had a hard time at SJC, but you were privileged. Eh? was all I could get out. You were Catholic, he said. So? I replied. This turn in the conversation was reducing me to monosyllables. Well, he said, in my whole life at CIC, I was only ever one thing. Me: Oh? Him: I was a Non-Catholic. At once, at Maracas, the sky clouded over. The breeze turned chilly. Sand lifted and blew into my face. Oh God Father in Heaven! To my everlasting shame I hadn't even seen, let alone paid attention to, the biggest discriminator of all. At our two schools, you were either Catholic, a member of the elect, or you were Other – the Nons. The non-Catholics. That poor, poor boy. Poor, poor Jimmy. Seven years of being nobody, being nothing but a Non. I feel shame all over again as I write this.

Among my classmates were maybe half a dozen non-Catholics. They were Hindus, Muslims, Anglicans and Presbyterians. Perhaps there were others who practised Rada, Orisha, Shango; maybe there were Shouters, Shouter Baptists or Spiritual Baptists, religions legally banned up until just before I started at the convent. The 'respectable' scorned those African-centred religions, and if anyone in my class belonged to such a religion they would never declare it. They'd probably mumble Anglican or some such harmless heretic Christian religion and hope it was never probed. Did they, these assorted Nons, feel othered when a teacher said, Catholics go to the chapel. Non-Catholics stay here. Catholics who want to join Girl Guides, go down to the library. Catholics remember that the Legion of Mary is going down the islands with Father Kennedy on Saturday. At the time, it skated right over my head. But how did they, the non-Catholics, the Others feel about the exclusion. I never wondered. That's the comfort of privilege.

There were those who seemed to manage the division. For a couple years, in sixth form, our class prefect was Lalita, a Hindu, who, to all appearances, comfortably straddled the two religions. Were Mary, Jesus and Joseph, the Holy Trinity, Xavier and Theresa and all those just more gods to add to her expansive Hindu pantheon? Were the Virgin Mary and Our Lady of Fatima simply avatars of Lakshmi? Lalita knew all the prayers, all the rituals, all the simmy-dimmy that goes into Catholic observance, so

maybe being a 'Non' wasn't all that bad? She did grow up to be successful
in banking and sit among the elite on the board of one of the major banks,
among the successful merchants, professionals and landowners, whilst I…
Could a little flexibility in these matters, a little insider knowledge, a little
common cultural reference points be helpful in the long run? They say the
right religion is a gateway to the next world, but it starts opening gates and
doors right here, in this one, especially when the dominant religion has a
way of switching back and forth with election cycles.

I knew that we girls who won exhibitions and came to the convent from
outside were an unwelcome addition to their enrolment. The school had
managed perfectly well as a fee-paying finishing school for the daughters of
the white elite and for a number of well-placed, non-white girls from
respectable professional and business families; it had also provided a place for
a couple of dozen daughters of Venezuelan presidents and generals and oil
oligarchs. These girls were boarders whose dormitory occupied a wing of the
school, a place to keep them out of temptation's way and adolescent mischief,
while they became proficient in English and in ladylike skills before their
return back home and early marriage to a suitable scion of a landed or
merchant or military family while the bloom of youth was still fresh.

Then there was us. A large grappe of rough girls from families with fluid
arrangements like mine, girls without roots, money or pedigree, girls from
low-class locations like The Plannings, Behind The Bridge, Laventille and
Belmont with a sprinkling from middle-class St James and Woodbrook,
and the girls from country districts who came in by train. We girls came
from what was scornfully referred to by Mère François as 'the elementary
school', as if it were one school we came from. Was this for her a generic
term as a category of school, or was it her lack of familiarity with pluralising
nouns in English? It was as if some mischievous deity, Eshu perhaps, had
dipped their hand in the mêlée of Trinidadian people and randomly
scooped up a mess of girls from all sorts of unmentionable and best avoided
home locations, girls of African, Indian, Indigenous or Chinese origins,
and from the many, many indeterminate, untraceable mixes from all sorts
of liaisons, some sanctioned, many not, and dropped us into the space once
reserved for the daughters of the white merchant class and the plantation-
owning cedula de la poblacion-descended Catholic, god-sanctioned elite,
and the Irish nuns who were sent from their homelands to protect them.
It could only have been with the intent of mischief-making, could only
have been Eshu who'd somehow set up the scenarios I found myself in at
SJC in the mid to late fifties. How did they manage with us? How did we
learn how to negotiate that *terra incognita* we'd washed up on?

The convent didn't have written rules, not like the Ten Command-
ments, which everyone knew even if we outsiders did not properly
understand them. I don't remember any list of things prohibited on pain of

punishment. But we learnt what was expected, what was permitted, what was tolerated and what was forbidden by word of mouth from initiates or by trial, error and consequence. So, for example, on that first day I learned that you don't open your desk without asking permission. Some other transgressions with consequence included: speaking in class, failing to have my veil for chapel, not doing homework, not having the right book for a class, sucking salt prunes in class, leaving school to go and find lunch elsewhere, bits of uniform missing, especially your badge or your veil. All of these breaches were recorded in marks against conduct or marks against application. You started every week like a freshly baptised soul with a clean slate, of a hypothetical five marks in everything. Then it was downhill from there, with marks breaking off from that five and tumbling down like rocks in a landslide on the newly-cut Lady Young Road.

Every four weeks there was an assembly of the entire school in the hall. We stood in long rows in our house groupings, facing the Mother Superior, a tiny shadowy figure whom we never came across in our day-to-day school life. I don't even remember her name and it was the same nun all my years there. Something twitches in my memory that it could have been a male name, some angel or archangel or cherub. Maybe Mother Raphael? This nun was not a teaching nun, but the head nun of the other nuns, and so the spiritual head of the school. It was to her that the school had to be presented, a sort of dry run for Judgement Day, with the Mother Superior as a Cecil B. De Mille understudy for the Almighty. For those not familiar with Judeo-Christian-Hollywood Biblical references, think of an inspection of the troops by the Commander-in-Chief. I think you'll appreciate that House Notes was not an occasion to be taken lightly.

For each house in turn, the girls who had an almost unblemished record for conduct, that is fives in all four weeks, were called by name to the front. One by one they walked up the aisle and stood facing the Mother Superior, bowed, and moved to the side to make a new front row. Those with an unblemished record in application followed. Then all bowed and filed back to their places within the ranks. Then came the bad girls, the incompetent girls. Those with a two out of five were called out, the uninitiated creeping out with head bowed, tears streaming, sobs barely suppressed, while the seasoned transgressors sauntered up with lip pursing, eye cutting, arm swinging bravado to stand in disgrace in sight of the entire judging community. For House Notes, think Salem. Think *Handmaids Tale*.

Never doing too well or too badly, I managed to remain undistinguished and invisible for six years, that is eighteen terms and perhaps fifty-four House Notes. I was neither good nor bad at anything much. During the lunch break and after school, we played rounders, netball and table tennis for fun, and I didn't distinguish myself at any of these to be selected for a school team, barely making the St Xavier's House netball team. My one chance of being close to rising above mediocrity came from my voice.

Once a year, each class lined up in the corridor outside the music room where Mother Helen, music mistress, sat at the piano. One at a time you went in to have your voice tested. Mother Helen would play a few bars and you sang it. While standing outside, you could hear one girl after another, girls whose normal speaking voices were clear, maybe even melodious, let out squeaks and crackles when in the presence of this diminutive nun as she played a note for the testee to *ma may me moe moo* up a rising scale. One after another they emerged, trembling and tearful failures. Mother Helen must have been told it was politically judicious to add some cocoa to the milk of her choir, for in my third year I was admitted as one of a couple of dark faces in her choir line-up.

Choir practice was on Wednesday afternoon at four o'clock, an hour after school was over. In the interim, choir members were expected to go home, shower, change and come back fresh and clean in street clothes to line up in the school hall, with Mother Helen conducting and Miss Thorne at the piano, to be drilled in church music or test pieces for the biennial music festival. Well, I did comply for a while. But then I didn't any more. There was little point in going home. There would be no water in the tap to shower – I'd have to go to the standpipe with a bucket and hope there'd be water there. And after that, fresh and clean, what would I put on to go back to school for choir practice? I had home clothes – outgrown school overalls – school clothes, church clothes that doubled as going-out clothes, and one or two old dresses for the cinema. Choir members wore nice dresses in cotton plaid with waists and belts or full skirts with blouses. I had nothing like that.

Mother Helen tolerated me in my school uniform for a couple of practices, but one afternoon when I'd come into the hall hot and sweaty after a particularly vigorous game of rounders just as practice was about to begin, Mother Helen, standing on the stage, sniffed the air to find the source of contamination, stamped her size-one black boot on the wooden floor, pointed straight at me and shouted, What is this creature doing here? You are an abomination! Get out! Get out! I got out. And never went back. It was more than forty years before I ventured into another hall to join a choir. There, Pat Bishop of The Lydian Singers said, If you can speak you can sing, go and sit with the sopranos.

It was not until I was an adult that I learned how Mother Helen and her ilk got the absolute power they had. This was different from the power of the Irish nuns, which was merely the power of being Catholic, nuns, and white. That *Cedula de la Poblacion*, dropped into the convent story earlier, was something I knew nothing about as a schoolgirl or young adult. The short version of the long story is that during the French Revolution and the Haitian Revolution, French plantation owners and merchants in the Caribbean who were royalists, and in fear for their lives and property, were invited by the Spanish governor of Trinidad to come with their enslaved workers and settle here. The conditions were two – first they must be Catholic and second they had to swear allegiance to the Spanish crown. Their inducement was thirty-two acres of land for each white man, each white woman and each white child who came, and an additional sixteen acres for the owner of each enslaved person they brought.

I've seen huge gilt-framed copies of the *Cedula* in the homes of descendants of the cedulites. There was a hierarchy among the arrivals; as royalists, many had titles such as *Baron, Chevalier, Compte* and *Duc*. Their enslaved workers cleared the land, built the great houses and their own less great quarters, and cultivated sugar cane and cocoa. At one time, each cocoa bean was worth its weight in gold. One cedulite descendant quoted me this little verse: *And this was good old Trinidad, the land of the red cocoa pod, where the Ganteaumes speak only to the De Verteuils, and the De Verteuils speak only to God.* It came as no surprise to me to discover just a couple years ago, long after her death, that Mother Helen, Soeur Hélène de L'Enfant Jesus of the Sisters of St Joseph of Cluny Paris, was born Yvonne De Verteuil.

A former neighbour and schoolmate, now deceased, was privy as a schoolgirl to a related aspect of our school life that she revealed to me when we were both parents of girls bound for secondary school and were determined we wouldn't send our girls to our alma mater – though why she was so adamantly opposed I'm still not clear. I hope the following may explain my confusion about her decision. She, the daughter of a coloured family who had been professionals for many generations, had entered the convent secondary school straight from the convent primary school. Girls who won exhibitions automatically got a place at the secondary school of their choice; girls from the private primary schools attached to the secondary schools also got in automatically. There was another group who were neither exhibitioners nor feeder-school pupils. These were the second stream of fee-payers, admitted after an entrance exam run by the school itself.

My friend told me that she, then a fourth-former, was assigned a singular responsibility on the day of the entrance exam at the convent. She was to take a close look at each examinee while they were writing the exam and against their name on the seating chart, she was to indicate the race of each girl. This woman described how, as a fifteen year old, she walked along each row and wrote Chinese, Negro, Dougla, Mixed, half-Chinese, Indian, brown-skin, white, half-white against the names of girls on the seating chart. You begin to understand the why and the how of the Hitler Youth and the Jesuits 'Give me a child before he is seven and he is mine for life.' I have no evidence as to whether this data influenced the weighting accorded to the candidates. For all I know, this could have been an early attempt at introducing inclusivity and ethnic diversity. Who is me to conjecture? Who is me to judge?

I've met women who, as convent girls, knew Mother Helen and Mother Columba. They have a view of these nuns that's diametrically opposed to mine. One says how much she enjoyed being part of the Mother Helen Chorale, another talks about Mother Columba's influence on her appreciation of English literature and of maths. Both of these people were ten to twenty years younger than me. By the time these girls encountered those nuns there had been Vatican II, Holy Mass had eased out of Latin, and the priest had begun facing the congregation, and the nuns of St Joseph of Cluny had morphed from Mothers to Sisters. I don't want to overstate the obvious differences in interpersonal relationships that sprang from that simple change in mode of address, how yuh does behave towards yuh mudda different from yuh behaviour towards yuh sistah, right, and the vice is versa, mother to child is not sister to sister. This, I am convinced, must have influenced our very different perspectives on life as pupils at the school.

Mercifully, life wasn't all school and nuns. There were some nice bits sneaked under the nuns' and Pappy's radar. There was home, home where the secrets were. Home of a mother who was not married to the man who was our father. Home with a father who only visited erratically, and then often brutally. Home of the ultimate shame of illegitimacy, which I had learned to hide from everyone outside. A woman, a stranger, once accosted me on the street saying, You have a Lafond face, and I said, Yes, I am a Lafond. She said, I see that straight away. I know the whole family. Who is you father Véné or Tebeau? Without the slightest hesitation, I picked one. Véné. How could I reveal to a stranger that I was born of a Lafond sister, who had the same last name as she always had and had perforce passed it on to me? It would drag my mother into shame. Yes. Home was another world. Kept separate from my other worlds.

Although home was small it never felt cramped because there was one place I could disappear into my private world – and continue to educate myself about things we weren't taught at the convent. We ourselves rarely bought papers, nor did the families who shared the house, but someone was able to get hold of old newspapers, no doubt collected as discards from somewhere else. These newspapers were meticulously torn into pieces the size of a page in an exercise book and hung on the door from a wire hook in each of the two cubicles of the latrine. The latrine became my reading room. The *Trinidad Guardian* was a local newspaper but it could have been from Mars because everything in its pages was strange to me, so I read it like a storybook, as something interesting but not quite real. I'd unhook the whole pile and flip through to see what caught my interest. *Mother To Chaperone Carnival Queen On US Tour Carnival Queen 1952. Miss Rosemary Knaggs will leave on her prizewinning tour of the Eastern United States on the SS Uruguay on September 14.* The article ran for a couple of columns – her many prizes, a brand new car, a radiogram, refrigerator, clothes, household items, furniture. I skim it and it's about where she's going and what she's taking and where she'll be staying and so on. It all seems unreal, even though it is about someone who lives here. I quickly lose interest and move on. *San Raphael To Get Water From Arima*. That, I want to know about, as I hope there are plans for Belmont to get water too, but the paper was torn off just there. I look through the stack to find the continuation but I'm distracted by, *Alluring Pictures, Temptations Cause Many Maladjustments*. What am I missing out on? It goes on, *Baffled people ask what's happening with our youth? Why are they so aggressive, so ill mannered, so rude, so immoral?* Well I am youth and I'm not any of these things, at least I don't think I am, so I am baffled as to why people are baffled. I skip over *Debut Party In South* because I know it will be Mr and Mrs and Miss somebody and tulle dress and sequins and seed pearl beading and diamante earrings and orchid corsage and handsome escort and dinner party, and all the Mr and Mrs who were there. *Grace Kelly, American Film Actress To Wed Prince Of Monaco*. Oh, no! Does that mean she won't be acting in films any more? I'd just seen her in *High Society* with Frank Sinatra and Bing Crosby singing, *If I could sing like Bing how happy I would be, lalalaboo, lalalaboo*, and Louis Armstrong with his trumpet performing the theme song and singing in that nice voice like waves stirring a gravel beach. I'd seen her, too, in *Rear Window*, which had me chewing the ends of my ponytail with dread all through. To leave that interesting life and go and live in a palace and just be a princess? *New H Bomb To Be Set Off. The United States will probably explode two hydrogen bombs in a new series of tests in the Pacific early this year and cause the greatest explosion the world has ever known. Premier Is Not Quitting. Press reports that Sir Anthony Eden might be replaced.* Ho hum. A photo of a girl wearing jeans sitting sideways to the camera on what looks like a wall. One leg is bent at the knee, the other hangs down. Her hair is cut short and she is looking away into the distance to the right of the photo. Who is she? *Seventeen year old Miss Meiling Wong seen on the roof of the St Martin's School of Art, Charing Cross Road… Miss Wong comes from Port-of-Spain Trinidad and is in London to study art*. You mean people go away to study art? How much good good money does a person need to have to go all the way to London to study art?

My other reading had long come from the Belmont branch of the Public Library, situated just two blocks down Pelham Street. I remember admiring the librarian, envying her unobstructed access to that treasure house, with her pencil-slim skirts with a slit at the back for ease of walking (but without the then requisite modesty pleat in the slit), short-sleeved shirt blouses and slingback high heels, hair neatly pressed and styled. And this lady ruled the one door, one room establishment. From her I got through all the popular series of that time – the Nancy Drew, Hardy Boys, Just William, Katy, *Little Women* series, as well as *Anne of Green Gables* and *A Tree Grows in Brooklyn*. My one disappointment was that you could only borrow two books a day. Every day in the school holidays I'd be there waiting for her at eight in the morning to hand in my two of the day before and get two more for the day. She wouldn't let me return them the same day and take two more to last me overnight. She said she wasn't allowed to stamp the books with the same date for Taken Out and Returned. So by three in the afternoon with both books read I'd have the long wait before the next morning with nothing to read. Bits of newspaper by candlelight in the latrine wasn't an attractive option, even though I didn't yet know about the dangers of methane and open flame.

Later in my youth it was from that library that I borrowed *The Origin of Species*, and which I renewed so often that I began to think it was mine. How different the world was when looked at through the theory of evolution. That everything was related, had come from a common source, that species evolved through mutations that suited their environment suddenly looked so obvious I wondered why no one had thought of it before. For me it was such a breakthrough in looking at the world that I could only compare its stunning impact on me with the process of learning to read. It was as if I had learnt to read by recognising whole words as distinct entities and suddenly someone pointed out that words are made of letters and letters have sounds and that letters can be rearranged to make new words – and the vast infinite possibilities in understanding and creating that insight had opened up. The creatures in the latrine were no longer ugly, no longer revolting. They were somewhere in the branches of evolution, sightless, breaking through the oily surface of their environment for air, breaking down waste, feeding, multiplying, adapting, surviving.

Everyone in the yard must have moved in a well-choreographed dance, because I don't remember any friction over the use of the kitchen sink, the lavatory stalls, the bleach stones, the shower or the clothesline. Marmie was a friendly, generous person and she readily gave way to others. Perhaps it was her way of avoiding conflict – for we were a vulnerable household without consistent male protection – or a way of earning credit for good behaviour from our neighbours. Marmie went to work, so we children had to fend for ourselves with me in charge, so we benefited from Marmie's kindness and generosity when we needed the benign oversight of nearby strangers.

My school years were spent in a world of girls and women, yet there was never a conversation that I remember about periods, menstruation, this particularity of femaleness, even among us girls. On one occasion I do remember Greta Edwards saying that having monthlies was a good thing, her mother had told her, because it shows you were not doing bad things. But apart from that, what we gleaned as individuals we didn't share as a group. You would see a girl rise from sitting and turn her head to look down at the back of her skirt and she would brush her back with her hand with a kind of self-conscious nonchalance as if she was checking for creases and had found one that needing smoothing. Sometimes, very rarely, a girl's blue uniform would have telltale dull smudge that she would discover for herself, and she would go to the toilet, switch the uniform round and wash the spot at the washbasin, letting the wetness air dry before emerging. Sometimes a girl would complain of not feeling well and sit out the once-weekly physical education class. These were your only clues that you were not alone with the problems of becoming a young woman.

And that instruction about a boy's thing and down there. Did anyone know any more about that than I did? The advice in *Seventeen* was along the lines of personal hygiene and about being nice to be near with *Mum* and *Odo-Ro-No* deodorants, *Neet* body hair removal cream, advertisements about hair – *Which Twin Has the Toni and Which the Expensive Perm* – and warnings about kissing and petting – whatever that last one was. The true-life stories in *True Romance* and *True Confession* went something like this ... *I was so excited to go on my first date with Bobby, the captain of the football team. We went to the drive-in. On the screen the stars were kissing. He turned to me and started kissing me. Then I felt him undo my bra. His hand went under my skirt. I felt as if I was swimming, in a dream, not aware of myself. When I woke up the movie was over and he drove me home. I didn't see Bobby the next week, but the week after I saw him leaning against his locker talking to Betty and I didn't like the way he was looking at her and the way she was smiling at him. I ran away and cried my heart out. It was only some weeks later, when I checked the calendar and saw that the date was a whole week after the red circle I had drawn, that I realised something was wrong...*

What did that mean? What had happened? The magazines never said. All you got was these coded messages, none of which you could apply to your own life. What use were stories about people with access to cars, dates, drive-in movies, popcorn, deodorants, lockers, when your world offered a bike, twelve-cents-a ticket-to-house Olympic Cinema, salt and fresh nuts and a bicycle saddle bag for your books? And yet it was to those foreign magazine sources I looked to for explanations and guidance as my own world gave little. Should I have asked somebody? Who would have known anyway? Those girls who seemed to have secret knowledge were described by the nuns as shameless and forward and those were not nice adjectives that you wanted bestowed on yourself. Even in our yard and on the street such girls were called hot-up and force-ripe.

What to make of the soft, plump, bee-sting buds that popped out on my chest where only small, brown, wrinkled-like-raisins nipples, were before? Of course, I knew about big women's tot-tots. Marmie used to pull out her milk-full bags anywhere and everywhere to feed my baby brother, nine years younger than me, but somehow I didn't equate my tender little swellings with my mother's heavy, floppy tot-tots, which I imagined were full of milk all the time.

I can think of one promising movie that could have revealed many secrets. The titillating advertisement ran, *No longer were they doctor and patient, now they were flesh and blood*, but *Not As A Stranger* with Olivia De Havilland, Robert Mitchum and Frank Sinatra, whose singing voice I was in love with, was Adults Only, twenty-one years and over. So neither home, cinema nor magazines were much help to me.

The nuns warned us about the sins of the flesh. Not the big sins of the flesh, not the real things. They left that to experience. What we knew of sins of the flesh was that St Maria Goretti, a little girl like us, was killed by a boy in her neighbourhood when she refused to give in to his sinful demands. We didn't know what those demands were. She was only twelve or thirteen and she was canonised and made a saint, because of her resistance to sin. I thought being Italian might have helped because the Pope lives in Italy, in his own country called the Vatican, and someone could have easily told him about Maria Goretti so he could make her an example for little girls everywhere. So we got hints about resisting advances from boys and men. But the lessons we got about sins of the flesh were about modesty and what we were cautioned against was immodesty – immodesty in behaviour and dress.

Father Graham was especially vigilant about immodesty in dress. If your bare arm was showing any higher than halfway between elbow and shoulder, he would put you out of his church. It made front page in the papers, with picture and all, when one bride didn't meet his standards. In the picture the bride was crying, her face looking down, so all you could see was the top of her head, the tiara and veil and, over her shoulders, covering her arms and her whole top, was a man's dark-coloured jacket. Father Graham had refused to conduct the marriage ceremony because he could see little glimpses of brown skin peeping through the little spaces in the guipure lace of her long-sleeved, high-necked full-length bridal gown. I don't remember anything like that happening to the country club debutantes who got married at St Theresa's or St Patrick's, whose gowns were usually a strapless underdress with arms, necks, chests and backs covered only with the selfsame guipure lace, but I suppose that it's harder to see light-coloured skin through the holes in white lace. Brown skin, black skin, has this rash habit of drawing unwelcome attention to itself.

Transgressions against modesty for us convent girls were things like laughing loudly and eating on the street, being seen on the street with a boy who is not your brother, wearing shorts or even pants, short skirts, tight clothes, pedal pushers, low-cut clothes, sleeveless dresses, skirts with slits at the back, and changing your clothes in front of anybody. Not even your own sister, they said. Turn your back. Avoid occasions of sin. Beware of falling from grace. Do only those things that were pleasing in the sight of God. I was sure that one of the sins of the flesh was having breasts, even my little sprouting buds. The nuns themselves did not have such protuberances. Their fronts were uniformly flat, encased in white garments; their silver and black heavy crosses hung from thick black cords like plumb lines straight from the neck to the waist, without the interruption of varying topography. With no breasts, no head hair, no bodies, arms, legs or feet, only white hands and white faces peeping from under dense layers of heavy white cloth, the nuns were our models of virtue. Modesty, chastity and obedience were the mantras of my school days and I was left to figure out how to apply them to my real life of growing up.

You would think from all of this that I was unhappy. That wouldn't be true. I don't think I ever gave a thought to concepts like happiness. If something hurt you, you cried. It could be belly pain, stubbing your bare toe on a stone, being hit or your best friend not speaking to you, or you saw in a film or read in a book something that was sad. If something you read or saw was funny, you smiled; jokes made you laugh. I'm not sure that any of that constitutes unhappiness or happiness. You just went along day to day without plans or expectations, just taking things as they came along, taking in life as it unfolded, feeding on whatever was on offer.

At school, our pop music sessions gave us sustenance, and these I remember better than conversations about ourselves. We had silly arguments. Fans of Pat Boone would extol his sweet sensitivity, those of Elvis Presley would sneer at such wimpish qualities. When we were fifteen or so, in Form Five, we would, after school, close all the doors and windows of the classroom and sing to Sue's guitar. Girls with access to a radio would try to write down the words of the top tunes in the Top Twenty when they were broadcast at night and compare notes, fill in the blanks and have full verses and chorus for us next day. We would be riotously, joyfully singing 'Tutti Frutti', 'Blue Suede Shoes', 'Rock Around the Clock'. We feigned lovesickness over 'Heartbreak Hotel', clustered around a roughly torn-off copybook page, deciphering a hasty pencil scrawl, oblivious to everything outside our own enjoyment of being there, unknowing of the past, uncaring of the future, just fully present in that moment of our lives. This was the second half of the fifties, just ten years after the end of the world war and an as yet unimagined Sixties sexual revolution ahead of us.

One afternoon, while the dozen or so of us had in full cry segued from 'Dream, Dream, Dream' to 'Hang Down Your Head, Tom Dooley', Mother Columba burst into the classroom, demanded to know what we were doing, and not quite believing it was just singing, threatened expulsion. Then she spotted Sue with her guitar. How many times was dear Sue, she a cedulite descendent, a convent girl from four years old, how many times was she our guardian angel, our get-out-of-jail-free card for us miscreants with whom she chose to affiliate? We got away with an unconvincing reprimand.

Birthdays were celebrated with house parties. I almost didn't go to Myrna's because of my can-can. Before the gentler princess-line shape for dresses replaced them, a tiny, belted waist above a big, wide skirt supported by a can-can underskirt was fashionable for a couple years when I was fourteen. Early can-cans were made of buckram. These required loads of starch to make them super stiff, but they collapsed under pressure at the back when you sat down, and generally sagged with humidity. One September, the Venezuelan boarders came back after the holidays at home with can-cans that stood out their skirts to an amazing near horizontal from the waist, so that if a breeze blew the outer skirt – the dress skirt itself – it would lift off like a tablecloth set on an alfresco picnic table. How pathetic our own buckram numbers appeared in comparison. I'm crediting Zena with getting this can-can upgrade available to us non-payols. Zena's mother was Venezuelan; Zena spoke commendable Spanish; her dad worked in a fabric store downtown so it was only a matter of a couple months, certainly well before Christmas, that Zena was sporting a Venezuelan style can-can. The gauntlet was thrown down for the clash of the can-cans.

Marmie went to town and bought the material. Alla cut the white synthetic netting material – so stiff you felt it could be used to make a cage for a small animal – to make five or six tiers, the first tier made of regular cotton or satin and close fitting from the waist to hips, but each subsequent tier was double the size of the one above, so at the end you had a voluminous cascade of scratchy stuff that had to be edged with bias binding otherwise your legs would look as if an angry manicou had been trapped within. For the party, I put on my pink cotton pique dress with the big, flared skirt that would have fallen way below mid-calf but I hoped the new can-can would lift it to a fashionable two inches below the knee. I put it on and looked at myself. What is this? I can't go out like this. What kind of can-can is this? I cried and cried and no amount of, but you looking nice, nobody will notice, plenty people will have one just like yours could persuade me. Why would anyone want something sticking straight out from the waist? This lasted until my younger sister Annette, who had grown faster than me and was already my height, said, Marmie, if Barbara don't want it…

At the party, we girls danced with one another, Castilian to *Alma Llanera,* bolero to *Besame Mucho* – which even now sends me into a romantic swoon – and to the much-loved Stanley Black LP *Cuban Moonlight.* This was played so often on the radiogram that Myrna's big brother came in and changed the record complaining, Allyuh going to wear out mih record. The secret of Zena's extreme skirt was revealed when she sat down and the whole creation flipped upwards for easy examination. Each tier was a double tier. One on top the other. Not six tiers, but six stacked on six.

There was also an undeclared waistline war. We'd all been to see *Gone With the Wind* and while the Civil War and the enslavement of people like ourselves on the plantations flew unregarded over our silly empty heads, we talked about Mammy pulling the corset strings tighter and tighter at Scarlett's insistence, so that Scarlett could score the advantage points of an eighteen-inch waist or was it fifteen, over that milksop whatshername who got the coveted Ashley in the end, but died – was it in childbirth? For me the high point of the film was Rhett's *Quite frankly my dear I don't give a damn* – a line I longed to use for most of my adolescence and early adulthood. Ah! the roads not offered. Anyway, waists.

Our scale of sizing ranged through magga (a condition which would now be deemed malnourished), to bony (with visible joints, including the knobs of spine bones), skinny (which is like thin), slim (with the right bits of flesh in the right places but not much), to thick (which would now be called plump), to bubbalups (which is well, which is). At school we ranged from skinny to slim, with very few outliers. The school uniform included a white belt at the waist. The drawing of the uniform showed a one-inch wide patent leather belt with a standard unadorned brass or silver buckle, with a pin that went into holes. Inevitably, we wore it too tight and the holes split and the patent leather cracked and the belt became ugly and had to be replaced. We conformed with the rule on width for a couple years until our growing female forms demanded something that would highlight our best features. Christina and June, Lalita and Helen had proper bosoms already at fourteen, some of us had just got our first bra, others not yet, but all of us wanted to look less like little girls.

I think it was Valerie who first came to school wearing the ultimate belt. How did these girls from well-placed families instinctively know their power? Valerie, from a posh coloured St Clair family of barristers and high colonial officials, came in one morning wearing a two-and-a-half-inch wide elastic belt that stretched and clinched at the waist, hooking together in an interlocking metal clasp at the front. Down to about fifteen inches, we guessed, as we watched her walking along and pausing in front the big mirror in the corridor leading from school to chapel, a mirror placed there, not for vain girls to admire themselves, but for the nuns to check their veils were fully flipped forward over the forehead band before going into chapel. Pilar, a Venezuelan boarder, upped the ante with a three-inch wide elastic belt; others tried with three and a half, the biggest in town, but by then the nuns' patience was worn thin or shall we say narrow, and we were reduced by edict to no more than one and half inches.

At the 60th anniversary Class of '59 reunion, I sat with a remnant of the close friends whom I made at the convent and who have endured with me all these years. These are people who know every thread that makes up the fabric of my life. They know the worn patches, the holes, the frayed edges. They know where the pattern is still bright and where the unused bits are. There is nothing in this world I could ask of them that they would not do for me if they could, and the same holds true for me for them. They never questioned my getting married in a registry office, refusing to baptise my children, or giving up on religion entirely. These women, and Sue who lives in foreign, are the convent's everlasting, precious gift to me. But I know, and this was evident from the fond memories of their schooldays that others at that reunion recounted, the delight and pride with which these other old girls modelled the five distinct sets of uniforms we wore during our convent years, I know that my feelings about my time at SJC POS was not universal among fellow alumnae.

Decades after my SJC life, I was walking from Earls Court where we then lived to the Chelsea & Westminster Hospital where my husband was a patient, when a woman crossed my path on the pavement. We continued on our way, then must have stopped at the same time because when I turned to look at her back, she too had turned towards me. Rosalind? Barbara? Rosalind had, since leaving school, lived in Europe as an opera singer. Of a Lebanese merchant family, she was one of the fair skin girls chosen to portray the Virgin Mary at school events where, dressed in robes copied from Renaissance paintings, she stood, as still as the statue facing the forbidden stairs, behind a gauze screen that made it all the more ethereal. When you looked at her in the tableau, you could think you were as transfigured as Bernadette, Luisa and chosen others, visited by apparitions of the Virgin. And here was Rosalind in London, with the convent years our only common ground. Rosalind, as one of the chosen ones, had been on more familiar terms with the Irish nuns than we others were. She described one who to me was a particularly hated memory, Mother Columba, as a thwarted thespian. Where she'd seen that, I'd seen The Wicked Witch on Her Broom. So blinded was I by the hurts, slights and indignities this woman had visited upon me that I never viewed her as a creature to be studied rather than one to react to. I saw that Rosalind had a point and thought that I should stand back a bit and get some perspective on this particular monster who had once loomed so large.

A giant of a nun, her white robes aflutter behind her, she'd first sailed into our form five classroom one languorous afternoon declaiming in ringing tones, *Quinquireme of Nineveh from distant Ophir, Rowing home to haven in sunny Palestine, With a cargo of ivory, And apes, and peacocks, Sandalwood, cedarwood and sweet white wine*. Who is this? What is she doing here? Those were the questions that invaded my head. What she uttered was utterly lost on me. Just now I looked it up. I Googled. Typed in what I remembered. Only the first few words – *Quinquireme of Nineveh* – that had registered before the shock had obliterated almost all else. The last bit, the *sweet white wine*, she'd said slowly with such relish that I must have registered the beauty of the soft repeated breathy wwuh – sswwuheet wwuhite wwuhine. It made me shiver in my spine and parts unknown. Did she say anything about what it was about? I don't remember. Did she say why she was there? I don't remember. Did we then open our books and go

back to our usual poem, *The Lady of Shallot*? I don't remember. But this I
do remember. That nun said she'd just come from St Lucia where she was
reading the poems of a young St Lucian poet. She then recited one about
the road to Choiseul. It was about the cliffs, the coastline, something about
the sea. It must be in *In a Green Night*, one of Derek Walcott's earliest
collections, and I have a copy.

This nun, Mother Columba Carthy, must have taught us in form five for
a while before she became our new Principal, but all I remember of that
interlude was our personal interactions. On one occasion she came up
behind me when I was sitting slumped, no doubt quite ungainly, across my
desk. Her voice boomed across the room, a thing of beauty is a joy forever.
It was my introduction to sarcasm and to its wounding power, which, to my
shame, I became quite good at.

On another memorable occasion, I think she was talking about the
severity of cold in winter in Ireland, and about people staying in the same
clothes for weeks at a time, not getting out of them at all, and when they
finally did take off their clothes to have a bath after a month of so, the outer
layers of skin would fall from their bodies like flakes of snow. A wonderful
image I'm thinking now, but at the time we were all scandalised that people
could be so stink and nasty not bathing for a month. I must have been
exceptionally appalled. Maybe I Oh geed rather too loudly, because she
strode towards me, grabbed my arm, and rubbed the inside of my elbow
until the day's sweat and dirt combined, and long strings of black vermicelli
rolled from under her fingers. She said nothing to me or to the class, and
though she didn't demonstrate the result of her experiment to anyone but
me, she gave me a look of triumph, then went back to the front of the class
and carried on with her anecdote, as if this interaction with a difficult child
was no more than yet another Station of the Cross along the long Calvary
of her life.

I always felt that we girls from the elementary school were regarded as a
large indigestible chunk of vermin that the convent, a caged boa constrictor,
had been fed by its captors, the government, and the convent, in its turn,
poured its emetics and purgatives down on us so as to expel us from its
body as quickly as it could.

Some girls left school after Form Five and by Christmas were at work.
Marie was in the blue skirt and white shirt-blouse uniform of a Barclays
teller while I was back in school uniform, put back in Fifth Form, now
among a batch of girls a year younger. I don't know why I was kept back,
nobody in charge explained, but I'm guessing it's because the nuns couldn't
easily put me out of school. I still had another year of free secondary
schooling, and keeping me back to repeat was the only way they could fulfil
their obligation to the government while denying me the opportunity to

advance academically. Many of my classmates were moved up to Sixth Form and were already immersed in new subjects with new teachers when one afternoon, close to the end of the school day, the school body was called to an assembly. Without warning or preparation, the Senior Cambridge results were read out to the whole school and you and everyone else heard what grade you got.

Uncle Carmie came by that afternoon. What you get? I told him. He nodded and smiled. I know you woulda get that. So what you going to do? I didn't have an answer. I knew that with that grade of certificate I could now leave school and look for a job, but I didn't tell him that, and I was glad I held my tongue. I hope you not thinking about leaving school and going to look for work, he said. You say you want to be a doctor? Well you have to get more education first. I couldn't tell him that I was powerless that I couldn't tell the nuns or ask the nuns to let me move up to sixth form to get more education, as he put it, and take the Cambridge Higher Certificate after two more years. The nuns made the decisions and everyone had to abide by them.

When we'd moved up from form four to five the year before, we met up with a couple of girls who'd been kept down to repeat the exam. Both Sue Quesnel and Marilyn Arneaud had got Grade One at Senior Cambridge, but I guess the nuns felt that they'd do even better next try and would be among the eight students in the colony who would be at the top of the list from Cambridge and thereby win a coveted House Scholarship and bring glory to the school – which they both did. Would I be kept down for the same reason? At the end of the next school day, Mother Francis Theresa came into my classroom. She told me I was to report upstairs to the sixth form the following morning. She didn't say anything to the other girls who'd been kept down with me, I think this was because they got only a second grade, though none of those who'd already been put in sixth form who also got second grade were demoted. It all seemed very vye-qui-vye to me, but you couldn't ask. Actually, it didn't occur to me to ask.

Which subjects to choose for Higher Certificate? I had enough distinctions and credits to choose anything that was on offer. My certainties were French and geography, so I needed just one more subject. I sat at the back of the class listening in on English. They were doing something they called Hazlitt, which was very amusing, and Wordsworth which was lush. Spanish was *Don Quixote*, but they'd gone too far for me to catch up, so I quickly abandoned that. Maths was impossible; only three girls had chosen it. What else? Latin wasn't on offer. At that time SJC didn't teach history because the Cambridge syllabus was history according to the Anglican version. We Catholics would surely go straight to hell if we studied heresy as if it were gospel, particularly that bit which the girls at Bishops (who did do history) called 'The Reformation'. I'd gone through school without any exposure to chemistry or physics, yet I wanted to do biology at HC, as I was still determined to become a doctor. There was no biology in the sixth form. I canvassed a few of my classmates whom I suspected might be interested. We located an unused alcove at the top of a flight of stairs and decided that could be our biology classroom; we borrowed a copy of the syllabus from the brother of one of us at school across at CIC and copies of the botany and zoology textbooks they were using and went to Mother Francis Theresa with our proposition. We would teach ourselves biology. She questioned us about how and why and where and who and finally she agreed.

The brother at CIC got his teacher to catch a stray cat, chloroform it and send it over to us when we had a fish tank set up with formaldehyde according to instructions. The syllabus said rabbit, but stray cats were easier to locate. Using the textbooks we followed the syllabus faithfully line by line for about a year until sometime in our second year we got a temporary teacher, a returning former SJC student who'd dropped out of an American medical school. She brought her big glossy medical human anatomy book full of labelled colour drawings. We spread it open on the table and hunched over it to study the drawings and since there wasn't much human in the syllabus, we adapted what it showed to the cat, which should have been a rabbit. Of the five who sat Biology Higher Certificate at Principal Level, only two of us got through, one with a pass and one with a credit.

It was a doomed experiment at the time but one that got traction with the convent authorities because they got hold of a suitable nun from some-where in their Caribbean convent schools network to start teaching chemistry and eventually physics in the lower school and this fed into a thriving and successful biology at HC in due course – never mind that even in the eighties, some quarter century on, it was reported that the head SJC nun gathered up all copies of the recommended biology textbooks for the then newly introduced CXC exam, the Caribbean successor to the Senior Cambridge and GCE, and taped together the pages of the textbook that dealt with the taboo topics of human reproduction in text and diagrams and with gestation, birth and family planning.

French in sixth form was interesting. A wide range of set books with Mère Rose for one paper, *Le Tartuffe, Le Cid, Lettres de Mon Moulin* and *Premier de Cordée,* and lots of translation of prose and poetry with Miss Rolston, for another. It was like being in another world of adventure, romance and danger with all that elegant language that your tongue, teeth, palate and lips had to contort differently to negotiate. Often when she handed me back my graded poetry translations, Miss Rolston would say, You're supposed to be translating what the poet has written, not give your interpretation, nor should you write what you think the poet should have said.

Mother Columba was our geography teacher. In lower sixth we were made to write a couple of exams at Higher Certificate level to get the feel of it. I did geography at Principal Level and French at subsidiary and got a distinction in geography. This encouraged me to ask if I could do the extra Scholarship Level Paper in geography the following year as well as the compulsory repeat of the geography along with my two other Principal Level subjects, French and Biology and the obligatory General Paper to qualify for a full certificate. Mother Columba agreed.

There were two of us geography scholarship students. The other girl, Sue Quesnel, and I were, and are, still friends. To her, born into a large well-off merchant class, French Creole family, I owe much. It was while still at school, from an introduction to The Field Naturalists Club, which her much older brothers ran, that I got to love natural habitats, as they were then called, at a very granular level. It was my first appreciation that here where I lived there were things, plants and animals, that you didn't find in books, but were real and worth your time and interest. Many decades later, stranded in Bristol, I relied on her emotional support, and, in our mid-fifties, she and I went on month-long backpacking adventures together – to India, then to Cuba, and later to Peru. Yes, friends for life.

Mother Columba had come into the school as a new broom principal. The first thing she swept away was the school uniform. We had grown quite attached to the one we were used to and resented the change, but we had to go along. She allowed our transition period to be as long as possible so that the old uniform was too tight, too short to be decent before surrendering to the new design – same colour, same material, but different overall shape. She also tried to tamper with the student hierarchy. In addition to the house captains and vice-captains at the pinnacle, Mother Columba Carthy wanted a head girl and a deputy head girl as well. Maybe that's what she had in St Lucia in her reign there. She wanted the captain of Holy Trinity House to be the head girl. Did the girl resist being drawn into possible controversy? Did Mother Columba's sister nuns try to dissuade her? Did she herself see that fixing what wasn't broken wasn't such a good idea? Dunno. But it didn't happen. My fellow geography scholarship candidate was the captain of Holy Trinity House and the head girl in prospect. You get the picture. I was a scholarship rival of Mother Columba's dou-dou darling, special student. Without either of us openly acknowledging it, that girl and I both knew that one of us was favoured and the other not. Dear sweet Sue shared her resources with me – books, magazines, bits of articles her brothers found for her. We saw ourselves as being in the trenches together and didn't let the blatant favouritism spoil our friendship.

Thinking about how it was in the sixth form, I think it was then that we changed from allegiance to our designated houses to becoming a group of like-minded adolescents. We girls, who up to then had been learning by rote and regurgitating for exams, were suddenly entertaining thoughts and ideas, questioning and engaging in discussion and debate. This was within the limits we knew were there, limits of church and convent expectations. There was still a distinction between town girls and train girls. I remember being a little envious of the train girls. The train girls left school promptly, not able to take part in anything after school, but they had a richer after-school life, I thought. While we town girls made friends within school and among our home communities, the train girls had all that and were also exposed to the whole range of boys and girls they travelled with from far-flung places like Barataria, San Juan, Curepe, St Augustine, Tunapuna, Tacarigua, Arima, Sangre Grande and Chaguanas. They hung about in the downtown Public Library and studied with girls their age from Bishops and boys from QRC and CIC and knew a whole lot more about places and people than we town girls, and this set them apart as somehow more knowing, more grounded. In the classroom, however, we were one, together as a cohesive entity, emboldened to be less conforming, to finding entertainment rather than discomfort in our school life.

One such source was Raoul Pantin's early manuscripts. Maritza sneaked out her brother's short stories written in school exercise books, boys' stories in the style of Zane Grey, stories of adventure set in an imagined Wild West that resembled St James, the west Port of Spain suburb where they lived. A small group would sit together in a free period and pass around the exercise book with the story of the day. Raoul was a prolific writer. We would take turns to read aloud, hardly able to suppress our laughter – which would have drawn unwelcome attention. We didn't know then that we were laughing because they were such wonderful parodies of popular Westerns. I think we found it funny that anyone could think that ordinary places like our island home was worthy of being in a book. Another source of delighted reading was Marilyn Arneaud's black book. In it she recorded all the sarcastic put downs, all the sayings, all the unusual phrases, all the acid comments that laced every interaction we sixth form girls had with Mother Columba and other teachers. During the day, whenever some-thing was said that was unusual, entertaining or wounding, it would be collected by those present and Marilyn would collate them in her book and that too would be passed around and read in a similar way to Raoul's stories.

I sometimes wonder what became of Marilyn's black book. I know she kept it long after, for on one of her rare visits back home from Toronto, many years later, we got together for lunch at Luciano's and she entertained us with readings from it. Then she silenced our laughter by announcing that she was going back to Toronto to marry a priest who'd left the clergy. For Raoul, the journey had just begun. He went on to become a much respected and admired print, radio and TV journalist and commentator, a playwright and screenwriter. He was held hostage in the national TV station during the Muslimeen 1990 coup and afterwards wrote and published his witness account of the terror of that time and he was able to testify at the Commission of Inquiry held two decades after. Little did we silly girls imagine what an adventure the Zane-Grey-lookalike-stories of his in the late fifties was a preparation for.

There was hanging about after school in the bicycle shed with a group of town girls, classmates and others to talk about what? Boys? Yes, there was some of that, mainly teasing one another about boys we didn't actually know but saw in the distance. Our mysterious body functions? I don't remember those conversations, if they even happened. Music we liked? Films we'd seen? Other people not present? I guess lots of those. Hour after hour, day after day and I can't recall one conversation. This, I'm figuring out now, is the essence of growing up, the growing into yourself process. It's the feeding of the roots, the new filaments of root hairs, unseen, getting into minute crevices underground and supporting the life of what's visible above. It is these sessions, I think, these unremembered passages that made my other lives less important, less large, so that most of the time I sailed through unawares and, I think, insulated from much unpleasantness. We spent two years on the brink of adult life, learning much in our subject areas, learning little about our own world, and learning nothing about how to move on after we had to leave. The exams came along, we sat them, and school life came to an end.

There was a culture of debutantes and debut balls in Trinidad, but it wasn't my culture, our culture. Upper-class families would host balls at the Country Club to introduce their just-out-of-school daughters to society and you'd see pictures in the paper of The Hon. So and So and Mrs So and So, all in formal ball wear, with their daughter, Marie Thérèse or Amelia Florence or Jacinta Eloise in a shimmering white gown, and there'd be a big chunk in *The Talk of Trinidad* gossip column listing the distinguished guests and the menu and the drinks and the toasts and the band and the music and who danced with whom until daybreak and the merry party moving on to the jetty to their boats, and continuing the celebration on one of the grand down-the-islands homes, Monos or Gasparee, just off Chaguaramas and The Base.

I wondered how it was that these just-out-of-convent girls could get away with all of that, dressing up to be on show, go up for the Carnival Queen competition too, have their pictures taken in the papers wearing bathing suits, have long stories written about them, where they lived, their parents, what they liked or didn't like doing, but I never heard any of that being referred to as *They're looking for attention or they're showing off*. Wasn't putting yourself in the papers and putting your business on the street attention seeking? I don't think the nuns thought so because when these same girls got married soon after their debuts, Mother Helen took her choir to sing at the wedding and the same newly-married girls, a couple months later, brought in their christened babies to show the nuns. Those girls had their debuts to mark their grownup state, but that wasn't us. For us ordinary girls at the convent, our rite of passage was school graduation. You graduated either after sitting school certificate, or two years later after higher certificate. Along with the exhibitioners, now guaranteed a sixth year of free schooling, I graduated after higher certificate.

Designed by Mother Columba Carthy, we wore identical white dresses of a heavy, figured satiny material cut in a princess line, fitted bodice, Sabrina neckline, a long full skirt with a modest can-can below to keep it standing away from the body, elbow-length white gloves, prayer book and rosary, a small hat-let of dress fabric-covered buckram topped with a wide, flat, white velvet bow, and white flat-heeled shoes. We had a service in the school chapel where there was the crowning, with a rose tiara, of La Rosière, the girl who best exemplified the ideals of the Convent. That year it was my classmate and friend, Annette Chow, who went on to become a nun and still is. Then we went off later to Bretton Hall Hotel on Victoria Avenue – the building, much modified, is still there – to a dinner and dance to the music of Pal Joey with your escort, some random boy you'd invited, a brother of a friend, a cute CIC boy you'd been spying on from the upstairs window of the sixth form classroom, or in my case with Jeffrey, the only boy I was ever friends with since the age of eleven.

I don't regret the six years I spent at the convent as a student, for they were among my most formative years. It was there that I learned at first hand how the unseen world I was born into worked then and still does now.

WINE

I left school in November 1959, just before my eighteenth birthday. When the Higher Certificate Exam results came from Cambridge with recommendations for scholarships, I was placed second for the one scholarship awarded to girls. One of my classmates, Bernadette Ashby, won it and went to England to study English. For boys there were four scholarships – one in each of science, mathematics, languages and modern studies. There was then no university in Trinidad, only the Imperial College of Tropical Agriculture. In Jamaica there was the University College of the West Indies, affiliated to the University of London, but I had no means of getting there. I awoke from my wild dream of going away to university, becoming a doctor and coming back home to lay a healing hand on a fevered brow. I had to have another look at what to do with myself. Since this was the fate of most of us, adjusting to normal expectations wasn't difficult. It involved moving away from schoolgirl convent life to living in mainstream Trinidad and finding a way to be.

And what could that way be? One option was to stay in the security of the convent by becoming a postulant as half-a-dozen or so of my year group did, and which, on many a Retreat Day, I, too, seduced by Trappist silence, intoxicated by aromatic incense and hypnotised by rhythmic repetitions of the many mysteries of the rosary, the rolling over and over of *Hail Mary full of Grace,* the hypnotic chanting of *Pray for us pray for us pray for us, have mercy on us, have mercy on us, have mercy on us* in the litanies, I fantasised that I could become chaste, renounce the temptations of the world and delights of the flesh and offer my life to God.

There were many attractions to the convent life. There was somewhere to live, with nice, clean comfortable quarters, where you'd be safe from the dangers of the outside world; you would have the company of like-minded people; you'd get to go away and study and become a qualified person; you'd get to see other countries when you were moved about; and though as young healthy girls the idea of security in old age and support in sickness were far from our thoughts, there was the certainty of heaven at death. It offered a way out of the struggle and hardship and the randomness of life outside, especially for those among us who were shut out of the nexus of wealth and power, those of us disadvantaged because of colour, class and gender. And how proud of us our families would be. At that time, to have someone become a priest or a nun raised the family above the level of common folk. After five or six years at the convent, many of us ordinary girls were more in tune with the ethos of Catholicism, the values of foreigners and the aspirations of an elite class than we were with our own families, the communities in which we lived and the island of our birth. The prospect of leaving the familiar convent forever and going back into the mainstream of Trinidad life must have seemed daunting to those of us who thought about it in any analytical way. So, with all of those advantages for the convent, why didn't I go with that flow of the current?

For many are called, but few are chosen – Matthew 22:14... and many more are not even whispered to. I didn't get the calling. I didn't even hear a whispered invitation. I now wonder whether the convent accepted bastards as nuns... Hmmm. Anyway, while I could see the attractions of the religious life, I didn't get the calling. So what was left? When I looked around I could see what was a well-trodden path. It was just this: Go out in the world. Get a job.

You know that bit in the Gospels, the Temptations of Christ, the time when he was in the desert fasting and Satan took him to the top of the mountain and showed him the wonders of the world and said something like, *You can have all of this if...?* From where I stood on the brink of my New World, I saw its wonders too and was sorely tempted. Suffice it to say that Jesus was made of sterner stuff than I. Finally I had the freedom to go where I wanted, with whom I wanted and for as long as I wanted. How could I not succumb? Girls my age went to parties and nightclubs, dressed up in the latest fashion, wore lipstick, eyebrow pencil, rouge and high heel shoes – glamorous girls like classmate Judith Miles' older sister, Gene – girls who eventually settled down with one of the boys or men with cars who pursued them. I know that that was a familiar and, on the face of it, successful path. As a member of the school choir I had gone with fellow choristers on enough Saturday after-noons to St Patrick's Church and St Theresa's to sing at the weddings of the country club type of girls who'd left school just a year or two before, and enjoyed the bits of wedding cake and Cydrax, the thank-you the bride's family sent to the convent. If a convent girl didn't join the nunnery, she went out chastely with a good Catholic boy, got chastely engaged, received instruction from a celibate priest about Catholic married love, got married in a Catholic church, had her first child soon after and had it baptised in a Catholic church on a Sunday morning. To get married to a non-Catholic was a serious failing, but not impossible. Lots of promises had to be made before such a union – called a mixed marriage – could be sanctified. Convent girls just did not have children out of wedlock. So I knew all the expectations. To get a job would make all of the above possible, for I would have freedom and money to spend how I wanted. Not such a bad prospect.

Armed with copies of my Cambridge School Certificate Grade 1 and

Higher Certificate with distinctions, and bolstered by carefully handwritten, respectfully phrased letters, I applied to every business place in town for a job as a clerk or some such, but I did not get one acknowledgement of receipt of my application. I applied to BWIA, British West Indian Airways, which, to a mixture of corporate fanfare – and equal measures of public acclaim and acrimony – had just taken on its first 'coloured' air hostess, Pearl Marshall. I applied to Barclays Bank, which had previously employed only white and a few Chinese girls – my friend Marie Ng Chow, pure Chinese, had left school after School Certificate and was already two years in Barclays as a teller – but was tentatively testing its palate beyond its regular diet of thick layers of cream and dabs of butter to dustings of cinnamon and – fingers crossed – gratings of nutmeg. I also applied to my alma mater for a teaching job. You can tell that desperation had truly set in.

It was February, Carnival season, when both BWIA and Barclays called me in for interviews – BWIA, as an airhostess, Barclays, as foreign exchange teller. I had never been on a plane, but I'd seen enough films to know in minutest detail the flying life: one week London, next New York, then Paris, Piccadilly Circus, The Empire State Building, The Eiffel Tower and Champs Elysée. And what was the job? To smile and serve drinks and food to the nice, well-behaved, respectable passengers. And the bank! Working on the foreign exchange desk, speaking French and Spanish to foreign customers, learning about money, learning how to turn the bills so they faced the same way, counting them fast, fast, fast, so they flipped through your fingers in a blur! Both offered exciting prospects of a new life, several rungs above the one I grew up on.

But while I was waiting to hear back from them, Mother Francis Theresa sent a message asking me to come in. The school needed a teacher urgently. I took the job. I was given a timetable. I was to teach Maths to the lower school and to the trainee teachers at the Catholic Women Teachers Training College, which at the time was housed upstairs above the school hall. It was after I had been teaching at the convent for a term that I heard the whisper as to why the school so urgently needed a maths teacher. It turned out that the woman I replaced was an Englishwoman who was married to a doctor, an Indian Trinidadian and, as the story goes, the nuns had got word that she had been seen in a swimsuit on Maracas Beach, walking with a man who was not the Indian doctor. This woman was a qualified teacher, a graduate with a degree in maths from an English university. I had been hired to replace her. And what did I know?

We'd had no decent maths teacher ourselves as students for three and a half years, until Joan Rolston came to our rescue in our last term of fifth form, a scant couple of months before our Senior Cambridge exams and, seeing our dire straits, decided she'd do her best with us in geometry, which I grew to love, especially the theorems. You had a statement to prove, so much logic! So much of: if this, then that, if that, then the other. I also loved the show-off Latin at the end of a proof – *Quod Erat Demonstrandum* – QED! Algebra she tried with us but we had struggled only as far as simultaneous equations. There was too much to do in too little time, but she at least taught us quadratic equations. As far as arithmetic was concerned, for us girls from the elementary schools, our various Mrs Thornhills had taught us right up to where we needed to be, except something called stocks and shares. This Miss Rolston had no time to teach us and so I still know nothing about such things. But I did pass with a credit at Senior Cambridge, the highest level I'd attained in Maths. Thus I joined the tribe of inadequate lower-school maths teachers. The brilliant Joan Rolston taught only the lucky exam classes at the convent.

Hardly had I put my feet under a teacher's desk, than both BWIA and Barclays offered me a job. Ah! More haste less speed wagged its reprimanding finger again. Too anxious, I'd fallen into the trap of taking the first one offered, and in a place and within a system that had thwarted and restrained me for six years. And here's the weirdest, bizarrest thing. It never once crossed my mind that I should go to the head nun and say, Look, something's come up that I'd really rather do. And furthermore, this maths teaching isn't something I know anything about anyway, so good luck with your search. Lord! the roads not taken. Geometry theorems again: if this, then that. QED. If I start recounting where my classmates in the airline business and banking industry got to in their lives and careers and compare it with myself in teaching – which was to become my lifelong occupation – I'd be writing something longer than *A Brief History of Seven Killings* or *The Bible* – though lacking the racy language, swift action, gratuitous violence, historical sweep and high drama of those two gripping books. Why didn't I choose what I really wanted to do? Why did I feel I couldn't leave? As they say, regret is a bitter pill that you don't need to swallow. So, stumbling blindly onto what became a life-changing course, I became a teacher at St Joseph's Convent Port of Spain where I had, a scant two and a half months before, shaken off the dust of six years of a schizophrenic existence where I was one thing in school, and another several different things outside, and which I was destined to endure for quite a while longer.

When I opened my brown pay envelope at the end of that first month and took out the sheaf of notes I was thrilled to count a whopping sixty dollars. I had never even seen so much money. My Uncle Carmie came by that first month. Yuh get pay? I said I had and I gleefully told him how much. So what yuh give yuh Marmie? When I hung my head he got my answer. Oh the shame! To my eternal discredit, it had never once occurred to me. I go back to what I said before – this in connection with we children's rudeness at Mrs Blanche's lunch-boarding arrangement – that children must be actively taught about empathy. My mother had spent eighteen years taking the best possible care of me and I hadn't given a moment's thought to the possibility that I, as a working grownup, should be shouldering some of the burden she'd carried willingly and uncomplaining for so long.

She had worked as a cashier at a Chinese grocery on Charlotte Street that didn't give trust to customers or staff, and later at Hi-Lo in St Ann's (also no trust), but where staff had first pickings of the little greaseproof paper packets of fragments of ham left on the slicing machine. These my mother converted, with the addition of two eggs, into a big omelette, shared among the five of us, a dish that for years defined the word omelette for me. Later, she worked in the laundry of the American base at Chaguaramas, where you were paid by the hour, outrageous and unprecedented at that time, though if you were even a minute late, an hour's pay was deducted. But you were allowed, in rotation, to buy sheets and towels that were no longer up to the standard of the residents on the base, at bargain prices. The items were snipped near the laundry stamp to show they were discards but when they arrived home they were greeted with incredulous joy as real sheets, real towels as in books, not bits of yardage to sleep on, not old clothes to dry yourself with. After that, she worked in the kitchen in the Mental Hospital in St Ann's, where she had to walk to work after a bailiff came home and took away her Raleigh bicycle. Marmie had spent all she earned in these places in taking care of us children, the basics as well as the extras, and I had never shown appreciation. I had taken it all for granted as much as I had taken for granted that what I earned was mine.

I still had three younger siblings at school, dependent on Marmie, yet it hadn't occurred to me that I should share a portion of my newly acquired financial independence until Uncle Carmie made me think. He didn't have to spell it out. He asked me one question that I hadn't thought to ask myself, and when I did ask it, I wondered why I had needed to be prodded. I gave Marmie twenty-five dollars. I opened a savings account at Barclays and deposited ten. That still left me with more money than I'd ever had before to spend entirely on myself.

Had I gone to either Barclays or BWIA, I would have been equipped with a set of company uniforms; as a teacher I was expected to buy my own working clothes. There wasn't a prescribed uniform but there were ways you could dress and ways you dared not, and because your whole convent life was teaching you to recognise decent from not decent, you instinctively knew the dress code. Miss Finn, a Canadian who was teaching at the convent at the time, was frequently spoken to by the nuns about her skirts that only reached as far as her knees, so that when she sat, her pink knees were visible, and about her sleeveless dresses which exposed her upper arms. At first, we straight-out-of-school new teachers wore the kinds of things we would wear as schoolgirls to choir practice or to church, but a few pay envelopes into the job and our wardrobes became more grownup.

Alla, Jeffrey's mother, made my new outfits – one shirtwaist dress with a flared skirt, two pencil skirts (one in what was then a very popular but daring colour, drab olive, the colour of Che Guevara's uniform), and one in a safe choice, chocolate brown, and four short-sleeved shirt-blouses. Each skirt worn twice, each blouse once, and the dress once in the five-day working week. Shoes – not black, not white – those were school shoes colours – but one tan pair and one oxblood, court shoes with a Cuban heel, size five. And matching handbags, of course. No teacher ever dared to wear trousers (there were no male teachers). The only man we saw on the compound was George, the gardener-handyman, whom we only ever saw in the distance, up a ladder, pruning a shrub or changing a light bulb.

And what about hair? What did we daughters of Africa do with hair in the early sixties to be fashionable? After spending schooldays with hair pulled back into a single plait or a ponytail, for graduation I had it cut shoulder length and straightened for the first time. At that time, while pressing hair with a hot metal comb was still common, hairdressers had got hold of Lontay, a powerful white paste which, when applied with a comb to kinky and very curly hair, makes it straight. The problem is that there's an inherent tension between application and successful outcome. If it comes into contact with the scalp, Lontay burns skin, strips skin, leaves painful raw wounds that scab over, yet if not applied at the root of the hair shaft, the kink at the root remains unstraightened and is a dead giveaway that your smooth, straight hair is a fraud. Overzealous application can also cause hairshaft brittleness, and hair to drop out in clumps. A careless hairdresser could send you home with straight hair and a scalp with third-degree burns, or hair with unsightly kinky roots but scalp safe. A fine balance indeed. Jaffry's replaced Lontay and was said to be less vicious, but both burned and stank of lye and I dreaded having to go to the hairdresser to keep up appearances. Not giving a damn and dispensing with all that nonsense came much later, but in those early years as a working girl at the cusp of adulthood, I at last had the opportunity and means to be 'beautiful' and I wasn't going to let that slip away. Hair that moved, hair that the breeze could blow, seemed an essential to set off the gorgeous clothes you planned on making.

Ah the joy, the sheer bliss of being able to walk into a store with money in your purse, the thrill of fondling silks and satins, cottons and linens, the excitement of choosing matching zips and contrasting braid and bias-binding and sifting through buttons to find ones that suited the mood of your imagined new garment, of fingering applique and lace, the security of being able to ask the shop assistant to cut three and a half yards of this and a yard and three-quarters of that, because your dressmaker had told you what amounts you'd need for the dress or the skirt or the blouse in the black and white picture you'd cut from the newspaper of a woman somewhere in Paris or London or New York at a fashion show, or coming down the steps of an aeroplane, or walking along a street, arm in arm with a man in a suit wearing a hat with a little dog on a leash leading the way. You wanted a dress like Doris Day in *Pillow Talk* with Rock Hudson or like Eva Marie Saint in *North by Northwest* – the dress with the bateau neckline – but how to wear a bra with that? Clothes for going out. Going out to new places. And oh! The places to go!

Out of nowhere came a life and people and places that you'd never heard of. Big sisters and brothers of friends introduced you to the life they'd been enjoying while you were shrouded in a convent uniform and your head was buried in a book. On Saturday mornings, I would meet up with school friend, Maritza, newly a library assistant, to shop downtown, then to Nanking Chinese Restaurant on Queen Street where we would indulge in food not cooked at home – wanton soup, fried rice, chow mein, chow har luk, char siu kai fan, followed by lychees in syrup and jasmine tea with a dried white flower floating in it. Then up to the top floor of Salvatori Building, the newest building in Port of Spain and the tallest, first time in an elevator and not a care in the world. On to the Penthouse, a club owned by the bandleader, Choy Aming. At night there were brass bands and dancing; Saturday lunchtimes was for liming and listening to small jazz combos. We weren't yet ready for night, so middays we sat at a table with Val, Maritza's so sophisticated big sister, a cigarette dangling from her fingers with long, neatly painted nails, and she introducing us to whoever came over to say hello to her. That way we got to know lots of big people, adults who were not in circles that any of our adults knew, many of whom were on the lookout for girls like us, just out of school – I could name a few but won't, but we were safe, because our grownups had laid some ground rules for us. What we got out of it was no more risky than ordering – like seasoned sophisticates – a Bentley which was no more than lime juice with soda water instead of plain water, and a dash of bitters swirling like red mist through the pale green drink, a maraschino cherry on a toothpick and a mini paper umbrella on top, to be drunk through a straw. We listened to what we thought were fascinating conversations about life, music, musicians, politics – conversations we hadn't heard before, and an unforgettable introduction to live jazz, our own jazz as well as American jazz.

There was Schofield Pilgrim on bass – Sco, whispering Sco from Barbados, teaching Latin at Queens Royal College, founding and mentoring the QRC Jazz band, facilitating musicians everywhere – he was always there in the Penthouse on Saturday lunchtime. Sco had this friend, a tall red fellow who was a smooth, arch-seducer of girls, not girls like Maritza and me, of course, only light skin girls, wannabe Jaycees Carnival Queen contestants and daughters of foreigners. It's a good thing I've forgotten his name or I'd be in trouble. There was Gerry Sankeralli from Cedros side, but who knew everyone in the city through selling insurance. He had a girlfriend who was a dancer in Beryl McBurnie's Little Carib Dance Company, so you got to know about bélé and piqué and so on, traditional creole dances you'd never seen or heard of. At the convent, the PE teacher was trained at the Morris School of Dancing, UK, and you learned the Sailors Hornpipe and the Maypole. What a rich life we found there outside the cloister, where we could sit for hours slowly sipping our one or two Bentleys, just liming and enjoying the gentle, easy, seductive ambience of jam sessions that were like musical conversations among budding composers like Andre Tanker, on his guitar, fresh out of school like us; stellar pannists like Bradley, Zanda on keys, and fresh off the boat or plane musicians like Stone on the sax. You'd leave in a daze, getting back home in a route taxi, all the while operating on autopilot because you were still in that cocoon of live music playing in your head. That early introduction to jazz became a lifelong love and nowadays when I need a mood boost, I'd as soon turn to Duke Ellington's 'Take the A Train' as to All Stars Steelband 'Woman on the Bass'.

These possibilities of life as a grownup were so different from the lives of any of the women I'd known. There's a song from the film *The King and I* (which I saw around then) that fits how I felt about this period of my life. 'Getting to Know You'. Yes, as the song says, I'd become *bright and breezy*. And I was learning lots of *wonderful new things ... day by day!* I was Anna and Port of Spain was my Kingdom of Siam. I didn't have Yul Brynner as my king, but that was fine as I was doing ok with Jeffrey, the one boyfriend I'd always had. There was a slow gradual long-term future inevitability to that, an unstated understanding that came from long familiarity, but I'm not segueing into that just now. It's a rabbit hole whose interlocking dark tunnels and blocked exits lay in the future and certainly didn't foreshadow or mar the pleasures of the unfolding present.

I think now that it was because I was seen with a steady boyfriend that I was saved from falling in with the sort of men, professional men, who were on the lookout for girls like me, a girl to whom they felt entitled as successful men, a convent girl new to the world whom they could, as they would put it, break in and train, and who, as a lover, could spice up a marriage that they felt had gone stale. I suspect, now, that having a girlfriend saved my boyfriend from the risk of possible rejection if he himself was on the prowl. So we were, I think, mutual shields for each other against attacks on our vulnerabilities. I am using the terms boyfriend and girlfriend, but we never referred to each other as such. It was the quiet, steady, unstated but all-consuming understanding of two children growing up together, doing things together.

As a budding photographer he was taking pictures of everything, everywhere. Even though we didn't own a car it was easy to get about. Step out onto the road in Belmont, raise an arm and a route taxi stops and takes you to downtown Port of Spain where you can connect to anywhere in other route taxis; it was only weather that determined where to go. Soon, sending negatives to develop and print became too restricting for him and he wanted to experiment, to have more control over the process. He had a darkroom built, carved out from his mother's carnival costume sewing room. Between Harriman's and Chan's we got all the equipment, the tank, chemicals, trays, enlarger, film. In the darkroom we'd take the exposed film and wind it into a black cylindrical tank, add developer liquid mixed from powder, shake the cylinder, wait for the ping on the timer, pour out the developer, pour in the stop, shake, shake, ping, pour out the stop, pour in the fixer, ping, open tank, take out negative strip, rinse, hang to dry. All this was in pitch-blackness, relieved only by one special dim light bulb – was it red? – that allowed us to just see but didn't harm the negatives or paper. I could never discern a good negative from a bad one. But I didn't need to. I was the assistant. Then followed the printing. The choice of paper, the trays with chemicals, the exposures, the drying, the discussion on the detail, the sharpness, the tones, the textures, the framing, the compositions: the pattern of shadows cast by fishing nets hanging to dry in Sea Lots; the wrinkles on the face of a wizened old man in a tattered straw hat, mending a net in Carenage; the reflection of a pirogue's bow in wet sand in Granville; the shadows on a rock emerging from churning foam in Matelot.

Developing colour transparency film for slides came next, with camera upgrades, bags of lenses, a telescopic tripod. And books and books on photography. Photography is an expensive hobby. He wasn't working. I was. I was active in the process. I was also the model, young and firm, perfect for experiments with skin tone and light and shadow and flowers and leaves and water – still, foaming, falling. But while for me it was fun, a dilettante's interest, for him it became a consuming lifelong profession. It took me a long while to feel I could take on something that seemed so technical, so hard, and I was already in my late fifties when I bought my first camera, a film camera at a time when digital cameras were already replacing them, to take to India. It went with me to Cuba and Peru, to Seville and Ferney Voltaire. I don't remember the model nor even the make and I have no idea where it is. Even with the smartphone always accessible, I rarely take a photo now. But I think I must have taken away something useful from that time because I get great pleasure in looking at a photo that someone else has made and trying to read it, read into it.

It was a custom now gone for people who owned cars to go for a drive. Not going from A to B with a purpose at B, but going for the sake of being in a car and driving. We, that is Marmie and us children, had no car, so every journey we took had a destination in mind. Only one childhood drive I remember, and that was when Pappy took us to see the oil refinery at Pointe a Pierre when I was about ten. What amazed me on the journey was the clouds. They were different from Port of Spain clouds. While ours in the North rose in big fat irregular masses that changed shape and colour every minute, theirs in Central and South were laid out in neat orderly rows, all the same size and shape, row after row. Clouds in the north looked like a person chasing a dog one minute, a gorilla or a cow the next, turning from white to grey or black. Those Central white fluffy clouds looked as if they had been drawn in the sky by a careful child who had never seen a real cloud but had been shown a drawing of a cloud. The other thing I remember about that trip is the smell of the refinery, a searing, unpleasant, rotten eggs smell that hit my head and my stomach, so that Pappy had to stop the car and pull aside for me to vomit into the grass verge. Drives were not a regular part of my experience before leaving school, but that changed later.

The uncle-in-law of another school friend who lived on Myler Street, just down from my home, had a tomato-red Volkswagen Beetle and he took us on long drives on narrow roads to unfamiliar places. My mental map of my home island – limited before to Port of Spain, Trois Roches and Toco, Carenage and Upper Belmont Valley Road, places I'd been with my mother and the one railway journey taken when I was in the last year at Tranquillity – became studded with new locations like Mount St Benedict, the Arima Dial and the lighthouse at Pt Galera, the acres of waving canefields in arrow on the undulating Central Range foothills, wild places like Los Iros on the south coast where the sucking sea came in and took back its sand from the beach, and Manzanilla on the east, arrived at after mile after mile under towering overarching coconut palms, the sea glimpsed through the crisscross of their slender, hundred-foot tall trunks. There was the tingling scent of sea salt and seaweed, the crunch of scurrying blue crabs beneath rolling tyres. However, at some point my friend's aunt, wife of the willing tomato VW owner, must have raised some concerns because he became less available. But I will record here my gratitude to her for affording me this expanded awareness of my island.

Mondays meant going back to the narrow focus of school where I was struggling with teaching maths. I didn't know or understand enough. Mother Angela would sit with me in the library at lunchtime and teach me what I was to teach the next day. In the afternoons, when I got home, I would work on all the exercises so that I'd be one jump ahead of the girls. I could see that the trainee teachers at the training college were better equipped. I was eighteen, fresh out of school, with absolutely no training or experience in teaching; these older women had been teaching for years and were in college to get certified as teachers, to be taught not only subject content but how to teach it effectively. My predecessor, as I soon learned from the trainee teachers, was a gifted teacher of the techniques of imparting knowledge, as well as someone who actually knew the subject. In the end, the more resourceful students ran the class and taught me, and the others. It was a humiliating and humbling experience repeated three times a week for two terms, until I was relieved of maths altogether and given the timetable of another teacher who was leaving to get married and go away to England with her husband. Now I became a teacher of geography and Spanish. With a distinction in geography at Cambridge HC I was happy with the change, but Spanish? Again only a credit, but somehow not as daunting as maths, because I had an ally – Madre Marina.

I first met Madre Marina in Form Three. Our set book was *Un Verano en España*. Once a week we read aloud round the class, one after another. Madre Marina was a stickler for pronunciation. *Puro Castillano* was her style. Every *z* every *c* was a *th* sound, not the heavy *ss* of the resident Venezuelan borders whose Latin American Spanish was all around us all day, who thought our Spanish, imitative of Madre's, affected. For home-work we had to translate a big chunk of *Verano*. I never did one word of translating myself, and I was not alone. I do not remember which day was *Verano* day, but let's say it was Friday. On Friday morning, Helen Guyadeen and a few other non-Catholics would be given all the copybooks of the girls who hadn't done the translation and during religious instruction or rosary in the chapel, she and the others would sit in the library and copy the translations they had dutifully done for homework into the exercise books of the transgressors. In spite of that I loved Spanish, though not as much as French, to which I felt I had a genetic affinity and which was to my mind a more sophisticated language, the language of diplomacy and all that. I would give my eyeteeth now for a copy of *Verano* to read in Spanish. I felt my ignorance most acutely when I spent a couple months in Spain and visited many of the places described in *Verano* and I was pulled back to that time when I paid it such scant attention and once again I found myself steupsing many times at my youthful folly.

I don't think Madre Marina was happy at the convent. She may well have found linguistic and cultural affinity with the Venezuelan borders who were her particular charge, and a degree of intellectual satisfaction with the sixth-form girls studying Spanish, especially with being able to discuss with them nuances of vocabulary and the ideas and mores in literature. I remember listening in to heated argument about *Don Quixote* and the nature of madness or was it eccentricity, or delusion. But I think that at heart Madre was homesick, more so than the other nuns, as there were at least eight or nine Irish nuns and a few local nuns, mainly daughters of the large families of the French Creole aristocracy, and a couple of French ones, but she was the solitary Spaniard. I think, too, that Madre was able to imagine our real lives outside the walls of the convent in a way none of the others could. Was this because she must have lived through the Spanish civil war and witnessed cruelty, violence, death and deprivation that none of the others would have? Not even the Irish potato famine could match that, and this made her as much of an outsider in the convent as we were. She constantly referred to herself as *fea*, saying that she had the face of a *burro*. It made me wonder whether some girls became nuns because no one asked to marry them, as they were not thought pretty enough. When I thought about the Irish nuns – tall, angular, bony, hooked chins and long thin noses – I could find merit in that assumption. But Madre's good heart shone through and I never thought her ugly with a donkey face.

Madre set me up to teach English to the Venezuelan borders after school. She got copies of the book I was to use with them, a formal old-fashioned English textbook with vocabulary lists, passages for comprehension and a list of questions; she arranged with their parents the fees that she thought appropriate, collected the fees and handed me this extra envelope of folded dollar bills at the end of the month. I sat with four newly arrived girls at a time at the back of the deserted art room after school for two hours, three afternoons a week, and they read aloud in English, did comprehension, practised grammar and we chatted about what they did and would like to do. We must have all enjoyed it, for I was never in want of a new little group, selected by Madre, when each set of girls got proficient enough to cope in regular class without assistance and move on. I imagined them becoming executive secretaries in the lucrative oil sector back home or working in the diplomatic service, or airlines or in industry, for Venezuela was far more advanced economically than Trinidad. Having fluent English set these girls up for sure success.

There was always a fluidity and ease of movement between Trinidad and the Main. Men went over to work in the oilfields so Maracaibo was a place that every Trinidadian seemed to know. Venezuelan young women lived as boarders within Trinidadian families while they learned commercial subjects – English, shorthand, typing and bookkeeping – in the many secretarial schools that acted as finishing schools for our own girls too. Venezuelans were such a normal part of the cityscape in those days that downtown stores had signs that read *Aqui Se Habla Español* and now, sixty years later, those signs have made a reappearance, assuring the tens of thousands of economic and political refugees from Venezuela newly resident in Trinidad, that Spanish is spoken here.

At that time, I, briefly, had another source of income, one that high-lighted major heights of incompetence that no one, least of all myself, had imagined I could scale. My cousin Junior – Edward – was working in a racing pool in downtown Port of Spain, somewhere on Duke Street near Pembroke Street, I think. Betting shops took bets on local races during our many seasonal meets, but the year-round mainstay of these establishments was English horse racing that seemed to go on all day every day at different courses all over England. Betting on horses was and is a very popular activity among us Trinidadians. You'd hear people talking with passion about which horse, which jockey they fancied in the 12:22 at Cheltenham, the 1:05 at Sandown, the 2:35 at Goodwood. There was an ease and familiarity with place names and form and pari-mutuel and odds.

The nearest I'd been to horse racing was to leave my home in Belmont with a couple of friends and cross over to the Savannah on race days and stand in excited terror right up against the two-bar wooden rail as the horses thundered by, flailing hooves flinging clods of turf in our direction. The jockeys, all adult men, but no bigger than ten-year old boys, in shiny colourful satin, did not sit on their horses but squatted over their backs, bottoms pushed out as if they were about to jump, leaning forward so their heads were hidden behind their horses' heads. My cousin bet a dollar, a whole dollar on the horse Mice Lutchman was riding and got back four dollars when the horse won.

English courses ran an eight-race card starting just after noon with only short intervals between races. With the four-hour time difference, it meant that our betting shops were busy from seven in the morning and continuing all through the day into the night as the pools added horse racing from an increasing number of countries to their offering. Anyway, the guy in charge of this pool, the manager, not the owner, asked Junior if he could find someone to work on Saturdays, a particularly busy day, as he wanted to be sure nobody who wanted to place a bet would still be standing in line waiting to be served when the bell rang and a race took off. It wouldn't be safe for anyone in the pool if a thwarted punter of an irascible disposition was to hear that his sure bet crossed the finish line ahead of the whole field. The new employee would have to write up the betting slips for the punters and accept payment for the bets. How hard could that be? I had not only Grade 1 School Certificate, but a Higher School Certificate to boot. I bet not a soul working there even got a place in high school. Yes. I was a shoo-in for the job, not least because cousin Junior was well regarded and his recommendation served me well. I shadowed a cashier for about ten minutes, then was called to man a cage because the waiting area was filling up and the day's card was about to start.

My first client approaches. Race five ten on five seven and eight to place and seven to win. I slide the carbon between the top slip and the duplicate and fill in the numbers that he called. He pays, I give him his slip and turn my attention to next in line. First race three six and one to place. Carbon between slip and duplicate, slip write up, hand over.

A-A A-A wha the mudder arse is dis? I tell she race five and she write seven! Move, move allyuh get out mih way. He pushes to the front of the line. The manager hears the commotion and comes out. He takes the offending slip, finds the duplicate, draws a double line across both and writes VOID. He writes out the man's bet in my book and hands over the new slip to the customer. He doesn't say anything to me. I can see a shuffling in my line, a voice reaches me, Like she eh know wha she doing. I'm completely flustered now. Calm down, calm down I say to myself. I serve customers without mishap until noon when the manager takes over and tells me to go for lunch.

There's lunch in a back room. Creole menu brought in from a woman who catered out of her home in nearby Corbeau Town. At the back of the room is a man sitting at a table by himself. He is short, very pale. His hair is slicked back. I can see red stripes of scalp between the dark strands. He is writing. A diamond flashes on the gold ring on his little finger. Black hairs spring from the back of his hand. He does not acknowledge my presence, but I sense he knows I'm there. His is an alert presence. A quiet menace emanates from him. When I saw Marlon Brando in *The Godfather* many years later I was reminded of that coiled, silent, reptilian power. I pick at the stewed chicken and pigeon peas pelau, something that I would normally have relished. A couple of the cashier girls come in. They sit at the table across from me, say hello, ask how I making out and talk about their lives. All in hushed tones as if in church. I go back to the cage for the afternoon shift. I am slow but I manage without incident. I am paid twelve dollars. I go home.

The next Saturday is uneventful, but on the third Saturday there are races in both Trinidad and England. The punters bet on both. I put the wrong race on a couple slips. They get voided by the manager. Now I am fumbling. I put the carbon in two pages down and a rash of slips do not have proper duplicates and there's a jumble of indecipherable writing under the carbon. Then I put the carbon in the wrong way up and the duplicate is at the back of the slip. I say, Just a moment, to the next person in line. I go to the manager and give him my messed up book. I'm sorry. I can't do this.

That was the last time I stepped out of my teacher's crease to lift my bat at some googly job that involved handling money and/or dealing with anxious customers. Had I gone for the bank job, who knows what level of financial catastrophe I might have caused, too many zeroes on a calculation, the dot in the wrong place? And with the airline, hot coffee on a favoured passenger's lap, perhaps, or not closing the cabin door securely on takeoff? So when I was offered an interesting private tuition job to supplement my teacher's salary, I took it.

The English wife of a local orthopaedic surgeon asked whether I would do homework supervision of their children after school a couple of afternoons a week. She would pick us all up and we would go to their home and afterwards she'd drop me home. Their home in Cascade was my introduction to a style of elegant and luxurious living that I never knew existed outside films and books. I'd been a couple times to classmate Carolyn's home, but no further than sitting with her the front gallery. It was a big two-storey house in posh St Clair and, I should imagine, full of nice things. But at the Cascade house I was inside the house.

Large, yet it didn't announce itself, instead it was airy and spacious and comfortable. There were visible, uniformed staff. When we got there in the mother's roomy estate car, the littlest girl ran towards the cook, all in white with an apron and cap, who scooped her up and popped some sort of biscuit into her mouth. Cook had prepared tea with baked offerings the likes of which I'd never seen before – thick, warm, floury raisiny things that you split open and buttered. There was a maid in a blue uniform with a white apron and cap playfully scolding the big girl as she was picking up the bags and shoes the children were dropping as they ran in. A yardman swept up leaves blown down from a massive samaan casting shade over the long driveway. In that house I was one of the family, moving from the dining room for tea as soon as we got there, to the large study where the children sat round a table doing homework, to the open patio with expansive views of the Gulf for little chats with the charming mother after the session. The children were my introduction to the ease and confidence and freedom that security, security of all kinds, bestows on those fortunate enough to be gifted it. There was a girl of twelve whom I was teaching at school, another girl of ten at the convent primary school, a boy of maybe eight at the convent boys' primary and another little girl, a wild free thing of three or four not yet at school. Years later, when I learned more about English society and class, I came to understand that my position and role with that family was as a sort of governess, paid help yes, but considered by the family to be socially not too far below them.

Not quite at the other end of the social scale but certainly very different was another family whose children I tutored. It was a Chinese family on Park Street, a block south of school. They lived on the top floor of a two-storey building, above their business place, a parlour that served sweets, snacks, drinks and sandwiches to workers, passers-by and shoppers on that busy thoroughfare. My two students, girls a year apart, were at the convent but they desperately needed help with schoolwork because their parents, along with an aunt, an uncle and a resident apo spoke only Cantonese and the fragments of English they needed for commerce. They naturally wanted their children to do well at school, get good marks, pass exams, improve from term to term, so I was to concentrate on the actual school-work, especially the homework, but what I'd learnt from my dealings with the Venezuelan borders was that the real need was bigger and wider than that. The apo remained in the room with us, playing with her baby grandson, but paying close attention to what I was doing and saying. So I had in the apo another student, and there was also a little brother of about ten who sat doing his own homework at the same table and would from time to time look puzzled and I'd ask if there was something he needed help with and spend a little time with him too.

But it wasn't these unofficial students I meant when I said the task was bigger and wider. I meant that these children needed acculturation. Their whole lives were bounded by school and shop and intimate family. They knew nobody but this small circle, had no friends from school or church, did not go outside to play, and had been nowhere but school and home and sometimes church. Such a limited life was not helpful for using English confidently. So I brought storybooks from the library and got them reading outside the school textbooks and there was much in those books, words and ideas and events that they could then use in writing and in conversation.

One day, one such story was about a boy and a boat and the sea. What is the sea? This from the little brother at the table. I first thought it was simply the word that he didn't know, and I went into a description of water, of vastness, of waves, of swimming and expecting him or his sisters to catch on and gleefully supply the Cantonese word. It didn't happen. It was the concept, the experience that they lacked. So yes, they had never seen the sea. These children lived on a small island, in a port city, and the sea was… Park St, Duke St, Prince St, Queen St, Marine Sq, South Quay and the wharf… the sea was five blocks south of where they lived and they had never seen it. How could that be? I decided it was my responsibility to remedy that.

When I became a parent myself, many decades later, I would never, never have allowed my children, my precious irreplaceable babies do what I asked of these innocent parents. Indeed, one Sunday morning my friend Raoul was taking his little Pilar, six, to Maracas Bay and asked if I'd let my Rhiannon, seven, go along too as sandcastle playmate. Is he mad, Paul and I asked each other. Has he completely lost his mind? When I told him no, Raoul said, So, you don't trust me? It was indeed so; we could trust nobody, not even Jesus-Mary-Joseph-Father-Son-Holy Ghost with any of our children at the sea. We couldn't have trusted ourselves not to follow Raoul's car up the narrow winding road cut into the Northern Range, over the watershed and down to the sea and then watch our precious child at the edge of the tumbling, sucking waves from behind a cluster of coconut palms, and then follow them back until she was safely home.

But back then I casually asked these strangers to allow their children to come with me into the unknown. It was a request to which they hesitantly – and after much unintelligible Cantonese twittering like agitated birds among themselves – agreed. Youth is a crass, thoughtless, entitled state. So on the following Saturday I found myself on Park Street, met up the two little girls – the brother who had asked the question wasn't allowed. The parents wisely thought I could manage two not three, and after all, a boy! I met them and we walked along Park Street to Green Corner right by Globe Cinema where the Carenage taxis queued up for passengers and we jumped in the first available one. All along the journey the little girls' eyes widened and widened until they looked as if their faces were only big bright eyes. Everything was new, never before seen.

We got off at Dhein's Bay, a small but fairly frequented bathing spot, with a narrow strip of shaley, grey-brown sand running just a couple hundred yards along very calm water that sent such tiny wavelets beachwards that they merely slipped into the sand without even trying to make foam. We took off our outer garments and hung them from a low branch of an almond tree. I was wearing a swimsuit; the little girls were in panties and vests, but this was quite normal at the time, for who had money for swimsuits? Even mine was a borrowed one, from my boyfriend Jeffrey's mother. I held their hands and we walked into the water. The water covered feet and ankles and then calves and knees and I said, Let's sit for a while. We did so that only their heads were out the water. Then they coaxed each other to splash about and I swam out a little way while watching them play and then floating on my back for a while, drifting into a reverie before I caught myself and looked around fearful that something awful might have happened to my charges, but they were there, looking at me with concern. I took the hands of one and took her out a short distance and had her kick and kick while I pulled her through the water; the other had a turn and soon they were happily taking turns. We must have been there an hour when another group came and the children of that party leapt in with such exuberance and confidence that my two wanted to be braver, but even foolhardy me knew where to draw the line, so we stayed in the shallows.

The girls didn't want to leave the water but eventually, when I checked their hands for wrinkly skin, they came out, sat on a fallen coconut tree trunk and we ate our sandwiches while drying off in the sun. One asked whether the land we were on was floating on the sea like the fishing pirogues we could see in the distance. They asked how did the sand get there; was this sea joined other seas? What were the small islands we could see halfway to the horizon? What were those giant metal balls piled up on the ground across the road behind us? How did coconuts get picked? Where did the road go beyond where we were? Who lived around there? What was the name of the big grey birds, and where did the sea water come from and why was it salty? We put back on our street clothes, crossed the road, hopped into a passing taxi and found ourselves back at Green Corner. The whole family was waiting for us in the parlour downstairs. You should have seen the smiles that broke the tension in their faces. The excited Cantonese chatter running up and down musical scales, the laughter, the huge relief and joy that greeted our return.

I went past the building on Park Street some weeks ago. It's still there, though many of those around it have been replaced by concrete several-storey offices. The family name is on an old, faded sign over the doorway of what seems still to be a parlour, but when I looked in it seemed to be manned by people of indeterminate ethnic mixtures. I wasn't surprised that they were gone. The early seventies exodus, precipitated in part by our

Black Power uprising, stripped us of the bulk of our Chinese population and many others, first and second generation immigrants for whom Trinidad was, in any case, simply a stopping off point, a welcoming and facilitating space where informal trade could be conducted without interference, where children could be taught English at free schools and get internationally recognised school certificates, where money could be made and saved, so the family, much improved, would be able to move up to the next level to Canada or America, where they would stay and raise their own new generation of first worlders.

It was as a teacher that I had my other noteworthy encounter with Mother Columba Carthy. Our brother school, St Mary's College, had a long tradition of putting on an annual theatre production of the Shakespeare set book for that year, with schoolboys in all the roles. In one memorable *Macbeth*, Anthony Jacelon, who was to go on to win the modern studies scholarship, go away to England to study law, come back and become an eminent barrister, sit on every noteworthy board, and subsequently go into politics and become a government minister, was Lady Macbeth. One of my fellow sixth formers was so taken with this actor that she'd stand at the window looking out after school to see him cycle by on his way home. We began to refer to him as Lady and had giggling fits at prayers when the words Our Lady were uttered. Of the three witches, one was Wayne Berkeley, who became a stage designer, Carnival Queen gown and costume designer and the top designer and producer of prizewinning Carnival costume bands and the first bandleader to transform that activity from a messy, casual thing into a smooth business operation. His brother, Oswald, was another witch. The name of the other actor in the trio I don't remember.

I'm guessing that our thwarted thespian looked on at what was coming from an institution that was not renowned for the arts, and thought it was time the Convent took up the challenge. Sheridan's *The Rivals* was one of the set books for English Literature at exam level and Mother Columba decided to produce this play with the girls taking all the roles. She told me of her plan and wanted me to be Captain Absolute. You know, she said, dashing, charming, a little roguish. Ok, I said. She found a wonderful Julia in Susan Goddard and an unbeatable Mrs Malaprop in the amazing Diana Wall. She then searched for a Lydia Languish. She did find a promising student for a role, but the girl, whose name I can't recall (who was really good in the role she was eventually given), was tall, way taller than me, so Mother Columba switched us, casting her as Captain Absolute and me as Lydia Languish. I was delighted. It was the role I'd secretly lusted after – a lead character who is a feather-headed, romantic, misguided, headstrong – but you know if you say you want something, that's your first sure move to not getting it.

Mother Columba made us learn our lines according to a strict schedule, had us read lines to one another, rehearsed us in a variable order of scenes to sharpen our responses. She designed the set; George, the school handyman, whose daughter was at school with me, built it. This had to be made in sections because the hall where the staging was to take place was in constant use. She designed the costumes, went into town and chose the fabric and probably sewed the costumes herself. She taught us how to speak to be heard at the back of the hall; how to move across the stage; how to have a convincing dialogue with another character while looking at the audience; how to speak behind a fan and be believed to be whispering while being heard everywhere; how to use the fan, not as if the day too hot and you want some breeze, but as an essential accessory to coquetry; how to hold and move your body like a real grownup lady with a suitor; gesture exaggeratedly for it to carry and not make it seem too much; how to move in the costume – long dresses with ruffles, tight bodices, clinched waists and wide skirts.

Most importantly, she taught us that when you say your lines they must not come out as tired and over-rehearsed, as if you're fed up with them and know them by heart, but must sound as if you had just thought of it, and when someone else is speaking, pay attention and react as if you're hearing it for the first time. Not one of us had ever been on stage before. But boy-oh-boy was it a triumph, a roaring success! It played to enchanted audiences. The newspaper carried a review which praised every aspect of the performance. I took all of that for granted. Lordy me. Sometimes you think you're the square on the hypotenuse but you're really the square on the smallest side, or not even in the damn triangle.

Recalling this, I realise that Mother Columba Carthy should have been a theatre producer or director, or costume designer, or a choir director (for she was choir mistress for a while and taught us interesting, different songs), or at the very least, been born a man, any ordinary man, any talentless man, any wayward lout, who then could do whatever the devil he wanted, and not be stifled, denied agency. Now that I've looked at her in the round, as it were, it makes me look again at those Irish nuns, not from personal acquaintance, but from what I'm now prepared to speculate on in the light of the world at the time, their world and ours.

Surplus, unmarried, Catholic daughters in big economically marginal families, what do you do with them? What can they do with themselves? This, I'm guessing, was the loudest answer. *Go ye afar, Go teach all nations, Bear witness unto Me, On earth in every clime, And I with you shall be, until the end of time.* They founded schools, lived in communities, adjusting to different personalities and tastes (subject to a superior and to the clergy), stifled their ambitions and buried their talents. They sweated under those restricting habits in our clime, ate what our alien soil produced. They were women with periods and period pain, feelings maybe for each other, maybe for someone back home, maybe for someone right here. They gave up mothers and fathers, sisters and brothers, country. They had no autonomy, could be moved from one location to another at a superior's whim, without consultation or notice. They could go out only with permission from the superior, had no money of their own, no possessions except what was allowed for work or worship. And they put up with us urchins.

How I would have wished for them to be free from the yoke of an authoritarian church and a craven, church-controlled state, even at the price of the difficulties they would have faced as ordinary girls, girls like Cait and Baba in *The Country Girls*. Those girls, whatever their troubles – and those troubles were mainly men – their lives had laughter, love, texture. They were alive. But I'm going to stop before I begin to feel too sorry for those nuns and forget that they, perhaps unwittingly, were instruments of a much bigger project, foisted on us when that Genoese sailor in the service of the Spanish crowns of Castille and Aragon, stumbled on these innocent happy isles and corrupted them irredeemably.

It's like that parable of the blind men in the forest who, on meeting an elephant for the first time, try to identify what they have come across. Each one touches a part and links it to something he already knows. The one touching the trunk says it's a snake, the one touching the ear says it's a fan, another at the animal's side says it's a wall, the leg is a tree trunk, the tail a rope, the tusk a spear. When I was at the convent, I thought I was dealing with snakes, fans, walls, tree trunks, ropes and spears. I was wrong. I was dealing with an elephant. And that elephant, the elephant of organised religion, of which the one I was brought up in was simply the then dominant manifestation, that elephant is still in the room, in this tiny room we call our island home, and it is squeezing the life of critical thought from many of the inhabitants trapped inside with it.

Many, many, years later, I was a graduate teacher for a long time at another Catholic School in Port of Spain, where lay Catholics ran the show, and the clergy were few and far between, thanks to Ireland's EU membership and the concomitant benefits to its economic development. But my experience at that school, when and if I do get around to recounting it, would have to be fictionalised. I don't have the court clothes or money for lawyers. But for many years after parting company with that institution under very unfavourable circumstances – I was made to leave – I avoided driving along the road where the school is situated around the time that the school day ended because, if I'd spotted a particular individual crossing the road as I was driving along, eye would have triggered a flash synapse to right foot, bypassing prefrontal cortex entirely, and my innocent car would have accelerated and plunged right through that individual's path. But there was always the possibility of collateral damage to some blameless child and I couldn't deal with that. *Ne nos inducas in tentationem* as that individual would say, since Latin remains their favourite language of communication with their god.

Why doesn't lightning strike where you want it to? I comfort myself with the thought that when that individual arrives at the mythical Pearly Gates, they will get the shock of their life to discover that god is not a Catholic, god is not Opus Dei and, most wounding of all, god is not even a man. How could it be, I often wondered, that there were people still stuck in the same way of viewing the world that had propelled me to leave. So much had changed in other aspects of life in the country, stirrings of change that began even in my last years as a pupil at school and in the teaching years that followed.

But what resistance there was to change! There were rumours flying around about what would happen when lower-class people, able at last to vote and stirred up by Eric Williams in his history lessons in the University of Woodford Square, decided they would remedy ancient wrongs, put out the comfortably entrenched incumbents drawn from the elite landowners and merchants, and put into power new people, better educated it's true, but of a different hue.

One day at school when I was already a teacher, word raced through the school with the speed and roar of a tidal wave. The men are coming! From one mouth to the next, one scream triggering a chorus of panicked screams, The men are coming, the men are coming. No one asked which men. Everyone knew men of their fearful imaginings were coming and while no one knew what else the men were doing in the city, everyone knew why they were coming to the convent and what they were coming to do – to the nuns and to us, the teachers, the girls. There was screaming, sobbing, rushing into classrooms, the locking of every lockable space and then waiting in silence, a listening silence. Eventually, as the silence became heavy, a few brave ones peeped out and saw that there was nobody. Nobody in the corridors, no one in the courtyard, nowhere were there half-naked black men wielding cutlasses, searching for us. We were safe. I emerged from the teachers' toilet where I'd locked myself in with Lorne, one of the girls who'd fled with me in that craziness, and who was followed by more. It was crowded in there, but the girls stifled their screams, quietened their sobs, afraid to alert intruders to their presence.

The fear of black men, the black bogeyman, and what they wanted from innocent women and girls was and is real, and, in the years that followed, stoking that fear remains a powerful political weapon, even now. When you think about it, about the history of the world, who has throughout time wreaked more havoc, instilled more fear, done more damage, inflicted more suffering, destroyed more lives, created more disruption to and on the people on every one of the six continents, including their own, than white men? So, if we were rational, who should we fear, who should we be running from?

What did we really know of the world, we children of the colonies? World news came via a daily newspaper and an evening paper. There was local radio plus the station at the American base and the BBC. We didn't have TV yet. So, in that comfortable cocoon of ignorance and indifference, what was the global event that got the nuns into a fever of excitement and had them herd as many girls as could squeeze into the art room, most sitting cross-legged on the floor (a position that would have on any other occasion earned a stern lecture about modesty), many others standing round the sides and at the back, the kind of setup that had there been a playful shout of fire, the stampede would have led to innumerable casualties and fatalities?

A crackling, fuzzy, spiky American voice coming from a radio plugged into the socket near the teacher's desk led us through the inauguration of the thirty-fifth President of the USA. John F Kennedy, a Catholic, an Irishman one generation removed, was the ruler of the free world. At last the world would be put to rights. At last Communism would be attacked with full force and would come crashing down as the Virgin at Fatima had promised. Contraception would be banned. A new world was dawning; and we were the fortunate ones to be welcoming it right there in SJC POS.

What else was going on in the world at that time, but didn't impact on me as forcefully? There was something about a war in Korea – the film *Pork Chop Hill* was about that. There was The Bay of Pigs in Cuba and there was Vietnam. All these events had to do with keeping Communism from spreading. In some places good people had to kill other people to prevent them from catching Communism. In other places, if you were communist, you kept other communists from catching whatever was on the other side of the Berlin wall. I was not particularly interested. I'd heard enough about the godlessness of Communism. At school we prayed Russia would fall, but my heart was not in that battle. I was already seduced by the glamour of Fidel Castro in his drab olive fatigues.

When I got hold of the Sunday paper what interested me most were the comic strips, colour insert and the cinema guide. It was mainly from conversations and overhearing others that I got any idea of my world and so my views were shaped by those of my messengers. I had two opposing sources – the *Trinidad Guardian* and The Catholic Church on the one hand, and *The Nation* and Uncle Carmie on the other. When I said this to Uncle Carmie, that I was in the middle of contradictions, he said, Well, Babs, that's good. You can make up your own mind which side you on. I couldn't talk to The Guardian or the Church or The Nation. But I could talk to Uncle Carmie.

When he comes by and I start with, The papers say, or Mother So-and-so say, or Father Graham say, Uncle Carmie would smile, because ah ha! he seeing an opening to a discussion and there's nothing he like more than a lil argument and considering how he home by himself, and he don't frequent rumshops, he can't get too much time with his fellow man, and therefore he had to settle for Marmie and me, as other family not able with him and all that politics talk. So when I say something that sounds promising, he would take off his cap, scratch his head with his one working forefinger, put back on his cap, push back the bench to give him room, lift the bad foot to lie across the other thigh and settle down to an ole talk.

He would listen to what I have to say, nodding all the while, so I'm encouraged to get it all out. So when I come home with something like, Father Graham say not to vote for the PNM because Williams bringing in birth control, Uncle Carmie asking, why that is bad? and I say, because the Pope say is against God's law to have birth control, and he answering, which Pope? and I say, the Pope, the Pope in Rome, the Catholic Pope, you know which Pope. He says, but the Pope only in charge of what Catholics do. Not everybody is Catholic. And I have to see his point; why should everybody do what the Pope say, even people who not Catholic? And I think about it for a bit, then say, England is in charge of us and England is Anglican. He say, that true, England is the Mother Country, but who really in charge? I look puzzled. He ask, who running things? And when I don't answer, he say, is the Legislative Council. Legco. Most of them is big Catholic. Is them who decide. And when I come with, they saying in school that Eric is dangerous. He want to interfere with the Catholic schools, he asking me, when and how? and when I can't say, he tells me not only when and how but also why Eric interfering with the schools, all the schools, not just the Catholic ones.

Just the week before this conversation with Uncle Carmie, while I was helping one of the nuns sort out book lists, I was laughing at a title, *My Family and Other Animals*, but the nun wasn't amused. I was reproved: People are not animals. But then I came across something interesting. Maybe she had left the room and I was left alone and idly looking around. I came across drawings of the floor plans of the buildings in the school compound. At first I didn't recognize what they were, but I was drawn to maps and I oriented the drawings so that I could place where I was standing and work out what was to the left, to the right, and ahead of and behind. The plans were annotated. Each room was numbered and named. The nuns lived at the school, so some buildings and some parts of buildings served as school for us and workplaces for them, others as home for them. On the plans, the school parts were lightly shaded and as I looked closer I could see rooms I knew were nuns' spaces, shaded, as if part of the school, labelled Sewing Room, Staff Meeting Room. The dormitory where the boarders lived was also shaded, but before I could read its function the booklist nun came back.

This came to mind when Uncle Carmie read aloud to me the bits of *The Nation* that detailed the terms of The Concordat between the new government and the Churches. The Church secondary schools would be required to fill eighty percent of their first form intake with pupils who had won exhibition scholarships from whichever primary school they were at. The school could fill the remaining twenty percent of spaces with pupils of their own choosing but taken from a list of those pupils who had passed the exhibition exam but had failed to win a scholarship. In exchange for this, the government would continue to pay fees for the exhibitioners, pay teachers' salaries, contribute two-thirds of the cost of new construction, contribute to maintenance, upkeep, and the overheads of running the school. The school could select its teachers and could apply religious criteria to the selection process; buildings would remain the property of the school and government would have no lien on them. Uncle Carmie folded the paper and placed it on the table. He looked at me. You see how Doc interfering. You know why? Of course I knew why. So that more children could get a good secondary school education and those schools were the only ones that could almost guarantee that.

And when I thought about what the school body, the nuns and the churches would get out of it, it sounded to me as if they were getting more than they were giving up. And they did. My old school expanded, absorbing some of the space formerly set aside for the nuns' exclusive use. Some nuns whom you'd never seen before were brought out as paid staff, teaching religion, doing odd clerical stuff. I'm wondering now what credible title was bestowed on the Head Honcho Insect Vector Control nun of my schooldays to secure her a government salary. Personal Hygiene Inspector?

As a footnote, the Concordat is sixty years old this year. Government has, in the meantime, built dozens of co-ed secondary schools that have no religious affiliation, even while the number of single-sex secondary schools run by religious bodies has escalated. In addition to the original Catholic and Anglican schools, there are now Hindu and Islamic schools, and others. Any attempt by any government to revisit the Concordat is met by firm resistance, not just by their religious bodies, but by the very vocal, powerful and influential alumni associations. This stymies any hope of reform to how schools are managed, and what is taught. I am a product of that system and by teaching in those schools I know now that I have contributed to ensuring their continued privileged status at the expense of the mass of children in desolate, deprived schools, left out of funding largesse, of excellence, of good exam results, scholarships to foreign universities. To them that hath it shall be given, from them that hath not, it shall be taken away, even that little which they have. I am deeply ashamed.

In mid 1961, almost two years after I left school, the government invited applicants with suitable qualifications to apply for a slew of scholarships.

There'd be interviews and successful candidates would be contracted to work for the government for five years after completion of the course. Most were scholarships to teach, as the dearth of graduate teachers was seen as an impediment to the future development of Trinidad on the brink of becoming an independent country. I was awarded a scholarship to study geography.

Where to go to study geography? I knew nothing of universities. Nobody I knew of, except doctors whom I didn't know personally, had been to university. There was, though, my cousin Val, eldest son of my mother's twin sister who had gone to Ireland to study, I think, classics as I remember him being fond of Latin and Greek. He came home for a fleeting visit just after I was awarded the scholarship. With him was his wife, a very pretty and friendly Irish girl, Violet was her name, I think, or was that just the colour of her eyes? They brought me a gift, a box containing a dressing table set: hairbrush, hand mirror, comb and a little glass jar with a lid for bits of jewellery. I have them all still, save the comb. They have been with me in the many, many uncountable places I've lived since then, one of the few things I have from that past life.

What did cousin Val reveal about living away? That it was cold. About university life? That you had to study hard. Two of my classmates had gone to Ireland to study right after leaving school, but I'd never heard from them after they left. I wasn't anxious about lacking information or anything like that; I write this here to show how skimpy was my knowledge, how few were my resources. In any case, not knowing any better, I guess I'd left it up to the scholarship awarding people to make arrangements and let me know what they'd fixed.

Towards the end of that year I got a message from Peter Carr, the young man who was looking after the business affairs of those of us who'd been awarded additional scholarships that I must come into the scholarship office in downtown Port of Spain. Somehow I'm remembering that this was in the building called Federal House, the local headquarters of the West Indies Federation. Once there, I sat across the desk from Mr Carr, who asked me where had I decided to go and study. I hadn't decided. I didn't know how to decide. He said, Which country? I didn't know there were places one could go to study apart from England and Ireland, and as I'd had enough of the Irish, I said England. He took out a book, opened it, and turned it sideways so we could look at the page together.

It was a list of universities set out in a table with subjects along the top. The list ran: Aberystwyth, Bangor, Cambridge, Durham... All offered geography as an honours degree. I didn't go further down the list as I knew that none of the places would mean anything to me except the obvious Oxford and London, so I asked for an atlas. As it turned out, the book had a map with the location of the universities. I chose Aberystwyth because it was on the coast and because it was the first on the list, I assumed it was the best. We must've filled in forms, but I have no recollection of any of the formalities that we engaged in once I'd chosen my university. A letter came to my home from Aberystwyth some months after to say I'd been accepted there.

I got a message early the next year that I was once again to go to the scholarship office to pick up the official note to take to a travel agent to book my passage to England. The next day I went to Lazzari and Sampson shipping agents. I told the person who was serving me that I wanted to get a boat ticket to England. He asked when I wished to travel. I said I wasn't sure. He said, are you going to study? I said, yes. He said, then you should get there by the middle of September. I nodded. I didn't know this until he said so. He pulled out a set of folded papers with fine print and ran a finger along lines saying, hmm, hmm, hmm, then he said, we have the *SS Antilles* leaving 31st August, a Friday. It will dock in Southampton in good time. What class do you want? I guessed this wasn't a timetabling question, about me choosing a group of children to teach, but I didn't know what it meant so I said I didn't know, and I showed him the note I'd got from the scholarship office. He looked up some more stuff and said, you can get a student discount. Let me see what I can give you for this. I said, thanks. He did some working out and then said, I can book you first class. I said, Thanks.

I had understood very little of what had transpired. So a ship had different classes. What does that mean? I grasped student discount because I saw him working out how much to deduct from the full fare. There was some talk about cabin number and deck and fore and aft and port and starboard and berth and upper and lower, but by then I was lost. There was only one thing I understood clearly. I had a ticket to go to England.

Two months later, the ten-member West Indies Federation fell apart when Jamaica left and Eric Williams pronounced that one from ten leaves nought. Jamaica declared itself independent and we did too, with a date announced for our departure from colonial status to independent nationhood. When I heard the date, I felt a chill. You know that story about Saul becoming Paul on the road to Damascus. And he saw a blinding flash of light and fell and saw the light? Was this coincidence of dates saying to me, *You are becoming independent on the same day as your island becomes Independent.* So was this a double dose of freedom? And what would it mean? Of course, the paradox of my willingly going to the former Mother Country when my homeland was departing, did not strike me at the time. I must have been too confused by the uncertainties of what might lie ahead to take any philosophical stance on it. I was looking with a kind of passive helplessness at the unstoppable days rolling onwards, one by one, to that day when I'd be leaving home, friends, the only life I knew.

I was unprepared for this voyage in the dark and I knew it. There was no one in my circle whom I could consult about what to take, what I would find there, what I would need. Gerry Sankeralli said he'd met a young woman from Wales and offered to take me to meet her. So we set off in his car, heading to the petroleum refinery at Pointe-a-Pierre where Rita Wynne-Evans was a contract teacher at St Peter's Private School, which catered for the children of the mainly expatriate managers at the refinery. We met in the clubhouse. She was friendly and gave me her family address in Machynlleth, a small town just up the coast from Aberystwyth, she said. But with respect to what to take, there was nothing I could buy locally that would be suitable because it would be cold there, far colder that anything I had ever experienced on a mid-December night in Belmont, she assured me.

So I packed what I already had, my clothes, a little red address book, my certificates and my acceptance letter from the university along with a matriculation slip. I didn't realise how crucial that last scrap of printed paper was until I was asked for it when registering for my courses at the university and discovered that without it I would be denied registration. There was more that I packed away, too. Any idea of becoming a doctor was one. But I was not unhappy about that. I trusted that something else was for me and I would only have to wait and it would come if I let it. I also lost faith in illusion, in the appearance of things. Marilyn Monroe had killed herself. And I had thought she had a perfect life.

In that period of winding down my life in Trinidad there was another change to our family. Annette, almost three years younger than me, got married to Richard Pantin, her long-standing boyfriend. Richard, Dickie to his friends and family, lived just down our street, our families were close friends, his dad is brother to my mother's twin sister's husband. That Annette and Dickie would one day marry was never in doubt. With me about to go as well, Marmie would be left with Carol and Tony, fourteen and eleven. At the time I didn't think about how losing the top half of her family would affect Marmie. If it had entered my head, maybe I would have thought, well, two fewer, more space, a gradual shedding of responsibility for Marmie. But now I see that it may have been a setback for her, a kind of dragging down, for she would have lost the balance and mutual support that comes with a spread of ages, and it would certainly have placed on her the full weight of bringing up the two younger ones on her own. But I didn't think about it at the time, neither as something good nor bad; I simply didn't give a thought to anyone or anything beyond my own concerns.

Because of this there was no opening for Marmie to talk to me about it, even though she would certainly have seen ahead to what life would be like for her and the little ones with us two gone. She would have had to harbour it all in her heart alone, for by this time Pappy had slipped into near irrelevance in our lives. He'd lost his control as we grew older, he hardly came by at all, certainly not after the day when we two older girls had pelted him with stones to his head after he'd beaten Marmie for the last time, and he had stopped giving Marmie financial support when I started working. Now I can tearfully reproach myself for being selfishly oblivious to Marmie's sudden awful predicament, but at the time I simply didn't give it a thought.

As to myself, how did I see my departure affecting my relationship with Jeffrey, my own long-term attachment? I think that to understand how it came about that I left and he stayed behind I need to go back to the context in which decisions like those were made. All of my school friends who went away to study immediately on leaving school were simply picked up by their parents and carted off to foreign locations. These were girls from families who'd sorted the application for a university place, got the accept-ance, knew how they were going to support their daughter financially and otherwise, arranged travel and accommodation, everything done and dusted while the girl was still at school. Theirs was a mapped-out and organised future and none of them was in a serious relationship; there had been no time for that as they were straight out of school.

Of those of us left behind, with no plans for the future and lots of time and opportunity to drift into a deep romantic commitment, many got married and became pregnant – in any order – situations that brought with them a kind of handle on the future. There were others, like me, coasting along, no plans, no ideas, no direction, waiting for Fate to throw something across our path, without us being aware that we were waiting. But even while not actively blazing a trail of my own, I was noticing what was happening around me to friends and colleagues as they seized capricious Fate and gave him a hard shake up.

Anne Marie, a fellow teacher a couple years older than me, had a boyfriend who got the chance to go to England to study. Anne Marie and Bertie got engaged, married and went off together. Marlene, freshly back from a Canadian university, met Jim who was going to England to study law, got engaged, married, and off they went. Myrna and Lance engaged, went to London, lived chaste separate lives for a year, then married and continued their studies together in matrimonial bliss. So, the usual pattern was the men going away to university, taking wives or fiancées with them, or simply going off alone like my god-brother, Lawrence and my good friends, Lennox Borel and Alloy Chow. I do not know of any girl setting off to study and taking a husband or fiancé with her.

Truth is, as the world was then, while there were many good reasons for a feller to take a wife to look after him in a strange land, and there were many excellent reasons for a girl to be unwilling to allow her boyfriend to go off to a strange land in the expectation that he would return to her when he completed his course of study. Smart girls quickly learnt from the abundant visible evidence of fellers coming back with foreign-acquired wives and the former girlfriends languishing in bitter spinsterhood. So yes, while there was plenty good reason for a girl to secure the ring and accompany, there was no compelling reason for a girl to tag along a husband or a fiancé. So even though Jeffrey and I were romantically bound to each other since schooldays, and I was wearing his ring – a circle of braided nylon fishing wire, so transparent you had to look closely to see it there – it never crossed my mind to make it formal before going away. But we did have an agreement that he would come to London the following year to study photography and work to support himself; I would continue my degree at Aberystwyth and when I finished and had to come back home to fulfil my contract, we would do so together and go back to the life we had before.

In the last week before I left, the excitement and anticipation I had felt vanished as if it was never there. Instead, I felt a numbness. I felt as if I had been turned into a pillar of salt.

Today, at the moment of writing this, it is Monday, the 31 August 2020. Today is the fifty-eighth Independence Day anniversary of Trinidad and Tobago. It is exactly fifty-eight years since I left home, that time of my life I'm trying to remember and articulate my feelings about. Last night I had written the first few lines above, that mini paragraph above this one. It was to be the opening sentences of the new paragraph I'd complete today, carrying on with the story of how I felt about leaving home. I went to bed trying to bring back my emotions of that time of leaving everything I knew for everything I didn't know. Towards the end of my night's sleep, in the wee hours of this morning, I dreamt about my mother. She has been gone twenty-seven years. Today I do not feel I can write more than just this one paragraph.

Yesterday, there was no celebration, no fanfare for the anniversary of Independence Day, no parade of army, police, fire services, health services, no crisp, blinding-white tunics nor knife-creased uniforms, no blazing brass buttons and belts, no shiny medals, no light-reflecting polished boots, neither prancing, gleaming steeds nor slow, open jeep with a standing Madam President taking the salute. There was no procession of the police band through the streets playing calypso and soca, followed by dancing revellers in the infinitely imaginative combinations of patriotic red, white and black that this carnival nation could conjure up. There were no fireworks, and so this morning I do not see posted on Facebook the seasonal laments for crazed pets who'd fled, the traumatised ones who'd stayed, the tranquillised ones that are still dazed. I see, too, that there was no Notting Hill Carnival yesterday, either. Its genteel residents did not need to flee their homes this year ahead of the invasion of the annual wild celebratory West Indian freeup. Neither here at home, nor there in the once Mother Country, are we West Indians in celebratory mode.

Covid 19 is in its second wave here. The number of active positive cases has rocketed from a handful in the early months when we were ranked number one in the world for our quick decisive response, to more than a thousand. To date, 22 of our 1.3 million people have gone forever, taken by Covid 19. Now in my seventy-ninth year I am what is called vulnerable elderly. Today, a new law makes wearing masks in public mandatory for everyone over eight, with a one thousand dollar fine for breaches. Flatten the curve is the mantra for this phase of the pandemic. We follow the WHO guidelines at every step; we look at what's happening elsewhere that's ahead of us in the trajectory of this unseen but present enemy and we take steps to avoid or mitigate. Like that day fifty-eight years ago, my island home is facing an uncertain future. And today, as on that long-ago day, so am I.

In the week before I was to leave home, as immovable as pillar of salt, I watched the arc of my days from sunrise to sunset turning irretrievably, the hands of the clock moving on, one tick, one tock at a time towards my departure. I did look back at what I was leaving, I did look with new recognition at everything I knew but hadn't taken the time to really know, seeing anew every place that mattered but I hadn't bothered to claim, everyone I loved that I hadn't realised I did till that moment when the heaviness of imminent parting weighed on me. So how could anyone know what it meant to me? I'd never said, never understood all that was me and mine and overlooked and taken for granted, dismissed as ordinary. I looked back and it was my lot to become Lot's wife. I didn't know then that it's a saying among those who turn to the half-remembered gods of the old continent that for us New World Africans salt is the worst of poisons, for which there is no antidote. It is what keeps us trapped in this space to which we were brought as captives to be bought and sold, chattel like cattle, with no autonomy over self, over time, over affiliations of language, religion, loves, even our children, for four hundred years. Eat salt and you are grounded, tied to this place forever. Eat salt and you'll be like Gang Gang Sarah, unable to fly back to the homeland, to Africa; you'll plunge, crashing into the sea. In the final days before leaving home, I felt I was all salt.

I had never been on a ship before nor on a plane. I had never left Trinidad, not even to go to Tobago. I had only ever lived in my mother's home with my siblings. I was going where no one I knew had gone before. I was going to a place where I knew no one. And I was alone.

At high tide on the afternoon of Friday 31st August 1962, mere hours after the red, white and blue was brought down and the red, white and black unfurled into the breeze for the very first time, the SS Antilles of the French Line winched up anchor, cast off its moorings and, with a little shudder, drew away from the harbour of Port of Spain. I could feel the throb of the engines at the heart of the ship as I stood at the rail of the deck looking over to where Marmie stood below, her arms at her sides, to where Annette, Carol and Tony stood with her, and I could not stop watching even as they dwindled and were no more and all that was left was the churn of cold glassy foam in the wake of the ship and an undefined throbbing and churning in me.

PEEL

It's like, at the end, there's this surprise quiz: Am I proud of me? I gave my life to become the person I am right now. Was it worth what I paid?
— Richard Bach

STRANGER

My first and only first class experience ever was on the *SS Antilles*, a then new luxury cruise liner of the French Line, the CGT, leaving Port of Spain on the 31ˢᵗ August 1962 destined for its home port, Le Havre, France, with stops in Vigo, Spain and Southampton, England.

I wish I could say I took advantage of what was offered. Truth is I didn't know what a luxury cruise ship or first class meant. I was twenty years old; I'd been teaching for almost three years in the same school I'd attended as a pupil. I had never been outside Trinidad before, not even to Tobago. I honestly didn't know that people got on a boat and stayed on it for a holiday. There had been the school graduation ball when all hundred or so of us, wearing identical Mother Columba-designed long, full, white dresses had gone to Bretton Hall Hotel after the school chapel ceremony and the crowning of La Rosière, but I am not stretching the truth to say that I'd never been to a proper restaurant, hotel, or a ball, which I suppose is where one is exposed to luxury. I didn't know what to expect.

Oops...not quite *never*. There was the time when Gerry Sankeralli, Maureen Marquez, Jeffrey and I went to the brand new spanking upside-down Trinidad Hilton Hotel for dinner soon after it opened. How could I have blanked that from my memory? It was memorable for lots of reasons, not least the menu. The chefs at the Trinidad Hilton had clearly researched our local dishes. What stands out now was the callalloo. At home, callalloo is a side dish to a main course. Its core ingredients are dasheen leaves and ochroes cooked in coconut milk with onions, a whole uncut hot pepper, garlic and a hefty bunch of green seasoning, mainly thyme and chive with the addition of pumpkin. Other ingredients are salt meat – pigtail or salt beef – plus blue crab. You know when it is ready when meat ingredients are soft enough and the ochro seeds go pink. You then mix it all up by swizzling it vigorously with a swizzle stick made from a barked tree twig with at least five little twiglets at the business end. The result is a thick green sludge composed of barely discernable ingredients with bits of animal sticking out. It is a signature Sunday lunch side-dish to baked or stewed chicken, pork or beef, macaroni pie, rice, stewed red beans and green salad. Plopped from a big pot spoon on to your plate, it spreads like viscous green lava, relaxing at its angle of rest quite happily alongside the other stuff, the meat, the rice, the whatever. I love callalloo: breaking open the crab gundy by resting it on the table and hitting it hard with the back of a spoon, teasing out the flesh from the legs after cracking them open with your teeth, picking up the salt-meat bits in your fingers and biting off the flesh and chewing the bones and spitting out the bits in your cupped hand to place delicately at the edge of your plate so it doesn't slide into the rest of the food.

The Trinidad Hilton had finessed callaloo, no-no-no, they'd alchemized it, like Rumpelstiltskin turning straw into gold. They had made callaloo into a refined soup. A first course. Served it in fat little bowls with little side handles, sitting on a plate with a soup spoon – I recognised this from those enforced lunchtime lunches with the nuns that I had to join on the day I was doing some sort of duty. That refectory soup was a thin lifeless Oliver Twist gruel poured from a jug passed around and you never asked for more. The Hilton callaloo was pure magic. Thinner than the Sunday lunch version and served without all the animal add-ons, but you could tell it was cooked with them in, because the flavour of the salt meat and blue crab was infused into its smooth blended deliciousness.

I have allowed myself to be carried away with that memory. So while it was not true I had no experience of luxury, I truly thought I had booked a passage to get from Trinidad to England on a boat whose business was simply to cross the ocean, give me somewhere to sleep and three meals a day. I certainly didn't know the first class ticket I'd been booked was for two weeks on a floating luxury resort.

I shared a cabin with a wonderful girl from Scotland whose name, to my shame, I do not remember – did it begin with an S? When she got back to her home in Perth, she wrote a letter to a friend whose husband was a lecturer in the Geology Department at Aberystwyth, which shared a building with the Geography Department, asking them to look out for me and make me feel at home, which they did. Indeed, they invited me to a lovely dinner at their home, and I committed the disgraceful faux pas of not bringing anything. It was only later that I learned that one takes wine, flowers, chocolate, some sort of thank you when invited to a meal in someone's home. The shame, the shame – this even though my cabin mate was my first and best teacher in matters of etiquette. She had joined the cruise as a holidaymaker further up the island chain and was already properly installed. She showed me where to stow my two pieces of luggage – a small brown trunk and a grey suitcase. In those days luggage didn't have wheels. Luggage was lugged, either by a porter or by oneself.

My companion, who shall be 'S', was kind enough to stop me from opening my trunk and getting out my own soap and towel, showing me that there was plenty for both of us to share; I'd thought they were hers. After I'd showered and put on a fresh dress – the one I'd boarded in was messy and sticky from all the sweaty hugging and salty crying that had taken place on the quayside – S and I went down to dinner at a table for two.

There in front of me are glasses, plates, bowls, knives, forks, spoons all
of different shapes and sizes, more for me alone than we had at home for
all five of us. Then the menu. A beautiful buff folded card, like a greetings
card. The company's logo, the ship's name and a little picture of it at sea,
all pristine white, with its red and black funnel, knife-edge front slicing the
ocean in two, the date and meal stated on the front and inside a list of what
was on offer, in gorgeous cursive print. In French.

I did French at HC and enjoyed the range of style and language we met
in plays by Corneille and Molière, entertaining stories of life in Provence
by Daudet and an adventure memoir by Frison-Roche. We had to translate
unseen passages taken at random from all sorts of other sources. I'd spent
a huge portion of my book allowance on a massive Cassell's French-
English-French dictionary, and I particularly delighted in translating French
poetry into English prose, although as I've noted, Miss Rolston wasn't too
happy with my free ways with translation. The huge omission in my
education was fine dining French. A limited farmyard vocabulary – boeuf,
porc, poisson, agneau – doesn't get one very far in first class on a vessel of
the French Line. And tout le monde who worked on that vessel spoke only
French. Not mainly French, seulement français.

So the waiter comes up to S and me and bows in my direction for my
order. Madame. Ten minutes later I realise that I should have nodded to S,
let her go first and when he got to me say, La meme chose s'il vous plait. But
I don't and I fumble at articulating two things that look like things whose
names I think I could divine. He looks genuinely confused, so I point at the
items I think I pronounced in impeccable French. He's still confused but
writes it on his pad. S reels off several items with aplomb. What is the matter
with what I said? I ask S. People don't usually order two hors d'oeuvres, she
says. I am still at a loss and she explains the menu to me. All the different
parts. The different courses. You choose one item from each if you want all
the courses. She is gracious. I am grateful. He brings my two items and her
one. I watch her with the cutlery. Use the same as her on my first. I start
on the second with new cutlery. He waits till we've eaten all, takes away the
dishes and cutlery. He brings her main course. Something piled prettily
with mini peas, tiny string beans, carrots no bigger than matchsticks. I am
starving. What I ate so far, two dainty morsels of I can't remember what,
filled only my teeth. So I point at hers and say, Moi aussi, s'il vous plait. He
doesn't laugh, bless him, and neither does she. Perhaps good training and
good breeding always come to the fore instinctively.

The waiter brings my real second course, but the appropriate cutlery has
gone with my second hors d'oeuvre so I am now stuck with a strange wide
knife that looks as if it couldn't cut butter in the sun. Before I could pick it
up, S summons the waiter with a little wiggle of her barely lifted hand. He
apologises profusely and brings me a fresh set of the right things. Phew! It's

plain sailing after that. S leads at the table, I follow. Breakfast, lunch, dinner for the duration of the voyage. By the time it was our turn for dinner at the Captain's table, I was Eliza Doolittle after dear Professor Higgins had wrought his amazing transformation, but regrettably without the gorgeous Cecil Beaton clothes. Thank you, dear S, wherever you are. I imagine that in your later life you went on to be a kindergarten teacher somewhere, wiping noses, holding hands, putting on wellies and coats. I hope you thought of me when you helped your little charges with these ordinary tasks. I certainly think of you when faced with a properly set table, and I see you in the person next to me whom I surreptitiously study for guidance.

Writing this reminds me of the irony of my involvement, a couple of decades ago, when with a colleague I used to conduct training courses in advanced business writing for corporate clients. One of the business's other training courses was in etiquette and sometimes we'd be training one group of employees in letters, memos, reports, proposals and the like, while another group was being taught the art of fine dining. For their final exercise they had to sit at table to eat a proper three or four or five course meal while their facilitator was watching and directing a video crew filming the diners. Those poor, poor diners. How my heart bled for them. There they were, quaking, running to the bathroom, squirming in their seats, sliding sidelong glances at one another for cues. It took me back.

That first night on the SS Antilles as I lay in the top bunk of that small metal cabin encased in a bigger, hollow metal space, I could be Jonah in the black belly of the whale cleaving its path through the dark unfathomed sea. I felt utterly helpless and very much afraid of the unknown that awaited me. I wondered about Marmie and whether she was worried about me. She would not know what to worry about, just like me. Her worry would sit in her as mine did in me, a dense lump of alien matter that my body didn't have the right enzymes to process. And that lump swelled and rose to my throat when I thought about Jeffrey.

That last evening, the evening before the ship was due to sail, I went over to his house to say goodbye. The front door was closed but unlocked. There was no one in the living room but I could hear through the open doorway the soaring strains of Moonlight Sonata floating from his mother's bedroom, the middle one of three interconnected bedrooms. I went in and sat on her bed. She turned down the knob of her bedside radio. What time tomorrow? Three. I could hardly say it. She was quiet for a bit, then said, You must go and look for Mario and Jill. I nodded. She looked at me long and puzzled as if she wanted to ask something or say something, but she didn't. Instead she settled back on her pillow and jerked her chin towards the front bedroom.

He was curled up on his bed, his face turned towards the wall. He was wearing the same shirt and shorts he'd been in all day. I shook off my slippers and lay on the bed behind him, spooning into his back. I put my arm across his waist. He took my hand and intertwined my fingers with his. The little braided nylon ring he'd placed on my finger pressed hard into our flesh. How long we stayed there, just like that, still and silent, I do not know but when I closed the door behind me each step I took as I walked home alone in the dark weighed heavier and heavier.

While dwelling on that memory I must have drifted off to sleep, for sometime later I was jolted awake. My first thought was earthquake, and I sat up in bed. When I looked around, I didn't know where I was. The rocking didn't stop. I lay back, closed my eyes and tried to calm down and focus. It came back to me. I was on a ship. On my way to England. It wasn't an earthquake. It was the seaquake motion of the ship.

While writing this, I googled the CGT, the French Line to see whether I could find anything about the enticements with which the SS Antilles must have baited its advertisements to lure its cruise guests into filling every cabin as they had on our voyage. I could find nothing, though I did find that the ship had ended its days in 1971 when it ran aground on a reef off Mustique – playground of the late Princess Margaret – ripping open its fuel tanks and catching fire. Fortunately, all were saved. I guess its early demise made the poor burnt wreck more interesting as a dive site than as a subject of charming social and economic history. One diver reports he collected melted champagne bottles. So clearly I missed out on the bubbly that was on offer. Was S teetotal? Hmmmm. My research threw up one website with something on the SS Colombie. Here's what I saw about the SS Colombie, which I believe must have applied to the Antilles too:

> First Class passengers had the use of the large Main Lounge, large Smoking Room, Nursery, Ladies room, and a Verandah Cafe on Promenade Deck, with a two deck high Main Dining Room on a lower deck. This luxurious Dining Room had wall length mirrors, with seating easily adaptable from long tables seating forty to small tables seating groups of eight, six, four and two passengers. The large Lounge and Smoking Room were both light and airy with wooden tables and beautifully upholstered chairs and sofas. The First Class Staterooms were very roomy with comfortable beds, two matching washbasins with mirrors above, and padded easy chairs and sofas. The First Class marble swimming pool was on a lower deck and of a generous rectangular size with adjoining changing rooms. Second and Third Class passengers each had the use of their own General Lounge, Smoking Room, Ladies Room, and Dining Rooms on lower decks.

Which of these amazing spaces did I visit? The Verandah Café on the Promenade Deck? No. The Lounge and Smoking Room? No. The First Class Marble Swimming Pool? No. Apparently there were also films, dancing, live bands, and live performances. I never went to one. I even failed to get a first-hand account of first-class life at sea from someone whom I knew had been a passenger on one of the SS *Antilles* voyages, despite there being quite remarkable coincidences in this discovery.

Miss Clare Stolls-Fox, a young English teacher, contracted to teach at Bishop Anstey High School, the elite girls' Anglican school, and rival of St Joseph's Convent, arrived from England on the SS *Antilles* on the morning of 31 August 1962 – the very same day that I left on that same ship to head in the opposite direction. I learnt this only a couple years ago at Clare's eightieth birthday party, where her long stay in Trinidad was being discussed. Now Mrs Clare Henderson – she married a Trinidadian ex-WW2 radio operator who knew the entire Lafond tribe and entertained me and himself by reciting their names in a rhyme – Clare and I have long been friends. We taught together at Bishops; she taught my two daughters and I taught one of her three. All six of our children had been friends at the same primary school and yet this uncanny coincidence of same ship, same date, took more than half a century to be revealed. When I discovered this I imagined Clare would be my reliable witness to the first class offerings on board the SS *Antilles*, for which her more sophisticated English upbringing would have prepared her and for which she would have been poised to take better advantage than I. But alas, I was foiled. Clare travelled second class.

And so I slowly slipped into the reality of where I was and why I was there. How did I spend my days between meals and bed on board a luxury liner of the French Line?

I want to be as accurate as I can in the telling here. I didn't keep a diary or a journal, so there's no record to consult, flesh out and animate. Everything I write is from memory and while memory is now somewhat patchy, I do recall a couple of things. For one, I wrote letters. Many, many letters. To Marmie and Jeffrey. To Marmie I wrote about the ship, my cabin mate, the food, the language and, to her, I said that studying French at school was a really big help to me on board. Those to Jeffrey were full of how I felt at the time, full of longing, promises, hope. I wrote about our intimate times together, from our first meeting, he ten, I eleven, the early teen years of slow and gradual exploration and knowledge of each other, to where we were, as we thought ourselves to be, secretly coupled forever. I relived those times in the telling, resurging in me urges that I could then write about in detail. And with the reviving and the recounting there'd be tears falling on the light-grey Basildon Bond notepaper, smudging the Quink royal-blue scrawl traced by the Parker 51. I drew hearts. I drew diagrams. I added lipstick kisses. I know I shouldn't be making light of the adolescent passion and eroticism with which I filled my love letters. And I know, too, that it's not fair, because at the time it was real and painful. But I can't conjure up that old feeling today and lacking that I won't be able to transcribe it into words with any degree of authenticity, so I won't try. Also, how I now feel about that time has been shaped and reshaped by events that followed, both soon after, and long after when we were both already old, and I fear I would diminish by analytical hindsight something that was at that time everything that mattered to us both. But it was letter after letter I wrote on the SS *Antilles*, bulging envelopes thick enough to threaten to split open the glued-down flap. They no longer exist, those letters. Neither the ones I sent nor the ones I received in return from either Marmie or Jeffrey. Too many moves for the three of us, too many new identities, too many new affiliations, so that things like letters that more secure, more rooted people tie in labelled bundles with pretty ribbon and store in the deep drawers of mahogany roll-top desks, preserved for posterity, we restless refugees shed carelessly or destroyed deliberately with each new life. I wonder now whether we, the uprooted children of Africa, Asia and the Americas are doomed to perpetual successive dislocations from one past and another and another.

Mercifully life on board wasn't all eat-sleep-cry-write letters because of a serendipitous sighting regretfully too far along in the voyage.

I discovered that Shirley Ann Innocent, a friend from school, was also on board. I'd been attracted by the sound of roistering on a lower deck and, glancing down, spotted her among a group of people having an uninhibited good time. That's how I would like to remember it. However it occurred, that encounter was my salvation.

Shirley Ann had quickly made friends with the Trinidadians and other West Indians bound for Europe and a *jahaji bhai* kinda thing had developed. During the day I went down to easy-going second class to join them in playing cards, liming and chatting. I discovered that whereas I could move freely from one class to another, passengers could not visit a class up. With my first-class privilege, I could go slumming, but to the other classes I was in a gated community with no passes for visitors.

Shirley Ann and I talked about what we were going to do. She was studying for a degree in Music at London University. I told her where I was heading and why. She told me it would be two weeks before classes started, so what did I plan to do? Jesus wept. I hadn't given it a moment's thought. I really didn't have a clue what I would do when the ship docked at Southampton. The ticket for the journey included the boat train to London Waterloo. Then what? Shirley Ann had her plans already set up. That is the benefit of adequate preparation. You know what you doing, and you know how you going to do it. Fail to plan and you plan to fail; sometimes the glibbest advice is for real. Shirley Ann was going to spend a couple of nights in Southampton at the home of another school friend – hers, not mine – Shireen Billamoria, whose family had emigrated to England a couple of years earlier. Why didn't I do the same and then go with her to London to her sister's, and after that I could move on to that place where I said I was going – what's-it-called-again?. When you're wandering aimlessly and uselessly and someone offers to tie things up for you, what do you say? So we disembarked at Southampton, Shirley Ann and I, now tied together for a two-week adventure.

How did I feel then about what would nowadays be considered foisting myself, without invitation, as a houseguest, on people whom I didn't know? I need to go back to not just myself as I was then, but back to that time, and to the people we were then. In the early sixties (still too newborn to have developed a character of its own), people were genuinely more innocent and more trusting. The usual narrative about unlocked doors, walking about fearlessly at night as well as day, welcoming visitors, sharing food, however little there was, was founded on actual real verifiable fact. At our home, Marmie served whatever she had cooked to whomever was in the yard at the time we were to eat. School friends stayed overnight when school activities kept them late; school friends who lived in the country lived by us during the week, returning home for the weekend. It was never a question of we don't have space; it was always, we will make space. One such schoolmate of Annette's who lived in Valencia was a regular visitor, and to this day Miriam Pierre and I regard each other as sisters. She refers to my mother as Mummy. Her sister Leeta, not a schoolmate, lived with us when she started to work in town. Bed sharing was as normal as food sharing, and I'm not talking here about the blood relations and other people Marmie adopted.

I don't know whether the Billamoria family experience in Trinidad matched mine. I did not know them. But as migrants to England they would have arrived and at first had no place of their own called home. So someone, a relative, a friend, would have taken them in, made space for them, for a few days, a few weeks, a few months. Though settled in their own home by the time we turned up, they had been there for a short enough time to have that early experience still bright in their memory. I'm guessing that a combination of back home living and recent history made it easy for them to be spontaneously welcoming. There's something else tickling a corner of my memory here. Why do I feel that while Shireen's mother was Trinidadian, her dad wasn't a Trini Indian? That he was real Indian from real India. Hmm, and if that were so, would it have added some hitherto unexamined complexity to the family situation?

So, waiting on the dock for the expected Shirley Ann, with me as an unexpected bonus, was Shireen, whom I recognised, and her mother, whom I'd never seen before. Why do I have a sort of shadowy memory of Helen Guyadeen being there – Helen whom I've mentioned copying translations into the copy books of us lazy Catholics during R.E. class? This former classmate had another memorable asset – the most gorgeous, enviable hair. Thick, shiny, black, she had it cut in what was then a very

fashionable style, a pageboy, and hers hung sleek and smooth to just at her
shoulders, where it did the most amazing curl under. Helen, when last I'd
heard, was studying in Ireland, both she and Carolyn Allum Poon going
there straight out of school, a couple years ahead of me, as so many with the
means to do so had done. Why I'm placing Helen there when I disembarked, when I haven't seen her nor heard from or about her for over half
a century, is beyond me, so for that reason alone I'm giving it credence,
because why else would I put her there? So here goes with the arrival in
Southampton one September morning, as I'd like to think I remember it.

Helen is there with Shireen and Shireen's mum. I'm relieved because
here is someone I know, who knows me. Helen's mum and Shireen's are
sisters and Helen was spending time with family. They took us home, gave
us lunch, and we must've chatted, caught up with news from home,
discussed future plans. Normal stuff. Then came bedtime and this I do
remember. Mattresses were placed on the floor. Was that two small ones
or one big one on the floor between two beds or two big mattresses for four
sleepers and no beds? Both mental images seem equally clear, but one sure
thing is we were all sleeping in the same room – Shireen, Helen, Shirley
Ann and I – and we talked deep into the night. The first topic was unusual.

As we lay down, the established duo said to us new arrivals, Listen to
your stomach. We did. Gurgle-gurgle, gurgle-gurgle came the sound from
our stomachs. I had never heard my digestive system at work before.
Shirley Ann was equally startled. Why is that? What's happening? They
found our puzzlement amusing, but could provide no explanation other
than it's what happens to your stomach here. We had soup as a first course
that night, and there was soup as a first course at supper at my hall of
residence at university, too. Could it be the soup? In my next life, when I'm
finally able to be the doctor I'd set my heart on becoming as a child, I'll
research this phenomenon. I know I'll get the chance next time round,
because it's no longer just one scholarship for girls. I think it's four hundred
they award now, and I'd get one even though I won't be doing the three
Maths subjects that often get the full marks that ensure a scholarship.
Maths is clearly the number one subject choice of many of the current crop
of young doctors you come across in public hospitals, because of the
accuracy and speed with which they count off the days of their internship
before dashing off to set up their private practice where there'll be rewards
worth counting.

The two seasoned girls took us shopping next day. Shirley Ann already
had a coat and a jacket – how did this girl know all that she knew? Looking
back, I realise I was dressed in that modestly old-fashioned way, like those
religious women who go round ringing unsuspecting doorbells and reading bits of Bible to whoever comes out. I was already shivering so much that
I had to be lent a thick cardigan before we set off. Buying warm clothes was

therefore high on the list, but pretty soon I exposed what was either a deep-seated phobia, or a simple lack of confidence: I do not like shopping. No, I hate, absolutely hate shopping. And in the case of buying clothes, I hate even more shopping for ready-mades. I do not like trying on. I do not like stripping down in a booth. I do not like looking at myself in a mirror. I do not like the feel on my skin of someone-already-tried-this-on of clothes from a hanger in a shop. I rarely know what size I am. My bust-waist-hips are not standard. What fits on top is too narrow below. If it fits below it's the shoulders hanging off, the armholes gaping. Now fabric is different. Fabric I love. I love silk. I love cotton. I love linen. I love prints, designs, weaves. I have bags and bags of cloth shoved in cupboards, tumbling off high shelves, yardage I couldn't resist when I set eyes on it. But I do not like to shop for ready-made clothes. Nor bras. Nothing you have to try on. There is only one kind of shopping I am a total fool for. Vegetables. On Saturday mornings, no matter what is already in the fridge, I come home with more bhaji, bodi, dasheen bush, pumpkin, caraillee, ochroes, tomatoes, breadfruit, sweet potatoes, cassava, arugula, melongene, pawpaw, sucrier, cucumbers, peppers, than I could possibly consume. If you want to see what lust looks like, just show me fresh vegetables and fruit.

At the first shop window on High Street, Southampton, there's a full-length coat. Grey and white speckles. Faux something with short hair. Faux something with much longer taupe-grey hair on the stand-up muff collar. That's it, I say. That's the one. I don't know whether they were delighted I'd hit the jackpot so soon or horrified that I didn't want to see more. We went in. I tried it on. It fitted. I paid for it with travellers cheques. Eleven pounds something – not even with the classiness that guineas would have conferred. Then they said, You'll need a mac. It rains a lot where you're going. They explained mac. I conceded. In the next shop window I spotted a red mac and bought it. Nine quid. Sorted for weather in just two stops. How's that for efficiency? I lived in the UK for a decade after that. Never bought another coat. Kiss the cross and hope to die.

How many days did we spend at the Billamorias? I can't recall, but one day Shirley Ann told me we were going to London. We arrived at Waterloo Station and at a kiosk there I bought an A-Z. I love maps. We picked up a couple of free foldout underground maps too. With these we worked out how to get to her sister's place. Shirley Ann went into a telephone booth to call the sister. I squeezed in too, to learn how the thing worked. You had to drop a thruppeny bit into a slot in a deep brass box, listen for it to clunk as it hit other coins, then pick up the handset, listen for dial tone and then rotate the dial to each number like a normal phone at home, except that in England the numbers were three letters followed by four numbers, so that you had to find the letters you wanted and that took time to look through and locate. The sister told Shirley Ann what time she'd be home and we followed the route we'd worked out and found our way there.

The sister's home wasn't in Shepherds Bush or Notting Hill where there were plenty of Trinidadian West Indians; it could have been in Goldhawk, or Ladbrook Grove, more rundown, notorious, almost exclusively Jamaican residential districts. (I can't ask Shirley Ann because she died quite young, a long time ago. I heard she had an aneurysm in her brain that struck while she was standing at the blackboard teaching a class back home in Trinidad.) I realised later was that it was a specimen of the type of area where West Indians were forced to look for a place to live and work in a city where there were as many *Room to Let-No Coloureds* signs propped up on windowsills as there were pigeons sitting on monuments of slave traders in public parks and *Nigger Go Home* graffiti – before some clever dick added to one such, *And Who Will Fuck Your Mother*. In this neighbourhood, the No Coloured signs were fewer, so there were plenty of people of colour around. I realised, too, that the finely calibrated colourism of back home – with all the distinct hierarchies from the lightest of chamois leather beige to the darkest of boot-polish black, had been flattened in this new space to a more democratic 'coloured', but not yet 'black'.

Shirley Ann and I did the London tourist rounds by double-decker bus, not a formal tour, just deciding to go wherever. We wanted to see Leicester Square where the cinemas were, Piccadilly Circus, Trafalgar Square, the Palace of Westminster and Big Ben. Berkeley Square, as in 'A Nightingale Sang', as performed by heart-throb Frank Sinatra, was on my list, but I had to leave that for another trip. Time was running out and I had to pay a visit to the Trinidad and Tobago High Commission at, I think, South Audley Street – that name surfaced out of the blue, so it must be right – but the last name of the very nice man there who told me what the scholarship gave me, hasn't. I think that I ought to ask Lenore, then Lyons, now Dorset, former captain of Our Lady's House at SJC POS, later career diplomat, whether there was a Keith Somebody who dealt with student matters in the early sixties, but I don't. The nice Keith person told me that the scholarship awarded me the following: passage to England – done – and passage back home at the end of three years when I was expected to finish my degree, train fare to the university and back after time was up, a one-off twenty pounds warm clothing allowance – spent in advance! – thirty pounds a month living allowance and I think twenty pounds a year for books. I was to set up a bank account when I got to Aberystwyth, write to them and let him know the account details and the money would be paid directly into the account on a regular basis. The money would not be coming from the High Commission but from the Foreign and Commonwealth Office, or did I just make that up? Anyway, he gave me cash for my train fare to Aberystwyth, the name I didn't know how to pronounce until I got there. I thanked him and left.

At Paddington Station where I went to buy my train ticket to Aberyst-wyth, what happened could best be summarised as At Paddington Station I Sat Down and Sobbed. The humiliation started at the ticket counter. I said, I want to buy a train ticket to, and I said it Ah-berries–to–why-th. The man, a pallid nondescript young scrap, who probably ended his working life at that very same window, gave that supercilious smirk reserved for the inferior, when we, in our clumsy efforts to ape them, slip up. He feigned a look-through of a list – luckily it starts with an A – came back quite quickly and reported, I don't have a station by that name listed. I said, but the train goes there. I can write it down for you. He looked discombobulated, let his shoulders sag even further and slid a pad and pencil through for me to write on. He looked at it, nodded and said, when do you want to go? I said, tomorrow. He said, single or return? I didn't know what that meant but I didn't say so because I was by then too afraid that if I uttered another word I would cry. I could hear the people in the queue, as I'd by then learnt to call what was really only a line, start to shuffle and mumble and I could imagine them executing that little pantomime they've perfected – that exaggerated way they have of lifting a left arm, right angles to the body, jerking it so that both jacket and shirt sleeves are pulled back to bare the wrist, crooking the elbow to bring the lower arm forward until the wrist is precisely eighteen inches from the face and looking at the watch with an expression of exasperation. Smart-Ass was waiting for me to answer so I said, *I don't know*. He said, are you going to come back? I said, yes, but I don't know when. I could hear snickers of amusement behind me. I could imagine the raised eyebrows. He said, you want a single then. I nodded. On reflection, I have been treated much more rudely at my own bank, at a branch where I had been going for many years. At least that railway clerk back didn't say, why didn't you say that before. He told me the fare; I paid, got my ticket put it in my purse and walked away, not looking at the queue where I'm sure knowing looks and knowing smiles were exchanged in a rare fleeting fit of casual camaraderie not witnessed since the Blitz.

Then I stumbled downstairs, following the sign that said Lavatory and entered the Ladies where to access a stall you had to drop a penny in a slot in a brass box on the door that operated a mechanism that allowed the lock to slide open. But I didn't know that and I had to wait there fumbling through a veil of tears until another person came in and I could observe how she did it – she looking at me as if I intended some nefarious plot against her – the worst I could imagine was bag snatching. After the demo, I went in, hoisted coat, dress, pulled down panties and let it flow, from bladder and eyes in about the same quantities. Then I blotted both sets of leaked-out orifices with those six-inch squares of that awful, slippery, thin brown paper that the Masters of the Universe passed off as toilet paper. My crude latrine newspaper had more absorbency, yet they could pass off this slippery material with the same pretence of superiority as they passed on what they called Civilisation. I adjusted my clothes, opened the door, washed my hands, splashed my face and went back up to the main hall of the station.

A scant three months later, back in London for the Christmas break, I could have, if I'd wanted to, looked for the clerk and said to him, I'd like a return ticket to Llanfairpwllgwyngyllgogerychwyrndrobwllllantysiliogogogoch. Please. But I didn't. As my mother Yvonne, infallible moral guide, would say, let byegones be byegones.

ARRIVING

When I bid farewell to Shirley Ann outside Paddington Station next day, it hit me that I was now completely alone to fend for myself for the first time in my two-decade life.

The train ride was uneventful; I remember only that we stopped in Shrewsbury, another name I learned to pronounce properly when I heard it spoken by local people, and I remember sheep and cows and trees, and buildings all of the same red brick, along the railway line with their backs to us and chimneys, and bridges and rivers until in the afternoon the train crossed a bridge over still water that reflected gold light into the carriage, and not long after it pulled into the station at Aberystwyth.

This was the end of the line. I got off with my grey suitcase – and there's something here that I'm very hazy about. I have a feeling that the cabin trunk was sent on separately from the ship to my intended address in Aberystwyth. Could it be the case that in those olden times you could have seamless collection and delivery over various transport methods without Amazon? I'm certain that I did get off the train with just the one suitcase and that I did have that brown cabin trunk for the rest of my time in Wales.

A tall young man approached me. Are you Barbara Lafond? I'm Trevor Spencer. From Trinidad. I came to meet you. How did you know I was coming? I asked. I checked the list of expected overseas students and saw a Trinidadian, you, were expected. How did you know I'd be on this train? I asked again. I've been coming to meet the train from London for the past three days. This is Freshers Weekend. I thought you'd be here for it. I had to ask what that was. He told me that first year students came the weekend before classes start to get to know the place. So is this the weekend before classes start? He looked at me as if I'd landed from Mars. Yes. Didn't you know? No, I got a train to come when I thought it might be the right time. Well it is.

Much later, I discovered that this young man, Trevor Spencer, went on to represent Trinidad and Tobago as one of our most distinguished career diplomats. And while I don't claim that his coming to meet me kickstarted his career, I can vouch for the fact that he made my first year a smoother ride than it would otherwise have been. He was kind and supportive even when, and of this more later, some aspects of my behaviour may have persuaded someone of lesser mettle to disown me. Thank you, Trevor, wherever in the world you are.

He takes my suitcase and together we walk across the road, Alexandra Road, and he points out the Geography and Geology Department building – it turns out he's a geography student too – we go along a road signposted, Terrace Road, and I say, where are we going? And he says, Alexandra Hall. Isn't that where you'll be staying? Yes. How do you know? He says, I asked. While I ponder on this, I see we've reached as far as we can go in that direction because there is water ahead all the way to the horizon. I ask, Is this how the sea looks in England? He says, be careful not to say that here. You're not in England. This is Wales. A different country. They speak a different language. I stop. I say, but I won't be able to understand what they're saying. He laughs, looks at my face to see if I'm serious I suppose, and I am. He says, they speak English too. We cross the road to the seaside. There is a long, very wide pavement with a railing on the seaward side. If you look over the railing, the sea is way below with a wide fringe of grey sand with steps to get down to the sand. There is a jetty leading out to sea. It's sunny, the sea is grey but where the light catches it, it sparkles like sea anywhere. How can the breeze be so chilly when the sun is so bright?

I'm openly gazing at the people, mainly young people, late teens, early twenties, in happy laughing groups walking up and down the wide pavement greeting one another. Some words I do understand so I'm guessing it's English; some conversations I don't. Could that be Welsh? Students, Trevor says. They're wearing thick scarves with wide stripes of dark blue and maroon or dark green and red draped around their necks, hanging loose in front. Their coats and jackets are not buttoned up like mine. The fronts of these coats and jackets flap open in the stiff breeze showing knitted garments underneath. I am wearing a bra and panties and a dress just like at home, but with my new grey and white faux fur coat over that. It will be many months before I learn how to dress appropriately for this new climate. My teacher will be pneumonia. Trevor points to a tall grey building at the very end of the grey road, rucked up against a dark grey hill. That's where we're going. I know my room number, it's sixty, and Trevor takes my suitcase up to my room. He says he'll check up on the weekend to see how I'm getting on. And he leaves.

I was twenty years old, and this was the first time I was in a room of my own. I did not treat this as a significant event, because it was never an ambition and maybe also because I was so accustomed to being, just being, anywhere I found myself that it did not strike me as remarkable. So it was with a quite a matter-of-fact acceptance that I looked to see what there was and where to put my things. There was a narrow bed, a desk with a cork pin board on the wall above it, and a wardrobe with drawers at one side. I unpacked.

My door is open and I look out when the door across the corridor opens and there is a girl coming out. She smiles and a dimple winks in one cheek. Her front teeth are slightly bucked, making her look sort of vulnerable. Hi there, she says. An American? Here? I'm Harriet Hendricks Hunter from Houston Texas, originally from Shreveport Louisiana. Mah daddy moved us there cause he's a Vice-President at Standard Oil. Those are places and things I've heard about and I nod and smile. I tell her my name and where I'm from. She asks where that is. I locate my island in relation to bigger places. A couple of weeks later she comes into my room waving pages of airmail paper. A letter from her mother. Isn't this a howl. My mom asked if you speak French. Seems her mother thinks Port of Spain is the same as Porte au Prince, Haiti.

At that introductory greeting, she tells me she's on a year's exchange from her university. Tulane. *Tha Harvard a tha Saath*. That's how she says it. I don't want to betray ignorance, so I don't ask about how people get exchanged. How did she pick here, who was she exchanged with, and why? She's doing political science over there, international relations it's called over here. She'd be going into her third of four years over there, but she'll be with the second year students over here. She's come over to Europe with a whole bunch of students and they toured Europe before she got here. London, Paris, Madrid, Rome, Amsterdam, all those European places. Took them a whole week. She's expecting her prints in a couple days. She'll show me the photos when they arrive. Are you going down for tea, she asks. I don't understand. She goes to her room and returns with a handful of printed papers. I got a whole bunch of stuff, she said. She shows me pages and pages about this building, Alexandra Hall. Its history and facilities, mealtime schedule and sample menus, staff names and functions, fee structure and payment deadlines, rules about times to be in by at night, guest visiting days and hours. I don't have that stuff to set me right, so I go down to tea with Harriet Hendricks Hunter from Houston, my new friend and, although fellow foreigner, my guide. She tells me much, much later that I'm the first nigra she's ever known. I'm dropping that and leaving it right there. But I'll add that I didn't let her saying that take away from the friendship that we had built up in the meantime. And we remained friends for years beyond her exchange year, my three years at Aber and my decade in Wales. I didn't ask her whether she got to know any other nigras back in the States and she didn't say. America is America and Tha Saath is Tha Saath.

That first day we sat at a table set for six and were joined by four other freshers. I, who had spent almost three years at home before I got the chance at university, was easily the oldest first-year student in hall. People my age were in their last year and would leave at the end of it. For everyone else in my year, only the summer holiday separated schoolgirl from university undergraduate. My tablemates were Jyotsna Bhadyia from Kenya, long hair in a single plait down the middle of her back, who wore only saris with a cardigan and coat every day for three years; Mysoon Rassan from Mosul, Iraq, poised and sleek, in classic European style – she immediately made me think of Farah Diba whom I'd seen in newsreels with her husband, the Shah of Persia; Joanna Mycock, from Colwyn Bay in North Wales, but not Welsh; Alison Roots from North London, who always had a genuinely earnest and interested look, leaning forward and peering through her glasses and a long blondish fringe. Alison and Joanna shared a room as did all freshers except overseas students. We were assigned more expensive single rooms, apparently a most enviable state which natives didn't qualify for until their second or third year. Privilege or discrimination? Only now the question arises. Then it was an unquestioned privilege and one I came to value highly for the easy privacy it offered me, while Joanna and Alison spent two years negotiating with each other for undisturbed time with boyfriends on weekends.

Freshers Week was great fun. I went to every possible booth to choose which courses I'd sign up for along with geography; you had to read for three subjects in the first year. I went first to the geography booth. Gentle folk. Fellers seemed okay, quiet, not bad looking, girls the same. Next I went to check French. The students, mainly female at that booth, were off-putting, too confident and sophisticated. I went to English, Welsh, German. None appealed. Everybody was studious looking – long, lank hair, glasses, as if they spent their lives in libraries. I didn't get to history or international relations because I stumbled upon geology. Tall, slim, long-haired, athletic young men in jeans and thick, cable-knit, roll-collar sweaters, leather boots with spiked soles, picks and hammers, maps and rocks, crystals and microscopes, bits of fossils. They promised adventure with benefits. I wouldn't be allowed zoology, my HC grade in self-taught biology, a mere credit, wasn't good enough to be let loose dissecting amphibians and small mammals, but botany said they'd have me. Plants are as nice as animals, I conceded, especially trees and seaweed. So my fate was sealed. I signed up for a BSc Honours in Geography, with Geology taken up to finals and Botany for one year.

The president of the students' union introduced himself as I was course browsing. Would I consider entering for Fresher Queen? I'd been seventeen, eighteen, nineteen, twenty – the ripe-for-the-plucking Carnival Queen contestant age in my own homeland – and nobody, not Cannings, not Sprostons, not JT Johnson, not SS Jaleel sweetdrink, not even Seemungals Variety Store on Belmont Circular Road (where I'd stopped to buy odd little things from age eleven and who must've witnessed and marvelled at my blossoming), no sponsor ever approached me to represent them at the Jaycees Carnival Queen competition. They picked the few fair-skin girls out from us mass of browns and blacks. Here in Wales, this feller was talent-spotting for a brown-skin girl from among the wash of blondes, brunettes, gingers and redheads. So I agreed and was the first overseas student to be crowned Fresher Queen at a gala dinner dance at the Ocean View Hotel ballroom, to which I wore one of my unsuitable dresses from home, a green silk one in which I passed a chilly evening among native folk sensibly swaddled in wool.

Then follows my shame. It was Snakes & Ladders with nose up in the air at the head of a snake and prattaps! Flat on backside at its tail.

At another event that weekend, some newly liberated freshers, now qualified to legally consume alcohol, and free of home and school shackles, went a little wild and inflated condoms as balloons. This is 1962. Then the word, condom, didn't seem in regular use – it was French letters or rubber johnnies. Those days you couldn't walk into a chemist or pharmacy and select a size, a texture, a thinness, a strength or even a flavour. If you were in a gent's hairdresser, you might be asked in a discreet whisper, Anything for the weekend, sir? So, getting their hands on condoms was quite a feat for the freshers, but inflating them like balloons on the promenade caused a huge bacchanal between Town (who had a seesaw relationship of mutual dependency and mutual animosity with students), and Gown (who had Janus-like, irreconcilable responsibilities for upholding *in loco parentis* and fostering intellectual and personal freedom).

The national press got whiff of the scandal and headed from the capital to that remote mid-Wales, provincial seaside town. They interviewed the usual suspects in town, gown and student body, and then, because it was freshers weekend, they interviewed the celebrity of the moment, The Fresher Queen from Overseas. The black and white photo in the next day's front page of a national newspaper did not do me justice and neither did the interview. I expressed neither horror nor condemnation of the freshers' behaviour, not because I was liberated, but because I, at twenty, had never seen a condom and was unaware of their intended use. It led to a lifelong distrust of both the press and newspaper photography.

The scandal also tested my nascent friendship with my fellow-exiles, especially the two Trinidadians, Trevor and his pal, Rudy, whom I was yet to meet. The only other person from Trinidad there, a girl who was at SJC a couple of years before me, didn't identify as Trini. She was Indian to the Aber community – and so was unembarrassed by my unseemly exposure. But all that passed and I entered fully into the rhythms of life in Aber and especially in Alexandra Hall.

Hall provided us with three meals every day. Breakfast was a fluid time, available from seven to nine. You came when you wanted and sat with your friends. On offer were eggs, bacon, sausages, toast, cheese with toast or plain sliced bread, baked beans on toast, cheese on toast, spaghetti in tomato sauce on toast, apples, bananas, tea, cereal and milk – that is fresh milk, unlimited and available round the clock in big jugs left on the serving counter of the dining room. I developed there a lifelong love of milk, real milk. I learned that when someone said tea they meant dried leaves measured out, put in a warmed teapot, scalding hot water poured over them, lid on pot, knitted tea cosy over, and left to brew for three minutes, poured into a cup into which a little milk had been put. I didn't like tea. It tasted like what it was, an insipid brown liquid leached from dry leaves and smelling like the stagnant slimy algae that coated drains. I'd been raised on cocoa, the drink of the gods. At home, logs of cocoa shaped from ground cacao beans, grated, boiled with condensed milk, a rich butter rising in little globules to the top and forming a skin that silked your lips with every heartwarming, grateful-for-life sip of cocoa tea was my idea of tea. My *camellia sinensis* affectation and addiction came years later – after sensitive and knowledgeable tutelage.

We came back from our morning classes for dinner, which is what I learned lunch was called. It was a formal meal. You didn't sit with your friends then, you were assigned a table with five others from all the year groups, with a final year student as the head of the table. The table was set with cutlery and with two serving dishes of vegetables. At the head of table was a stack of six plates and a little book with our names where attendance was recorded by the head of table. When we were all seated, the head of table went to the counter and brought back the main part of the meal. I absolutely loved food in hall. It was new. It was different. I couldn't understand why the natives kept complaining about hall food and missing home food. The other overseas students, they missed home food. Not me. I loved hall food. It was an adventure, an exploration in new ways of preparing meat and fish, vegetables, fruit, eggs, milk and cheese, butter. Meat, two veg, pudding is the dismissive summary I know, but just you open up each of those categories, and see what interesting stuff is inside.

It could be shepherd's pie, a casserole of beef or lamb; fleshy chunks of cod in a white sauce; cheese pie; minced beef stew. The head of table spoons a serving on a plate and passes it to the girl on her left who passes it round the table till everyone has a plate. Then the two bowls of vegetables are passed round. One is always potatoes – tiny whole ones with skin on, peeled boiled ones, or peeled, boiled, mashed ones – and the other of peas or cabbage or cauliflower or green beans or carrots, or those wonderful tiny, tight little cabbages I met there for the first time – brussels sprouts. Oh, the vegetables! There is salt, black pepper in glass shakers and mustard in a little stainless steel pot with a hinged lid and a tiny stainless steel spoon, its handle poking through a hole in the lid. At the first lunch I picked up the mustard. Everyone at the table looked sidelong at me as I spread it lavishly over my green beans and potatoes. I thought I knew mustard. I'd seen people in films draw thin, parallel, yellow lines of mustard over the thick line of ketchup along the top of their hotdog. They then would bite in, lick their lips and chew. I discovered to my everlasting antipathy that English mustard does not work in long lines. It works in tiny dabs at the edge of the plate. Otherwise it brings tears, coughing, choking, swollen tongue and raw lips. It is a lethal weapon. I imagined I had discovered, mouth first, that deadly mustard gas written about in WW1 poems, though it is, of course, not the same.

The main dish at Sunday lunch was a platter of sliced meat. Beef with horseradish sauce and Yorkshire pudding, pork with applesauce or lamb with mint sauce. Chicken hadn't yet become a mass-produced meat item, and the hills around were dotted with sheep; cattle came from family farms nearby, and I guess pigs too. Aberystwyth was a market town. On Mondays, farmers came with live animals to the market near the railway station. There must have been an abattoir, but I can't remember one, perhaps butchers with shops in the town actually butchered. The rare vegetarian or religion-restricted girl had a vegetable rissole instead of that delectable array of cooked animal flesh. There was dessert, called pudding or sweet. There I met apple pie, blackberry pie with top and base of shortcrust pastry, sponge pudding, spotted dick, jam roly-poly, apple crumble, trifle, fruit salad, and, best of all, heaven-sent lemon meringue pie, a Sunday special, all served with custard sauce or whipped cream poured from a passed-around jug.

Supper was informal, back with friends to recount the doings and happenings of the day over soup – brown Windsor or tomato – followed by what? For the life of me I can't recall. On Sundays there was an earlier meal instead of supper. Called high tea, it consisted of salad – lettuce, tomatoes, cucumber with bottles of salad cream (a sort of thin, pourable mayonnaise), beetroot and onions pickled in vinegar, gherkins, hard-boiled eggs, Cheddar cheese and Caerphilly – which I'm still in love with! – and thick slices of ham, and fruit salad with cream for dessert. Bread? I don't think so. I don't remember bread at any meal except breakfast. I guess we had a cold meal on Sundays because kitchen staff went home after their labours over the special Sunday lunch.

The staff were such kind, gentle ladies, always wanting to make sure you were happy and enjoying what they'd prepared. I'll say more. I never met an unkind person in all my decade in Wales, except perhaps one potential landlady who refused us accommodation and I'm not going to rub in why. And she was apologetic, saying honestly that she didn't think she'd be comfortable sharing a kitchen and bathroom. And, quite truthfully, neither would I. At this distance of time and place, I see her as someone who would very likely have been moved by time and circumstance to be more open; she may even have eventually thawed to accept the wrong sort of neighbour or, who knows, in-law.

At the helm of Alexandra Hall was Miss L. Powys-Roberts, our Warden, who had an elegantly appointed suite of rooms on the ground floor where she called in any girl she had reason to see. A tiny lady, with short, permed, mousy hair, a pastel twin-set, a just covering knee-length skirt of Welsh wool – a kind of tweed of deep mossy green and russet – sensible brown Oxfords and skin-tone stockings, with a PhD in History and a self-effacing manner. We saw her only at Sunday lunch where a rotation of students were invited to join her at head table, rather like the captain's table on an ocean liner. She ran things through subordinates, but she had a firm handle on everything. She knew every one of the almost two hundred girls in her care. When you lunched with her she knew your name, where you were from, what you were reading, who you were seeing and what time you came in at night (and maybe what you drank at The Bluebell). But only the first three came up in conversation. Like the queen, she spoke to everyone and engaged the table in chat about current uncontroversial topics, the weather especially, about which there was always much to say.

Sometime in the second week of every term of the nine terms I spent in Alex, I would find a note in my pigeonhole inviting me to an audience with Miss Powys-Roberts. My hall fees were overdue. And every term I would say the same thing. My scholarship allowance is thirty pounds a month. It comes into my bank account at the start of the month. Hall fees are sixty pounds a term, therefore I can't pay fees until the beginning of the second month of the three-month term. Of course, I did pay then, but it meant I had nothing by way of spending money for two months. At the start of the third month, my thirty pounds made me financially flush for the first time in the term. She understood, and graciously let me go into arrears every time, but I still had to go in and explain. The other residents, the local girls, got a means-tested grant, a free sum of money based on parental income that came at the start of every term and so could pay their hall fees on time. My Iraqi friend, Mysoon, got a fifty-pound a month scholarship allowance and I think her hall fees were covered separately. So I alone was a consistently bad debtor.

Trevor Spencer was on a Trinidad scholarship too, and his allowance was the same as mine. How did he manage to pay his Pantycelyn Hall fees on time? It wouldn't surprise me to learn that Trevor had the presence of mind to come to Wales with a float that enabled him to be always ahead of expenses. He told me long after that I could have written to the High Commission and asked for an advance, say two months at the start of the term, but I never thought of doing that. And apparently, I could have got a grant to go on holiday. But I didn't know. If I were to draw up two columns: What I Didn't Know and What I Did Know, the first would run to three or four pages while the second would be at best half a page.

Nurse Evans was our Matron at Alex. A sweet old lady – wait, she can't have been more than fifty-something; how arrogant is twenty to deem fiftyish old – she took care of the girls' health. It was she who, when I'd been in Aber less than a term, alerted one morning by the cleaner that I was still in bed and unable to rise from it, sent for the doctor, quick, quick, quick, and he came with his black bag, took my temperature, felt my pulse, listened to my chest, looked at my throat and pronounced bronchial pneumonia. What cured me? I don't remember. I don't want to say antibiotics because I'm not sure they were in common use back then, but what was cured was my urge to run outside onto the promenade in the flimsiest shortie pyjamas at night as Texan Harriet HH and I had done, when we'd spotted through our windows the phenomenon we'd only seen in the movies, to catch on our upraised faces and stuck-out tongues the first snow flurries of winter, that winter of 1962 of record-breaking meteorological legend.

Our porter-guard-watchman-security-janitor at Alex was Mr Jones, another old person. He, I think, was really old. He moved around with dignified care. He kept the register of resident girls' goings out and comings back in. You wrote your name and time of going out in a ledger open to that day's date and signed the time when you came back in. This register kept tabs on our movements, but it was also useful when the one phone in the building rang and the girl on phone duty had to find the person for whom the call was intended. How grateful you were when, on glancing at the book, you could say to the caller, sorry she's gone out, instead of having to check her room number on the residents list, run up flights of stairs to knock and announce a phone call, or be greeted by a sign on the door that said, In TV lounge, and you'd run back down to the ground floor where you'd come from to find said callee. At ten o'clock on weeknights and Sunday nights, and at eleven on Saturdays, Mr Jones shut and locked the door. He'd come out a few minutes before and flash the light over the door to warn everyone stealing a last snog with their boyfriends against the railings of the promenade that time's up. If you were out after that big front door was locked, you had to ring the bell to be allowed in and no doubt had an audience with Miss Powys-Roberts the next day.

We couldn't have been more than two weeks into our first term when one of my tablemates suggested going to the hop. This was a regular Saturday night dance held in a basement space somewhere along the front. Most hop attendees were freshers who hadn't yet hooked up with a boyfriend or girlfriend. Jyotsna said she had some work to do and Maysoon reminded us that she was engaged to someone back home and didn't go out to places like that. I, too, had told everyone I was engaged, but more of that later. When we got there we went straight to the bar and, with glasses of either yellow or orange soft drinks, joined other girls lined up along one wall. The boys stood along the opposite wall, clutching half pints of beer. Over on that side, there'd be jostling of one another, an occasional burst of laughter, a spilled drink. We girls would be chatting, not really paying attention to one another, but casting sidelong glances at the other wall.

Someone was playing records – the word deejay either as person or an occupation wasn't common yet – and the amplified sound came from just a couple of speakers fixed high on the walls. It took about an hour, and maybe two unaccustomed half pints, for the boys to agree among themselves who would form the scout party to make a recky of the other side of the room, having already decided which of the girls they would approach.

I once read some advice in a photography book that struck me as a deft bit of psychology. To find models to practice your photography on, it said, go to your little local beauty contests and, after the results are announced, go to the second or third-placed girl and ask her if you may take her picture. With the winner mobbed by photographers, your girl, downhearted, would be grateful for the attention and one pretty girl is as good as another.

At the hop, I watched the approaching boys as they walked towards us girls, and yes, indeed, they singled out those they felt were less likely to rebuff them, yet passable enough for the boy to feel he'd got an attractive girl in his arms. By the second dance the boys got bolder and soon the dance floor was crowded. I did get asked to dance, but reared on bolero, calypso, waltz and castilian, with a passable effort at cha-cha, I wasn't up to whatever it was and after a couple of failures and much more soft drink than I liked, I went back to hall. The hop wasn't for me. I didn't understand it as a way for boys to meet girls. It seemed so premeditated and obvious. Anyway, I was too old to join other freshers in search of amorous adventure and besides wasn't I promised to someone back home?

And there was something else that baffled. It was to do with money. Everyone had limited means, as did I, but there was a way in which people kept a running account in their heads that was puzzling. After a lecture, a group of us would walk up to a café for a hot drink. A cup of tea was sixpence, coffee – not a popular choice – was more, seven or eight pence. If I was in the line ahead of let's say Lucille, and I said to her, keep us a seat and I'll get yours and I brought the two cups over and handed her the tea, she'd want to give me the sixpence and when I refused she'd say, I owe you one, and next time, the very next time, she'd insist on getting my coffee and I'd be rummaging for the odd penny or tuppence to make up the difference. And everyone was like that. It's not going Dutch, everyone paying for themselves, it's a scrupulous attention to trading relations that made any encounter involving money uncomfortable for me, and while I adapted eventually, I could never bring myself to regard it as a natural way of doing things. It isn't that they weren't generous; the girls would come back after a weekend at home laden with homemade treats to share. Laverbread cake was a new excitement for me – all we do with seaweed back home is make seamoss drink – and they were kind to put aside your supper if you'd run off somewhere and would be back late, and they would lend you their notes if you skipped a lecture. People never specifically asked for reciprocity, but the money basis of exchange always seemed implicit. It jarred to hear someone say, my dad bought me this jumper, or my mum bought me this pair of shoes. It's the *bought* that got to me. It sounded so transactional. In my head ran all sorts of thoughts. Of course, mum and dad paid for things you own. You don't work. They do. You live in their house. They're supposed to buy your jumpers and shoes. Why, I wondered, why not *gave*? Oh what nice gloves, I say. My sister bought me them, comes the answer. I gave up. It's just a verb after all.

Culture shock. What a wonderfully handy term. So complete, so all inclusive. I wish I had it then. How comforting it would have been to replace the self-defeating words I had to describe my mishaps – clumsy, stupid, ignorant, know-nothing misfit – with *culture shock*! Dear Stuart Hall, where were you when I needed you most? But I wasn't the only overseas student, as we were then called. How did the others among my friends deal with culture shock? I think that Jyotsna and Mysoon were more focused than I and steadfastly put their studies first, so that as long as they understood what was going on in the lectures and were able to produce work of the required standard, they didn't feel the need to preoccupy themselves with what was going on around them, nor to fight or question it. I envied the easy accepting way they slipped into the way things were done.

I'm trying to figure out why it was not so for me and I go back to my first Aber friend, Harriet HH, and I'm beginning to realise that of all the new people I met, she was the one whose accent, vocabulary, references I understood most readily, for while we were poles apart in wealth, expectations, family life, race and class, what we had in common was a culture. For her, it was a lived culture, for me a received one, but I knew what she was talking about, and we spent time together without the need for interpretation or explanation. We had a shared background of comic books, magazines, films and pop music, so when she came back from shopping one day with bathroom scales, I immediately understood how important it was for her to know and record her weight. Daily. *Seventeen* magazine had instructed American girls about weight/height ratios and the relationship between a girl's figure and her chances of being asked out on a date. The English and Welsh girls didn't see bathroom scales as an essential item, didn't know or care about their weight, couldn't fathom her obsession. She went shopping again and came back this time with a record player into which an LP fitted snug like a foot in a shoe. We sang along with Ray Charles and Betty Carter to 'Baby it's Cold Outside' and probably accepted the lyrics and performance as a clever seduction and perfectly acceptable, if outside our own experience, so when I posted a link to the You Tube recording on Facebook just a couple years ago, I was a little taken aback when it triggered a barrage of comments about the sleaziness, bullying, gaslighting, patriarchy, MeToo, male-female power imbalance in the song.

Since I now know terms like lens and prisms, I took the pushback on the chin.

That I understood Harriet does not translate to Harriet understood me. Harriet wanted to be understood. I didn't. I wanted to understand. Besides, I suspected that if I talked about myself, my family, my life back home, what I did there, no one would find any points of similarity to connect with. There was nothing of me and mine that had come into their lives before to make a point of entry for me, and I brought nothing to pioneer Trinidad into my new space. I didn't bring either music or dance, nor cuisine or craft. So, while I was ready and willing to learn, I didn't feel in a position to teach. Come to think of it, none of us four, no, three Trinis brought with us anything culturally specific. I think we saw ourselves as West Indians, even though at that time there weren't other islands represented. Rudy White, tall, big, handsome, head-turner, so brilliant that he got a first in philosophy and the following year a first in English, played sport. He was on the university rugby team, though meeting that sport for the first time in Aber. Trevor Spencer, tall, good looking, suave, well respected as a debater, played cricket. And there was me. All of us adjusting and shaping ourselves to fit into our new milieu. Integrating.

Was Harriet HH happy at Aber? On balance I don't think so. From what I'd gleaned from her and films about American universities, they were big sprawling, manicured, glitzy-glossy campuses with all mod cons, in which students were tightly organised in clubs, teams, residences, with lots of activity centred around membership. There were big games in big stadia with teams and allegiances, matching sweatshirts, cheerleaders, dating, drive-ins. It seemed an interlinked, homogenous social scene, closely monitored by staff and representative of a single social class. Students had their own cars; their rooms were outfitted as private suites; people knew the status of one another's parents. In Aber there was none of that. You were pretty much on your own to do what you wanted, how you wanted. No one held your hand. No one cared that her dad was a VP at ESSO.

It might have helped if she was happy with her courses, but she wasn't. How could she be? Poor girl, to have arrived, the lone American, in the middle of the Cuban missile crisis. Try as she might to defend Florida, a mere dozen miles from Red Castro, she faced stiff opposition from those who objected more strenuously to the crescent of American placed ICBMs pointing at Russia from Turkey. When that simmered down, there was the old grievance of the Korean War for fellow students to revive, until the USA, wasting little time, found itself getting more deeply involved in Vietnam to make her life even more miserable. The simplistic explanations of these events that she had learned back home, about the evils of Communism, the domino theory, and the righteousness of American exceptionalism could not stand up against her fellow students' deeper, more complex, more nuanced analyses that stretched back in time and space, with an awareness of that long history of Empire and almost half of world coloured pink and which was coming to an end. The debacle of Suez had taught many younger Britons about the folly of overseas expeditions. It might have helped, too, if Harriet's hair had held the curl she'd carefully put in with setting lotion, rollers and a salon-type hood hairdryer she'd bought for her Saturday night date with Jim, and it had not collapsed into its natural limp state on exposure to Aber's legendary damp, after half an hour. It might have helped, too if she, after running her hand through Jim's enviably wavy locks, hadn't compared it to a sheep's fleece, at which he took umbrage and the evening cooled rapidly thereafter.

Over the course of her year in Aber she kept up a correspondence with Felipe, a man she'd met in Madrid when she did that whirlwind European tour at the start of the year abroad. That provided a lot of comfort for her, and fodder for our mealtime conversations where she had a sympathetic and supportive sisterhood in her trials. Saw a letter with a Spanish stamp in your pigeonhole, someone would say and we'd hear about Felipe missing her, telling her to visit soon. That awful Dave, we'd say, commiserating when in her tutorial she'd been painfully wounded by an anti-American barb from the said fellow student.

But if Harriet and I shared New World perspectives, there were some things the English and Welsh girls and I had in common. Our school systems had major exams at eleven, sixteen and eighteen that determined our futures; we had read the same literary texts and admired the same authors; the same laws governed us; we shared a constitutional monarchy. We drove on the left. We said pavement, policeman, post, lawyer, murder, tomahtoe, not sidewalk, cop, mail, attorney, homicide and tomaytoe. We said 'going out with', not 'dating steady'. But that's a different kind of commonality and I don't know the correct terms to use to distinguish them. Harriet's presence, our shared hemispheric view of the world was like a hand in front of the sun, hiding everything, everyone else. When she was no longer there and I began to know the other girls better, I discovered how lucky I was to be at university in Wales where many students were Welsh and rural; they were the first in their family to go to university and were financially dependent on their grant. We found we had such a lot in common, including enough ignorance of shared if problematic colonial history to make for easy and equitable relations.

The quote 'There's no such thing as bad weather, only unsuitable clothing', summed up what I realised with every trip from my warm, centrally-heated room to the world outside where reality bit so hard it forced me to admit I had to get more appropriate clothing. But where and how to start? Not having built up a suitable wardrobe over time like the girls around me, starting from scratch seemed an insurmountable challenge. I'd need different kinds of clothes for different occasions, I thought, just like home. Aber wasn't a fashion mecca and what I saw in the shops – twinsets, tartan pleated skirts, straight skirts in wool – didn't appeal. Everything seemed too heavy, dull, muted, monochrome, discreet, as if the purpose of their clothes was to blend in with one another, as if their skin colour didn't do that already.

One miserable, chilly, late October afternoon, with the sun long in declension and the clock reverted to GMT, I, aiming to avoid the howling wind and flying spume coming off the Irish Sea onto the promenade, diverted from my usual route back to hall, choosing instead an unfamiliar back road. While I was walking past a nondescript one-window-one-door shop, a low shaft of light bounced off something in the window and into my eye. I looked in and saw it was rows of medals hanging off ribbons that had caught the light. I stopped and stared. It was my wardrobe road to Damascus moment. For there in the window was a range of clothing so unlike anything I was accustomed to that it seemed a perfect match for a situation also unlike anything I was accustomed to. Away with feeble feminine compromises, I decided there and then.

I pushed open the door and set a big brass bell hanging over the doorway into a frenzied clanging, causing a figure standing on a ladder along some shelves to turn around. He came down, placed his palms on the counter between us and said, Prynhawn da. I answered Bore da, which I knew meant good morning, but I didn't know the one he said and didn't catch it in time to repeat it. All the goods that weren't on display in the window were behind the counter, stacked on the shelves he'd just climbed down from. I pointed to the jeans and he looked at me as if trying to gauge my size. He said, let me see, in that warm, singsong English of the Welsh, so like the Trini accent I could close my eyes and believe I'm hearing someone back home. He climbed up and brought down a pair. I opened my coat and held the jeans against my waist and hips. Hmmm, maybe a bigger size? I told him so. He climbed up again and got down another pair. This pair promised a better fit. I told him I'd like two. He showed me that there were three colours, really all sludgy tones of the original colours – sludge greeny, sludge bluey, sludge browny. I waved away the bluey. I asked, Sweaters? He looked puzzled, so I pointed. Oh jumpers, he said, and pulled out thick sweaters with roll necks and turtlenecks. I asked for thick socks and tried on a pair of tough lace-up-front shoes. I told him I had no money. He told me about layaway goods. Two pairs of jeans, two sweaters, two pairs of socks, one pair of shoes were wrapped in brown paper, like a package to post, and placed under the counter. I made a small deposit and promised to return at the start of November when I would once again be in the money. Diolch yn fawr, he said as I was leaving. Nos da, I answered. Good night in Welsh; he/she/it/you formal give/s us in Spanish. Hmmmm.

What is the point of war, I pondered on the way back to hall, a thought triggered by those medals in the shop. All that carnage, all that distress, all that destruction, all that squander. I think armies and navies are a waste of lives and money. But that Army & Navy Store saved my life for very little money. It was my sole source of student clothes for the three years I spent at Aber. I decided, too, that presenting as beautiful was also a waste of time and resources and abandoned make up – which at that time was only lipstick and eyebrow pencil, since face foundation and powders for skin of my hue hadn't yet been invented. Oh the freedom that comes with not bothering about one's looks. Food, shelter, clothing sorted. What else. Hmmm. Why am I here? What am I supposed to be doing? Take a look at Jyotsna and Mysoon for guidance. Are they running around crazy like a cockroach that you chasing to slap with a slipper? Well?

The University College of Wales, Aberystwyth, had a highly recognised Department of Geography and so I shouldn't have been surprised to discover that there were one hundred and twenty students in the first year. The professor, Prof Bowen, a diminutive, lively Welshman, gave the first lecture, while a technician projected a few slides of maps of the town. Aberystwyth should really be Aberrheidol, the Prof said, as it was nearer the mouth of the Rheidol than the Ystwyth further south. We learned about the history of the town, its growth, its economic life. And finally if you look north and you can't see Constitution Hill, he said pointing to the map, it's raining. If you can, he added, a note of triumph in his voice, it's about to rain. There was a laugh and an audible groan. Alexandra Hall at the northern end of this wide sweep of Cardigan Bay abutted Constitution Hill. That titbit of meteorological insight proved so accurate that my red mac got much more mileage than the other coat, and with the frequent washings that necessitated, it faded to pink. Too late I discovered that people didn't wash their macs. It was worn outside, so it didn't matter if it was dirty. I couldn't figure out how that was different from shoes, but I didn't make it a discussion issue.

Prof Bowen was our lecturer for a foundations of geography course, the actual name of which I don't recall, but it dealt with how the subject started and morphed over time, where it had got to, and where it might go. There were courses in meteorology where you had to cut out the British Isles weather map of the previous day's weather from the back of the newspaper and follow the track of air masses and fronts and, referencing wind speed and direction, make forecasts about the probability of precipitation, including the type, time, duration, cloud type and amount for a range of locations. I loved that game. Over the three years, we studied geomorphology, anthropology where the lads snickered at slides of naked Nama Hottentot females, settlement geography, agricultural and industrial geography, statistical geography and a whole lot else. My two years with geology was just as intense, more geomorphology, of course, along with palaeontology, stratigraphy, petrology, maps and polarising microscopes, fossils and field. Both these subjects were in adjacent buildings, but to get to my one year of botany I had to hike up Penglais Hill against an icy wind to one of the new buildings on an enormous building site, the future location of the whole university and where Pantycelyn, the spanking new men's hall of residence, was located. A serious young lecturer took us through cells and plant function in a lab; a darling old man took us in the field through gardens and woods, rock pools and shorelines, both riverine and marine.

It strikes me that, though I chose my courses using what, even then, I knew were superficial and frivolous criteria, I got lucky. In all three, I was exposed to the range from broad, sweeping canvasses, across eons of time, and massive landscapes, to the smallest pointillist detail – an individual person to survey, a plant cell to examine under a microscope, a crystal to flash back and forth in polarising light. We went from the sky to very deep underground, from Pre-Cambrian to the present. It was everything, everywhere. It was the lecture room, the library, the lab, the mountains and sea, the towns and villages, every kind of transport from walking to hitchhiking, to bus and train, breaking up rocks to expose the tiny coppery egg-shaped coprolites of dinosaurs, or chunks of basalt, or ammonites or mapping land-use in a small Welsh town. You know how in Big Bang Theory it says that after the big bang, bits of atoms and molecules and dusty matter floated in space, then started going round and round, forming whirling clouds and then coalescing into spinning masses of fire, finally cooling to form solid planets, or something like that? That's how I feel about my experience of being a student at Aber. As if I had been aimless, scattered, amorphous bits before and Aber brought them together to coalesce, shaping my worldview, shaping me.

I turned twenty-one just before the first term exams. Harriet, Alison, Joanna and their respective boyfriends, Jim, Alun and Owen took me to the Ocean View Hotel for dinner and drinks. Coming of age was celebrated as a big event and to mark it I had my first cigarette, offered by Alun. That evening, I didn't get my own, but after cadging the odd one off others and sampling from Woodbines to Players, I settled on Silk Cut, and by the time Christmas break came, I was a five-a-day smoker. At the break everyone went home. I think I remember Harriet meeting up in London with her year-abroad, fellow Tulane folks under proper *in loco parentis* supervision arranged by her university. As for me, I'd written to Mario, a friend from home who'd come to England maybe five years earlier and was living in London with his wife Jill, an Englishwoman from Bristol. I was to stay with them while university was closed. I found my way to their flat on Milson Road, Shepherds Bush, just behind Olympia, as Mario described, and there got my first real taste of West Indian life in London.

Mario was a musician – that is, Mario uses to beat pan with Dixieland around Carnival time back home. He was the youngest of the three older half-brothers of Jeffrey, my back-home, informal betrothed, to whom Mario referred not by name but as 'de boy', as in, so yuh sennin fuh de boy to come up too? which is the only thing he ever asked me about his back-home family, his mother, brother or grandmother, old friends, neighbour-hood, birth place, and that only once in all the three weeks I spent with him and Jill. But Mario, my informal, expected-to-be half-brother-in-law, was a good friend. He didn't have a job, but that didn't mean he didn't work. It is hard work to find yourself clean and tidy early on a Tuesday morning every fortnight outside the dole office to get your weekly unemployment payout, especially if you was up late the night before liming in a club with Russ and de boys and dem after a gig. Mario, as a seasoned ex-colonial, had London-based West Indian friendships to forge and maintain, hustles to organise, and girls from Europe to introduce to London life and British customs.

Mario was charming and persuasive and lots of fun. In other words he was a damn nuisance to Jill who went to work diligently every morning at Dereta, a clothing factory that made ladies' outerwear. She was appalled at my awful, newly-landed-immigrant black and white faux fur coat, though she didn't say so. She simply offered to get me a good wool one at staff factory price. I could see that my coat was vulgar and pretentious in comparison; I didn't need the comment from a fellow student, later friend, now deceased, who told me that when she first saw me walking into Alex Hall, she thought I was a planter's daughter. I read this as planter meaning white plantation owner or overseer of a sugar or cocoa plantation and daughter as in female, mixed-race child from his illicit, perhaps forced, union with an enslaved or servant woman. But to give her the benefit of the doubt, maybe she was thinking of Dido Belle, mulatto daughter of an English aristocrat and herself raised in England as an aristocrat. It was just my bad luck not to have fallen under Jill's expert tutelage on stepping off the SS Antilles, instead of being with a group of similarly untutored fellow Trinidadians. I would have been firmly guided away from the tat I'd invested in, towards more appropriate and more upscale wardrobe choices.

Jill was sweet. I liked her a lot. She was welcoming, patient and kind. Also long-suffering, as anyone married to Mario had to be. How a nice girl like her landed up with my scampish half-brother-in-law-to-be I still can't fathom. On mornings, after Jill had gone to work, Mario and I would hang around in the flat keeping warm, talking about our lives, which was mainly me listening to what London was like for him. He knew every Trinidadian around and even a few Jamaicans too, though he thought the latter took offence too easily and lacked a sense of humour. Dey doh make joke, everything was serious for the boys from The Hawk and The Grove, and Dey doh like calypso, is only ska wid dem. Then he'd suddenly look at his watch, jump up and say, Oh shoot, dress quick, I suppose to meet up the boys ten o'clock and is half past nine already. You keep me here talking nonsense all morning, and we'd get into his car and skate round to someone's house where the boys would be in rehearsal for their gig in a club weekend nights, and is just not only the musician boys there, is other fellers playing cards, and they'd rehearse and we'd go back to the flat and Jill would come home and tell us about her day, what they were making, the designs, the special orders. Imagine that, I say, delivering the spring collection in December, and she says, all our new collection is already in the shop windows and I ask, you mean people buy new coats every year and she says, Many do, and we'd have dinner.

Nights, when Mario went to meet up with the boys again, Jill would say she's tired, feet sore, wants to watch a bit of telly, but you go with him, she'd say to me. At the club, he and the boys would be playing on a little stage in the corner, and there'd be just one or two of the other fellers I'd met that morning, stylishly dressed, sitting at a table near the musicians, tapping ring fingers on their glass along with the music if it was calypso, like if is bottle and spoon at a house fete back home, or tapping feet and nodding head if it was jazz, which it mostly was. And they'd be with girls, very pretty girls, beautifully groomed, fashionable girls, girls from home who dressed in ways that said: Look at me, look at my long lush ponytail, my smooth face, my careful make-up, pouty red mouth blowing cigarette smoke, my long shapely red fingernails, my nice coat unbuttoned to show my slim shape in a well-fitting jumper and short skirt, my fishnet stockings with the long straight back seam and my slingback pointy-toe high heels. How I admired and envied the calm assurance of those girls sitting in groups of two or three, chatting and laughing, girls who'd found a way to make this place their own – a nice little West Indian corner in the room. Around them the natives sat at little tables, drinking and talking loudly above the music and above their own voices. Once in a while, one of the locals would come over and sit with our lot and one of our girls would stub out her cigarette and get up and go with the man to dance, I supposed, but if they were going to dance, why did she take her coat and handbag? I didn't see her come back, and while I'm there, the other girls leave one by one with guests.

We put up a tree one day and decorated it, not a big one because my folding bed and suitcase in the living room took up lots of space, and we went on Christmas Eve and bought gifts for Jill – no clothing items of course – and I had my first British Christmas with friends in their home and it was a happy time. On Boxing Day, we went to their friends' homes, making music, dancing, singing, eating, drinking. At one home, I remember the French wife of one of the musician fellers sitting at a window with their baby boy on her lap – was the child's name Marcus and hers Marie? – and she was singing 'Autumn Leaves' in French, in a wistful, tristesse sort of way that somehow wasn't out of keeping with the season of merry, because everyone there was from somewhere else, and was once someone else, and had within them buried longings that came to the surface, especially after a few drinks. A woman, someone's sister, a very recent arrival, swaddled in innumerable layers and an overcoat, sat so close to the paraffin heater to keep herself from shivering that people kept telling her she'd singe her coat and catch herself afire, and she said she's not bothered, she was so cold she would at least be warm enough at last.

I went back to Aber and heard talk that the sea had frozen over Christmas. The record for the lowest temperature in that part of Wales had been broken and throughout Britain it turned out to be one of the bitterest winters on record. I also found that a box for me had been delivered to Alex Hall. I took it upstairs. Marmie had got a cardboard box, maybe from the shop across the road, packed it, sealed it with tape around every edge and across and over every opening. Then she'd wrapped it all in brown paper and taped that up too. It took a full ten minutes of running a knife and a scissors' blade along the tape, using scissors to snip and fingernails to pry it open. And when I did, for the first time in the more than four months of gradually shedding my old life and slowly adapting to my new space, I was yanked back home and I sat on the floor and cried.

Marmie had sent black cake, sorrel liqueur and ponche à crème. I could see her soaking the dried fruit in cherry brandy and rum in the big stoneware jar with a tightly fitting screw-top lid for months in advance for the cake; tearing the red fleshy sepals from the prickly seedpods of sorrel and steeping the sepals in rum to draw out the colour and flavour, straining it after some weeks and bottling the heady liqueur; whipping a dozen eggs into a foam with a length of lime peel – the citrus zest to cut the eggy smell – and adding to it condensed milk, evaporated milk and rum for the ponche à crème and pouring the mixture into a rum bottle and corking it tight-tight. She'd wrapped each bottle in layers of newspapers, because it had a long way to go in the hold of a heaving ship, and packed them one by one in the box, more newspapers crunched between the bottles. She would have checked the date for last parcel post to England and got someone to drop her and the box to the post office. Marmie, hugging the box on her lap, Marmie thinking of me, but unable to visualise what I looked like, what I'd be wearing, where I'd be and what *there* was like, but maybe imagining my face, my joy at receiving these reminders of home and proof of her love and thoughtfulness. I pulled out each bottle and unwrapped it: the ruby red sorrel liqueur, the creamy ponche a crème. I opened the tin and smelled the black cake. Then I put everything back into the box, closed the flaps and pushed the box under my bed. I didn't want to see it. I didn't want it to be seen.

A cardboard box begged from a grocery, the brown paper wrapping, the newspapers, the badly cut or torn tape of different colours and kinds, the address in ballpoint written in capitals once, then over again though not quite exactly on the first letters and over written again to thicken the letters to make them more visible. An address of seven lines: Barbara Lafond, Room 60, Alexandra Hall, University College of Wales, Aberystwyth, Wales, United Kingdom. If there had been more space I guess the next line would have read, The World. And the things inside. How could I explain the contents when the idea of difference as a positive wasn't on the horizon of a yet to be imagined imaginary, when things not familiar were scorned, things foreign, food foreign, you held your nose at, even European things like garlic, a culinary staple back home? To smell of garlic was thought of as repulsive as smelling of bodily waste. So how could I share what had arrived, my homemade fare, with my friends?

It's true everyone shared whatever they brought from home after weekends away – Welsh cakes, Victoria sponge, laver bread, fudge – but those were their things, things that already occupied common cultural space, a place in conversations, in books, in films – things you could compare: my mother's Victoria sponge with yours, my grandma's fudge with yours. Where and how would my mother's homemade fare fit? How credible a comparison would black cake in an old biscuit tin, which one sliced with whatever knife was to hand and served on a side plate, and the slice taken to your mouth with fingers, how could that stand comparison with, let's say, the Christmas pudding of Christmas carols, of Charles Dickens? This was pudding lifted out of the steamer, unveiled from its mesh bag, to expose a light brown dome, plump with preserved vine fruit, decorated on the top with an artificial holly berry and leaf cluster and placed in the centre of a Royal Doulton oval dish at whose side rests a purpose-designed pudding slicing tool, a little trowel-like object, one edge serrated one smooth, and a jug of whipped cream or brandy sauce at the side? At least these two items, black cake and Christmas pudding had something in common – the ingredients – if not the manner of cooking or presentation. But where would I start with sorrel? How do I explain a bush with flowers like hibiscus – like what? I hear – and sepals growing thick and reddening when the flowers fell off and a seedpod fattening green and maroon with prickly hairs? Or in the case of ponche à crème, how to account for the use of condensed milk? I was ashamed. Ashamed of home, of my mother's efforts which cost her much, but seemed so pitiful here, that Christmas offering whose primitiveness I'd shoved under the bed. Nothing was up to the sophistication, the civilisation of what I thought I had merged into. I couldn't bear to think that where I had come from, who I really was, could, if others saw this box, be so easily, so irrefutably, exposed.

When I came in from lectures the next afternoon, there was a note in my pigeonhole from Miss Powys-Roberts asking me to see her. I thought it was a bit early to ask about hall fees; it was only the first week of term after all. But it wasn't that. She apologised about an accident in my room that morning. When the cleaner pushed her broom under my bed, the broom knocked something, and it was only when what she thought was blood began to spread over the floor that she realised something was wrong. She knelt, peeped under the bed, saw the box, pulled it out, its base now soggy, the contents soaked. She cleaned up everything. Luckily the broken bottle bits and splinters were within the box, so the floor was free of hazard, but regrettably one bottle was broken and the contents lost. The other items were cleaned up and were now on my desk. She regrets the box had to be thrown away. Miss Powys-Roberts knew how precious things from home were and she was sorry that one item was lost.

As we say at home, you can run but you can't hide. Everyone now knew that the sight of blood flowing from under my bed made the cleaner's heart almost stop in her chest, how it had turned out to be alcohol – it had such a strong smell she almost passed out. It could have been spirits, but she didn't know what kind as she doesn't have anything to do with spirits. There was another bottle that didn't break with something white in it and a biscuit tin. The supper table of friends was tense with curiosity that evening. I heard there was an accident in your room this morning. Yes. Package from home. One bottle of liqueur broken. I'd repacked it badly after opening. Liqueur? Yes, you know, like Cointreau. But not citrus. Other fruit soaked in rum. That must be fantastic. Yes. It is. The other things? Come up and see. I took my supper knife upstairs and when the others came by, I passed round to them, as they sat on my bed, little squares of black cake, rechristened rum cake, served on the upturned lid of the biscuit tin. Jyotsna and Mysoon couldn't eat it for religious reasons, but half the cake went that evening. As for the ponche à crème, rechristened eggnog, it enlivened everyone's bedtime milk drinks for many weeks after. It was only much later that I learned that, at that time, many working-class British families made something very similar for Christmas – and used condensed milk.

My next letter to Marmie was full of gratitude and appreciation, how happy I was to have a home Christmas sent to me, and how much I and everyone else enjoyed everything. I did not mention anything about the fate of the sorrel liqueur because I thought it would have taken the shine off the trouble and care she took in making it, packing it and sending it and would have denied her the satisfaction over my imagined pleasure in receiving it. But I did tell myself that I was a fool to have behaved the way I did and I reminded myself that once again I had demonstrated that I was unworthy of her.

That first winter was hard. To wake in the still quite dark, walk through biting wind and rain to lectures, hands and feet and face so cold they had no feeling, I couldn't be as accepting, as stoic as everyone else. No, not me, I wanted to fight it and rage against it. I now know that weather is something you work with not against, and if I were to be transported back there I'd leave hall on mornings wearing a knitted hat with earflaps or a balaclava, have on my feet stout tall boots with three pairs of socks, the outermost oiled and waterproof, a thermal vest and long johns, woollen trousers, inner jumper and outer cardigan, thick wool scarf, fleece-lined leather gloves, full-length sheepskin coat, but instead, see me flapping around in bra, panties long-sleeved jumper, jeans, socks and boots, knitted gloves, scarf and gradually fading red mac. Too many things to put on to go out into the world and, when you enter a building, too many things to take off. Things to forget, to leave behind, to lose; too much advance planning, too much need for awareness of weather fluctuations and foibles; too many decisions about layers and weights and collars and scarves and hoods and hats and caps; too much, too much, too much of everything, and you had to be there, and be on time always and regardless. And on top of that, the walk back in the dark, not along the promenade, not by the sea, because there'd be pebbles the size of duck eggs flung over the railing, over the promenade, over the street and over the four storeys of Alexandra Hall, even onto the back road which was the winter entrance and exit. The front door and windows up to two storeys were boarded-up against winter storms – like the shop windows and the plate-glass, curtain-wall facades of office buildings at home at Carnival. I'd get back in and welcome steaming supper soup and be glad of a central-heated room, a warm bed to snuggle into and read, happy to push aside essays due, labs not written up, stratigraphy maps not decoded, happy to be in bed with Graham Greene in the company of the howl of the wind, the boom of waves exploding against the sea wall, the rattle of the window against its frame. Winter is for hibernation and humans are fools not to learn from animals who know when to shut down, even those with the benefit of stored fat and thick fur coats.

Spring edged in cautiously, unsure it had the upper hand, since summer itself, coming up from behind, could not be relied on to push forward with any degree of assertiveness. So it was that winter clung on in pockets of frost and little piles of snow becoming greyer and greyer as they shrank. I'd find myself walking on the sunny side of the street, when there was one, eschewing shade, doing the opposite of what I'd instinctively do at home. Fellow students changed from coats to jackets, shed gloves, changed from boots to shoes, as if by doing so they could coax the weather into following suit and become more balmy. I didn't trust those human efforts; instead I looked for signs in nature. On my walks up Penglais Hill to botany I was happy to see snowdrops and crocuses in the front gardens of homes I passed and the air around the trees was lit with a soft green glow. But what I longed for, what would have defined spring for me I didn't see, so that when geology field trips for Easter were announced and my name was on the Devon and Cornwall list, I was disappointed. I wanted the Lake District and Wordsworth and Ullswater and daffodils fluttering and dancing in the breeze. As luck would have it though, Lucy and Gareth, lovers in the first flush of euphoria, under threat of being torn asunder for an entire ten days by being on two different trips, on hearing I didn't want Devon and Cornwall – which I learned later was the hottest ticket in town – were thrilled and grateful to make an exchange, and thus it was settled that I'd be going to what I thought of as Daffodil Country.

A group of us hitchhiked to Keswick where we were to stay, with daily hikes into Skiddaw and Scafell, Helvellyn, Honister and Shap. We chipped into frozen rills to expose pretty pink, white and black-flecked granite, excavated ancient crustaceans, separated layers of crumbly slate looking for fossils and did all manner of mapping dips and strikes of folds. It was then I developed a kind of joint inflammation. I'd come back after a day of axing and hammering and chiselling in the cold and wet, have a hot soak in the bath and sit by the roaring, open log fireplace not able to bend a knee if my leg was outstretched, or stretch it out if bent. Every joint was painfully frozen from cervical to coccyx, from shoulder to metacarpals, hips to metatarsals. I slept with the electric blanket on all night to be able to get out of bed next morning and go out walking and climbing for the duration of the field trip. And nowhere, not by the lake, not on the fell, not in the dale, nowhere, nowhere did I spy one single daffodil.

The field trip ended, the group disbanded, everyone went home. As the lone overseas student there was only one place I could go. I took the train back to Aber to find Alex closed. The only student hall open was Pantycelyn, the men's hall of residence, which was open to women for the Easter break. I arrived there on the evening of Holy Thursday. The office was closed until the following Tuesday. I hadn't thought ahead about any of this. I hadn't booked a room. My joints hadn't eased up and I couldn't go around the town looking for accommodation. Rudy and Trevor took me in and housed me illicitly in a friend's vacant room until I could legalise my status. Most students had gone home for the holidays, but us overseas students would have been stranded if it weren't for this special arrangement. There were also third-year students who chose to stay on, engaged in intense swotting before final exams. It must have been as early as the Saturday when the boys and I had a falling out, probably over some trivial matter to do with something back home, some petty rivalry between sports teams perhaps that got to be bigger, noisier, more personal than it should have and I left their room and hobbled to the communal bathrooms to cool down, which in my case means to cry. And that's what I did.

What if? What if the boys and I hadn't quarrelled? What if we had, but then settled our differences amicably? What if I hadn't gone to the bathroom but had gone back to the borrowed room? Or having gone to the bathroom, hadn't cried? But none of those other things happened because the alignment of the planets did not allow, the script was written and the action was already playing out. A voice from the adjoining cubicle asked if I was OK and when I didn't answer, there was a knock on the door. What if I'd said, Go away you nosy bastard? But I didn't. I opened the door, he came in, we sat side by side on the edge of the bath and I stopped crying. He offered me a Balkan Sobranie. We sat there, silent, side by side, in a cloud of warm, fragrant soothing smoke and when the glow along the black cigarettes reached their gold tips, he stubbed the ends in the lid of the cigarette tin and put it in his bathrobe pocket. He asked if I'd be all right. I knew that I would be.

The next morning I spotted him among a group of three fellers with their breakfast trays heading towards a table some way from ours, but facing us. I asked Trevor, who is that feller? He said, which one? I said the tall one. He said, the ginger one is Norman. I said, no, not that one. He said, you mean Paul Jenkins. I said, I suppose so. Who is the other one? He said, Pete Davies. As I passed their table to go to the buffet, he joined me. You all right? I said, yes. He stayed standing there, so I added, thanks for yesterday. He said, that's OK. I walked on and he returned to his friends. Trevor and Rudy finished breakfast and went off to their rooms. Rudy was studying for finals in philosophy, Trevor for second year exams. I should've been studying too; the upcoming exams would decide whether I would get into the honours degree programme, but all my books were in Alex. I wondered whether the geography and geology library would be open, but it was Easter weekend, so maybe not, and in any case they were down the hill and walking was still painful. Where to go, what to do with myself?

I saw the three fellers get up and clear away their stuff. I saw him saying something to the other two and they went off. He came over and sat across from me. You're all right now? I nodded. You're sure? Yes. I'm fine. If anything's wrong between you and them. He looked in the direction in which Trevor and Rudy had gone. Oh, no. Actually they're helping me out. I launched into an explanation about field trip, no accommodation, Trevor and Rudy letting me stay in a friend's room until I sorted myself out on Tuesday. He said his name and I said mine. He said, I know. I said, I know yours too. Thanks for yesterday. He said, what about today? Anything you're unhappy about today? I said, not yet. He said, Pete and I are going up to Cwm Woods. Want to come? I said, how far is it? He said, pretty far. We're going in Pete's car. Leaving around ten. If you want to come, meet us here. I didn't leave the dining hall until he was gone. I didn't want to be seen struggling to get up, hobbling along to the stairs, painfully taking each step two feet at a time, but at ten I was back downstairs, a little more flexible for having moved around, and we set off in Pete's black Morris Minor, me in the front passenger seat, him in the back, for which I was grateful, aware that my limbs couldn't have manoeuvred into the space behind the front seat of a two-door car. Even so, I couldn't easily get out when we stopped; my knees didn't want to unbend and I had to be helped out.

We walked along a little dirt path through the rows of trees that flanked the roadside and when we emerged into the more open woodland my breath was snatched away, for all around the air was a haze of blue mist as far as you could see, an abundance that went on and on, the most spectacular bluey-purpleness underfoot and everywhere, thousands upon thousands of tender spikes covered with row upon row of delicate purple-blue flowers. And there, at the base of tree trunks, there shone a glowing golden light, the longed-for clusters and clumps of buttery yellow daffodils. It didn't look real, it looked staged; so much perfection. When I could walk no further I lay down among the bluebells. He lay beside me and took my hand. We looked up at the sky through the trees. The softest of green, so subtle it looked silver hung way overhead, a mesh of newly minted leaf buds against a crisp blue sky. So much newness, so much promise, so much hope. I felt overwhelmed by a joy that must be the way freedom feels when you've come out of captivity. We didn't speak. What do you say when there's nothing to say and so much to feel?

We shouldn't, of course we shouldn't. We shouldn't have been squandering his last term, his last few weeks before his finals. He should have been immersed in his international relations, in his geography for his joint honours. But there was an urgency that we didn't talk about. He would soon be leaving. He knew it and so did I. We didn't want to let a moment go to waste. So on weekdays when supper was over, he'd come down to Alex and we'd spend the hours together before he had to leave to get back before his hall shut for the night.

In Alex, except on weekend nights, most girls stayed in. There was a TV in the lounge and the girls sat and watched their familiar programmes. Since TV came to Trinidad only after I'd left, watching TV wasn't a habit I'd developed so I never went into the lounge. Of the girls who went out, many were off to the library or to meet up with friends to study. A few were out to meet up with boyfriends. Some went to the Students Union where it was said there was a bar and TV and a lounge, but in the three years I never set foot there, and I think that's because the whole concept of a common room, an indoor gathering place, was alien to me. I know why people gather indoors to be warm and companionable in weather that is generally hostile, but for me, where I came from, there wasn't an equivalent. Gathering places for like-minded people would be places like the Country Club and the golf club for the upper classes. The rest of us met up in small family and friend groups in each other's homes or stood at corners, in the shop, at the standpipe, or at the beach, botanic gardens, savannah, race track, river.

Young people met at house parties; men met in rum shops. But for us – at least the people I knew – there weren't clubs. So, no Students Union, no Alex TV lounge. So where did I go to be with people outside my hall group and my classes? I went to the ground zero of community life in Wales when I lived there. The pub.

The Bluebell! Ah! such happy memories are located there. It's there that I saw, openly stated and clearly identified, class distinction and its easy acceptance. Pubs had two bars; one, a spit and sawdust room for ordinary folk where the beer was one penny a pint cheaper, and the other, the saloon, a bit posher with higher priced beer and a range of spirits. In both, patrons played darts all night long. The Bluebell was not a students' pub. It was a place that locals frequented. Paul and I became regulars in the saloon bar there. At nights, the patrons sang, led by a local – a bank manager I heard after, whose name I don't recall – whose one opening note, in stirring baritone, was the signal for an informal choir to fall in. Hymns and patriotic songs in Welsh were the staple. The rich baritones, the ringing tenors, and you, you who'd left your native land before you'd even heard one note of its new national anthem, you whose only national anthem had been *God save the Queen* or was it *Land Of Hope and Glory*, you were Welsh with them, joining in *Mae Hen Wlad Fy Nhadau*, followed without a break by the rousing *Canlon Lan* and *Cwm Rhondda* and you were swept along into feeling a deep Hiraeth for where, for whom, for what you cannot tell. It's not specifically located anywhere, but it's real enough to bring you close to tears.

On those evenings, after Paul's couple of pints of draught Hancock's Best Bitter, my three or four whisky macs – haven't had one for more than half a century, yet I can close my eyes and conjure up the fragrance of Stone's ginger wine rising on a waft of nose-tingling whisky vapour – we leaving near closing time, us two swaying along the promenade, down to the far end to kick the bar for good luck, arm in arm, still singing. And there were nights when, back in my room, delirious with love and careless of consequences, we didn't part till it was safe for him to be seen and mingle with the next day's guests.

DESPERATE NOTES

The night before my wedding I said to Marie, there's something I'd like to tell you. It was Easter of my final year at Aber, and Marie, my only friend from home and the sole stand-in for my entire family, had come that afternoon to Bristol from Surrey where she was training in midwifery at St Helier's Hospital. She must've been saying her night prayers or something because it took a moment before she turned my way and, when she propped up on her elbow to give me her full attention, I said, I didn't tell Jeffrey I'm getting married.

And I hadn't. I hadn't seen him for over a year and we weren't in touch. Once we'd put him on the train back to London, I thought of him as finished business. Yet it bothered me that the night before I was to marry someone else, I hadn't got news to him that soon it would all be formally over; that we were at a final parting of ways, definitely set on separate life journeys. I don't suppose that rationally I should have been bothered. But there was a niggling guilt about the shabby way that whole break-up had happened and I know that how I behaved then could be thought cruel. But my sensible self said, What do you owe him? Do you owe him anything? To the last question I could answer both yes and no.

Yes, I owed him in that we had an agreement, an unstated but understood agreement that we'd be together always. It had been so since we were teenagers. And when it was time for me to leave home and him, to go far away, I'd left with the promise that he'd follow in a year and our lives would go on as before. I was wearing his ring, had been since I was fifteen, that plaited circle of transparent nylon fishing wire. Yes, I owed him, because in my early letters to him I'd written about the way we used to be, letters full of the past, the longing, the sense of loss at being apart. In that first year of our separation, I had said nothing to him about the changes in me, changes in my way of thinking, changes in my way of being and I think that while these were real, they were so gradual, so organic that I was unaware of them in a conscious, analytical way. If I gave any thought at all about myself in my new life, it was more in the context of events and people, not so much about the effect those were having on me, shaping the malleable impressionable clay of me, so that I was a different person by the time we met each other again at the end of that first year. I wasn't aware of this and I didn't show him either, not through any reflection on my part about my new world. Now I can see that my letters, those pages of consolation, of revisiting the old life, could be read as a cowardly palliative, avoiding the inevitable truth, and that through them I had failed to prepare him for the new me. So yes, maybe I did owe him something.

No, I didn't owe him anything. Hadn't I paid my dues over time, both back home when we were together and when he'd got to England? Once we'd first parted, once I'd become independent, reliant only on myself for negotiating a new world, I had begun to feel the weight of him, the weight of his dependency on me. I'd begun to feel that I'd carried him too long and I was tired of it. You're wondering about carried? Well, I was always ahead of him, born a full one year two months and nine days before, so I was the one who did HC while he was doing Senior Cambridge; I was the one working, teaching full time, while he was dithering about whether to carry on at school or get a job, which he did for a bit, then he decided he would go back to school to do his Higher Certificate. I didn't have that luxury but, because of me, he did. I'm trying to remember whether he stuck it out and I'm reasonably sure he didn't, but not because he'd got a job, no, because he had a safety net, for while he was experimenting with a hobby that would become a career, I was working. How else do you think the darkroom got built and equipped? And cameras, bags, lenses, tripods, film, consumables? Expensive stuff for an expensive hobby for a dedicated single-minded purist. The passion for photography was at the early learning stage and nothing he produced was paying, except a flurry of orders at convent graduation time when I was teaching there.

But back then I hadn't shaped it in my mind that I was carrying him; I think I saw it as me just going with him, along the road he was travelling. At the time, I didn't have the words and ideas to allow me to think of myself as either a benefactor to a budding artist, or maybe an investor in the future of a good prospect, which would yield dividends on which we could both live comfortably when he got famous. That kind of analysis is what I'd now give to someone else's similar situation, but I hadn't the tools to assess myself then. How he managed financially after I left I don't know. I guess that since he was living at home with his mother, she picked up the tab, or maybe he worked as a photographer at events, but I never got around to asking him when we met again, because it wasn't the kind of meeting that allowed easy catching-up.

He arrived in Southampton on the *SS Colombie* and took the boat train to London. Paul and I were waiting for him on the platform at Waterloo. I introduced the two of them, but I didn't say what Paul was to me, why we were together. Much later he told me he'd assumed Paul was a friend from Aber whom I'd asked along to help with the luggage. We took a black cab to Milson Road, Shepherds Bush, to the basement flat where his half-brother lived. He was to stay there with Mario and Jill until he found his feet, meaning until he could afford to pay rent somewhere. We had a cup of tea and when Paul and I made to leave I said, I'll come by tomorrow morning around nine to take you to the place where I got you the job. He said, you're leaving? I thought you'd be here with me. I shook my head. I have to work tonight. I'll come back tomorrow.

You didn't tell him? He doesn't know? Paul asked when, back at our room, I was getting ready for work. No. I didn't. I couldn't tell him. He might have decided not to come. I don't know whether I thought this was going to be the start of a conversation, but when the silence grew heavy I looked around over the back of the sofa where I sat tidying my hair to where Paul was standing, his back to me. His voice was matter-of-fact when he spoke. And would that have mattered? He didn't turn for my answer but continued to look up towards the dingy pane of glass that was our only source of light from the outside. Yes it does matter. Because he needs to live in a different place. Do a course. Learn something. That's how I answered Paul. To myself I added, to grow up, to learn to fend for himself. Otherwise he'd be back home waiting for me to return and carry on looking after him. And I'm not ever doing that again.

The next morning I took Jeffrey to the greengrocer's. The owner was the father of a boy I'd met at Aber. My first Christmas, the Christmas just past, Ben had invited me to spend a weekend with his family in Gravesend, Kent. I asked the dad whether he'd agree to hire a friend from home who needed an offer of employment before he could be allowed to enter the following summer under the new Commonwealth Immigration Act. This nice stranger, who told me he was a true-blue Tory, all for the Queen and the Commonwealth, agreed to help. At the greengrocers that first morning, Jeffrey was handed gloves and an apron and shown a sack of potatoes he was to get the dirt off so they could be displayed to advantage. Yes, I know. What degradation! What sacrilege! An artist's hallowed hands forced to engage in menial work! Shame, isn't it?

I'd by then left my daytime job at The Contented Plaice, a high-end fish and chip restaurant on the river at Kingston-on-Thames, so that I could support Jeffrey while he was settling in. Now, while Paul waited up late for me, having done a day's work at a printery, I was working nights in The Blue Lagoon, a nightclub in Mayfair, in the heart of the posh West End. It was someone's South Sea Islands fantasy, marrying Gaugin's Tahiti with the musical *South Pacific,* with a ruthless time-managing American in charge, who'd fire you for being two minutes late and did so right on cue when inevitably I transgressed. As a cocktail waitress, I released my hair from its ponytail restraint, slipped a paper hibiscus behind an ear, tied a coconut palm patterned sarong around my waist, threw a paper lei around my neck and served tropical, sunset-coloured drinks with little paper parasols, maraschino cherries and pitted olives on toothpicks to lone men seated at little tables scattered near the fake waterfall – real water, fake pool, live fish, fake coconut palms – and real lonely men who asked me if I'd go back with them to their hotel for a drink and just talk – I just want to chat, nothing else – after they'd been turned down by other waitresses and maybe thought me an easy mark.

What could he want to talk about, the man with the lost face that looked as if it hadn't seen sun for a decade, a pink circle peeping through sandy thinning hair on the top of his head as you bent over to place an orange Honolulu Hula Hurrah on the little table. What conversation could there be that's worth the offer of twenty quid to a girl he knows works for three quid a week, plus tips? No, sorry, I'm busy, was what you said. You didn't say that you wished there weren't so many lonely people. That you would have liked it if someone else had accepted his offer, if only so that the world's quantum of unhappiness was reduced by one person, but it couldn't be you, since you were already failing in relieving the misery of others, misery you had yourself inflicted. You didn't say that you were lucky to be going home to someone who was waiting for you. No matter it wasn't a West End hotel room, but a scruffy one-room space.

We were paying three quid a week for the room. There was a one-burner gas ring on an oilcloth-covered table and a gas fire into which you dropped a shilling to get a few minutes heat which you needed, even in the summer, to keep off the chill and damp. There was a lumpy grimy sofa that served as a bed. There was a stained cracked washbasin with a tap. The one toilet and bathtub up the stairs served the entire house of six rented rooms and the landlady's apartment. I was paid three pounds a week and Paul three pounds ten shillings. We ate boiled rice into which a can of soup, usually cream of mushroom, was poured near the end of cooking time. We made toast with cheap white bread held by a fork against the gas fire. We made tea. We were having a happy adventure, delaying life's real decisions, except the one big one I had foisted on us.

Roger, a Belmont and CIC (St Mary's College) friend of Jeffrey's was already in London; he'd been there a year or more. He was doing a hairdressing course at Helene Curtis and working there. His Trinidadian fiancée had arrived around the same time as Jeffrey, but Roger had moved on in his tastes and things were strained between them. We went flat hunting and located something in Bayswater. Pooled resources allowed the three of them – Jeffrey, Roger and his fiancée – to move in. I think everyone assumed that I'd move in too, to make two couples, but I explained that since I was going back to university in a couple of months anyway it would make no sense for me to change my arrangements. I told him I'd rented a room for the whole summer. I didn't say I was not alone.

London is a big city, but not so big that people who know one another can't find who they're looking for, and it wasn't much more than two weeks after he arrived that I was found and found out. I was getting ready to go to work, the dinner rice was on the stove, and Paul was due any moment. When the bell rang I looked up out the basement door to see Jeffrey standing there on the top step leading to the main house and told him to come down. He came in and looked around. How often had I seen him do this, sweeping his eyes around the room, his artist's appraisal of a new setting, but never before was it an assessment of my space, of me in my space. I could see he found it interesting in a smug, amused way. He wouldn't take off his jacket. He sat on the edge of the distasteful sofa and with a shake of his head refused an offer of tea. I was grateful for that. I would have had to take the simmering rice off the burner and put on the kettle. He'd been there five minutes and not yet said a word when Paul came in from work, turning his key in the lock and taking off his mac and hanging it on the peg behind the door before turning around and seeing Jeffrey sitting there, head bent, attention fixed on his hands clasped between his knees, not acknowledging the sound, not turning around. I've only come in for a cup of tea, Paul said. I've agreed to do overtime on a rush job. He put a finger to his lips, stopping in my throat the question I was about to ask about this unusual overtime business. He made a pot of tea, drank a cup and went out, leaving us. We still hadn't exchanged a word but we both understood what was what between us. All that was left were recriminations to be voiced and admissions of failure to be assented to. There could be no justifications. Nothing that would be accused could be weaselled out of. And even that was almost predictable. That script had been written by both of us in our heads from the moment he climbed off the boat train and set foot on the platform where Paul and I were waiting for him and for our futures to be divined.

No, I didn't tell him that I was seeing someone else. Ok, so I lied in not saying, and yes, by continuing in my letters to avow my devotion to him, yes, it's true I was guilty of gross deceit. No, I couldn't tell you. Yes, I guessed you wouldn't have come if you knew. But I still wanted you to come to London. No, not for me. For you. For you to better yourself. Yes, it's true that washing potatoes in cold water isn't bettering yourself. Not yet. But being here is better than being back home. Here there are more opportunities for you. Look at Mario, your brother. What was he doing home? Sitting down in the back room in a merino and short pants, scratching. Beating pan Carnival time. Isn't he better here? Ok, he's a big man with friends from home, agreed. But what about Roger? Look at Roger. He came here, no job, no friends. But now he's studying and training while working. Yes, I know he's a hairdresser and you are not. But photographers work too. What about Norman Parkinson? Maybe he could do with an apprentice. He's in Tobago lots of times and must know that West Indians are not stupid. Look, I'll continue to help until I have to go back to university. Until you're settled. That's all I said, but not all I wanted to say.

What I wanted to say, what was playing silently in my head was: What were you doing for yourself in the year since I left except waiting to come here? I bet you weren't walking around like Cecil, taking snaps of people hoping they'd buy the photo, or sending a photo to the papers hoping they'd print it, or looking up banns to seek out prospective brides and show them your work so they'd hire you to do their wedding album. Oh no. You're too proud to do any of that. You'd expect to have a studio in town, like Chan's, and people would hear how wonderful you are and come in and request an appointment. Not so? And how would that happen? But for me to say that out loud would've been too truthful and too painful for both of us, painful for me as I would have had to admit to myself that I had spent time and money and had worked at anything honest that came my way to prop up someone who felt it was beneath him to get a job and work for someone else, and it would have wounded him to have that thrown at him at that insecure time along with everything else I had presented him with. I was all too conscious that a word once spoken does not come back.

I dropped in at the greengrocers to check on him a couple times in the next week, but he would find something at the back to be doing when I came and so I stopped for a while. Then I felt I should see him and looked in again. There was a strange young man restocking the purple plums. I asked if Jeffrey was there. He didn't know who I was asking about. Ben's dad, at the cash register, said that a young woman had come to tell him that Jeffrey was in hospital. What did she look like? She spoke with an accent like you. But she looked Chinese. That would be Roger's fiancée, I said, she's from Trinidad too. He looked puzzled but I didn't stop to explain our nation of immigrants even though he was someone whose country had organised those many voluntary and forced global migrations that populated the Caribbean and other places in the empire, while now denying entry to very folk they'd scattered willy-nilly round the world. But I did owe Ben's dad for opening up the gap just that little bit so Jeffrey could squeeze through. So I thanked him and went on to the Bayswater flat. He was there. He'd been in hospital for just a couple days. He said he'd had food poisoning and needed rehydrating while the toxins were flushed out, but he was better and would be going back to work. Privately, the fiancée told me that it wasn't exactly food poisoning. He was taken in to have his stomach pumped. He'd been having trouble sleeping so he got some pills to help him sleep.

Paul and I went back to Aber at the end of summer for the start of my second year. He had no real business to be there; he'd graduated with joint honours in International Relations and Geography before we set off for London. I went back to Alexandra Hall; he found a bed and breakfast and continued to live off his London savings. We met up between my classes, spent evenings together at the Bluebell or in my room. We went for walks.

We had no plans. We were coasting along as if life was an infinite holiday we'd been gifted.

We'd been back in Aber about a month, when I got to hall late one Friday afternoon, bleary-eyed after an intense petrology lab staring down a polarising microscope at slivers of shale, schist and slate, and drained by the trek along the promenade against a biting wind off the Irish Sea, to find I had a visitor waiting in the lobby. Jeffrey was sitting curled up into his coat, head slumped into his chest, eyes closed. A duffel bag lay at his feet. I touched his shoulder, and he lifted his head. How tired and beaten he looked. I couldn't take him up to my room; it was before visiting hours but I did take up his bag so he'd be free of it when we decided where to go. But where to go? I had no idea where the common, warm, neutral places were. He didn't want to go to a pub and neither did I – too many people, too little privacy. I couldn't take him to the Bluebell where I would have gone if he hadn't turned up, because Paul was there, pulling pints while the publican's wife was up in Llanbadarn Fawr helping their daughter with a new baby. He said he wasn't hungry but I told him that if we were to sit somewhere out of the cold, we had to go where food was sold. The daytime cafes that did non-alcoholic drinks and snacks were closed. That left the Chinese and the chippy.

He toyed with a spring roll and let his jasmine tea go tepid while I waited for him to say something. I didn't ask him why he was there because I knew it was to do with us, him and me, but whether he was there for an explanation, an apology, a reconciliation, a final parting of the ways or a row, whether he had come to say he was going back home or he was staying on in London I couldn't guess, but I did know he had taken the one train from Paddington to Aberystwyth to see me and that the one train back to London had already left. We walked back to Alex, not along the prom where lovers strolled, their arms wrapped around each others waists under their coats, but along the pavement, past the windows of terrace houses behind whose drawn drapes the blue light of the TVs flickered.

We sat at the edge of my bed. I tried with pleasantries. How was he, the job at the greengrocers, Mario and Jill, Roger and fiancée, the flat and so on. He told me he hadn't seen much of them; they were not doing well. Then he said, why are you asking me about these things; is this how you people talk in this hypocritical place, pretending interest in things that don't matter. You know you're not really interested and neither am I. He got up from the bed and went over to stand near the desk. He seemed to be looking at what I had pinned on the corkboard. There was a mini Trinidad and Tobago flag, a list of books I'd asked the librarian to reserve, the outline of an essay due in a week's time, the Welsh National Anthem written phonetically, but from the way his head was tilted, the way it was turned, I could tell that his gaze was focused on an eight by four black and white print of a photo of me he'd taken at a day-long shoot at L'Anse Noir where we'd found cool, sheltered, secluded caves in the cliffs backing the foot-searing black sand, me in a white swimsuit, smiling flirtatiously through hair swung forward while ducking under sea-grape bushes to lean into the frame, one strap of the swimsuit slipped off a sun-reflecting shoulder and resting halfway along the upper arm, so that the effect was that of an accidental décolleté, a playful gamine caught unawares.

His attention was still on the photo when he continued. Let me ask you something. I was at home. Minding my own business. You said you wanted me to come. I came. I am here. What are you going to do with me now? I didn't answer. I had no answer to give. He left his question hanging there, forcing me to dwell uneasily on it, and when the silence grew uncomfortably long and heavy he answered it himself. Since it looks like you don't want me any more, what am I to do with myself? All I could say was, I am sorry. Things have changed. He turned to me. No. Things have not changed. It's you that changed. You have become like them. Talking out the side of your mouth, saying one thing and meaning something else. He turned back to the corkboard and the photo. Why do you keep this? Haven't you left all this behind? Me and you? Then? Or is it here to haunt you? Like how you keep a crucifix over your bed. Oh! Wait a minute. Something's missing. He walked around the room, looking closely at each wall, even though a glance from one spot could have covered it all. Where is the crucifix? Where is the chaplet? You mean you don't even have a chaplet hanging up somewhere? Tut-tut-tut. Don't tell me you gave up church too. He laughed. My-my-my. His voice was rising. Who would have thought God and I were so intimately connected? The all-mighty and not-so-mighty, but the two of us brought down with a single stroke. But it's funny how he and me get to be in the same bracket. He was getting louder now. Because you used to be always running to confession, relating to some Father our business, and after absolution I is Satan self; you keeping away, saying you avoiding the occasion of sin, playing you is nun for a week or two. But when the itch start up and it had to get scratch, it's back to me and confession time again.

He said nothing for a long while and I wondered what he was thinking, wondered whether he was reflecting on our time together with pleasure or with regret. I know that what I was feeling was sadness. I knew that the blame and hurt that was flung at me was my due for handling this whole business so clumsily. I should have told him. I should have left him back home to make his own life where he was, or make his way to England if he chose to. I should not have made the decision for him. But then, I was simply carrying him as I'd always done, taking responsibility. And he was right. What was I going to do with him now that I didn't want him? What was he going to do with himself?

When he spoke his voice was low, resigned. So, you drop God and you drop me. He came to stand right in front of me. I wouldn't look up into his face. Tell me, he said, almost in a whisper, how you dealing with sin now? Or, maybe here, he paused and waved an arm around the room, but I felt the gesture go out beyond the room and Alexandra Hall to encompass Aberystwyth, Wales, Great Britain. Maybe here, in this place, nothing is sin.

The sound of the buzzer rang through the hall. Visitors had to leave. I had half an hour before the front door was locked for the night. I picked up his bag and motioned that we were leaving. He followed me down the stairs, us two silent and separate among the whispering couples stealing a last embrace. Out the door and into a night of drizzle so fine you only knew it was there when you looked up and saw it, a fine spray of splinters drifting in cones of light under the street lamps and right into my deceitful heart. I pulled up the hood of his coat to cover his head and wrapped my own head and neck in my university scarf. He didn't ask where we were going or what my plans were for him. It was as if he'd surrendered to fate, or to me. I myself wasn't sure. I was counting on Bryn from Geology who was in a flat along the prom. Rhodri, his flatmate, had gone home to Pontypool for the weekend. Maybe something could be arranged there? As we neared his flat, I spotted Bryn swaying towards us, happily sozzled after his post rugby booze up. I put out my hand to stop Jeffrey walking as I went on quickly to intercept Bryn. I didn't tell him much, only that a friend was visiting from London and had missed the train back. He agreed to let Jeffrey use the sofa in the sitting room. We went in and in the absence of proper bedclothes made a nest of spare coats and Rhodri's blankets for Jeffrey to sleep on. He shrank back from my attempt at a hug and cheek kiss, but from his slight nod when I said I'd be back in the morning I knew he'd understood. At the door Bryn said not to worry; my friend would be all right with him. I ran down to the Bluebell hoping to catch Paul and bring him up to date, but the pub was closed, probably with him still inside clearing tables, wiping them down, putting up the chairs and mopping the floor, replacing the darts, washing glasses. But what was the point of knocking or calling out as there wasn't time and what could he do now anyway. Tomorrow is another day and if I hung about I wouldn't get back before Mr Jones locked me out.

It was still dark when I went round to Bryn's next morning. He came to the door barefoot and dishevelled. I followed him down the hallway. Sorry to get you up so early, Bryn. He put a finger to his lips and continued to the kitchen, pulling the sitting room door shut as he walked past. Was wondering how it went last night, I whispered. Bryn filled a saucepan at the sink, placed it on a burner, struck a match, turned on the gas and lit it. He blew out the match flame and put the spent match back into the box. He picked up a teapot and pointed it towards me. I nodded. The whispering, the silent gesturing was making me uneasy. Hey Bryn, everything's OK? He didn't answer. He measured a heaped teaspoon of leaves from a PG Tips packet into a teapot, poured in the boiling water, jumping back quickly as the flow of water caught the rim of the teapot and sent a wide scalding spray towards his feet. He rubbed his eyes, looked at the floor, opened his mouth as if he was going to speak, but instead he shook his head and glanced towards the sitting room. I followed his gaze and my palms began to sweat. It had to be about Jeffrey. This hesitancy. Why else was Bryn, blunt Bryn, being so cagey? He picked up the teapot, poured tea into two mugs, added milk to both, passed me one, dropped two lumps of sugar into his and stirred. Bryn, what's going on? How was last night? He took a couple sips before he answered. I've had better nights. I stopped, the mug halfway to my lips. Why? What happened? He looked into his mug, fished the teaspoon from the sink and stirred his tea some more. He clinked the spoon against the rim of the cup and dropped it back in the sink. He looked directly at me for the first time. What is he to you? I mean is he just a friend? Or…?

Gosh Bryn, I'm so sorry. I should have explained. We used to be together, back home. But I broke it off. He came unexpectedly yesterday. I still don't know why. Last night, did something happen?

He pushed his free hand through his hair. Look, I don't know how to say this, but he's not well. I slumped to sit on the floor, my back against the doorframe. Last night your friend asked me for a glass of water and when I gave it him he shook some tablets from a bottle. I asked him if he had a headache and he said I suppose you could say so. I said that's a lot for a headache and he said this will make it go away. I told him goodnight and went to my room. I had just fallen asleep when I heard someone puking. I thought, Rhodri had too many again, shouldn't mix his drinks and I was drifting off when it struck me it can't be Rhodri, he's away. I went to the bathroom and there was your friend, leaning over the toilet bowl, sticking his finger down his throat and puking so hard I thought his effin liver would come up. I said, are you all right? And he said, I don't know. I said, was it something you ate? And he said, I think I got it all up. I asked how he was feeling and he said he was much better. Anyway, I gave him a glass of water to rinse his mouth and got him to wash his hands. He was still wearing what he came in. His trousers and shoes got a bit pukey. I offered him a cup of tea to settle his stomach and he said it was Ok he'd be all right. I went back to bed and tried to fall asleep but something kept niggling so I went to the living room to check up on him.

I found him slumped across the arm of the sofa. I said, you all right? He didn't answer. I went closer and saw he was asleep. He didn't look comfortable so I shook his shoulder to sort of wake him and help him lie down properly. He still didn't wake. I turned on the light and my eye caught the bottle of pills. I looked at the label. It wasn't aspirin. It was something long but it said take one at night. I had seen him take more than one. I shook him harder and he half-opened his eyes. I said, look mate what's the matter. What are you trying on here. He said leave me. I'm sleepy. I said, no mate. No way are you going to sleep. Not here. Not on my watch. Come on. I hooked my shoulder under his arm and yanked him off the sofa and dragged him along to walk around the sofa and down the hallway and back again till he was walking better. I made coffee very strong and black with sugar. I made him drink it and we walked some more until he was properly awake. I asked if he was all right. He nodded. I said is something the matter? And he said it's a serious case of ta-bank-ah. I said what's that. And he said that is unrequited love. And I said that's it? I told him, you got to get someone to requite it. If you look around, you'll find lots of girls out there happy to requite. That's my experience, I told him. You pull yourself together, I said. Plenty fish in the sea. I picked up the bottle of tablets and I said, if you don't mind, I'll have those. I think you've had enough for one night. And I took it away.

I sat there on the floor trying to take it all in. Bryn reached down and took away the mug. The tea, undrunk, had gone cold. I got up and made to go to the sitting room. Bryn held my arm. He's sleeping fine now. I need some kip too. Come back in a couple hours. I'll keep him here. Give him some breakfast. I thanked Bryn and told him I'd clean the bathroom, the least I could do. He gave an exaggerated yawn and went to his room. I scrambled around, found his cleaning materials, and started to give the bathroom a thorough going over.

Tabanca my arse. How dare he get to be so pitiful? OK spoilt. I'll take some blame there... Christ knows I've pampered him... nothing was too expensive, no demand too unreasonable... his mother too, well she set the tone, favoured him the youngest of her four boys from three different fathers... his the only one who put her in house and gave his last name to his son and when his dad died on one of his trips back home to China... his mother had to work hard just to maintain the two of them sewing carnival costumes for Sally, making shirt collars in the Elite factory... she was so good careful... neat and keeping her head... their two heads above water... yeah that's before I start working and he look to take up this hobby... other people collect butterflies and postage stamps but not him... with him it hadda be different and exclusive... click click click... another roll of film finish... and oh I could do with a long focus lens for carnival pictures, and by the way this morning the postman dropped off that Hasselblad brochure we sent for... one thing after another... mea culpa mea culpa mea maxima culpa... but I'm done done done with that emotional blackmail crap. Time he got a grip.

By the time I was done scrubbing, the bathroom gleamed to showroom standard. I bet those two fellers never had it so clean. I guess I should have extended my reach to the kitchen. It certainly looked as if it would benefit from some of my still unworked-out rage, but my stomach reminded me I'd skipped breakfast. I hurried back to hall to see what food remained, even more determined than ever that I was having no more, no more of this. I can't. I can't be held eternally responsible for messing up. It does not deserve a life sentence.

Back at Bryn's, what do I find? The two of them sitting on the sofa in the living room with Bryn's little camera and a scatter of photos between them. I sat through endless talk of exposure and light meters, and composition and paper and shadow and angle and focus and definition, and then I went to the kitchen and made a pot of tea and brought in a tray with three mugs and milk and sugar and poured, and they sipped and didn't look my way, didn't wonder how tea had magically appeared, and I cleared up and I looked at my watch and went to the kitchen and brought in a damp rag and sponged off the puke spots from his trousers and shoes and picked up his bag and said, Come on or you'll miss the train. On the way I stopped off at Paul's digs to see if he was up and about, and to let him know what was going on. I found him just about to leave; he was going up to hall to find me to go for a walk as it was a fine day. I told him that Jeffrey had arrived the day before and I was taking him to the station to get the train back to London. He said he'd come with us for the walk. Jeffrey would have none of it. I don't want to see that man. I said, Well you don't have to. I told Paul I'd meet him outside the station after Jeffrey's train left.

I bought the thruppeny platform ticket and went through with Jeffrey to see him board. He stood stiff and unyielding as he allowed me to give him a hug. He didn't hug me back but he seemed to be listening while I said I was sorry for the way things turned out between us; that I'd write him to find out how things were working out for him in the care of Mario. He gave a brisk nod when I finished speaking and he turned away, walking towards the train. He got on without looking back. He sat near a window where I could see him, but he kept looking straight ahead and he didn't return my wave when his carriage jolted as the engine started.

I watched the train pull away with him on it. It got smaller and smaller until it shrank to nothingness and all that was left hanging over the tracks was its flimsy ghost, grey and frail, already turning to tatters in the wind. Benediction. The distinctive piercing scent of incense burning, smoke hovering in puffs over the pews, rising in faint blue wisps long after the censer had been closed. *Ite missa est*. It is over. I knew I'd done the only thing I could do. But I didn't feel I'd done it right.

I walked back along the platform to the turnstile. Hurried footsteps behind me caught me up. He hooked his arm through mine so that we were walking step-in-step. I thought we were meeting outside, I said. He pressed my arm tightly to his side. Just making sure you didn't get on that train.

LOVE LETTERS

Paul's parents were upset that he hadn't lined up his next stage after graduation. No, that's not quite accurate. Upset is when you order coconut, ginger and rum ice cream with crushed cocoa nibs topping and get two scoops of vanilla with yellow, blue and pink sprinkles instead. So, let me revise that. They were disappointed. They were confused. They were fuming. They saw him as drifting, aimless. There was good reason for the way they felt, at least from their perspective. They would have liked him to do some post-grad course, or get a job that had training and prospects, get into some profession as they'd done – both of them teachers, his dad a headmaster, his mum a part-time literacy skills teacher in an infant school and otherwise housewifeing. No, they didn't want him to go into teaching, they didn't think he'd like that, but can't you just pick a profession, any profession, for heaven's sake, boy? What did he think life was about? They'd sacrificed for their children, not like some of their friends who'd spent their money on expensive holidays and new cars and shiny appliances and fancy restaurants. He was the eldest; they'd invested in his posh Queen Elizabeth Hospital schooling –Bristol's leading independent school – all those uniforms and kit, pricey public school tat, even though he was on a scholarship, and right after that came his means-tested university education. Had he forgotten that there were three younger ones looking up to him? What kind of example was he setting them? Why did he go to London last summer if it wasn't to look for career opportunities?

Directly after his final exams, he and I went to Bristol to his parents on my way to London. It was the twenty-first of June, which in theory I knew as midsummer day, and I remember saying to his parents that I was disappointed that it was already the middle of summer and that things were only going to get colder afterwards. They laughed and assured me that things were going to get warmer until the end of August. Since I'd arrived early the September before and things were already cold, I wondered if that could be correct. For supper, his mum had prepared soup and mushrooms on toast. The only mushrooms I knew were the dried black Chinese ones that cooked flat and somewhat rubbery. I'd never had white mushrooms before, and certainly not on toast. I'd had beans on toast in hall, but the bean sauce made the toast soggy enough to be manageable with regular cutlery.

How was I going to deal with crisp, crumbly, buttery toast and small, wobbly, grilled button mushrooms? I don't think this was meant as a test of my table etiquette – those welcoming people were too innocent of life beyond their own experience to imagine that I'd only recently given up using just a spoon to shovel up meals, had only just been introduced to toast as a knife and fork item. I watched to see how the other diners handled their knife and fork, skewering the mushroom to the toast below with the tines of the fork, holding them together immovably on the plate, then working around it with the knife to cut out a small square of toast, and bring fork to lips. It worked. How much of my life have I spent at tables not my own, with my eyes fixed, not on my own hands, on my own plate, but sliding sideways and across at the hands and plates of others?

At the table there was lots of small talk with big talk sandwiched within it. How big was my family, did my mother work, what did she do, what did my father do, what was I doing, how did I get there, was I planning to go back after, and as to the summer break, where was I going, did I have family here, was I going to do sightseeing, if so I must visit Kew Gardens – wonderful tropical collection – did we have rhododendrons back at my home? No, I didn't know that flower, except by seeing the name in books. Is that how you pronounce it? I'll certainly try to get there, though I'd be staying with friends and trying to find a job to keep me afloat and busy.

They would be off to spend the summer at their caravan parked all year at Brean; they'd be leaving as soon as schools closed, but before that, before Brean, they would go with Paul to Aber for his graduation. Brean? Oh it's a place in Somerset, a wide stretch of sand on the Severn estuary, not very far; lovely there on the beach in the summer. The tide goes out very far and you've got to be careful that you aren't caught out there, on the sand when it comes in or you'll be stranded in deep water; there's a very strong current. They go every year; they know all the families who have caravans there; the children have grown up together summer after summer. I don't know what questions to ask, what conversation to make. What is a caravan? Is it like the covered wagons in westerns, horse-drawn gypsy caravans in picture-book stories, or strings of camels attached by ropes crossing the Sahara? Do I say something about staying in a rented house by the sea in Toco? No, because that would be about Marmie, and I didn't want to be drawn into talk about my father, or Marmie pawning her gold bracelets to meet the cost, or forfeiting three weeks' pay as a grocery cashier to do this for us? Could I talk about Trois Roches, no wide beach, no tide ambushing the unwary? Does crab-hunting at full moon, or rainflies divebombing into hissing gas lanterns count? I don't say anything about any of these.

As I write this now, October 2020, I see Mia Mottley of Barbados talking on YouTube about our lack of cultural confidence in the Caribbean, when we have so much that is world class. She lists some of our greats, in every sphere of human endeavour, and they are many, disproportionately large to our population size, and I, a child of colonialism and last century Irish Catholicism, I know what Mia means about lack of cultural confidence, which, on that long-ago day in Bristol, I would have named silencing shame.

Paul's little sister, Dinah, then nine or ten, sweetly surrendered her room to me for the night. Next morning, Paul borrowed his mother's car to take me to Temple Meads Station for my London train. I'm almost positive that at that time his parents did not see me as a threat to their stability. I think they saw me as a university friend, someone who, as an overseas student, would welcome being invited into an English home, meeting an English family and enjoying real English hospitality. At worst, I'd be a passing fancy, but with him having left Aber, and me there another two years and due to go back where I came from right after, this visit was hello-goodbye for all of us. That was how it was the summer before, but there we were in September, Paul and me, back in Aber for the new term of my second year, where I was meant to be, but as far as his parents were concerned, where he wasn't.

I know that Paul understood all this, about their hopes and expectations for him, that it was only fair that he should be done and dusted, before they moved on to the next child in line, a promising, hardworking, serious boy in sixth form. And yes, his delay in getting on with the business of a career could be seen as setting a bad example to the others, and while he understood that these were real concerns for them, it bothered him that they weren't prepared to let him be, and just cut him loose to find himself. They kept sending him brochures and newspaper clippings with job ads and kept encouraging his well-placed uncle to write him well-meaning letters with suggestions and advice, anxious that he'd be left behind. He would be at the bottom rung of the ladder of success, and he'd find it hard to catch up and he'd be sorry he frittered away this opportunity.

But Paul wasn't aimless. It was simply that his aim wasn't stated, not to them, not to me, perhaps not even to himself, but it was understood as a given to the two of us. His aim, and mine too, was not to lose each other. That's all. And that necessitated his being where I was committed to be, in Aberystwyth. I think, too, that the whole business with Jeffrey and me and him in London the previous summer, and more recently in Aber, showed us how easy it was for people to drift apart. Jeffrey and I had spent all of our teen years tied to each other, but as soon as I was no longer in that space, away from the confines of him and home, it all seemed to me a pointless commitment and I think that without either of us voicing it, both Paul and I, who had known each other for only six months, feared that what we had holding us together would be under severe strain if we lost sight of each other. But for him to come back to a university town that he'd just recently left, without a stated purpose, would have raised questions for any one concerned about his future, and three months after his graduation his parents were beyond simply raising questions. They were frustrated with what they saw as his dithering, and angry that he wasn't moving on. For goodness sake, he wasn't even moving away.

Paul's close friends had gone their ways. Pete Davies, his best friend, had gone to a job in Liverpool. Norman, another friend, had simply disappeared. But there was Godfrey, still there as a student with his wife, Gwyn, and their baby. Godfrey was his first friend in his first year. He'd had to retake a year because of missing a term or so to sort out his life when he and Gwyn got married. She'd had to carry on with her job in the library and they both had been looking after their new baby. It had been a struggle to make ends meet, but Godfrey was there for a fourth year in a tiny caravan parked in an often rain-soaked field outside town. You approached it in boots, pulling them off, heavy with mud, and leaving them outside, under the caravan. This had only a paraffin stove for heat and water had to be brought in by bucket. They had a motorbike with a small sidecar, low to the ground, hardly bigger than a pram really, for Gwyn and baby to ride in, but Godfrey was happy, really happy and content with his new life as a suddenly responsible adult. Maybe Paul saw Godfrey and Gwyn's situation as not bad, not bad at all, not something anyone could see as anything but successful on its own terms. They became not just Paul's friends but mine too, and we spent many enjoyable evenings up in the caravan. Paul would be reaching into his long riding mac to pluck a newspaper-wrapped supper from against his chest, where he'd kept it warm on the long cold wet trudge, and us four would then be chasing down crisply fried, vinegary cod and long limp pale fingers of potato chips with a flagon of cider that we'd brought from the off-license.

When he saw a 'Help Wanted' sign hanging on the door of an electrical goods shop in town, Paul walked in and convinced the owner or manager that although he had a degree, he was willing to take the job if he'd have him. It afforded him the means to continue living in Aber. He found digs at Nant-yr-Maen on Portland Street with a family who let rooms to students on a bed and breakfast arrangement. The husband was a Pole with curious eyes, one blue, one brown, the wife Irish, and I seem to remember they had three boys under five. Paul was comfortable enough there, a single bed in a room with a desk and chair, sheets changed regularly, one bathroom shared with the whole family, but at least on the same floor as the bedrooms, breakfast of eggs, bacon, toast, tea, TV and a cuppa on evenings in the family living room if you were prepared to watch ITV with the family. That was them and Paul. But how did they react to me?

Aberystwyth is a prosperous market town, the only one of its size and importance in mid-Wales. That's how Harriet HH's guidebooks would probably have described it. But at heart it was, while I lived there, a seaside town that depended on visitors for much of its livelihood. During the term, it was students; in the summer it was day-trippers and other longer-stay holidaymakers, as well as researchers and conference attendees. It had an economic ecosystem in which many benefited and some prospered, whether farmers, business people, home owners, ratepayers, landladies, students in halls of residence, landlords of pubs, restaurateurs, proprietors of bed and breakfast rooms, cafes, hotels, the crazy golf course and one-arm bandits, the pier hawkers with naughty postcards and tawdry keepsakes, sellers of sticks of Aberystwyth rock, cans of Welsh sea air, candyfloss, and the butcher, baker, candlestick maker and all. The trade-off on the part of the townsfolk was a willingness, or at least a resignation, to welcome, or at least to tolerate, people from a variety of countries, speaking a number of languages and presenting a range of skin hues.

So Paul's landlord and landlady were friendly enough to me as the girlfriend of one of their lodgers. But that went through a rocky patch when, once again, my ignorance of cultural norms caused a bit of bother with the folks at Nant-Yr-Maen. Of course, house rules prohibited my going up to Paul's room, but one day I dropped in the electrical shop and was told he'd called in sick. I went to his digs to find he had been in bed all day, feeling unwell and the landlady said I could go up and see him. He looked awful, and was feeling worse – sore throat, headache, chest pains, temperature. I went to the phone box on the street corner and called Dr Pryce who said he'd make a house call that evening after surgery. I gave him the address. I went back to hall, had supper and went to bed.

After my ten o'clock lecture next day I went to check on how the doctor's visit had gone. The landlady came to the door. Oh, she said. It's *you*. She said the *you* with distaste and I wondered why she was in a bad mood. She continued. You can go up for five minutes. Paul was sitting up in bed reading *Private Eye*. You're looking much better. What did the doctor say? He tossed the magazine aside, shifted so I could sit on the bed and made a mock sad face. Bronchitis. Then he brightened. But I should be all right in a couple days. The chemists sent over some stuff. He glanced towards his desk at a cluster of small bottles and paper bags. What's up with her downstairs? I whispered. He gave a wry smile. She's upset because she wasn't expecting the doctor last evening. He went on to explain that people don't invite others to someone else's house. I said, sorry. I didn't know. Then I thought about back home where people, anyone, friend or friend of friend, could just drop in, uninvited, and be offered hospitality. And you'd be so relieved if a doctor came when someone's sick, you wouldn't care about how or who. On my way out I went to the kitchen to say I was leaving and to tell her I was sorry. She took the chance to get it off her chest about what I had done wrong. It had been embarrassing to her to answer her doorbell to someone whom she wasn't expecting, to greet the doctor unsuitably attired and to take him to a patient whose room and person she hadn't prepared for the doctor's visit, as befits the landlady of a respectable household. She was the one to call the doctor, not me. It was her home not mine, nor any of the lodgers. No, she didn't mind the doctor's visit. A sick person ought to get medical attention. What she objected to was my thinking it was permissible for me to send for the doctor to come to her house without asking her permission first or, more appropriately, asking her to make the appointment. Back in hall I pictured her opening the door to Dr Pryce. He, mohair coat, pinstripe three-piece suit, crisp white shirt, knotted striped tie tucked in waistcoat, black bag held in brown leather-gloved hand, gleaming Oxford brogues; she, house dress, cardigan sleeves pushed up to elbows, faded apron, felt slippers, hairnet; the hall, toy-strewn; the patient, untidy in unmade bed. She was right of course. I didn't think. I didn't know. I didn't ask. I had caused her real distress, avoidable if only I'd done the right thing. And my self-pitying tears soaking my pillow were of no use. After a few frosty weeks she once again invited me in to join them for a cuppa when I dropped by on an evening. I now wonder whether she, Irish immigrant, and he, Polish war refugee, may have remembered themselves as new arrivals also making one or two grave cultural errors, and they had then come to see me as a fellow stranger in a strange land?

At the electrical shop, Paul's job was easy and afforded him the opportunity to meet and mingle with townsfolk, whom students rarely meet on equal terms. He learned new stuff like how to change a plug, a fuse, an electric cord on a lamp and felt proud of those achievements. I had one of those 'what a small world this is' experiences in that shop. Apart from the man in charge and Paul, there was a girl working there. One day, when I came by to meet up with Paul, he called her over to introduce us. He said that I was from Trinidad. Trinidad? she said. A girl from my town who was in class with my sister went to Trinidad to teach. I don't suppose you'd know her. Her name is Rita Wynne-Evans. Yes, the very same Rita Wynne-Evans that Gerry Sankeralli had taken me to meet at the Pointe-à-Pierre refinery. I was able to tell Paul's workmate that I had indeed met her, that she was well and seemed happy with her teaching job and had made lots of friends among the expat and local engineers and so on. I also added that Rita had told me I should visit her family in Machynelleth to let them know I'd seen her. Yes, you should, said the new friend. They'd love to meet you and to hear about Rita's adventures. Sadly, I never made it to Machynelleth. Life got in the way.

   I think Paul would have carried on working in the electrical shop for the two years until I completed my degree. We had no responsibilities apart from each other and we were happy, very carefree in our happiness, and we didn't have the time or inclination to think about what next. How he got wind of Cardiganshire County Hall needing an assistant town and country planner I don't recall. I don't think his dad spotted the ad in a newspaper, cut it out and sent it by post to him because by then things were a bit chilly between them. I think it must have been Paul himself reading the classified ads and this one jumping out at him. He applied and got the job. The County Hall was in Aberystwyth. He would start work right after Christmas. He would stay on at Nant-Yr-Maen.

I imagined that the only changes would be buttoned-up shirt and tie instead of open-neck shirt and jumper, sleeves buttoned at wrist not rolled up to elbow, and the gift of Saturday afternoons free to do as we pleased, but there were other changes that I didn't at the time foresee. Eager to share the news with his parents, we headed to the phone box at the far end of the prom. Through the glass I could see him chatting animatedly, the tall piles of thruppeny bits shrinking as he dropped them one by one through the slot. I imagined his parents taking turns to speak into the receiver, sometimes talking over each other, the many questions they would be asking – his dad wanting to know more about the job itself, what it would entail, the salary, is it pensionable, prospects, training; his mum interested in what he would need by way of new clothes, where he would live, holidays – and him answering he didn't know yet, wasn't sure, he'd wait and see. I thought about the two different journeys the conversation was making – one from his parents, hugely relieved at him seeming to have secured a foothold in a worthwhile future, to himself, completely in the present, happy to have at last good news to share with them; the other through telephone wires from 69 Cassell Road, Fishponds, in secure suburban Bristol, under the Severn estuary, over the Brecon Beacons with red kites circling overhead, by-passing Caerleon and King Arthur's cave, the pits and tips of the collieries, Tiger Bay, Cardiff, Shirley Bassey, Aberfan, Plynlimon, Devil's Bridge and the Rheidol, to the red phone box beside the sparkly water of Cardigan Bay. I thought, too, that my mother knew very little of me and what I was doing and with whom or why, where and when, and I wondered whether that mattered to her or to me as much as Paul's doings mattered to his parents and their opinion of him mattered to him. And whether what separated us, Marmie and me – the physical distance across the vast ocean, the many latitudes and longitudes drawn between us, the difficulty of keeping in touch other than by infrequent letters – was all that made the difference.

The 'real' job brought the expected change in his parents' attitude, restoring familial harmony to their relationship, but there was something else too. It somehow made him a person about whose life and career choice they could have grownup conversations – it was as if he, by getting a job that met with their approval, had moved up in some way to become something of an equal. And now, as I'm thinking about that period, I can see that it also marked a turning point for us, a gradual but discernible change in ourselves, and in the way we saw ourselves together. What had started off as a student romance when we met the Easter before – with all the exploration and excitement of such things, spiked as it was for both of us by our stepping outside our norms and engaging intimately with 'The Other' – had grown into a love affair by the time we moved to London in the summer, had become a serious attachment just by his coming back to Aber with me, so when he chose to stay on in a real job with a career path, what we had together began to shape itself into something else (something that I think we romanticised in our friends Godfrey and Gwyn), a new *bravez danger* attitude to the future that made us feel invincible, made us indifferent to warnings. For, oh yes, weren't we strong enough as a pair to vault over any hurdles that stood in our way, silence all naysayers?

Hall closed for three weeks for the Christmas break. There was an exodus of students from the town and digs were lying empty. I got a room to tide me over until hall reopened. Paul was due to start the new job on the first working day of January but was needed at the electrical shop for at least the week leading to Christmas, when he was expected in Bristol and where I, too, was expected. I was anxious about this because I could no longer be thought of as simply an overseas student friend passing through on the way to London as I had been in June. It was six months since Paul had not joined the family in Brean after graduation, but had come to London to be with me, had gone back to Aber with me in September and he had found ways to secure himself there. I could not trust that their relief at his getting a real job was great enough to cancel out their concerns about what was almost certainly to them a tricky situation, tricky for many reasons apart from the one that grabbed you at first sight.

When our own eldest went through babyhood, infancy, primary school, secondary school, first boyfriend, off to university, it was all first time, first time for everything, for her and for us. We had no template to work from. It was trial and error and we made mistakes in choices and judgements, some bad, some less so. But all of that came later, and I know now that the first child is the test case, the experiment that as a parent you're almost bound to fail at – at least as often as you don't. Paul's parents were as worried about him as much as they were dismayed.

On Christmas Eve, we got there by train. Paul's dad picked us up at Temple Meads. At the house, his dad took my coat and hung it with his in the cupboard under the stairs. He pushed open the door where the rest of the family was gathered and motioned me in. It was like that scene in the fairy tale where, with the princess asleep in the tower, a fairy waved her magic wand to freeze the entire household in whatever position they were. I could see that they had been doing little fiddly things, inconsequential things like gift wrapping, hanging ornaments on the tree, reading, watching telly. But when the door was pushed open and I was framed in the doorway, everyone was motionless, eyes fixed in my direction. His mum broke the spell and rose to greet me, holding out her hands to mine and leaning in to kiss me on the cheek. I'd learnt sufficient good manners by then to say, thank you, Mrs Jenkins, for inviting me. She laughed. You're to call me Mum.

On Christmas morning I was anxious to run downstairs and give presents and open presents, but Paul whispered it wasn't time, presents were opened after the Queen's Christmas message. What time is that? She gives her message after lunch, starting at three. Lunch was big and orderly. Hall had trained me about proper table etiquette, about a table having a head, about assigned seating, who's on the right, who's on the left, who's next to who, napkins and all that, so I think I conducted myself irreproachably. They tried hard to give a good impression of themselves, not in a way to show how fine they were, no, not at all, the dad was from South Wales, mining stock in his family's past, and although his generation had done well for themselves, he had no illusions about his past and his place in the world. The mum's dad was a school headmaster, so already a middle-class head start, and she'd gone to a posh girls' public school – named after a slave owner whose statue, venerated for over a century was, just this year, tossed into the Bristol harbour. This was also the school to which Dinah, Paul's sister, was destined to go at eleven. They wanted to make as good an impression on Paul's friend as I wanted to make on them, his family.

Dealing with a cultural neophyte is like teaching a child new things; everything moves in one direction. So let's say Paul's mum is making an apple pie and there's grunt work to do, sous chef stuff. I say, Can I help? and she says That would be lovely. There's Granny Smiths in the larder, maybe four? Of that I know one concept. Four. So she's got to show me that Granny Smiths are the big green apples and the larder is the walk-in cupboard with thick, cool, slate shelving. Then there's the peeling. I can figure that out, but which knife, oh a peeler? There's such a thing as a peeler? A tool not a person? And a corer too! Slice thinly. Which way? Across or down? Short crust pastry and school cookery memory kicks in. But here margarine and shortening are called fat and there's something called suet which is actual animal fat. And a darling little funnel you put in the dish among the filling to keep the pastry lid from collapsing into the pie. There's a brush just for dipping into milk to sweep over the crust and then the thumb indentations along the edges to scallop-seal the lid to the base. Some people do it with a fork, but I like this way. How does your mum do it?

The dad took me round the garden. There were cordons – pears and apples – along one wall, a big apple tree with a swing hanging from it as in a child's picture-book, a rhubarb bed, bamboo tepees a relic of last summer's runner beans, roses, wisteria, forsythia, and much else I didn't know and wouldn't recognise when things grew leaves again. On Boxing Day, he took us in the car to an arboretum, and I saw the care and love and investment that a place can devote to things they love and cherish, even if it's just trees and shrubs. All of it, in and out the house, was new. And I knew I would take in only a small amount of this teaching and be as dumb and as useless next time, if there was to be such.

How much easier it would have been for them if he'd gotten involved with a girl from there, from Wales or from England, like everybody does, everybody they know does. A girl with parents they could meet and assess, with families they could trace, from landscapes they could relate to, and professions or even jobs – people they knew. Certainties, commonalities. After the first child you learn a little about how to deal with the second and by the third, you think – 'whatever', but Paul's parents didn't know that, and neither, when it was our turn, did we. So at that time, that first Christmas, I'm guessing they saw all the uncertainties and all the woeful certainties ahead that such a relationship would be encumbered with; something they would have preferred not to have to deal with and, as loving parents, would have preferred for him to avoid. However, whatever they may have discussed in private, I'll never know because they were the epitome of hospitality and kindness to me, and I must've taxed their energies to breaking point. How they must've slumped in their chairs in the lounge and exhaled deep and long after we'd left. A guest like me could only take and take and take and be able to give very little back. We went back to Aber before we needed to, simply for time together, snug, warm, intimate and domestic, before he went back to Nant-yr Maen and to his new job.

The new term went by. Paul was enjoying his job and getting more and more interested in town planning. Then it was again Easter and for me field trips. This time both geography and geology trips, so just a short time to fill in between. I stayed with a friend in Porthcawl after our geography field trip, then Paul and I went to his parents for the Easter weekend. Then came the third term of my second year. A job in Cardiff City Planning Department came up. Paul applied and got it, leaving Aber at the end of June, just as I was setting off for Trinidad to research for my final year dissertation. And just like that, we were parting. I was going back home, and Paul was going to Cardiff to live and work.

I'd been away less than two years, yet when I got to the only place I'd known for more than twenty of my twenty-two years, I didn't feel that home was Home. I was a stranger in that I had changed. My clothes were wrong, my accent was wrong, the things I wanted to talk about and to do didn't fit. I was in a strange land, a new one with a flag, an anthem, national songs and watchwords that I knew nothing of. I had just one good schoolfriend left there, Maritza, she of Penthouse Saturday lunchtime, and she was my salvation. She was at the Central Library on the Savannah at the time, and I would walk over from home and meet up with her there. Her big sister, Val, had got married to a Brazilian and they took Maritza and me wherever they were going – the beach, clubs, limes. I got some suitable clothes made and spent most days doing research, conducting interviews, chatting with people, reading back copies of newspapers, reading journals, getting my material together. I visited Jeffrey's mother who lived round the corner from home. She knew that Jeffrey and I had broken up. She didn't reproach me. In fact, she asked me to take some stuff back for him and I agreed, saying I'd leave it with Mario. I told her about Jill, what a wonderful girl Mario had got.

We had a phone at home by then and Paul and I would chat once a week. He was staying at his Aunt Bet and Uncle Joe and their younger daughter, Eryl, in Whitchurch, a Cardiff suburb, and flat hunting for somewhere nearer his work in the Civic Centre. I spent six weeks back home and never once thought about remaining there, never imagined giving up university, but when I got back to London Heathrow and Paul picked me up, he said he wasn't sure I'd come back until he saw me. All I remember of that day of return was a wave of exhaustion sweeping over me, a tiredness, a letting go. I slept all the way from the airport to the flat and immediately went to bed, sleeping through the day, through the night to next morning and I awoke in a new place, the flat he'd moved into.

The flat was the ground floor of a large house on Kimberley Road, Roath Park. Upstairs lived Mrs Evans, the owner of the house, an old lady, quite bedridden. Sometimes you'd hear a bump and Paul would pause and listen and dart upstairs. She'd fallen off the bed and had to be helped back up. Or she'd repeatedly knock on the floor with her walking stick because she wanted something. Her son came by every morning and every evening, but because he lived somewhere else, Paul would sometimes have to go to the corner phone box and call the son's home if there was an emergency, when he couldn't lift her back on the bed by himself.

Our flat was very spacious, many more rooms than we needed or even wanted, especially as it was full of stuff that Mrs Evans herself didn't want. In the drawing room, the front room, dark drapes, lumpy living-room furniture, huge, worn, dusty rugs, a fireplace that didn't work. But there was a bedroom, a small dining room, a kitchen and a bathroom, a garden at the back, and for the first time we had a proper place of our own. For the remaining month of the summer break I was an idle housewife while Paul went to work. I explored the neighbourhood, found two corner shops for staples, a long narrow park bordering a stream with an abundance of wild flowers on its banks – cow parsley, large white umbelliferous inflorescences, like the Queen Anne's lace flower so beloved for bridal bouquets back home. On Wellfield Road there was a wider variety of shops, including a Co-Op, a gents hairdresser, a ladies hairdresser, a baker, a greengrocer, a butcher, a launderette, a doctors surgery, a library, a much bigger playing field, mature trees lining the pavements, street names like Balaclava and Kimberley, Mafeking and Ladysmith, which, innocent of history, I didn't know were Boer War names, nor what the Boer War had been about or when.

We became good friends with Paul's cousin Lyn and her husband Mac. Lyn was like a pixie, slim and tiny and bubbly. From her I learnt about stuff like the class difference between earning a wage and receiving a salary. A bright girl, she'd given up teachers training college to work instead in the office of the big steel mill, GKN, in Newport. She told me that she preferred winter to summer. I could not imagine anything more outrageous than that statement. I asked why? Because, she said, in winter you could dress smartly – a dress and matching jacket and a coat with a skirt that goes with it, or you could mix and match with blouses and make many different costumes. I realised that by costumes she meant outfits, where back home costumes meant Carnival – something quite different.

From Lyn, too, I learned something about the cultural practices of young couples. There was the one called 'boys night out' – those evenings when Mac met up with male friends at the pub for drinks and darts and Lyn was dropped off at her parents and picked up again after the pubs closed, with Mac coming in to have a cuppa with Joe and Bet before leaving. Did Lyn have a girls night out, too? I don't remember. Booking a holiday was another ritual, planned and booked in winter, followed by actually going away on the holiday itself, cheaper in spring and autumn than in high summer. You couldn't call it a holiday if you were simply not going to work. You had to actually leave your home and go somewhere else. These rites were somehow sacred, not to be tampered with. Paul and I went out with them on evenings for drinks, had them round for dinner and went to theirs. I now wonder whether that kind of meeting up had a name in people's schedules, but at the time it seemed spontaneous and we enjoyed it. Then it was time for me to go back to Aber and start my third and final year and leave Paul behind in Cardiff. He rented a car and took me there, leaving me outside Alex, waving.

Not since at Paddington Station two years before had I felt so totally unmoored. Not on leaving home for the first time, leaving my family, friends, known places and people, Jeffrey, all the things that mattered and defined me; leaving those was an adventure, a striking out to explore the unknown. Standing there, on the promenade in Aber without Paul, I felt abandoned. When I looked around for those whose mere presence was reassuring, I realised that many had gone. Trevor Spencer had graduated and, smart lad, once again had his business sorted. I heard he was off to do postgrad and train as a diplomat in Switzerland. After getting a first in philosophy, Rudy White had added another first, this time in English, after another year. He'd got married to Alwyna, a Welsh girl and fellow student. They had a little boy, Andrew, and were living in Devil's Bridge, not far from Aber. Godfrey and Gwyn and their baby had gone too. Worst, the rhythm of daily life with Paul, which had shaped most of my life as a student, was no more. But it was my third and final year, only geography now to contend with and I pulled into my little circle of Alex Hall friends. I was lucky to have tutors and lecturers who took a special interest in me. There was James Taylor, my Latin American studies tutor and dissertation supervisor, who wanted me to stay on a couple more years and do research under him for a PhD, and Harold Carter, whom I absolutely adored – he was so careful, so thorough, so curious about whatever he was teaching that he excited his students into sharing his love of settlement geography, especially urban geography. Paul used to say that it was Harold Carter who'd inspired him to take town planning seriously, so I fancied that if a PhD was really on offer, that's what I'd like to pursue, but I'd have to get a good degree first.

That autumn term Paul came to Aber on weekends, overnighting illicitly in my room, but friends knew, not by being told, oh no, that I wouldn't do, but by adding two and two correctly. Others guessed, too, so that when the fire alarm was sounded one Saturday night and we resident women in nightclothes rushed down the fire escape onto the back road for a roll call to be taken, and rooms were checked to make sure no one was sleeping through it all, Joanna and Alison asked how Paul had been able to make himself invisible during the room check. On other weekends, though fewer, I went to Cardiff. Christmas break came and this time Paul came to Aber to pick me up and we went to Cardiff where Paul was at work until Christmas Eve. Then we set off by train to Bristol for the weekend.

We still couldn't be open about me staying with Paul in his flat in Cardiff. We knew that to be honest about our domestic arrangements would force his parents to form an opinion on it, perhaps to want to discuss it with us. It would be awkward and embarrassing for us all. It would change our relationship with them – he with his parents, them with me – and it would put them in a position of having to decide how much of it the other children should be exposed to. I don't doubt that they guessed that in Cardiff we were living together, but our official story that I was staying in a bed and breakfast at a Mrs Thomas on Pen-y-Lan Road satisfied everyone. Tellingly, no questions were ever asked about Mrs Thomas, the accommodation, the breakfast, the cost, nothing. It was a way of preventing an unwelcome intrusion into their protected lives. Don't trouble trouble, as Marmie would say, although I don't think that she would have been at all scandalised if she had known, not because her morals were laxer, but because she was more realistic about life. After all, my next younger sister, Annette, was married and a mother and my youngest sister, Carol, at nineteen, also had a son. And let's not forget how all four of us came into the world.

Christmas came and went. We went back to Cardiff and then on to Aber for the second term of my final year. I wanted to be in Cardiff with Paul more than anything, so I wrote to the High Commission in London asking them to forward to Trinidad my request to do the Diploma in Education at the University of Wales, Cardiff, in the last year of my four-year scholarship. I pointed out that since I was expected to teach on return to Trinidad, this additional qualification would equip me better. I left the matter in their hands. Crunch time for the dissertation meant visits in either direction were fewer, while scheduled phone calls became more frequent. Winter made travel difficult, anyway.

One afternoon, sometime early in March, I picked up post in my pigeonhole to find an envelope with a Trinidad and Tobago stamp. Everyone home wrote me on air letters, so this was an unusual piece of correspondence. The address was typed and that made it even more formal. I tore open the envelope as soon as I got to my room and when I read the letter my heart dropped. It was from the government department that dealt with my scholarship. It stated that since my course of study, the BSc Honours in Geography, was due to be completed in a few months' time, I was to return to Trinidad and report for duty at the Government Teachers Training College, St Vincent Street, as a Lecturer in Geography immediately on my return to begin my contractual obligation of five years service in a government educational institution. I waited downstairs near the phone booth for Paul's call that night and when it came I read the letter to him. He listened. He said, let us get married.

It is a truth, universally acknowledged, at least in the UK, that an unmarried man in possession of a job is in want of a wife before the fourth of April, the end of the tax year, so he could get a tax refund. Consequently, there was fierce competition for a slot to have a marriage performed and registered in the weeks leading up to that critical date. It would never have happened if it weren't for Paul's parents. Paul's mother was persistent in her search at every registry office in and around the Bristol area for the narrow window that my Easter field trip would allow. She got us a space at the Bristol Registry Office for the third of April. That date was Dinah's birthday and I felt bad about usurping her celebration. But she would have none of my apology. That dear little child said that it was the nicest gift she could have got, an answer that was the most generous one I could have hoped for. It helps me now in my dotage that each year I remember her birthday and am forced to scramble around my memory for everyone else's.

Paul's mother was, though, disappointed that it wouldn't be a church wedding. She was a regular member at Christ Church, Downend and, as head of the Young Wives Group, our insistence that it must be a civil ceremony put her in a quandary. How would she explain this to her fellow parishioners, and what would she tell friends and family? She found a solution. She told everybody that because I was Catholic and Paul Anglican, we'd decided that we should be married in a neutral place. Paul and I were amused at how quickly she came up with this truth-defying but plausible explanation, and very grateful for her coup in landing us a space in the lovely old Quakers Priory in its new function as a registry office. All of this, of course, was relayed to me by phone as we were in three different places.

As it happened, conversation at supper that evening – the evening of the letter from the government telling me to return at once – which I didn't tell anyone but Paul about – concerned a girl in hall who had got gifts from her merchant navy boyfriend who'd returned from a tour of duty in the Far East, and she was selling off some of the gifts she hadn't any use for. I went along to her room. Among the items were two lengths of heavy embroidered Malayan silk. I took a three-yard silvery white piece with tiny birds embroidered in black thread. It cost me one pound.

I went off to Cardiff. Paul and I had by then decided on a car and we bought a new, light-grey Austin Mini – FKG 122C. Why do I suddenly think it cost somewhere around five hundred pounds? We paid cash. He'd been saving since the time he was working in the electrical shop, adding a pound at a time to his Post Office Savings account. This was popular among his parents' generation as something you started your children with when they got to about ten years old, and friends and family would give them money as gifts for birthdays and Christmas. I was new to that, so my financial affairs were conducted at Barclays Bank. Of course, I now know about Barclays and their lucrative financial dealings in the whole enterprise of the enslavement of Africans, my own ancestors, but you can't go back in time to transfer your account to the saintly Post Office, can you?

We drove to Bristol the weekend term ended, so that Mrs Evans, across the road from Paul's parents, could take my measurements for a long-sleeved cheongsam style jacket with black frogging fastenings on the front of the jacket and a fitted knee-length slim skirt. I had to leave right away to join my last field trip, to Yorkshire. I got back to Bristol a week before our wedding. We went into Broadmead to choose a ring and both of us immediately loved a very wide gold band with a raised pattern of roses and vines. I think it cost fifteen pounds. The flowers and vines are worn yet discernable and the ring still has its deep twenty-two carat gleam. Paul and his mother had sent out invitations to his family on both his mother's and father's sides and to a few of his parents' close friends. Paul invited one friend, Geoff Northover, who was at QEH with him and at Aber as a geography student in my year. As for me, there was no family, but there was Marie Ng Chow who came up from Surrey. From hall were Vivienne, Joanna and Jyotsna. Harriet HH had Harrods deliver a white Wedgewood tea service as a wedding present. I still have it, and the breadboard and breadknife from hall friends is in constant daily use.

The day before the wedding Paul and I went to Heathrow to pick up a package from my mother. Back at the house I opened the long box. Under layers of white tissue paper were pink and white anthuriums and white orchids, the end of each stem plugged into a glass vial of water. No one had seen any of these flowers before, and as I named them and passed them around for admiration and questions and comment, I felt a pride I hadn't felt before about where I came from, who I came from, what had made me, who at the core I was. A church lady made a little bouquet and a bandeau of the orchids. The anthuriums were put in tall vases.

The reception was held in Paul's parents' back garden in unseasonably warm dry weather. Rented tables were laid with white cloth and decorated with little posies as centrepieces; the garden was in full bloom with spring flowers. The buffet lunch was rotisserie chicken quarters from MacFisheries with potato salad and green salad made at home. There were bread rolls and butter with lunch, cheese and biscuits after. There was wine, beer and our favourite, Taunton Natural Dry Cider. There was a two-tier cake from the Cadena Cake Shop. There was tea and coffee. Every detail had been worked out by Paul and his family when I was in Aber and in Yorkshire. There were toasts and speeches. My mother phoned from Trinidad to speak to me and Paul and to his parents. A friend of the family made a little movie. Vivienne brought her camera and exposed a roll of colour film; someone else, I think either Vivian or Philip, Paul's younger brothers, took black and white pictures. In all there must've been about fifty people at the reception, and everyone said how much they enjoyed the occasion. It was perfect. There was nothing I would have changed. Everything was a wonderful gift.

We went on honeymoon to Wessex as we were both immersed in reading and rereading Thomas Hardy at the time. We stayed in bed and breakfasts for a blissful sunny and dry two weeks, going from one Hardy location to another. In those days you could go right up to Stonehenge and touch the massive upended rocks, lie on the grass in their shade. We visited the chalk downs with Iron Age giant white horses and a man, the Giant of Cerne Abbas, complete with erection and wielding a club, giant figures scratched into hillsides along with long barrows and burial mounds. We went to Avebury, to Winchester Cathedral, Salisbury, Dorchester, following Hardy references in *Tess of the D'Urbervilles* and *The Mayor of Casterbridge*, and to Poole and Purbeck, looked for fossils at Lyme Regis, and walked along Chesil Beach to Portland Island.

So much has been written in poems and songs, novels and plays, so much portrayed in film about love and how it feels and what it does to a person who is in love, to two people who are in love with each other, that I dare not try to say anything more than that we were happy, perhaps without knowing that it was happiness we felt. We didn't name it. We simply lived it as our new life.

Near the end of the fortnight, we drove to London to the Trinidad and Tobago High Commission and asked to see the High Commissioner. Sir Ellis Clarke met us without an appointment and was his cordial and suave self, but I did get admonished for not informing the Government of Trinidad and Tobago of my intention to marry. He agreed to look into my request for spending the fourth year of my scholarship in Cardiff, working towards the Diploma in Education. Then we headed back to Cardiff via a one-night stopover in Bristol, for the first time sleeping together in the same bed in his old room in his parents' house, and then onward to Aberystwyth after a couple days.

A few more classes, submission of the dissertation, defence of dissertation, intense swotting, exams, and it was over. Goodbye to Alex and friends. Joanna had landed a teaching job in a posh girls' boarding school in the south of England, her own posh girls' boarding school background not a handicap. Voluntary Service Overseas in West Indies destinations captured Alison and her fiancé Alun, off to Barbados, and Mary to St Vincent. Vivienne and boyfriend were moving to Devon. Jyotsna and Mysoon were going back to Kenya and Iraq. Lucy and Gareth were getting married and were going to be back in Aber, Gareth embarking on a PhD. I was off to Cardiff and, just so, three years of close association disappeared. We came back for graduation, my friends with their parents and Paul and his parents with me. Everyone stayed in hotels. We saw one another briefly in and around the town, but I found those meetings awkward. When we met they had their parents in tow and to me it seemed that my hall friends and course friends were speaking differently – was it a different accent or a different vocabulary? In that short time they had already moved on and now belonged to a world I didn't know.

Are you sure you don't want to stay on and do the PhD? But Dr Taylor was only being playful. He knew I was set on a different track.

FEAST

Does being married make you different, I mean does having your relationship sanctioned in some way – civil or religious – make you a different person, so different in the eyes of others that you warrant a different level of courtesy? In the corner shop, the proprietor who had looked at me askance before, guessing at my questionable relationship with the tall young man I would be seen walking with arm in arm, now wiped his hands on his apron and came forward with, and what I can I do for you today, madam? All at the flash of gold on the ring finger of my left hand. It was plonk in the middle of the sixties – of Glastonbury, the Beatles, free love, the pill. But for most people it could still have been the forties or fifties. Living together without benefit of clergy or state sanction is, nowadays, in the third decade of the twenty-first century the preferred option of most couples. Saves the fuss, bother and expense of a wedding and, a little later on, divorce. Cohabiting couples have the same rights and responsibilities as married ones. Anyone of any sex or gender – or neither, or both, or one and the other sequentially – can marry anyone else, or not, with or without benefit of clergy and of state. Children can be born out of a test tube conception, with eggs or sperm from any number of donors, in a surrogate womb, and can legally belong to any, or all, or none of the parties involved. Such freedom was not imagined in 1965, so my local grocer in Cardiff was impressed that Paul and I had got married and greeted me as Mrs Jenkins. The ugly duckling had turned into a swan.

I was on holiday between universities, while Paul was at work. I'd put on a bikini, spread a towel in the back garden and lie there sunbathing and get lost in reading for hours at a time, then get up and prepare a little lunch before Paul got home. We'd eat and listen to the The Archers on the radio, he'd go back to work, then I'd be out the back again, with a quick trip indoors for tea preparation. It was in that state, with a towel hurriedly pulled around me, that I answered the front door early one afternoon to my Alex Hall friend Joanna and a young woman, the sister of Joanna's Paul, her Aber boyfriend. They'd come down the valley from Merthyr Tydfil, where his family lived, to Cardiff, to do some shopping. Joanna and her Paul were getting married, and they would be moving to Derbyshire, where he'd got a job in a technical college and all of that would be happening in a couple weeks' time, and would we attend their wedding. After Jo and her Paul went to Matlock, we were in touch for the first few years, then not any more, and it bothers me now that our friendship has that hanging loose end, especially as I was the second godmother to their first baby, a girl, whom I never saw in the flesh. There are so many people from that time whom I've lost, not least Trevor and Joanna, Harriet HH, Jotsnya and Maysoon. I looked up Harriet HH in one of those USA search sites and found someone with her name in Austin Texas, age, one year less than mine, next of kin, mother with a name sounding very Louisiana, very Southern belle, something like Lauralee, age ninety-something. It all fitted. I called the number and the person who answered, a male voice, said there was no one by that name there. Recently, I went on a google search for Jo. Up came an announcement of the death of her dad, quite recently, this century at least. Her name was there too. I thought I'd saved it but now I can't find it, and a new search doesn't get me back there. My mind was on Maysoon during the Weapons of Mass Destruction period, the shock and awe advance of American troops. Was she all right, I wondered. Did Maysoon mark herself safe on Facebook after the blowing up of the mosque in Mosul, her home town? I don't like these voids, this unfinished business. All these people mattered in Aber, made my life there rich, full. They have no business disappearing.

But there are others with whom I still have contact. A few years ago I went back to Aber where Alun and Alison had bought a home up the hill. After their stint in Barbados, from where they had visited Trinidad, staying with my mother for a couple weeks, they'd moved to Germany, teaching at a camp school for the British Army on the Rhine, and raising their two children there, and afterwards retiring to Aber. They had another home in France where they play boule in the summer and one in the Pyrenees on the Spanish side where they skiied in winter. Mary Denny came to Trinidad to stay with us in Cascade and keeps up with a card and a newsletter at Christmas. Two years ago I looked her up in BT white pages and called her. We met up on my last visit to London. She brought me up to date on Gillian and Marion. She's still in touch with the people she taught in St Vincent those long VSO years ago.

I started at University College Cardiff in the civic centre, accessible from home, and settled back into the rhythm of being a student. Paul was taking classes in town planning, and all was well but for one thing. My periods, which were always regular but painful and heavy, became so debilitating that I had to be out of normal life for two or three days every month. I'd recently also developed period-like pain halfway between periods. My GP, Dr Naysmith, referred me to the clinic at Cardiff Maternity Hospital. There, a very kindly gynaecologist, Mr Tindall, took me under his care. Endometriosis was his diagnosis and he recommended surgery. This was close to the end of my Dip Ed year and I had the surgery right after the exams. Mr Tindall greeted me the morning after the surgery with a copy of the day's newspaper publishing the University exam results and there was my name with a first and the Dame Olive Wheeler Memorial Prize award. He told me what he'd done to my innards, removing endometrial tissue from around ovaries, bowel and some of what could be safely disentangled from around the fallopian tubes.

The surgery brought two results. The first was great relief and I was able to be like other women with only mildly inconveniencing periods. In the era before laparoscopy, the second result was a long scar just above the pubis bone which in time led to loss of muscle tone and a tendency to slackness in that area. This looseness was the first of the many saggy flops, alpagat flaps and deepening craters I now lift with one hand to scrub under and burrow into with a soapy washrag held in the other hand, along with those inner creases of my joints that Mother Columba brought to my attention that afternoon in the distant past when she took me to task for making a mockery of the early spring, flaky epidermis-shedding of her Irish childhood.

With the new freedom of menstrual normalcy, I began to look for work. I put my name down with Cardiff Education Authority for supply teaching. In the meantime, the school where I'd done teaching practice, a Catholic grammar school for girls, asked me to do a maternity cover in their humanities department. That meant not just geography, but history. Ah history! My own Dark Ages spanned from conception to twenty-three. I knew nothing of the history of my own country, my own region, my own hemisphere. Everything I knew about the past was from fiction, newsreels and Hollywood – and the latter mainly he-men Biblical stories and Westerns. The form four group, that is the pre-GCSE class, was studying the Tudors. This was before BBC period drama brought *The Six Wives of Henry VIII* and *Elizabeth R* into every home and, of course, it predated the wonderful Hilary Mantel trilogy by over half a century. So my resources were the students' textbook and the school library.

As a lapsed Catholic in a Catholic school, negotiating this tricky period in Catholic history was a minefield, particularly as I was completely ignorant of the complexities of the Reformation. I quickly realised I should have been more cautious in accepting, once again, the first job I was offered. Thousands of teaching jobs were advertised in *The Times Education Supplement* every week, but I didn't look. I learned some interesting history, but what I learned about Catholicism in Britain was most telling of all.

In Britain, at that time, Catholicism seemed a religion on the defensive and in the shadows. It is the underdog, the defeated, and it was the Tudors who made it so. In the Tudor period, Catholic royalty, archbishops, priests and nuns were executed, the monasteries were dissolved, churches desecrated, church buildings destroyed and church land dispossessed. Catholicism became a religion regarded as treasonous and, for centuries after, Catholics were subject to legal and political discrimination. It was not until 1829 that Catholics gained basic, but still restricted, civil rights. To put this in context, this is a mere nine years before the chattel enslavement of Africans in the British West Indies ended. The derogatory view of Catholics persists in some quarters; Catholics are still referred to as Papists, particularly in Northern Ireland.

When I was at school at the convent in Trinidad, we sang a hymn whose chorus goes like this: God bless the Pope, God bless the Pope, God bless the Pope the great, the good. I won't write out the verses in which his many virtues and titles are extolled. Of course, the hymn is about a generic pope not any specific one, so I guess Papist as Pope follower is as unspecific as that hymn, but being in the UK and teaching Tudor History in Cardiff did wake me up to the realisation that Catholicism was not the dominant religion everywhere that growing up in Trinidad had led me to imagine.

It was refreshing for me to be in that space after a lifetime of Catholic superiority and judgement where Catholicism, thanks to that infamous Cedula de la Población, still called the shots and essentially dictated government policy on public holidays, the funding and entry policies of schools, among so much else. I learnt, eventually, that Catholicism had brought genocide to the indigenous, and sanctioned the capture, transportation and enslavement of African people and their descendants for centuries. To this day, historically, for a small elite, being Catholic still determines who owns and controls land resources. If I'd only known the word *schadenfreude* back then in Cardiff, I would have been able to label my feelings and would have derived some satisfaction from knowing it was a permissible thing to feel, nothing to be ashamed of, feelings I'd once identified as spite and malicious glee, feelings that caused you to think or exclaim, It good fuh allyuh.

So there I was teaching (and rapidly studying) something about which I knew nothing and, to boot, the Catholic version of that period of English history, when Catholicism was abolished as the state religion, and Henry VIII ousted the Pope to become head of a new church. I had to teach this history to Catholic teenagers in a country whose national religion and monarchy disputed the Catholic version. Of course, in order to pass the exam, the girls had to learn both sides of the story and everything was couched as if there were two versions of the truth, a situation I wasn't to meet again until alternative facts became established as part of the acceptance of parallel truths in our own 'Information Age'. I survived, but I'm not sure the girls did. My difficult tenure ended with the return of the regular teacher.

There's one connection with that time that's nothing short of uncanny.

On the first day that my eldest daughter started as a student at the University of Warwick, she discovered that her neighbour across the corridor in hall was also called Rhiannon. They became instant friends and my daughter was invited to spend the weekend at her new friend's home near Cardiff. In conversation, the mother, learning I was a teacher and that Rhiannon had been born in Cardiff, asked whether I ever did a maternity cover at the Catholic girls' grammar school. My daughter didn't know and the mother insisted she phone me to ask. I remembered the mother as the science teacher at the school. We'd had the same gynaecologist; her daughter and mine, namesakes, were born in the same hospital around the same time.

Paul and I moved home round about that time. Mrs Evans had died and her son wanted to convert the house into two quite separate dwellings. There wasn't much available in Roath Park where I'd grown to feel at home, and flat hunting led more than once to Paul finding somewhere suitable, getting excited, getting me excited too, taking me to see it and discovering that it was no longer available. It was the shared bathroom that made one prospective landlady uncomfortable, and I must admit that even with my twenty years of latrine sharing, three years of communal hall bath and toilet arrangements, I, too, was reluctant to share a bathroom with strangers.

I think that back home, because we had our own cubicle in the latrine, there was a certain privacy and furthermore it wasn't an inviting space, with the ineradicable stench of accumulated years of excreta mingling in varying proportions with the intoxicating vapour from rotting guavas and the damp lingering earthiness of layers of fallen leaves. There was also your awareness of the unidentifiable sightless creatures swimming in the oily dark ooze just a few feet below the seat (along with the urgent need of another family member) that determined that you went in, did your business, and got out – even though it was an opportunity to catch up on scraps of old news. Using the outdoor, open-air shared shower was as casual as bathing under a waterfall or at the standpipe, both locations being communal, so you felt there was nothing personal about these places. They were anybody's. In Alex, there was also the collective anonymity of a row of toilets and a bank of baths – no showers there – and in that sense it was like home, save that home's primitiveness was replaced by modernity. The very collectiveness of the arrangements left no space for any sense of being an individual user.

But in a private home it felt different. There I felt uneasy about using a shared toilet, leaving my lingering odour for another person to judge me by; using a bath where another person's body had been submerged for a once weekly wallow (the norm in those days), and even when cleaned after use, I could imagine the slimy grey watermark left by their shed skin, their sweat, dirt, bacteria and mould in the soap scum, their verrucae and athletes' foot spores on the floor. I think a mutual squeamishness, as much as anything, decided that we couldn't live like that, either. Estate agents weren't then the established breed they have since become. It was the classified ads that got you everything from a job to a home to a car to a pram. We found a studio flat in the top storey of a new three-storey block of flats just outside the city, in Rumney Village, off the A48, the Newport Road. There was one big room with a sofa bed, a three-bar electric fire, some shelving and cupboards along one wall, a dining table and two chairs, a small alcove over the stairwell, a bathroom and a kitchen with a stove and sink and wall cupboards. It was perfect. Marwood House, Kinross Court, 56A Ridgeway Road, Rumney, Cardiff was our home for almost five years.

How Mrs L, the head teacher of the local Catholic primary school and owner-occupier of a flat in a block just up from ours on Ridgeway Road got wind that an unemployed teacher was on her doorstep I never knew, but early one afternoon I answered the door to a tiny smiling woman who introduced herself, asked to come in, and over a cup of tea offered me five days teaching a fortnight in the reception class of the infants department of her school. It was a job-share with a maternity-leave returning teacher who wanted part-time, three days one week, two the next. I took it. Although my teaching practice included a stint in a primary school in Splott, I knew next to nothing about teaching very little ones, and even as the eldest of us four back home and being responsible for the younger three since I was eleven or so, I was pig-ignorant about the actual management and care of little ones in a school setting, never mind in a foreign country and culture. I thought my common sense would see me through, but common sense is not as common as you think.

The children in the reception class in those days were rising five, that is they'd have their fifth birthday during the school term they entered. I now know quite a lot about four-year-olds, having raised three of my own and having lots of contact with my grandchildren, but back then I hadn't realised it wasn't a teaching job I'd taken on, but childcare in a school setting. It was taken for granted that since the practices were so normal and everyday, surely everyone knew what to do without being told. Not me.

Very little children, I found out, are not miniature versions of homo sapiens; they are homo-not-yet-quite-sapiens. There were four elementary things I didn't know how to manage with this subspecies, namely coats, milk, dinners and toilet. This was a time before the introduction of teaching assistants to manage such practical things, to allow the teacher to concentrate on teaching and learning. In those days, when children came into the classroom on mornings, you as teacher had to help them off with their coats, one by one, make sure the knitted hat and mittens are shoved into the coat pockets, lead the child to the screened-off area with the coat hooks, supervise the hanging of the coat and say, Kevin, which is your coat, what colour is it? so Kevin knows which and where when it's time to go out and play. And you do that again after play. In the era before Margaret Thatcher, the milk-snatcher, changed all that welfare state support and brought Victorian rickets back as a late twentieth century childhood affliction, milk was free, a full-cream third or was it half-pint for each child every morning, delivered to the classroom, fresh and cool, in a crate, and left outside to keep cool in nature's fridge. The first day I brought in the milk crate at break time, I had to be prompted by Coleen, a savvy little girl who'd taken me under her wing, to tell them to line up, that I had to take off the gold foil cap for them, that I had to make them sit down to drink it. After the scrum, I found the mop and a cloth behind the screen, thanks to Coleen.

On Monday mornings, you collected dinner money, a small payment to offset the cost of school lunch. Since the school served a brand-new council estate housing young families from the more crowded and deprived dockland area, many children were receiving the means-tested free lunch. I, not knowing how to interpret the symbol on the alphabetical list, asked one little boy for his dinner money, only to be told by a chorus, Patrick gets free dinner, miss, while poor Patrick did his best not to be seen, by closing his eyes and lowering his head. You also supervised the children at dinner, made sure they ate, did your best with manners and mess, and made sure they washed their hands before and after.

Toilet was another challenge. You had to help them lift up and pull down their layers of clothes, wipe and or blot, get clothes in order again and wash hands. I got back home after a day with infants vowing that I would never ever bring a child into the world, kiss the cross and hope to die. It was too much work.

I met up with the other teachers at lunchtime when I wasn't on dinner duty. It was a time of cordial interaction and I got on well with everyone until I got into an argument with Mrs K – everyone was Miss or Mrs, I never heard any teacher called by her first name there. The rules about abstinence from meat and fasting in Lent were strictly observed by practising Catholics, so that on Wednesday and Fridays good Catholics would not eat meat and would instead have fish or other seafood. When the topic was being discussed one day in the staffroom I opined that the rule was silly and led people to abuse the intention of sacrifice, that I couldn't understand why expensive smoked salmon was within the edict but cheap meat paste was a transgression. How could a person feel holy when indulging in luxury while condemning as wicked someone eating a substandard meat-based item. Mrs K was high up in the school hierarchy and I could see the other teachers present feigning busyness with their desks rather than coming down on either side of the argument. When Mrs K responded, it was to tell me that if we didn't follow rules, there'd be anarchy. I surrendered with a limp, you could say so, and the heat went out of the discussion. But it wasn't the weight of Catholic dogmatism that was wearying – Lord knows I'd carried that burden long – it was dealing with the minutiae of little children that was beyond me, so when the job-sharer was ready to return to full-time, I was relieved to be reassigned.

My next teaching job was in a Catholic high school for boys. It was to teach maths. Maths to boys in the R stream. R stands for Remedial. The school had, I think, six or seven streams or levels of achievement. I met the man whom I was to replace. I should have been warned from observing him. He was tired, beaten, dishevelled. His nails were a thin line, a mere sliver of nail, just above the nail bed, badly bitten down, and yet still managing to be grimy. His hair was untidy, overgrown, curling down the back of his collar and spreading in a fan over his ears, his shoes scuffed and dirty. I should have read my fortune right there, but I took the job. Talk about the sins of the parents being visited on their children. With those children you wondered what their parents had done. It was hell, pure and unadulterated. I didn't know what to do with them, the R boys. They knew what to do with me and with all the teachers assigned to the R stream. I got pitying remarks from the rest of the staff who taught from A to G streams; the rest of us R teachers huddled at lunchtime in a corner of the staff room recounting the day's trials. It didn't matter that I knew no maths; the boys, seemed destined never to know any maths. I soon gathered that my job was to go in, try to stop them from killing one another, and to get out sufficiently alive to repeat the process the next day.

Salvation came from an unexpected source – the City of Cardiff Education Authority. All schools were to become comprehensive and co-educational. That meant that the boys' school was to merge with the girls' school on the same compound. The geography teacher in the girls' school was being promoted in the new system and I got her job. As the merger was being settled over a term, the head of geography of what was the boys' school moved up to deputy head and I became head of geography for the whole massive school of a couple of thousand students. I guess someone felt that, as I was still intact after my R experience, I had the mettle for the job. I also, belatedly, solved the mystery of why I was being sent only to Catholic schools. It was my application to Aberystwyth, where in the religion line of the form, I'd unthinkingly entered Catholic. All my documents thereafter bore that visible sign, so I, with the hidden stigma of being lapsed and fallen from grace, was being sent to teach in Catholic schools where, if my lapsed condition was discovered… a situation, I think, known as double jeopardy.

By the Easter of 1966, Paul and I had been together for all of three years and married for one. Our life in Cardiff, just the two of us in our own space, was one of excitement and discovery, not just of each other and in our work, but in the everyday business of learning to be independent, self-sufficient adults away from family, away from the past. It was to do with responsibility for rent and electricity, laundry, income, expenditure, balancing needs and wants, savings and entertainment, none of which had been a concern of either of us before. We didn't take it as seriously as we ought, I suppose, too much caught up in the novelty. For me, at least, it was a kind of grownup dolly-house, the adult version of childhood make-believe with dolls, and mini tea sets and mini kitchen ware. But Paul and I also threw ourselves into cooking, real grownup cooking.

In those days you bought the ingredients for your meals almost every day. Milk was delivered outside your door each morning and you paid for it by leaving cash in an envelope stuck into the neck of one of the washed-clean glass bottles that you left outside at night, but everything else you picked up from the shops yourself. Root vegetables such as potatoes, carrots, parsnips, onions, garlic, beetroots could keep in a basket for a week or more, but green vegetables would tolerate little more than a day, so on the way home from work I'd be thinking what meat or fish I'd buy and which seasonal fresh vegetable and fruit. This would occasion stopping in more than one shop, because supermarkets hadn't yet penetrated the commercial life of Great Britain where the small, independent, specialised shopkeeper still held sway.

You could get half an eighteen-inch cucumber, a few tomatoes, a head of cauliflower, leeks, broad beans, a cabbage, a cardboard punnet of strawberries or plums at the greengrocer's; a quarter pound of Caerphilly from the cheesemonger next door; two lamb crops from the butcher or a couple of fillets cut from a plaice from the fishmonger just along the rank of shops at the bus stop where the steep rise on the Newport Road plateaued. The last shops before you turned left onto Ridgeway Road were a dress shop, a wool shop, the launderette where we went on Saturday and, at the corner, a branch of Barclays Bank. For bread you'd have to cross the busy Newport Road at the pedestrian crossing and choose something hot and fragrant, straight out of the oven. None of these items required much preparation and, with at most a scant half hour from shopping bag to table, it hardly seemed like cooking, and we wanted a greater challenge.

The flat came with a four-burner New World Gas Cooker with eye-level grill and an oven under the burners. I'd give my eyeteeth now for one of those sensible sturdy stoves. Our first big purchase was a fridge, not a common kitchen appliance among our friends in those days, but we were serious about this cooking lark and saw ahead of us mounds of perishable ingredients and lots of cooked stuff to be stored. Which fridge to buy came after a careful study of *Which*, the new consumer magazine that guided the uninitiated postwar generation through the minefield of choice for which their parents could offer little useful advice. I think we got an Indesit, not well known at the time, but worth every farthing we spent on it – was it thirty quid? What to cook was decided by TV and the weekend *Guardian* and *Observer*. We were not going to simply replicate the food around us. We were going to be adventurous.

One April Fools Day, less than a decade before, *Panorama*, the respected BBC TV news report, showed a spoof clip of a family purportedly in Switzerland harvesting spaghetti from trees. Thousands were fooled; cooking and eating spaghetti wasn't yet common in the UK, and requests poured in to the BBC from home gardeners wanting to know where they could get seeds for their own spaghetti trees. I don't know why, but recounting this I feel not amusement but a little sadness. Food has moved so far from its source now that it's hard to connect a juicy steak on a plate with a live bovine creature, let alone global deforestation. But let me get back to the new cooks in Cardiff with a stove and fridge and utensils and tools ordered by mail and cheque from Habitat, with newspapers to suggest what and TV to show how.

Step up Philip Harben, *The Grammar of Cookery*, TV series and Penguin paperback, revised edition, 1966. Yes, I've still got my copy, but with back cover lost, I can't quote the price, but was anything more than 2/6 – two shillings and sixpence – in those days? Grammar. The foundation of everything, the why. Why add an 's' to some nouns, and an 'es' to others to pluralise, why dovetail a joint in wood, why seal a piece of meat with heat before roasting? If you know and understand the why you are not at the mercy of detailed instruction, you can experiment with some confidence in the outcome. Week after delightfully anticipated week, *The Grammar of Cookery* led us through the physics of heat application and the chemistry of the material being cooked, with protein as the foundation material. We roasted lamb, grilled fish, fried eggs, stewed chicken – using heat through the application of hot air, radiation, contact with hot metal and immersion in hot liquid. We learned how gluten, baking powder, eggs and yeast work. We baked bread and Yorkshire puddings, filled shortcrust, raised, choux and puff pastry with fruit, steak & kidney, chopped pork, cream and cheese. We made crèmes caramel, meringues, pancakes, jam.

I think our greatest delight in cooking with Philip Harben was converting egg yolks and olive oil into mayonnaise and its companion sauce of egg yolks and melted butter into Hollandaise and Béarnaise sauce. Oh the wonder of those two simple ingredients along with an emulsifying agent, the tension of the exacting process, the magic of seeing it coming together, the sheer alchemy of these humble things adjusting to one another, merging together, and transforming into rich, smooth, creamy, wantonly decadent, wickedly calorific sauces that would lift a humble potato or cauliflower, a piece of beef, a slice of chicken breast or a cod fillet to unimagined gourmet heights. I remember too well the pain, the horror of seeing the first streaks, the first globules at the separation of oil from yolk, butter from yolk, the frantic attempt at rescue with drops of vinegar, the agony of restarting and slowly incorporating the earlier disaster – and the pathos of discarding irremediable failures. Through the entire season of

The Grammar of Cookery – was it twenty-six episodes? – we cooked and we ate, cooked and ate, cooked, ate, cooked, ate.

We went on a diet for a fortnight after that, aiming for each of us to lose a pound a day. Paul drew up a chart on graph paper with date and weight in stones and pounds along the axes, and we recorded our weight at the same time on mornings just before breakfast. Thank you Harriet HH for your handed-down Aber bathroom scales, which I still have and which are, regrettably, still woefully accurate. We existed on Weetabix, skimmed milk, tea and coffee – both black – grilled fish and steamed vegetables. The two his and hers lines on the graph dipped day by day, until each was lighter by fourteen pounds. Then with grammar somewhat secure, we were ready to add vocabulary, complex syntax and a variety of accents to move our expertise from cooking to cuisine.

Enter Elizabeth David and her range of continental experiences gained while living in France and Italy, distilled into food, her rhapsodies on trips to farms and markets, encounters with people, with ingredients on trees, vines and in fields, and her observations and conversations teasing out recipes from traditional cooks and housewives, landladies in bed and breakfasts, cooks in bars, bistros and cafes. As much as the actual recipes, this collection of five cookbooks is filled with stories of travel, history, anecdotes from people met on the way, descriptions of landscapes, farming techniques, foraging, notes and references from older cookbooks and lots of advice on choosing ingredients.

The leek is the national vegetable of Wales as the daffodil is the national flower, both in season in spring, around the first of March the feast day of St David, the patron saint of Wales. All that to say that leek and potato soup is a popular Welsh dish. Under the guidance of Elizabeth David's *French Provincial Cooking*, we made the traditional simple soup starring those two humble vegetables, then progressed to crème vichyssoise glacée whose origin she describes thus: *Based on the ancient formula for potage bonne femme, the leek and potato soup known to every French housewife, the iced vichyssoise was served for the first time by Louis Diat at the Ritz-Carlton in the summer of 1917.* Now how could anyone sit at table and consume this delectable cream-enriched cold thick soup without imagining oneself dining at the Ritz?

And so it was with everything we cooked à la Elizabeth David. Mashed potatoes became pommes mousseline; a pork and beans stew, cassoulet. Much to my delight there were legitimate, sanctioned, acceptable recipes for things we ate regularly at home but which in the context of Great Britain appeared unseemly. Salt-fish buljol, pig-foot souse and tripe boiled with vegetables are named morue aux tomates, la salade lyonnaise, and tripes à la mode de Caen. For the last dish, this is how she describes the special vessel in which it is cooked: *a special earthenware pot rather the shape of a flattened-out teapot, the small opening of which ensures the minimum of evaporation.*

But where to get pigs feet, saltfish and tripe, let alone the authentic tripière cooking vessel, in Cardiff? Even Ms David thought the effort to prepare this dish beyond the ordinary home cook, but gallantly directed the intrepid to Escoffier's *Guide to Modern Cookery* for the recipe. We couldn't replicate, of course, but I was excited to read these recipes aloud to Paul, happy beyond reason to find Miss Clara's souse, Marmie's tripe soup and buljol as proper recipes in a proper book about a proper country's traditional food.

When I saw the film, *Julie and Julia*, many, many years later, I sat in the cinema alone and could not stop the tears, and they weren't from laughing at the comedy. Julie, a blogger looking for something interesting to blog about, challenged herself to cook every one of the five hundred and twenty-four recipes in Julia Child's two-volume cookbook *Mastering the Art of French Cooking* in the three hundred and sixty-five days of a year and to document the experience in her daily blog. This is a pleasant enough story for a film by itself. However, spliced with that story was another, that of Julia Child entertaining herself by training as a cordon bleu chef in Paris in the fifties, while her husband worked as a diplomat. So there was a restless early twenty-first culinary neophyte working her way through the cookbook recipes of a culinary goddess whose mid-twentieth century cooking life in France is also being told in the film. The poignancy of the parallel with Paul and me experimentally cooking while following Elizabeth David's food journeys through France and Italy was too real to not bring on a helpless hiraeth of longing, loss and regret.

HEART

In November 1968, I discovered I was three months pregnant. How did that happen? Jusso-jusso? After five whole years together with the birds and the bees? But then again, maybe we now felt secure in the medical issues around my fertility, what with the endometriosis, the twisted tubes, the blocked channels. It wasn't as if we'd harboured unfulfilled longings for a child, for a family beyond us two, because, well, we got married simply because we didn't want to be apart. And that was all. Us two. And now this, this level of serious commitment, for which we were unprepared. You can't bring a small dependent human being into the world and carry on regardless; even the evidence of our own eyes everywhere around us wasn't going to convince us otherwise. We were not persuaded by the seeming ease with new life teeming everywhere, the effortlessness of much younger parents with babies in prams, toddlers in strollers, older children skipping along the pavement outside our window. There were mothers cheerfully parking unguarded prams with both sleeping and alert infants outside shops and going in, spending ten, fifteen, twenty minutes with no line-of-sight, confident that not only would their baby still be there, but that it hadn't choked on their own vomit, wasn't sucking a lollipop given by a passer-by, had not been smothered under its own blanket, or that a dog tied nearby wasn't licking its little face. We had such fears but, truth is, while our fears embraced such possible, imaginable disasters, they went way beyond. We were afraid of the world.

We'd learned to deal with the hurts and disappointments the world around us casually inflicted, shielding each other as best we could, but we feared we were ill equipped to guard and protect a small vulnerable person. In April of that year we'd celebrated three years of marriage, and while it was a cause for celebration, that same month was a cause for disquiet. For years we'd watched on TV snatches of what was happening in America. Malcolm X, aged only thirty-nine, who'd done so much, was assassinated a couple of months before our wedding; we watched the Selma-Montgomery march, heard the speeches of Martin Luther King Jr, dear MLK, trusting prophet of non-violence, he whose mission was to show white people that black people were worthy of being accepted into the family of human beings from which, in America, the land of the free, they'd been left out, cast as they had been as only three-fifths human and chattel at that. We watched the more direct Black Power message, that whites would not concede unless we show them our power, because in the land of the free they only understand power. We listened to the message of the Black Panthers, of our own Stokely Carmichael, Kwame Ture, of whom I was immensely proud, a Belmont boy, born the same year, and schooled at Tranquillity Intermediate, too. So much, so much accomplished, but that April of the third anniversary of our marriage, news came from Memphis that Martin, also only thirty-nine like Malcolm, had been assassinated and the civil rights movement was both aflame and shaky. Robert Kennedy, USA Attorney General, younger brother of the assassinated President John F Kennedy, and thought to be sympathetic to the demands of people of African descent, was also killed that year. There was open, state-sanctioned warfare between white power and black aspiration.

We weren't so naïve as to believe that it couldn't happen in Britain. The year before we got married, Smethwick, Birmingham, had returned to parliament a Conservative candidate who'd won with the slogan, *If You Want a Nigger for a Neighbour, Vote Liberal or Labour.* Over the years it had not got better, but worse, with sporadic incidents of black baiting and attacks by gangs of white youths on black people. In late sixties Britain, the Labour government under Harold Wilson was moving to bring in the Race Relations Act. We were anxiously awaiting that. It would supposedly end discrimination in housing and employment on the grounds of race, things that affected us personally. While we trusted Wilson's public declarations that he was as much opposed to racial discrimination in Birmingham as he was in Bulawayo, we feared that the UK parliament did not share his position, because, in the ranks of the opposition Conservative shadow cabinet, racial tensions were being stoked.

There came Enoch Powell and his rivers of blood speech in which he asserted that having in Britain people who were not white was making the country unrecognisable to the native population, and that was a change for the worse. He said that allowing immigration led to racial street violence, that white people would be inflamed and forcefully object. As a prominent politician, Enoch Powell brought respectability to racism, and much of white Britain was not the side of the Conservative leader who, after Powell's inflammatory speech, sacked him from the shadow cabinet. Support for Enoch Powell and his views was so great that strikes and marches were organised in his favour.

We watched the TV news at night in disbelief. The sight of dockers marching, members of unions marching, ordinary white people marching, shouting, hoisting placards into the air as if they were their own raised fists: WE WANT ENOCH. ENOCH HERE, ENOCH THERE, ENOCH EVERYWHERE. BACK BRITAIN, NOT BLACK BRITAIN. KEEP BRITAIN WHITE. ENOCH FOR

PM. A Gallup poll at that time found 74% of the British people supported Powell's call for immigration control, and 60% were in favour of repatriation. Attacks on black people became more open, more common, sanctioned. The swastika, a feared and hated symbol of a scant couple decades earlier was now adopted as a symbol of whiteness and appeared as common a graffito as *Nigger Go Home,* and there were even more *Room To Let – No Blacks* on signs propped up on windowsills.

We saw a difference between the two countries. In America, Black people were marching for equal rights, while white entrenched authority was fighting back. In Britain, the offensive came sections of the white population who were the marchers, rallying behind Enoch Powell to demand an end to black Commonwealth immigration and the repatriation of black people. A white minority was prepared to engage in the open intimidation. We were afraid. Afraid of what the world we lived in could do, would do, to a child of ours. In the schools where I taught I saw the way in which black children, and mixed-race children, were automatically considered less intelligent, less capable, less worth the effort of attention, and were also considered more aggressive, most likely to be troublemakers. Paul too, as a schoolboy, had witnessed it all in the classroom. All around us the easy assumption of white superiority, black inferiority was as much an unremarked but natural phenomenon as breathing. We didn't talk about it; we didn't need to. We were watching the news together, reading the same newspapers, so we knew and understood the same things. What was there to say? Could I make accusations about his country without putting him on the defensive or making him take on a country's shame and guilt, hurting him when in his own life, his own choices showed otherwise? It would be unfair. It would be cruel and unjustified.

It wasn't that we avoided talking to each other about wounding things; we talked about hypocrisy, that people who supported Enoch Powell and his publicly stated views – that people who were not from Britain should go back where they came from – could not see that it was hypocritical to also support Ian Smith in Rhodesia – the Bulawayo reference made by Harold Wilson. In Rhodesia, Ian Smith, leader of the minority white settler population had declared UDI, Unilateral Declaration of Independence, supported by sections of the Conservative Party in Britain, with their talk of supporting their kith and kin. Smith and his party were creating an apartheid state, seizing land and assets and corralling Black Africans into zones where rights and opportunities were restricted. It staggered reason that the people who supported the expulsion of black people from Britain and supported the minority white settlers and their desire to stay and own and control huge swathes of Africa, saw no hypocrisy there, so entrenched was the belief in white supremacy. So, we knew, without giving it voice, that we were afraid for our child who we had to try to shield from the hurt that we knew many others would try to inflict.

There was another unvoiced worry about bringing an innocent child into the world. A personal worry, a worry that something would go wrong. Nowadays, I am struck by the easy assumption by parents-to-be that all shall be well and all manner of things shall be well. There's the early public announcements and displays from the first missed period, the full maternity wardrobe of stretchy dresses and bulge-enhancing garments, the public exchange with friends and strangers about the baby bump, the rush to prepare a nursery, to know whether boy or girl so as to choose the wardrobe, the colour and décor of the room, the names, the godparents. I marvel at this confidence when I remember our own reticence about the forthcoming event, how we told Paul's parents only after four months when there was a measure of certainty, that it wasn't a fluke, how we wrote my mother after six months, and broadcast to no one, leaving people to see for themselves. We were so much crossing fingers that we made no tangible preparation, except that in the eighth month Paul brought home a Mothercare catalogue and we sat at the edge of our sofabed and ticked off the items that were listed for newborns – everything white, simple, neutral. He would buy it all when the baby was born, indisputably present. It was a sort of superstition, not calling the attention of the gods of fate to ourselves, lying low, under their jealous radar, not wanting to put goat mouth on our tremulous hopes for our lives together. So we stayed quiet. Paul's mother got his dad to bring Dinah's cot down from the attic where it had been stored. They cleaned it up and kept it in Bristol until it was needed. They couldn't understand why we weren't nest-making and we could not explain our uncertainty, our cold fear of the unknown, the medical unknown. No, it wasn't the medical unknown we were afraid of, it was the medical known. It was fear of the known.

It wasn't that either of us was indulging in anything that could harm a baby. Following a bad chest cold some three years before, I'd given up smoking, and so had Paul a few months after. I hadn't been taking any medication that could raise a red flag. I think our main problem was that we knew too much. Once the pregnancy was confirmed, we read too much about babies and pregnancies and we focused on the warnings and the unfavourable outcomes. We'd followed the thalidomide tragedy, we'd read about the frequency of spina bifida in South Wales, and the high odds against either happening to us meant nothing. To the one who is the one in twenty, or the one in a hundred, or the one in a million, it is none of those odds. For that one, they are the one in one. And it wasn't only the race worry and the medical worry. We harboured fears of forces striking out of the blue.

What if our child, whom we thought we'd saved from everything that could go wrong, was in a primary school, sitting there looking at the blackboard and listening to the teacher, and the hill behind the school, the hill which had supported our child merrily tobogganing on pieces of packing cardboard the Christmas before, what if, one October morning after three weeks of heavy rain, that hill suddenly lost its cohesion (it was only barely compacted waste from the pits), and changed its nature from hard-packed spoil to liquid slurry and, rushing headlong, it swallowed our child's school. Just up the valley from where we lived, there among the coalmines, the hollowed pits and raised tips of waste, we saw the horror of Aberfan, the living nightmare of over a hundred children in Pantglas Junior School buried alive under a mudslide. So while harbouring voiced and unvoiced fears, we held our breath for nine months, just waiting.

In spite of our fears, the pregnancy was easy. There were none, not one of the many inconveniences that are common to others, no morning sickness, no bloating, no tiredness, no swelling of joints, none of that. The two things that happened health-wise were unrelated to the pregnancy. Early on, I got pneumonia. Dr Naysmith made a house call, prescribed something and dropped in almost every day to see how I was getting on. Then, towards the end of the pregnancy, I couldn't lift my head, couldn't move from the bed. The visiting doctor from the same practice diagnosed a dislocated neck. He had Paul keep my shoulders still while he held my head in both hands and pulled it away from my body. It hurt. It hurt like hell. I didn't feel anything click or bounce back in place, but I was able to get up, although for days afterwards I couldn't turn my head and every movement jarred.

I joined a dressmaking evening class, free, as were so many such classes, funded by the local authority and held in school classrooms at night. I bought a versatile Simplicity pattern and made a pinafore of dark green-flecked heavy Welsh wool to be worn over a jumper and tights for everyday use and a long-sleeved woollen orange dress for special occasions. These served me well and were the only garments I ever made. I bought a pretty red dress with long sleeves and another one, also long sleeved, in green. Afterwards, they remained in storage in Paul's parents' attic until, many years later, Dinah had the use of them. I carried on teaching until four weeks before the due date and went on three months maternity leave. Paul and I attended weekly classes on natural childbirth run by a wonderfully matter-of-fact midwife, Sr. Presdee, at the Maternity Hospital, and where I was still under the care of Mr Tindall.

The due date, the first of May, Labour Day in the UK and much of Europe, came and went and no labour started in our home. A week passed and still no sign of a baby coming. Mr Tindall decided on an induction. On Tuesday 13, May 1969, with Paul, Mr Tindall and midwives in attendance, our first child was born. And just like that, the 'we' who'd been most important to ourselves was no more. Only one person mattered to us, this perfect little eight-pound four-ounce person.

Among the blue Marks and pink Emmas, her little pink wristband said only 'Baby Jenkins', for she had no name, yet. We were waiting to see what would suit the new person. We had a book – I still have it – a slim stapled pamphlet, *Names for the Welsh* – five hundred Welsh Christian names – compiled by Peter Hourahane, published by The Trisket Press, Merthyr Tydfil, 1964. Price half-a-crown. An alphabetical list from Aderyn, f, a bird, to Ystwyth, m, from the river Ystwyth. She remained *the baby* of no fixed name, although we'd chosen *Rhiannon, f, A heroine from The Mabinogion*, quite early on, and, after almost six weeks of debate, with the deadline for birth registration looming, we decided on no middle name because our choice, Isobel, did not win favour with the only grandmother present, who was concerned about how the name would be treated. But oh, said she, her schoolmates will tease her by saying, is a bell necessary on a bike? So she was given one name only. I hope she has finally forgiven us and now thinks, as I do, that *Rhiannon* is a regal name, one that needs neither the embellishment, nor prop, of a runner-up, second-choice middle name.

It was a good time to have a baby. Britain was generally kind to its people in those days. Yes, I do remember officialdom as being kind. New mothers stayed in hospital for nine days, being taught stuff like bathing baby, feeding baby, changing baby. A health visitor, a midwife, visited the homes of newborns every week to check on the progress of baby and mother. There was a nearby clinic for children where you could get vitamin drops, powdered milk, inoculations, all on the public health, the National Health Service. I swear I was so impressed by the level of care that if the baby had been a boy, I think *Aneurin, m, One of the earliest Welsh poets,* whose namesake founded the National Health Service, would have been a strong contender. In those days, although there was no family allowance for the first child, there was a weekly allowance for each subsequent child. This, I'm guessing, was to encourage larger families to make up for the losses of life and of opportunities for marriage and children during the war years. I am wondering now whether, at that time, government decisions weren't focused just on the next election, but on the long term? You know what I mean – the idea of a government looking ahead to things like anticipated work force needs fifteen, twenty years down the line, tax-base requirements twenty years into the future. This would explain much, would explain stuff like milk for school-age children and tuition-free university education supported by means-tested grants.

How have things changed! Nowadays to get an additional allowance for a third child you've got to prove you've been raped, or, as they put it in officialese, the child is the product of a non-consensual conception. Yes. That's a fact. These days I wonder if anyone is checking the population pyramid, where we wrinklies sit like a badly balanced beam over the narrow column of kiddies? Or do governments expect that the current pandemic (and those that follow) will wipe out us oldies so the social and economic burden that we represent will disappear and allow resources to be redirected to more important pet projects – the tangible physical legacy stuff, like motorways, luxury apartment blocks and offices? You can almost see the brass plaques, the engraved stone. But back in those days, fifty-something years ago, I remember a Britain that was trying to take care of all its citizens, even those on the lowest rung, in a more even-handed way.

As for us two, our lives were completely absorbed by *her*. She was all that mattered, even though, in truth, we had no idea how to manage this new wonder of our world. What did I know about baby care? Nothing that fitted our particular circumstances. My brother Tony was born nine years after me and I remember him as a baby very well. Marmie and he shared her bed. His piece of the bed was spread with a rubber sheet with a cotton sheet over it. She lay down with him to feed him and when she left him to get on with the rest of her day, she made a soft wall of pillows around him. When it was her bedtime she lay next to him and fed him when he woke up in the night. In the world of my own past, babies did not have their own sleeping or transport arrangements. They were offshoots of their mothers and families, sleeping with them and being carried around by them or other family members, so they were either in someone's arms or in someone's bed.

I know that this is now the much vaunted modern co-sleeping trend in the developed world, but back then, the late sixties and before, breast feeding was not common and the cultural practice of having your baby sleep with you or lie in your bed would have been deemed primitive, akin to strapping your baby on your back while tending the fields. In any case, even if I was tempted or brave enough to try to do like my mother, we had no bed.

We opened the sofa at night to sleep on, and on waking up closed it for seating and to make floor space. We kept our little one in a large roomy pram we'd bought new for thirty pounds. The frame folded for easy transport and the baby carrier part lifted out. This wasn't so common at the time, having a dual purpose transport and sleep item. Everyone we knew as new parents had a cot in which the baby was put to lie between feeds. We did, eventually, have Dinah's cot brought over from Bristol and it fitted snugly into the alcove above the stairwell, but we didn't do this until our baby was showing signs of wanting to do alarmingly dangerous stuff like trying to sit up. In her pram. Several feet off the ground. Over a hard stone floor.

But long before this, in the days when I lay in hospital, surrounded by all the doctors, nurses, midwives, cleaners, and meals brought to my bed, I dreaded taking my fragile, helpless, dependent one home. I was puzzled by the other new mothers complaining about how long they were forced to be there, how desperately they yearned be released, how they pined for home, to be with their new babies on their own. But not all were like that. Let me close my eyes and think back to the ward where eight or so of us new mothers were lying there with our babies. It is visiting hour on that second day. Paul's parents have come over from Bristol to see their first grandchild and are cooing and fussing over her. Paul is here too, looking proud and happy. In the bed next to mine, on my right, there is a young girl. A man and a woman stand beside her bed. They do not hug or kiss her. They do not look happy. They do not look at the baby in the little bassinette beside the girl's bed. They speak very little to each other and to the girl. They do not stay and their goodbyes seem to be just a nod in the girl's direction. When they leave, the girl turns her face away from me. The next morning the bassinette with her baby is gone. After breakfast, she gets up and packs her things into a duffel bag. She leaves the ward and doesn't come back. I now wonder what happened to her and to her baby. As for us, baby and I and Paul came home after nine days. I was filled with fear and trepidation to be suddenly cut off from twenty-four-hour support, completely on our own.

What are new babies essentially? Inscrutable beings who must be fed, who must be changed, who must be handled with care, who must sleep, who will cry and not be able to say why, and who won't easily be comforted. This enormous business of baby – especially the baby sleep business, the baby feeding business – were such fraught issues to us new parents. They had been handled as far as I remember with so little kerfuffle by my mother, though I only thought about this long after. It's not that we lacked advice; we had it, loads. We bought books. We read them. Actually, we studied them as if for exams, life exams. The books had Rules, Schedules, Routines. When baby should sleep. How often baby should sleep. How long baby should sleep for. How often baby should be fed. When baby should feed. How much food baby must get, and how often at one week, at two weeks and three, four, five and each and every number of weeks old.

We got a plastic bucket with a well-fitting lid for soaking nappies, two dozen terrycloth squares, as many nappy liners and thinner muslin nappies, a pack of big safety pins, each with a slide-over safety head and the green sterilising powder to be measured and dissolved. We got a bowl for sterilising bottles and teats. Paul saw the whole business as a test of scientific efficiency. He experimented with folding the nappy for maximum absorbency in the right place and came up with a kite shape quite different from the rectangle recommended in the books. We bought a spin dryer and a drying rack that fitted over the bathtub. We had the books and the equipment, but we were still fumbling greenhorns. For practical word-of-mouth experienced advice there were Paul's parents, or I should say, Paul's mum. She knew how to deal with a baby. She'd had four.

I can see her now. Mum with baby number one, both just five days home from the Aberdare maternity hospital where she'd gone to be with her husband's parents for her lying-in, as the port of Bristol was under bombardment and the hospitals weren't functioning normally. So here, back home in her Bristol kitchen, in their own home, bought before they got married, is Mum and her baby number one, her darling two-week old Paul, born a scant week after her own New Year's Day thirtieth birthday. Her stockinged heels rise from her carpet slippers as she places her hands on the kitchen counter to look out of the kitchen window. A flurry of snow drifts over the garden. A few flakes fall through the white cat-net hooked to the hood and stretched taut over the tonneau cover of the big navy-blue perambulator parked on the lawn. Baby will be fine though. She's wrapped him well in his blanket. She has lit the fire in the lounge fireplace to get the room warm and cosy and she is now preparing supper for herself and husband. He will have had midday dinner at school with his fellow teachers, but supper is the only time they can have a relaxing meal together and she likes it to be a nice time. Wartime rationing has limited what she can get from the shops, but their *Dig for Victory* allotment has yielded potatoes, carrots, winter cabbage and turnips. In the larder there is the bone from the shank of lamb that was Sunday roast and Monday's shepherds pie. It will boil up nicely as stock. She will make a soup. Always welcome on a winter evening. She peeps out again. The pram is shaking. Baby is probably crying. She checks her watch. It is only half past two. His last feed, the third of the day, was at twelve; he's not due another until three. It'll only be a bit of wind. It'll pass and he'll settle.

She takes out a vegetable peeler and chooses a knife. She'll get on with preparing the vegetables while the stock is simmering. At seven minutes to three, as she slides the potato and turnip cubes, the carrot discs and the cabbage ribbons from the wooden chopping board into a basin of water, she looks out of the window. The snow is falling steadily, the pram is rocking. Next week he will be on a four-hourly feeding schedule and she won't be so rushed. She unties the bow and lifts the rose-patterned apron over her head, lays it across the back of a chair, opens the kitchen door and steps onto the back porch. The colder air triggers an involuntary shiver. She slips off her indoor slippers, pushes her feet into galoshes, and throws on a raincoat, opens the back door to the garden and steps out. The pram is wheeled in and parked in the back porch. She takes off the raincoat, changes footwear and lifts out her little one.

In the lounge a low fire radiates warmth. Baby lies across her lap while she unbuttons her sweater and unhooks her maternity bra at the front. She puts him to her left breast, the one at which she nursed him last at his earlier feed. She guides him as he snuffles around, finds the nipple, latches on, his little cheeks pumping. She checks her watch and after ten minutes she lifts him off, puts him upright against her chest and pats his back until he burps. She switches him to her right breast for five minutes, another burp and it's over. She fixes her clothes, changes his nappy, carries him to the back porch and puts him in the pram. It is not yet four o'clock, but the sun has gone. Baby will stay snug while she finishes cooking supper and gets herself ready to receive homecoming husband, new daddy. She drops the vegetables into the lamb broth, puts on the lid, brings it all to a boil, then lowers the gas.

At the hall mirror she glides a pink lipstick over her lips and presses them together, checks her teeth, pats her hair, smiling ruefully at her reflection. She hasn't had a perm in three months, a luxury and a self-indulgence frowned on while the nation's sons and brothers face death at the front. Her husband's brother, Joe, was last heard of in Burma. She understands, but still, it's only human to miss the cheerful bounce of curls. A key turns in the lock. She checks her watch. It is three minutes past four. Hubby is home. She hears the scrape of his winter boots on the front door mat. His outline wavers behind the knobbly glass-paned door as he takes off his boots, hangs his coat, hat and umbrella. She checks that her sweater is properly done up. She is smiling happily when hubby opens the door and steps into the warm welcome of his loving family.

That rosy picture of organised motherhood was my gold standard and what I aspired to as I sit on the toilet, baby at one breast, the other unused breast leaking a spreading patch of sticky translucent bluish-white liquid down the front of my pyjama top. I wince when the sting of salty urine flows past the stitched wound of the cut, what's it called? Episi...something... I blot with a wad of toilet paper and look at it. Red slime. When will this end? It's been three weeks already. I cradle her, still on the breast, in the crook of my left arm while with the other hand I pull a fresh pad from the pack, jam it onto my crotch, pull up panties and pyjama bottoms. As I turn to flush, the doorbell rings. Oh god, that can't be the health visitor yet. Jeezanages, what's the time? I don't want to believe it's ten already. I hurriedly flush the toilet. The swirling water spirals the red discharge and takes it away. I wash the one hand that was dealing with that business, switch baby to the other arm, wash the hand that wasn't involved. The mirror is over the washbasin. I don't look up. I know what's there. Greasy face, big dark blots around red eyes. Tangled hair loose, wild. I go with my baby to the door and open it.

Good morning. And how are we today? Health visitor is crisp, sweet-smelling, smiling in her smart blue uniform as she comes in with her little black bag, like a doctor's. We sit side by side on the sofa bed and she pulls out her notebook. So, Mrs Jenkins, how are we doing? Feeding time now, is it? I nod mutely. So when was the last feeding? I don't answer. The tears are falling on my baby's head. She is feeding all the time, I say. Is she? Let me see how she is feeding. Is this how she usually feeds? I nod. Let's try something else. She rests her notebook on the sofa and lifts my little girl off the breast, cradling her head in her left hand. My little girl is now lying along the health visitor's left arm like a glove puppet. She swings her arm towards me and rests my baby's head against my left breast. My little girl nuzzles at the nipple. Is that all she does? Let's see. She squeezes my daughter's cheeks and her little mouth opens wide. She then takes my breast and places it far inside my little girl's mouth, so far that the nipple has disappeared and only a halo of dark aureole is visible around baby's mouth. She sucks and sucks. I feel the milk moving down inside my breast. It is the very first time in the three weeks since she was born that I get this sensation of the milk being pulled, being suctioned out. How is the sleeping? asks health visitor. I say, She doesn't sleep. She cries all the time. She feeds all the time. I am crying again. I am weary. It'll be better now, she says. Just make sure she latches on properly and she will feed better and sleep better. Shall we switch sides? She detaches my baby and places her on my right breast. Baby opens her mouth wide all by herself. I put all of the nipple and much of the aureole into her mouth. She suckles hard. I feel a wave of shame wash over me. I was doing it wrong all along. I was starving my poor little baby. No wonder she couldn't sleep. Couldn't stop crying. Couldn't stop trying to feed. How could I do this to my poor precious little girl? I am truly making a mess of this business that millions do so naturally. I can't stop crying. Health visitor takes baby. She says, You might want to wash your face. She'll be fine with me. Wash my face? With both hands? A forgotten skill from a barely remembered luxurious past. I wash my face. I drink a glass of water. I put on the kettle for tea for two. And I so want to believe that things will be better from now on.

And things did get better, at least with the feeding. I was producing so much milk after a couple weeks that I was able to use a manual pump donated by yes, you guessed right, the wonderful NHS, to express enough extra milk after every feeding to fill the sterile containers that were left outside my door early morning and picked up the following morning to be given to the syringe-fed, tiny premature babies in hospital who couldn't suck hard enough to get milk from their own mothers, who themselves weren't producing enough milk. It was what, I guess, you could call remote wet nursing, but of course, valuable though it was, you can't do that nowadays, not with all the viruses about that are transmitted through body fluids. I never did match Paul's mum's clinical efficiency, her certainty, but in time it ceased to bother me that I wasn't performing up to some unattainable standard. If we were only fudging along, it didn't matter; we were all three of us well, baby's weight was finally going in the right direction and she was growing; all were getting some sleep sometimes, and who could ask for anything more? We couldn't, not when we saw on the news and read in the papers what was going on in the world.

When I think about Paul's mum's world and mine, first babies some twenty-seven years apart, I can't help but reflect on how, while in some respects our circumstances were similar, there were more ways in which they were wildly different. When our first babies were born they were welcome both in their immediate families and in the country into which they were born – in the sense that there was adequate provision for them at home, with state support for health and wellbeing. But Mum's baby was born in the Second World War. Britain and its allies were fighting against Germany and its allies. You knew who were the goodies and who were the baddies. Everything around you, the news, the newsreels, the commentators, the posters, the conversations, everything confirmed those positions. You could feel at one with families in the Blitz in London and welcome the displaced into your communities; you must have applauded the bombing of Dresden, celebrated the dropping of the two atomic bombs on Japan and VJ Day, and wept for those brave boys on the front in the Far East. But for us it wasn't so clear-cut, it wasn't so easy. Where were our affiliations, our loyalties? Which sides did we take in the conflicts we saw and read about?

I couldn't understand, we couldn't understand, how the British government could have such contradictory positions on independence for colonies. Why, for example, did they allow the break-up of the West Indies Federation? I loved the idea, loved being politically part of an archipelago with our common past, our common people, common language and traditions, a physically similar and culturally similar grouping. Why did Britain create a weak structure with continuing colonial status and allow it to fall apart and, at the same time, fight to enforce federation in Nigeria, itself a recent colonial construct of different peoples, different languages, customs, histories, ethnicities. Why give support to the federal government and the army, sending troops, aid, weapons to crush the Igbo people in Biafra? I couldn't figure it out. Nigeria is such a big country with so many millions of people, so why not let one part separate, go its own way?

Kwashiorkor, a new word, became a familiar one. Night after night, the news brought scenes of children with bloated bellies and stick-thin arms lying listless and dead-eyed in their mothers' arms, or their bigger sisters' arms when the mother was killed or captured by the federal troops. There were the troupes of orphaned children wandering around, running away, trying to evade capture by their own army or the invading army. It was not just men fighting, but children too, without real weapons but with makeshift guns and projectiles, in the forest, in the swamp, with all of Europe and Britain against them. Why not let them go their own way? What was so sacred about this federation that was different from my West Indies, or Central Africa, or East Africa – all of whose falling apart met with little more than a shrug?

Paul explained about oil. About the European companies in the Niger Delta. About the politics of oil. I understood then that when power takes sides it's not about good and bad or right and wrong, it's about where power's interest lies. It could be economic as in Nigeria, could be political as in Vietnam, could be strategic, like Suez, could be just a case of who blinks first as in the macho contest over Cuba. I held my baby, my well-fed happy baby and cried for those other babies, and I felt ashamed of living in a country that thought its own babies worthy of care and attention but, could so casually support that kind of atrocity against other people's babies all for the sake of the profits of their oil companies.

I'm writing this today, the seventy-fifth anniversary of Hiroshima and when I think about that I have to stop. I have to look up from the laptop into the world outside my window. I focus on the palms silhouetted against the sky from which colour is rapidly draining, I listen to the chorus of maybe a thousand or more tiny croaking frogs no bigger than my thumbnail, who wake at dusk to sing to one another till dawn. I have to do this to help me regain the composure I need to carry on, because thinking about power and how it is used makes me so angry, and thinking about Hiroshima makes me sick with despair about the seeming inevitability of science being prostituted to the malign purposes of power. We know that one day those weapons will be used again in anger and we will all perish. I believe our fatalism about this inevitability makes us not care about the planet, gives us the freedom to hasten its destruction.

But let me go back to the last year of the sixties, when my baby was new and thriving and fly-covered babies were starving elsewhere, and planes were being hijacked and Yasser Arafat's proposal for two nation states side by side was rejected, and refugees were fleeing ahead of armies, and ordinary people working in rice paddies had napalm rained on them by planes flying low overhead, and in the midst of all this we all lived in a yellow submarine and a man walked on the moon. But while Paul and I bore witness to everything else, we could not, we did not, watch the moon landing. We could not. It didn't seem right or fair. To us it was not man's greatest technical achievement but a testament to man's perverted priorities. And my view on that and on so much that's happening now – with Mars, Palestine, Covid 19 and looming climate disaster – remains the same.

Back at that time, Paul and I were like jellyfish, swept along with the winds of change, the tide of local and the current of international events, tentacles trailing through the agitation of the world and responding with anxiety. As things worsened on the world and the national scene, you wondered how much worse before things hit rock bottom. And then, quite slowly, things seemed to us to get better.

I think now that this was not a change in the world around us, but a change in ourselves. While we continued to let in the world, it was, apart from the TV news at night, more through print, much less through the screen. We spent more time with *The Guardian* daily newspaper, *New Society*, *The New Statesman* and *Punch* weekly magazines. It was a filtered exposure, measured, reflective, more balanced. It wasn't immediate, raw and painful. I think that, by learning about events that had happened, rather than the bombardment of events actually happening in our faces, we were able to detach ourselves from the world of chaos and disaster and be less fraught about our own impotence to change it. This has stayed with me. I haven't owned a TV for more than twenty-five years; I stopped taking newspapers – *Time, Newsweek* and even the *Guardian Weekly* subscriptions. I depend on the internet to do a quick catch up of the world of events and the world of ideas. Thinking about this is making me somewhat analytical about the things I do now in my day-to-day life, things I once did automatically without serious thought. And it seems to me that if I'm not at an event, live and present, it holds little interest, whether it's cricket, a concert, carnival, a play, a steelband or a dance performance. It must be live and me present, or I shan't be bothered with it. I must hold the book in my hand, weigh its changing heft, and adjust the balance across the bones and ligaments and tendons of my hand and wrist as pages move from one side of the spine to the other; I must inhale the chemistry of print and paper, feel the varying rough and smooth textures of pages and covers, let my bedside lamp throw light and shadow on where my eyes are focused or not. Could be age, eh.

So, at the cusp of the seventies, Paul and I withdrew, pulling in our tentacles from the maelstrom. We had a small dependent human being who had her own concerns and needs that we had to attend to and just so, jusso, global became local, became domestic, and care for the world became care for this one precious person who was ours to care for and no one else's and we found that there was joy and delight and surprise and pleasure in the minutiae of each minute of our lives. Additionally, this new life sobered us up to the realisation that we couldn't be as impulsive, as careless about the future as before. Even so, we were still so lacking confidence in our skills in our roles as parents that we didn't refer to each other as Mummy or Daddy and so Rhiannon called us by the names we called each other, and this caused some amusement among the people around us and concern within Paul's family.

Paul was still working in the Cardiff City Council Planning Department and having found it an enjoyable and intellectually stimulating career had decided, even before our baby was born, that it was time to qualify as a chartered town planner. This meant buying books, studying, and writing exams spread over a couple of years. I was interested in what he was doing and we had something else to chat about, to discuss, apart from the insurmountable problems of the world. About this time, too, we made two purchases that changed our leisure time, which of necessity was spent at home. We bought a colour TV so as to watch Kenneth Clarke's *Civilisation* series; we knew that the black and white one wouldn't do it justice even though we'd watched the riveting *Forsyte Saga* drama series without the benefit of colour. The other purchase was a rather expensive record player, a turntable, with speakers and an amplifier and a collection of classical music records. Deutsche Grammophon and the Berlin Philharmonic under the baton of Herbert Von

Karajan performing Beethoven was a staple and, by drawing us into complex and uplifting sound, it kept out some of the hurt and pain of the world outside our bubble. So please don't tell me now that Von Karajan was a Nazi sympathiser and turn the spotlight of revisionism over our blissfully blind and ignorant past. Would I buy his work now? No.

In the meantime, our little one was growing, doing magical new things every day. Everyone's baby is wonderful, perfect, but I swear ours was far and away the most exceptional baby ever. She was walking before a year, talking in fluent sentences by fifteen months, could identify by name all the flowers in the scrupulously maintained and labelled flowerbeds at Rumney Hill Gardens, where she and I spent the whole long idyllic summer of 1970, and before she was two she could identify every make of car we passed on the road. I know now that this was because we talked to her, and with her, constantly naming things, and she picked up everything that was said, sorting and storing rhymes and stories. A favourite picture book, *The Owl and the Pussycat*, she could recite by heart, something which I can't do now and Lord knows I've read it innumerable times to my other two children and my nine grandchildren.

We had friends among those with children nearby. Sandra, a midwife on night shift, was always welcome when she brought her Catrin to play with Rhiannon, so she herself could catch up on sleep. My school friend, Sue, lived across the Severn in Western-super-Mare, and she would come on Saturday afternoons over the new Severn Bridge with husband, Steve, when he had a hockey game in Cardiff. But our closest friends at that time were Tom and Dee Carter. Tom also worked in the City of Cardiff Planning Department, Dee was a teacher, and their first baby, Sophie, was just a couple months younger than ours. We met up in the park, we went to each other's homes for tea and for dinner. A really compatible friendship; both Tom and Dee were genuinely open and generous and the best of what you'd call down to earth. I remember early in my breast-feeding drama saying to them that I was not sure if I could continue with it because of the difficulty, and maybe both of us would be better off if she had the bottle. Other new mothers I saw at the clinic bemoaned the unendingness of it, the mess on clothes, the confining of mother to baby. They extolled the ease of bottle on schedule and of dad being able to take over the feeding at nights. They didn't like the thought of their breasts being dragged down when an infant feeds. Tom said, But that's what they're there for! At first I thought he meant the infant, being there to feed and be fed, but then I realised he meant breasts, and their purpose in mammals. That moment, that comment, crystallised for me why we were friends. It encompassed something beyond how we voted, the newspapers and weeklies we read, beyond a shared view of the world. It was shared values.

The onset of colder, rainier weather in the autumn of 1970 brought home to us that the studio flat, once thought cosy, was too cramped for the three of us, but since we were in the throes of Paul's final town planning exams – to prepare for which he'd taken three months unpaid leave – we thought we'd leave looking for somewhere bigger for a while. But then something happened that made that need urgent.

One morning, before the Little Ben alarm could shock me out of sleep, I felt a touch on my arm. I opened my eyes. It was Rhiannon. How did she get here? I turned my head to check. Paul was still asleep next to me, so he couldn't have lifted her out of the cot. At seven the night before, he had put her to bed in her cot wedged into the alcove, pulled up the side of the cot and fastened it, drawn the little curtain that separated the alcove from the main room and made a final check on her around eleven when the words began to blur on the page he was reading. All of that I was processing in silence, still doubting the reality of what I was seeing. But when she said, Barbara, I shook him awake. Paul. Paul. He opened his eyes. I said, She got out by herself. When she heard that she looked shy and proud, as if this was another achievement, like going to the potty by herself, or recognising and naming all the animals in one of her books. Come, he said, show me how you did it.

He lifted her over the still fastened side of the cot and we watched as she piled her soft toys in one corner of the cot, climbed onto them, held on to the corner post, swung her legs over the side and rolled onto the window sill. She scrambled to a sitting position and stood. She was two storeys up, the windows were kept slightly ajar and unhooked, and if she leaned against one of them there was nothing between her and the concrete pavement below. Her babygro, a neck to toe sleeping suit of towelling, had no sole grips. I could feel my own feet slipping, sliding out of control. I moved to get her down. Paul's arm blocked my way. She walked along the windowsill out of the alcove. At each window I could feel myself leaning against it, pushing against it, stumbling against it, falling against it and down, down, down, but she carried on into the main room with the big, fixed, plate-glass window, got as far as the window box of purple-heart tradescantia blocking her way, but where the table was jammed against the windowsill, she crossed over, lay down on the table, wriggled backwards onto a chair and slid off onto the floor. I, too, was on the floor by this time, crying in loud gulps.

The thought of us sleeping unaware of what she was doing, what could happen, unaware that it was even something that she could do, that we could have found out by a cry, a shout, a soft thud of something falling, or heard nothing and found her missing in the morning, or a neighbour, a passer-by, the milkman ringing the doorbell. You put away knives, scissors; you stick strips of toilet paper on the corners of tables and counters to dangle and wave as a warning of danger; you keep the Milton and cleaning materials high up; you sterilise everything she could touch; you put your hand in to check the temperature of her bathwater; you feed her solids out of a jar because don't trust the safety of what you yourself have cooked to eat; you strap her little torso into a harness and reins to go for walks together; you never, ever, leave her even for a minute alone with someone else, not even her grandparents; you pull up the side of the cot and secure it; you leave the windows slightly ajar for fresh air and go to sleep.

Paul let down the side of her cot and had Rhiannon play a game of getting in and out with the side down. This was to be the way she'd get out thereafter. But we knew that was only an emergency stopgap. We had to find a bigger place. All around us, young couples just starting out in professional careers were buying their first homes. Those upstairs with a new baby, he an architect, she a teacher, bought a house nearby on Ball Road. Kathryn and Thomas bought a flat on Kennerleigh Road. Tom and Dee bought a house, a lovely three-storey house in a quiet corner just off the civic centre. They referred to the area as Poets' Corner – were they on Southey Street or Wordsworth Avenue? Paul's younger brother, Philip, and Jacqueline, his French girlfriend, went over to Nantes, got married, came back and bought a house in Plymouth where he was teaching.

I admired their certainty, their confidence in the future, that they should see as far ahead as a twenty-year mortgage, or understand buying and selling houses well enough to know that the place where you lived was property, an investment, not just a roof over one's head, knew about trends in house prices, neighbourhoods, gentrification and so on. We knew and understood these things too, in theory, but we were stymied from going along that route because we did not have the confidence in the future that everyone else seemed to have. In the back of my mind and somewhere in his, there lurked a knowledge that I, and by extension, he and she, were not of the same world as everyone else, that one day my past would catch up and I, and they, would have to face up to my responsibility elsewhere, in a place I'd left physically, mentally, emotionally and of which they knew little and for which they felt less. Time, place and new commitments had dulled that sense of responsibility to elsewhere, yet I, we, didn't feel quite free to embark on putting down roots. I'll say here that feeling of impermanence, of insecurity, must have been very deep, because we were fifty years old before we moved into a home of our own.

But after Rhiannon's windowsill adventure we did start house hunting, scouring the evening paper for suitable property. I didn't favour an old house. I didn't know anything about hanging wallpaper or putting down carpets or pointing bricks or dealing with boilers. I wanted something ready-made with central heating. We saw a nice, new, well-appointed semi-detached house in Llandaff. But it was three storeys, bedrooms on a floor above the living room and kitchen. Does that mean she'd be napping in the day, upstairs, by herself, while I'm busy downstairs with laundry and cooking? What if she wakes up and I don't hear? What if she tries to come down the stairs? Oh, you can get gates fitted at the top of the stairs. What if she climbs over the gate?

A three-bedroom, one-bathroom detached bungalow in Rhiwbina Village came on the market. We went to see it. A privately owned development, Rhiwbina, on the northern edge of Cardiff, is across the main road from Whitchurch, a council estate where Paul's Uncle Joe and Auntie Bet lived. Rhiwbina, once a pre-war garden village, was growing, like so many, into a commuter suburb. To recommend it further, Paul's Uncle Trevor and Aunt Hilda lived there in a bungalow nearby on Clôs Yr Aer. Set in a row of similar homes, each with its tidy front garden complete with neatly trimmed privet hedge and big blowsy hydrangea shrub and a larger back garden, a park nearby, mature trees lining the streets, a row of shops within walking distance, the bungalow was perfect for our needs. Paul's gross salary of one thousand nine hundred and fifteen pounds per annum as a senior planning officer qualified him for a twenty-year mortgage on a five-thousand-pound house. We had savings to cover the down payment. The cheque was written and signed. Paul was to meet with the lawyer transacting the conveyance on Wednesday morning at ten.

On Tuesday, around noon, there was a ring at the door. I opened. There was a man I didn't know. He said, Are you Barbara Lafond? I said, yes. He said, I am here to deliver this to you in person. He handed me an envelope and asked me to sign for it. I did. He turned and went down the stairs. A car started up and drove off. I stood there with the letter in my hand. I didn't open the envelope. I left it there until Paul got home. I was afraid of setting off a bomb I knew I couldn't deal with, not with just us two, me and her, at home, alone. I waited for Paul to come home, for him to defuse it, to take away the awful power I knew it must have.

TIME

You must have seen the envelope on the dresser when you came in, but you must've sensed its portent as I had, for it was only after dinner, after you'd read her story and put her to bed, after we'd watched the news, after we'd tidied up, that you reached for it.

You slit the envelope with the ebony letter opener, the one with the carved head. You pulled out the single-folded buff sheet, opened it and read it silently. You folded it back and slipped it in its envelope. You rested it on the sofa between us. You didn't look at me. You looked straight ahead at the three glowing bars of the heater. You rubbed your chin with your left hand. You took my hand. You said, It is from the Government of Trinidad and Tobago. You paused. About the scholarship contract. I nodded. You went on. They want repayment. The amount they spent. I was afraid to ask but I had to know. How much? How you must've tried to grasp the enormity of that figure before answering. You looked at me. Your voice was hardly more than a whisper, It's more than four thousand pounds.

You remember the movie where the accused, on being found guilty and sentenced, laughed and laughed? I remember the scene but not the name of the film. A bizarre reaction, I know. Hysterical. I didn't laugh. Instead my response was just as ridiculous. What ran through my head was Sinatra crooning, 'The party's over'. Trite, yes, when you consider that everything I thought about myself, about who we were, about what our lives were going to be was a mirage.

If we had been allowed to get old together, we would have done what old people do, what I'm doing now, going back, trying to understand. We would have spoken about it, that time that loomed as large then as a giant's hand to our face, blocking distant but vast and brilliant constellations. We might have, with time, been able to put that time into perspective. But alas, it was not to be one of our gifts, that late-life empty space together, with nothing, no one, but each other. So we never got to talk about the past, what we did or didn't do, what we talked about or avoided talking about, those niggles and prickles we felt chasing around inside our restless heads but didn't, or couldn't, utter to each other or even to our own selves. We were alike in that way, you and me. We felt that if you didn't voice a fear, didn't name it, it wasn't real. To put it out there, give it a shape in the mouth and a sound in the articulation would be to give it life, an act of creation, the word would be made flesh and would dwell among us, our creature to harbour and nurture. Was this the unspoken reason why we'd been so long hesitant to embark on anything permanent, planting a fruit tree or painting a wall, bringing new life into the world or getting a home of our own? And once we'd taunted fate with an act of will, deciding to buy a house, something planted permanently on the ground, something immovable, we were shown that it was not a straight, smooth path we were on; we were at a fork in our journey through an unexplored landscape, thick with fog. It would have brought me comfort to have reminisced with you about that time, but I know that you will trust me to be as faithful to it as my memory will permit.

We'd managed the stay of execution for five years; with each demand, each letter from the High Commission in London, I could cite some new reason for me not to return immediately. There was the diploma in education, my gynaecological problems including surgery and years of treatment, pregnancy and a new baby, your professional exams. This bought time, enough time for us to feel secure.

We were a day away from signing another contract, a twenty-year mortgage loan of five thousand pounds to buy a house. What could we do? We knew we did not have, and could never have, the means to repay the scholarship as well as buy a home. It had to be one or the other. I didn't want to face that decision. I tried to block it from my mind, pretend it hadn't arisen. I had my own wonderfully absorbing interest. I was a mother of a little girl. That's what I was doing with my day, with my life. It was the most important thing I had ever done. Go back and teach for five years. Go back to a place I didn't know any more, to do something I no longer had any interest in. And what of Rhiannon? How would that work, me at school and she, where, how? And what of you? What would you do?

You had a good job right there in Cardiff. You were excited about your latest project. You remember Thornhill, that brand new residential neighbourhood? I have a picture on my desk that I took of you surveying that greenfield site, the back of your hair, the front of your jacket, your scarf lifted by a strong breeze. It was an exciting time of renewal; even brownfield sites were being brought back into new use. Everywhere planning departments were expanding as new towns were being built. Right there and everywhere there were amazing prospects for someone like you, young, qualified. I was in despair, unwilling to even think about leaving Cardiff, leaving Wales. I was happy right where I was. We were going into our own home, becoming rooted, weren't we? The more despondent I became, the more you tried to get me to see that it was a waste of energy to rail against what we couldn't fight and win. I think you recognised the inevitable and were more hopeful than I that somehow things would work out, that we'd be all right.

I wrote again to the High Commission in London, through which all correspondence passed, agreeing to return as soon as it was possible for my family to accompany me. I sent copies of your qualifications, including membership of the Royal Town Planning Institute, with a request that consideration be given to employing you in government service. There was a shirty reply about your interest in working in Trinidad not being any of their business, but that the request had been forwarded through the appropriate channel. I feared to open the door when the bell rang. I had visions of being carted off to a debtors prison or forcibly repatriated by the police.

Where to get advice, who could help? There was no one I could talk to. No one in the High Commission to give me the inside dope on how these matters are handled, no one back home who could make discreet enquiries. Marmie, the one person interested enough to take on my concerns, was no longer there. She'd been in New York a year already. We had no phone, neither did she; we relied on letters and with her so far away from those who'd put in train that summons, we were at the mercy of officialdom, just us and them in an uneven negotiation, without an intermediary. So we waited for their response and reasoned that if they wanted you, they'd get back. Days went by, then weeks, the days greyer and shorter, the nights darker and longer and soon Christmas with your parents, which I was dreading, as of course they'd been told and I knew their worst fears about us were coming to pass, that I was responsible for their son leaving a promising future for an uncertain one far away in an unknown place.

It comes to me now, reflecting on that Christmas 1970, how important ritual is in creating space and time for quiet thinking and for saying things without words. Seasoned by then in British Christmases, I could be more helpful in the kitchen, and as your mum and I stood side by side, rolling out pastry for mincepies, cutting the shapes with a scallop-edge cutter, placing them in the pie tins, filling them with Robertsons mincemeat – you remember back then that the jars still bore the golliwog trademark. Made right here in Bristol, she'd say. Biggest jam factory in the world, your Dad would add. We were mixing the dried fruit and spices for the steamed plum pudding, working in unison but with a bottled up anxiety about us leaving, you and me and their first long-awaited grandchild, going to a place they knew nothing of, under conditions of duress. It was not like their second cousins who'd long-ago gone to Australia, willing exiles, about whom, every year at Christmas dinner and over the plum pudding and brandy sauce, a story was told that provoked laughter and horror and never got stale with the annual retelling. Now that pent-up anxiety of hers was slowing down the process, making her walk with heavy steps, smiling forced smiles, but both of us keeping a rhythm going, doing what we were doing because it's what we do, what had to be done, and I could only squeeze her shoulder, showing I knew, but couldn't help, for what promise could I make to dispel the well-founded worry?

And that worry hung about the Christmas tree, the Queen's Christmas message, the opening of gifts. That year, for the first time, I wasn't given a nice, long-sleeved woolly jumper, nor fleecy slippers, nor knitted hat, but a silk scarf – its being more suited to our future remaining unspoken – and the day moved on, night settled in, and the gloom was lightened the following day only by the arrival of Margaret and Ron and their four children, people who were great friends of your parents, but didn't know of our impending fate, so we could laugh and chat and have high tea and make as if. And then back to Cardiff after what we all knew was our last Christmas in Bristol, but of which not a word was said.

I think about that now when I am here without you, without our children and their children. Covid Christmas 2020 is looming. If I last till then – I'm not being gloomy, eh, I'm just being real. We vulnerable elderly cohort with co-morbidities, which simply means the inevitable deterioration of organs with increasing age, are the highest risk demographic. Check out how quickly I absorb and fling about new jargon, age notwithstanding. Aren't you amazed when you remember me and that Commodore 64, how you and Gareth, he a mere schoolboy of fifteen, tried in vain to get me to at least try with it. If I last till Christmas, I shall be alone, in the sense that our family is scattered and inaccessible, borders closed in many places, lockdown enforced in more and more, quarantine compulsory in most, the few available airfares impossibly high and health risk certain.

But I know that wherever our children are with their own children, when they are putting up their Christmas trees, or cooking, or setting the table, or listening to parang and carols, they'll be thinking of us and of the Christmases of their childhood, and in the ritual of preparation and enjoyment they will perform their personal and our collective history. They will discard some things and add new things and grow that history, but something, some things of the past will be embedded there, like secret fragments of DNA waiting to pop out and manifest in a new unforeseen generation. Our children may or may not talk about childhood memories with their children, but whether they do or they don't, they'll be reflecting on our many Christmases past in Cascade with Marmie and Auntie and they'll remember it, you and I know, as a happy time, as I remember those years with your family, who loved me and welcomed me, when everything they knew and saw in their world told them that it was fine and normal not to.

The government of Trinidad and Tobago sprang into action in the new year, in the way 'sprang' happened back then. A minimum of four weeks for a cycle of correspondence, but there was by April a three-year contract offering you a job as a town planner with a salary less than you were getting in Cardiff, but it was something and with me teaching at a salary even lower than yours, we thought we might manage; after all we would have to. You were to start work on arrival in July, me in September at the opening of school.

You remember the problem we had with the technicalities of leaving? By the way, no one has 'problems' now. They have issues and challenges. However, what we had was a problem – neither you nor I had a valid passport. The Citizen of the United Kingdom and Colonies, the one I'd left Trinidad with had expired; so had yours. It seems funny now, doesn't it, to remember that whole families had to be on the same passport: husband, wife and minors – children. You filled in the forms and sent them off. By return, you were instructed that I couldn't be on your passport unless I registered as a British citizen. We looked at that form, at the grounds on which to apply. Either marriage to a British citizen, or personal right through having lived in the UK for more than five years. How we debated the implications of that choice! Through marriage meant that if anything should happen to you, we reasoned, that would leave me exposed in an Enoch Powell Britain or a Trinidad we didn't know, and how would that affect Rhiannon? Personal right seemed to offer better security. We never imagined how our decision on that simple binary choice would prove to be problematic later on, but that is another story. So with my citizenship secure in June by way of Section 12(2) of the Commonwealth Immigrants Act 1962, the one single passport with you, me and Rhiannon came in the post and we were fit to travel.

Worldly goods were disposed of quickly: the wing armchair to old Mrs Evans downstairs. Do you remember that we had to save our sixpences, florins and half-crowns for her to use in shopping when decimalisation came in, and how you sat with her on evenings and explained to her about the new currency, its Ps and Qs, using actual coins and pretend purchases? Gosh, that makes me feel such an old fool now – here's me trying and failing to resuscitate my iPhone 6 in an age of iPhone12Pro, and there's our Gareth messaging me, saying stuff like 'sunk cost fallacy' about my search for a battery replacement and begging me, Please let me buy you a new phone, Mamacita and me saying, No darling, you got your own expenses. And where do I turn? The only one, he or she up in the firmament, who could help with winning a lotto ticket, is evidently continuing to pay me little mind, not even prompting me to buy the ticket – probably too busy with assisting his followers in making America great again and unleashing new scourges and pestilences on humankind? But who is me to criticise? Is only me, a child of lesser gods.

The chair to Mrs Evans taken care of, the spin dryer to Sandra, the fridge down to Bristol for home fridge overflow, small bits and pieces of household stuff passed on all around to whoever wanted it. Books and records and record player and toys and some clothes, some pots and pans, crockery, utensils, the packers took care of – three huge wooden crates sent to

Southampton dock to be there just after the Sunday June 27 arrival of the Fyffes Line Glasgow-built *SS Camito* from its extreme southern leg, Trinidad for bunkering and discharging passengers and goods, then to Kingston, Oracabessa, Montego Bay and Port Antonio to collect bananas, the real reason for the journey to the West Indies. What fun we had singing and teaching Rhiannon, *Come Mr Tallyman, tally me banana*. Distraction, spurious distraction, but surely the condemned are allowed a last cigarette?

We were due to sail on Wednesday June 30th. On the evening of Monday 28th, we two adults, in the flat that had been emptied of our possessions, ate a makeshift early supper of tinned mackerel in tomato sauce, said goodbye to neighbours and got into our mini to head over to Bristol. That night the two of us were taking turns in the bathroom with vomiting and diarrhoea. We talked about that night for years after, remember? Never ate tinned fish again. Next morning the doctor came by and diagnosed food poisoning. We spent Tuesday in bed. On Wednesday morning Mum and Dad took us three to Southampton.

There was some trouble on the docks and the *Camito* hadn't completed offloading. We could board but sailing was delayed. Your mum and dad went back to Bristol, making it an easier goodbye, a more protracted goodbye lasting some days, during which you went to the nearest phone box to report on the progress of the offloading, but I think more for something to do, an activity with a purpose. For them being at home in Bristol, and us in a familiar town, and still there in the UK, somehow made the departure less real for them. Something to chat about on the phone that wasn't about us going far away, but about how quickly bananas ripen sitting on the dock in summer heat versus packed away in a refrigerated hold.

It was a limbo time, neither here nor there. I, too, was neither me nor not me. I was leaving a me that I had become, student, wife, mother. I was taking you and her with me, the two precious beings that made me the me I had become. I was taking the two of you to somewhere where there was an old me locked in layers of past life like a fossil, a place where I'd have to become another me, not this one, to fit a changed environment that I knew very little about and for which I felt not excitement but apprehension.

That I do not remember the date nor the day that the *SS Camito*, as reluctant as I, finally pulled away from the Southampton dock to set sail for Trinidad, to arrive there on a bleak Sunday morning 11th July, I shall leave to psychiatric or psychic interpretation. This I do know. We stood on the deck and watched the coastline slip away. You held Rhiannon in your arms. I wrapped both my arms tight around you, clinging on to the real, solid and reliable that I would count on to see me through this uncertain passage and beyond.

ABOUT THE AUTHOR

Barbara Jenkins was born in Trinidad in 1941. She studied at the University College of Wales, Aberystwyth, and at the University College, Cardiff. She married a fellow student, and they continued to live in Wales through the whole decade of the sixties. In the early seventies they returned to Trinidad.

Since she started writing in 2008, her stories have won the Commonwealth Short Story Prize Caribbean Region in 2010 and 2011; the Wasafiri New Writing Prize; The Canute Brodhurst Prize for short fiction, The Caribbean Writer; the Small Axe short story competition, 2011; the Romance Category, My African Diaspora Short Story Contest; and the inaugural The Caribbean Communications Network (CCN) Prize for a film review of the Trinidad and Tobago Film Festival, 2012. In 2013 she was named winner of the inaugural Hollick Arvon Caribbean Writers Prize. Her debut short story collection, *Sic Transit Wagon* (Peepal Tree, 2013) was awarded the Guyana Prize for Literature Caribbean Award. Her debut novel, *De Rightest Place* (Peepal Tree, 2018) was shortlisted for the Royal Society of Literature Christopher Bland Prize.

She completed her MFA at the University of the West Indies, St Augustine, Trinidad, in 2012. She spends her time reading, writing, singing in a choir, serving on the boards of two NGOs and seeing in person and virtually her globally-scattered three children and nine grandchildren.

ALSO BY BARBARA JENKINS

Sic Transit Wagon and Other Stories
ISBN: 9781845232146; pp. 180; pub. 2013; price £8.99

The stories in *Sic Transit Wagon* move from the all-seeing naivete of a child narrator trying to make sense of the world of adults, through the consciousness of the child-become mother, to the mature perceptions of the older woman taking stock of her life. Set over a time-span from colonial era Trinidad to the hazards and alarms of its postcolonial present, at the core of these stories is the experience of uncomfortable change, but seen with a developing sense of its constancy as part of life, and the need for acceptance.

The stories deal with the vulnerabilities and shames of a childhood of poverty, the pain of being let down, glimpses of the secret lives of adults, betrayals in love, the temptations of possessiveness, conflicts between the desire for belonging and independence, and the devastation of loss through illness, dementia and death. What brings each of these not uncommon situations to fresh and vivid life is the quality of the writing: the shape of the stories, the unerring capturing of the rhythms of the voice and a way of seeing – that includes a saving sense of humour and the absurd – that delights in the characters that people these stories.

In the title story – a playful pun on the Latin phrase on the glory of worldly things coming to an end – the need to part with a beloved station wagon becomes a moving and humorous image for other kinds of loss.

"Barbara Jenkins writes with wit, wisdom and a glorious sense of place. In stories that chart a woman's life, and that of her island home, this triumphant debut affirms a lifetime of perceptive observation of Caribbean life and society."
Ellah Allfrey, Deputy Editor of *Granta Magazine*

"Barbara Jenkins mixes a lyrical prose style with a close and humane eye for the human condition[...] She is a major new talent emerging in Caribbean fiction."
Monique Roffey, author of *Archipelago*, winner of the OCM Bocas Prize for Fiction 2013 and the OCM Bocas Prize for Caribbean Literature 2013

De Rightest Place
ISBN: 9781845234225; pp. 278; pub. 2018; price £10.99

"Often wickedly funny, always profoundly Trini, Barbara Jenkins' debut novel assures her 'rightest place' among the vital new chorus of women who are redefining the English-infused Caribbean."
— Robert Antoni

Indira Gabriel, recently abandoned by her lover, Solomon, embarks on a project to reinvigorate a dilapidated bar into something special. In this warm, funny, sexy, and bittersweet novel, Barbara Jenkins draws together a richly-drawn cast of characters, like a Trinidadian *Cheers*.

Meet Bostic, Solomon's boyhood friend, who is determined to keep the bar as a shrine; I Cynthia, the tale-telling Belmont maco ; KarlLee, the painter with a very complicated love-life; fatherless Jah-Son; and Fritzie, single mum and Indira's loyal right-hand woman. At the book's centre is the unforgettable Indira, with her ebullience and sadness, her sharpness and honesty, obsession with the daily horoscope and addiction to increasingly absurd self-help books.

In this warm, funny, sexy, and bittersweet novel, Barbara Jenkins hears, like Sam Selvon, the melancholy behind "the kiff-kiff laughter", as darkness from Indira's past threatens her drive to make a new beginning.

"Forget all the old-time books, here is one about the Trinidad of today, teeming with life and up-to-date Trini humour and steamy sex scenes. The action largely takes place a pub in Port of Spain and follows the antics of a wide cast of local characters of all races, religions and social classes. In the middle of it all is Indira, whose lover has recently left her, and who, at the beginning of the novel, takes stock of her assets in life. "Young, good looking, nice body," she writes, admiring herself in the mirror. Read it first yourself, and then press it into the hands of the Trinidadians in your life."
— Claire Adam, *The Guardian*